Military English
군사영어

Military English
군사영어

2017년 3월 15일 초판 발행
2020년 3월 15일 제2판1쇄 발행
2023년 2월 25일 제2판2쇄 발행

지은이 | 조용만 · 최병욱
펴낸이 | 이찬규
펴낸곳 | 북코리아
등록번호 | 제03-01240호
주소 | 13209 경기도 성남시 중원구 사기막골로 45번길 14
        우림2차 A동 1007호
전화 | 02-704-7840
팩스 | 02-704-7848
이메일 | sunhaksa@korea.com
홈페이지 | www.북코리아.kr
ISBN | 978-89-6324-688-8(93740)

값 25,000원

제2판

Military English
군사영어

조용만 · 최병욱 지음

북코
리아

저자 서문

　대장금과 같은 드라마와 K-POP으로부터 시작한 한류 열풍이 동남아를 넘어 유럽과 남미를 파고들더니, 싸이의 〈강남 스타일〉과 공군 병사들이 패러디한 〈레 밀리터리블(Les Militaribles)〉이 유튜브에서 돌풍을 일으킨 적이 있다. 방탄소년단이 세계적인 가수 대열에 합류했고 봉준호 영화감독이 골든글로브상을 받고 비영어권 영화는 꿈꾸기 어렵다는 아카데미상을 타는 등 이제는 한국음식, 태권도, 한국 화장품, 한국 의류, 한국 드라마, 아이돌, 걸그룹과 같은 콘텐츠들이 지구촌을 누비며 아예 K-Culture(한류 문화)의 열풍을 일으키고 있다. 또한 〈태양의 후예〉라는 드라마가 군대병원과 외국 파병을 무대로 젊은이들과 여심을 달군 적도 있다. 이런 것들은 한국의 젊은이들이 얼마만큼 세계를 무대로 뛰고 있는가를 여실히 보여 주는 사실들이다.

　이러한 시류는 군 내부에서도 소리 없는 아우성으로 전파되고 있다. PKO(평화유지작전), 외국의 무관 및 보좌관, 외국 군사교육기관과 군부대의 연락장교와 같은 파견 임무에 장교 및 부사관들은 물론, 병사들까지도 앞다투어 지원하는 모습으로 나타나고 있다. 그리고 해외 업무를 담당하는 전략 정보 분야의 인기가 과거의 보병 작전 특기를 능가하다 보니 정보병과의 지원율이 그 어느 때보다도 높다고 한다.

　그러나 외국으로 나가는 혜택은 열정과 욕망만으로 주어지는 것이 아니다. 한국군의 특수한 사정상으로도 연합작전은 한국군에게 군사영어의 필요성을 더욱 증대시키고 있어 군사영어를 창군 초기부터 교육하며 강조하고 있지만 쉽게 터득하기가 어렵다. 그럼에도 불구하고 지구촌화와 국경선이 없는 세계에 살고 있는 현대 군인들에게 있어서 연합작전은 한국뿐만 아니라 전 세계의 모든 국가가 공통적으로 시행하는 필수의 선택이다. 예를 들면 유럽의 EU나 NATO에 가입되어 있는 국가의 군인들이나 ASEAN에 속해 있는 국가의 군인들은 대부분의 작전과 훈련을 외국군과 함께 하거나 단독 국가의 훈련도 모두 연합작전을 가상하여 훈련한다.

이러한 요구사항을 충족시키기 위해서는 의사소통이 자유로워야 하고 단순한 언어의 공유가 아닌 인식과 이해의 공유가 선행되어야 하는데, 이를 위해서는 언어의 극복과 더불어 문화의 차이도 이해해야 하며 실시간 전장 상황을 공유해 보고 군사교리와 작전예규에 근거한 전문 군사지식을 알아야 한다. 영어를 아무리 잘하는 사람도 군사용어를 모르면 당황할 수밖에 없고 대화가 잘 진행되지 않는다.

필자가 한국의 대형 교회에서 미국인 남성과 함께 예배를 본 적이 있었는데, 예배 후 그와 대화를 하는 중에 필자가 말하는 내용은 알겠는데 군사용어의 의미는 모르겠다는 고백을 받은 적이 있다. 또한 공군작전 사령부에서 최고 실력파 공군 통역장교가 machine gun을 몰라서 지상군 통역은 필자에게 부탁한 적이 있었다. 이처럼 군사영어는 정말 쉽지 않다.

필자는 육군사관학교에서 영어를 전공하고 영어연극 공연을 수차례 했으며 외국 군사기관에서 2년간 공부를 했으면서도 영어를 제대로 구사할 수 없었는데, 연합사에서 6년간 근무하면서 미군들의 영어와 문화를 익혔다. 그리고 육사에서 국방정책학을 영어로 강의하면서 생도들의 영어 실력에 어떤 문제점이 있는가도 알았다. 또한 서울과 용인 소재 대학교의 군사학과 학생들에게 군사영어 1과 2를 강의하면서 얻었던 경험을 바탕으로 군사영어 교재를 편찬해야겠다는 다짐을 하고 10여 년간 자료를 수집하였다. 아울러 NATO 국가 군인 및 민간인 대표자들과 다국적 실험에 2년간 참여하면서 국제적으로 통할 수 있는 필수 군사영어 교재를 만들어서 사병 및 부사관으로부터 고급장교에 이르기까지, 단계별로 접근하기 쉬운 초·중급 영어에서 고급영어 수준까지 습득할 수 있는 교재를 편찬해야겠다고 다짐하였다.

    그러나 너무나 많은 자료를 어떻게 엮어야 하며 어떻게 하면 가급적 많지 않은 분량으로 편집할 수 있을까 고민을 하면서 수십 번 고치다 보니 오히려 졸작이 되었다는 느낌을 지울 수 없다. 모쪼록 군사영어의 선배님들과 후배님들의 정성 어린 채찍과 조언을 받아 다음에는 더 좋은 교재를 편찬하였으면 하는 마음이 간절하다. 끝으로 교정과 감수를 맡아 준 조영휘 군과 Emilee Jennings, 그리고 출판을 도와주신 이찬규 사장님과 관계자 여러분께 감사드린다.

2023년 2월
집필자를 대표하여
조 용 만

Contents

Military English II

Contents

Appendix

Military English

I

Unit 1 | 군사영어 역사와 교육체계

1. 한국군과 군사영어

한국군은 창군기부터 오늘에 이르기까지 미군으로부터 각종 군사제도, 무기체계, 군사교리 등을 도입하여 군대를 발전시켰고 많은 장교들이 미국에서 군사교육을 받았지만, 그 수요를 다 충족시킬 수 없어서 군사영어학교를 1945년 12월에 설립하였다. 그리고 1946년 남조선 국방경비대를 창설하면서 군사선진국의 문화, 교리, 전술 등을 습득하기 위하여 영어는 필수가 되었다. 또한 1953년 한미상호방위조약에 의하여 한국군은 연합방위체제를 선택하게 되었고 이는 미국으로부터 각종 군사적 도움을 받아 부족한 전투력을 채우게 되어 한국군의 국방비를 줄이는 데 획기적인 역할을 하였다.

〈표 1-1〉 한국군과 군사영어의 역사

1945.12. 한국군 창설과 동시에 군사영어 학교 설립

↓

1946.1. 남조선 국방경비대 창설: 군사선진국 문화, 교리, 전술 등 습득을 위해 언어 장벽 해결

↓

1953.10. 한미 상호방위조약: 연합방위체제 선택(국방비 절약)

↓

PKO 등 연합작전 및 훈련: 한국군의 필수 및 미래 　- 해군, 해병대, 공군 장교: 연합작전 및 훈련 빈번 　- 연합사 장교들 영어 실력 상이: 육군이 대체적으로 저조

그리고 연합방위체제의 전투력 향상을 위해 고안된 팀스피리트, 을지포커스, RSOI[1] 등 한미 연합연습과 육해공군 및 해병대는 각각 미군의 counterpart들과 세부적인 전술전기를 연합으로 익히기 위하여 영어가 필요하게 되었다. 그 이외에도 지구촌 곳곳에서 이루어지고 있는 평화유지작전, 평화재건작전 등에 많은 한국의 젊은이들이 참여하여 한국군의 위용과 우수성을 떨치고 있는데 여기에는 영어가 또한 필수적이다.[2] 이를 요약하면 〈표 1-1〉과 같다.

부하들의 생명과 전쟁의 승패가 달려있는 실전상황에서 영어가 얼마나 중요한가는 다음과 같은 사례를 보면 잘 알 수 있다. 서경석 장군이 월남전에서 중대장일 때의 일이다.[3]

도망간 것으로 판단했던 적이 다시 사격해 왔다. 처음보다는 훨씬 조직적인 것 같았다. 높은 지역으로 올라갔다가 중대 전 지역을 관측했는지 중대본부 지역과 다른 소대에도 적탄이 정확하게 날아왔다. 포로가 되거나 포사격에 쓰러진 동료들을 구출하기 위해 우리 병력이 빠져나오자마자 전열을 정비하여 다시 덤벼드는 것이 틀림없었다.

다시 포병을 불러서 총소리 나는 지역에 포사격을 실시했다. 대대 상황실에서는 미군의 무장헬기가 곧 도착할 것이니 유도해서 운용하라는 연락이 왔다. 당시 헬기는 대부분 미군 측에서 우리를 지원하고 있었기 때문에 미군 승무원과 한국군 사이에 언어의 장벽으로 인해 임무수행 중 마찰도 생겼고 웃지 못할 일들이 많이 일어났다. 특히 부상자가 발생했을 때 보급용 헬기의 조종사를 총으로 위협해서 사용하는 경우와 격전 시 적의 지상화기만 올라오면 아무 곳에나 병력을 내려놓고 가려고 했을 때 마찰이 많이 생기곤 했다.

---

1) 2020년을 기준으로 연합사의 큰 연습은 을지프리덤 가디언(Ulchi-Freedom Guardian: UFG)과 키 리졸브/독수리(Key Resolve/Foal Eagle)가 시행되고 있으며, 최근에는 UFG를 을지프리덤실드(Shield) 또는 을지자유의방패연습이라고 부른다.

2) 2019년 기준 해외파병인원은 UN PKO 627명, 다국적군 324명, 국방교류협력 149명 등 총 1,100명이다. (출처: 국가지표체계, http://www.index.go.kr/potal/main/EachDtlPageDetail.do?idx_cd=1715, 검색일: 2020. 1. 19.).

3) 서경석, 『전투감각』(서울: 샘터사, 2003), pp. 215-217.

무장헬기 두 대가 공중에 나타났다. 대대에서 우리 중대 호출부호와 주파수를 알려 주면서 중대장이 미군과 의사소통을 할 수 있으니 직접 날아가서 지원하라고 요청해서 왔던 것이다. 지난번 미군 전차가 지원되어 함께 작전을 한 적이 있었는데, 이때 주섬주섬 전차 소대장과 몇 마디 주고받은 것을 보고 의사소통이 가능한 것으로 판단한 모양이다. 아는 체도 함부로 하면 이렇게 난처하게 되는가 보다. 사실 무장헬기가 지원 온다는 연락을 받고 무척이나 고민했다. 우리 작전에 지원받는 것은 고사하고, 잘못하면 오폭을 받을 수도 있었고, 무장헬기를 사용하지 못하고 돌려보내면 중대장이 말 한마디 못해서 지원차 나온 헬기가 빙빙 돌다가 그대로 돌아갔다고 알려져 상급부대와 중대원에게 고개를 들지 못하는 창피와 망신을 당한다는 것이 더 두려웠다.

나는 중대원이 배치된 선을 따라서 여러 개의 좌표를 따 놓고 그 점을 따라 원을 그렸다. 그리고 원을 따라서 중대가 갖고 있는 녹색연막을 분대별로 한 발씩 터뜨렸다. 나를 찾는 조종사에게 내 말을 알아듣거나 말거나 세 번 반복했다.

"You see green smoke, smoke inside my soldier, you no fire. smoke outside enemy, you fire. Mountain enemy, you fire……."

조종사가 알았다고 주위를 빙빙 돌더니 우리가 포를 쏘던 쪽으로 로켓과 기총소사를 해 주었다. 몇 바퀴를 돌면서 지원사격을 하고는 날아가 버렸다.

지금 생각하면 너무 엉터리 같은 영어 솜씨라 부끄럽지만 의사소통은 그런대로 된 것 같아 정말 다행이었다. 공지작전이나 항공기 운용 및 군사영어 교육은 전혀 받은 일이 없었기 때문에 얼마나 당황하고 쩔쩔맸는지 모른다. 당해 본 사람이 아니면 그 고충을 이해하지 못한다.

서경석 중대장이 미군의 지원화력을 받기 위하여 사용한 영어는 문법적으로 설명하기가 매우 어렵다. 그만큼 비문법적인 의사소통을 했다는 이야기다. 그러나 우리는 여기서 두 가지 중요한 점을 발견할 수 있다. 첫째, 비문법적인 의사소통이지만 상황이 절박하고 눈으로 현장을 보면서 의사소통을 하면 통한다는 것이다. 둘째, 군사영어는 간단명료해야 한다는 것이다. 긴박한 상황에서 가장 빠르고 정확하게 상호 의사전달이 되어야 한다는 것이다. 이 점이 '법보다 주먹이 앞선다'는 전장상황에서는 더 중요하다는 것을 알 수 있다.

그러면 실제 야전에서 군사영어는 어느 정도 필요할까? 대략 네 가지 수준으로 구분해 생각해 볼 수 있다.

첫째, 대대급 부대 이하의 소부대 전술 수준으로 이는 병영 생활, 복장, 기본훈련(사격훈련, 체력단련 등) 분야와 소부대 작전명령 등의 기본 전투 및 전술 관련 분야의 영어가 필요하다고 할 수 있으며 주로 소부대급 지휘자(관) 및 참모에게 필요한 수준의 영어를 말한다.

둘째, 연대급부터 군단급 이하 부대에서 주로 사용하는 영어는 부대지휘절차, 공격 및 방어와 관련한 전술 분야의 영어이다. 여기에는 전술 개념을 설명할 수 있는 교리와 관련된 군사용어, 부대지휘와 관련된 상황판단, 참모판단 등에 필요한 군사영어이며 주로 중령급 이상 중견급 장교들이 필수적으로 알아야 할 수준의 영어가 이에 해당될 것이다.

셋째, 야전사와 합참 및 연합사를 포함한 연합훈련 간 긴밀한 협조가 요구되는 작전술급 내지는 전략 및 정책적 수준의 제대에서 필요한 군사영어이다. 주로 중·대령급 이상의 장교가 습득해야 할 수준의 영어이다.

넷째, 군사외교의 차원으로, 국제정치 이해를 바탕으로 집단안보, 군사동맹 등의 외교안보정책과 관련된 분야의 영어이다. 최근 육군은 군사외교를 담당할 전문가 양성의 필요성을 느끼고 군사외교 지역 전문가 제도를 도입할 정도로 이 분야의 장교가 필요하다. 한·미 동맹의 틀을 기본으로 한 군사외교의 다변화, 전문화를 위한 노력에 박차를 가하고 있는 한국군에서는 군사외교의 두 축인 지역 전문가(regional specialists)와 국제군축 분야의 사안별 전문가(arms control specialists) 양성을 위한 투자가 점점 증가할 수밖에 없을 것이다.

2. 군사영어의 특징 및 양성 교육체계

군사영어는 군에서 연합작전 수행을 위한 타 국군과의 의사소통을 위한 하나의 매개체로서 일반적인 의사소통체계와는 상당히 다른 점을 가지고 있다. 가장 특징적인 점은 군대문화의 특성상 매우 간결한 문장 구성을 보이며, 문장 속의 단어는 대부분이 약어로 이루어진다는 것이다. 이를 좀 더 세부적으로 살펴보겠다.

첫째, 수식어나 미사여구를 생략하거나 거의 사용하지 않는다는 점이다. 이는 의사소통상 혼란과 착오를 방지하기 위하여 문장이 단순해야 하며 긴 문장을 사용하지 말아야 한다는 것이다. 예를 들면 실제로 지상군 구성군사의 임무는 다음과 같이 기술할 수 있다.

GCC's mission is to be prepared against NK's provocation, to carry out operation plans on order, and to train and prepare for mobilization in peacetime.

둘째, 사실과 가정에 기초하여 꼭 필요한 내용만 언급하고 여타의 사사로운 감정 개입이나 사실에 기초하지 않은 상상적인 내용은 언급되지 않는다.

셋째, 명령문, 작전계획, 예규 등은 명령형 또는 지시형 문장이 주류를 이루며 각종 브리핑 문장은 서술식보다는 개조식 문장을 주로 사용한다.

넷째, 약어 또는 두문자어를 많이 사용하며 약 15,000여 개 정도가 사용되는 것으로 알려져 있다. 예를 들면 "COL. What's the relationship between DEFCON and WATCHCON?"이라는 문장에서 COL은 colonel(대령)의 약어이며, DEFCON은 defense와 condition, WATCHCON은 watch와 condition의 두 문자를 가지고 만든 약어이다.

다섯째, 일반영어와 전혀 다른 뜻의 단어도 사용된다. 예를 들면 rifle range에서 'range'는 '범위', '방목장' 등과 같은 일반적인 의미가 아니고 '사격을 하는 장소'의 의미로 사용된다. live ammunition은 'live'를 '실제'라는 의미로 사용하여 실

〈표 1-2〉두문자 및 약어 사용의 예

두문자어(Acronym)	약어(Abbreviation): 단어를 줄여서 표현	
– NLL: Northern Limit Line(북방한계선) – IRBM: Intermediate Range Ballistic Missile – OPLAN: Operation Plan	– Dec.: December – CPT: Captain – exam: Examination	– Sgt(SGT): Sergeant – ad: Advertisement – 5 bns: 5 battalions

탄이라는 용어로 사용된다. 'surprise'도 '놀람'의 뜻이 아니라 '기습'이라는 의미로 사용하고 있고, 'position'도 '위치'나 '입장'이라는 뜻이 아니라 '진지'라는 의미로 사용된다. 이와 같은 두문자와 약어를 몇 개 더 정리해 보면 〈표 1-2〉와 같다.

이처럼 특징적인 새로운 언어에 적응시키기 위하여 한국군은 양성교육과 임관 후의 보수교육으로 나누어 많은 노력을 기울이고 있다. 먼저 학교교육기관 중에서 장교의 대다수를 차지하고 있는 몇몇의 학교를 대상으로 살펴보면 다음과 같다.

첫째, 육군사관학교 영어교육은 1, 2학년은 교양기초로 Academic English를, 3, 4학년은 Military English를 전원 이수하도록 되어 있고, 선택으로 War in Media, 영문학 속 전쟁읽기, 군사실무영어실습, 시사영어, 실무군사영어 등 군사영어 비중이 점점 커지고 있다.[4]

둘째, 육군3사관학교에서는 3학년 때 영어강독, 청취, 회화, 작문, 시사영어, 뉴스듣기 등을, 4학년 때는 군사영어 강독, 연합실무영어 1, 2, Military Briefing 및 Writing 등을 이수토록 되어 있어 세계화시대의 추세에 맞춰 군사영어의 강도를 높이고 있다.[5]

셋째, 국군간호사관학교에서는 통합영어, 영어토론과 발표, 현장실무영어를 필수로 이수토록 되어 있고, 선택으로 Creative Reading & Discussion, Advanced General English 등을 이수토록 되어 있어 생도들 영어 구사능력 향상을 위해 많은 노력을 하고 있다.[6]

---

4) 육군사관학교 홈페이지, https://www.kma.ac.kr:461/kma/2195/subview.do, 검색일: 2023. 1. 30.

5) 육군3사관학교 홈페이지, https://www.kma.ac.kr:461/kma/2195/subview.do, 검색일: 2023. 1. 30.

6) 국군간호사관학교 홈페이지, http://www.kafna.ac.kr/user/indexSub.action?codyMenuSeq=81995591&siteId=afna&menuUIType=top, 검색일: 2023. 1. 30.

넷째, 일반대학의 ROTC 및 군사학과 학생들은 『Military English I』또는 기타 교재를 선택하여 2-4학점 정도로 회화 및 독해력을 중심으로 학습하고, 군사용어에 대한 이해와 일부 브리핑에 필요한 부분은 암기식 학습을 하고 있다. 특히 군사학과 학생들의 경우, 대부분의 학교에서 토익 점수 획득 목표를 부여하고 있고 교양 영어까지 수강을 할 수 있기 때문에 영어에 관심이 있는 학생들은 많은 시간을 영어 학습에 할애하고 있다. 또한 부사관을 희망하는 대학생들이나 부사관학교 간부들도 군사영어를 열심히 하고 있어 군사영어는 이제 군인들에게는 필수가 되었고, 이러한 추세에 부합하여 대부분의 교육기관에서는 영어 학습 시간을 증가시켜 편성하는 추세이다.

한편, 임관 후에 실시되는 영어 학습 방법에는 국방어학원에서 실시하는 군사영어반 교육이 있다. 영어 과정은 영어과정은 고급과정(24주), 중급(24주), 중급단기(14주), 유학준비과정(8주), 단기기초(8주), 연합실무(4주), 통역사관(6주)으로 편성되어 있으며 제2외국어 과정은 중국어, 일본어, 스페인어, 프랑스어, 독일어, 터키어, 인니어를 각각 24주 동안 학습하고 러시아와 아랍어반은 40주를 학습하도록 편성되어 있다. 이를 운영하는 목적은 단기간 내 집중적인 교육으로 어학자원을 확보하기 위한 것이며 단계별 교육을 실시한다.

이러한 내용은 조금씩 변경될 수 있기 때문에 관심 있는 사람들은 합동군사대학의 홈페이지를 확인하면 도움이 된다.[7]

한편, 야전부대에서는 부대별로 홈페이지를 운영하여 개인별 영어 학습을 지원하고 있다. 국방부에서는 〈Live English〉를 〈군사영어〉와 통합하여 다양한 형식으로 영어회화에 중점을 두어 학습을 지원하고 있다. 육군에서는 경기도 영어마을에서 개발한 e-Learning 학습 콘텐츠(찾아가는 영어마을)를 전산망에 탑재 운용하고 있다.

이러한 점을 고려하여 이 책에서는 군사영어가 필요한 다양한 독자와 추세에 맞춰 "Military English I"에서는 영어와 한글을 병행 사용하여 군사영어의 기초

---

7) 합동군사대학교 국방어학원 과정 홈페이지, http://new.mnd.go.kr/user/indexSub.action?codyMenuSeq=70206&siteId=jfmu&menuUIType=sub, 검색일: 2020.1.19.

에 해당되는 군사영어 인사 표현법, 계급 및 제대, 참모부별로 많이 사용하는 군사 용어, 제대별 명칭, 병과체계, 소총과 탄약, 통신, 독도법, 전술통제 수단, CAS 지원 요청 등을 다루었다.

"Military English II"에서는 참모편성과 업무, 의사결정 절차와 작전수행과정, 공격 및 방어 작전, 작전명령 양식, 군사리더십 그리고 브리핑 형식에 맞춰 국방백 서를 근거로 한 브리핑 예문 등을 수록하여 수준 높은 군사영어 실력을 습득할 수 있도록 단계별로 구성하였다. 그리고 여기에 사용된 text들은 모두 미군 최신 교범 과 과거 연합사에서 사용했던 실무영어 참고서적에서 인용하였다.

Unit 2 | 군사영어 인사 표현법

1. 초면 인사

⊙ **초면 인사**(상급자)

_____, it is a great honor to meet you.

_____, 만나서 영광입니다.

예〉 Major Gates, it is a great honor to meet you.

게이츠 소령님, 만나서 영광입니다.

⊙ **초면 인사**(동급 및 하급자)

Nice to meet you.

만나서 반갑습니다.

⊙ **다시 만났을 때**(상급자)

It is an honor to meet you again, sir.

다시 만나서 영광입니다.

⊙ **다시 만났을 때**(동급 또는 하급자)

Good to see you again.

다시 보니 좋습니다.

How have you been?

그동안 어떻게 지냈습니까?

◉ **수차례 이상 자주 만난 경우**(동급 또는 하급자)

Always a pleasure to see you.

항상 당신을 만날 때마다 즐겁습니다.

2. 자기소개와 안부 표현법

◉ **자기소개**

I am CPT Kim.

저는 김 대위입니다.

I am commander of 3rd company.

저는 3중대장입니다.

I am director of Security Policy Division at ROK MND.

저는 국방부 방위정책과장입니다.

◉ **안부 묻는 법**

How is _____ doing?(이름 또는 계급+성)

_____는 어떻게 지내고 있습니까?

예〉 How is Mr. Cho Yong-Man doing?

조용만 씨는 어떻게 지내고 있습니까?

How is Sergeant First Class Kim doing?

김 중사는 어떻게 지내고 있습니까?

◉ 날씨 표현법

It's really beautiful, today.

오늘 날씨가 정말 좋습니다.

Everything is green in June.

6월이 되니까 주변이 푸릅니다.

It is a little bit raining outside.

바깥에는 비가 조금 내리고 있습니다.

The weather has turned very hot over the last few days.

날씨가 지난 며칠 사이에 매우 더워졌습니다.

This is the most beautiful time of the year in Korea.

지금이 한국이 연중 가장 아름다운 시기입니다.

What a wonderful day. I think our meeting is blessed with such a beautiful weather.

날씨가 좋습니다. 날씨도 오늘 회의를 도와주는 것 같습니다.

◉ 속담을 이용한 표현법

There is a Korean old wise saying, "A deep friendship can melt ice in the severe winter."

"깊은 우정은 한겨울에 얼음이라도 녹일 수 있다"라는 오래된 한국 속담이 있습니다.

There is a Korean old wise saying, "A journey of a thousand miles begins with a single step."

"천 리 길도 한 걸음부터"라는 오래된 한국 속담이 있습니다.

⊙ 세미나 및 토의 중 표현법

• 우리 측 대표단(참석자)을 소개할 때

Let the Korean delegation introduce themselves from my right(left).

오른쪽(왼쪽)부터 각자 자기소개를 하겠습니다.

• 회의를 시작하자고 제의할 때

We have a lot to cover today. It's good time to start. (So why don't we get the meeting started.)

오늘 논의할 의제들이 많이 있습니다. 회의를 시작하는 것이 좋겠습니다.

• 회의 중 휴식 · 오찬 · 만찬을 제의할 때

(If you don't mind) let's take a ten minute break. Shall we go to luncheon(dinner)?

10분간 휴식하는 것이 좋겠습니다. 우리 점심(저녁) 함께 하실까요?

• 종료 후 격려

This meeting was a good opportunity to be exposed to such a wide variety of ideas.

다양한 아이디어를 들을 수 있어 좋은 기회였습니다.

The meeting was very valuable(successful, helpful).

회의는 매우 유익했습니다(성공적이었습니다).

⊙ 확신 표현법

I am sure that your effort to promote our relationship will be rewarded in the future.

우리의 협력관계 증진을 위한 당신의 노력은 향후 보상을 받게 될 것으로 저는 확신하고 있습니다.

⊙ 정치적/사회적 현안 표현법

What are your thoughts on ＿＿＿?

＿＿에 대하여 어떻게 생각하십니까?

예〉 What are your thoughts on the recent outbreak of avian influenza(AI)?

최근 발생한 조류 인플루엔자에 대하여 어떻게 생각하십니까?

I am deeply concerned about ＿＿＿.

본인은 ＿＿＿에 대하여 깊이 우려하고 있습니다.

예〉 I am deeply concerned about the recent political unrest in Thailand.

본인은 최근 태국의 정치적 불안에 대하여 깊이 우려하고 있습니다.

It is the policy(stance) of the Korean government that ＿＿＿.

My government's stance on the issue is ＿＿＿.

＿＿＿은 한국 정부의 정책(입장)입니다.

예〉 It is the policy(stance) of the Korean government that we will not recognize North Korea as a nuclear power.

북한은 핵보유국으로 인정하지 않겠다는 것이 한국 정부의 정책(입장)입니다.

You can say that again. / You said it.

당신 말이 맞습니다.

That makes two of us.

그것은 내게도 해당됩니다. (나도 같은 입장입니다.)

I fully agree with you.

저도 전적으로 동의합니다.

You said a mouthful.

지금 하신 말씀이 아주 중요한 말씀입니다.

⦿ 최대의 경의 / 호의적인 표현

Thank you for a great dinner and your welcome words.
당신의 이와 같은 훌륭한 만찬 접대와 따뜻한 환영사에 크게 감사합니다.

I would like to express my deepest appreciation for your great support(hosting dinner).
당신의 성원(만찬 주관)에 깊은 감사를 표명합니다.

I'm looking forward to your continued support and cooperation in the future.
우리는 앞으로 당신의 지속적인 지지와 협조를 기대합니다.

Let's work together for a bright future ahead.
밝은 미래를 위해 우리 함께 일해 나갑시다.

I am very pleased that we could exchange valuable ideas on the North Korea issue(the matters of our mutual interest).
북한 문제(우리의 상호 관심사)에 관하여 귀중한 의견 교환을 하여 대단히 만족합니다.

I hope that your government continues to support my government's position on this issue.
귀 정부가 이 문제에 대해 우리 정부의 입장을 계속 지지해 줄 것을 바라고 있습니다.

⦿ 건강 회복 기원

I hope your wife gets better soon.
당신 부인의 조속한 쾌유를 빕니다.

⦿ 건배 제의

I would like to propose a toast to the everlasting friendship and the alliance between our two countries.

우리 두 나라 간의 영원한 우호관계와 동맹을 위하여 건배를 제의합니다.

I say "위하여" in Korean, then you can repeat my word, "위하여", which means "cheers".

한국말로 제가 "위하여"라고 하면, "위하여"라고 따라 하세요. "건배"라는 뜻입니다.

⊙ 안부 / 환송 인사

Please send my regards to your family.

가족들에게 안부 전해 주십시오.

Please give my best regards to _____.

_____께 안부 전해 주십시오.

I hope we can get together again soon.

I'm looking forward to seeing you in near future.

조만간 다시 만나 뵙기를 바랍니다.

Tip 1	**초면에 미국 사람들에게 결혼 여부, 자녀 유무 등을 묻는 것은 실례** 한국의 문화는 정(情)의 문화이지만 미국 사람들에게는 불편함을 주는 질문들임. 그래도 물어야겠다면 "Can I ask you a private question?" 하고 어느 정도의 분위기를 조성한 후 묻는 것이 바람직.
Tip 2	**여성에게 아름답다고 이야기 하는 것도 실례** 한국인의 정서에서는 여성에게 아름답다고 이야기하는 것을 미덕으로 생각할 수 있으나, 미국의 문화에서는 이를 성적인 표현으로서 성희롱으로 생각할 수 있음. 여성에게 beautiful이나 wonderful과 같은 표현은 가급적 삼가야 함.

Unit **3** | 작전실무용어 해설 **I** (인사/군수 분야)

Rank and Promotion (계급 및 진급)

⊙ Technique of Smart Expression

- When did you get promoted to the rank of major?

  * Get promoted to: 진급하다(Pin on)

- When did you make Major?

◎ 각 군의 장교 계급

구분	육 · 해병 · 공	육군	해병 · 공	해군	
소위 O-1	Second Lieutenant	2LT	2nd LT	Ensign	ENS
중위 O-2	First Lieutenant	1LT	1st LT	Lieutenant Junior Grade	LTJG
대위 O-3	Captain	CPT	Capt	Lieutenant	LT
소령 O-4	Major	MAJ	Maj	Lieutenant Commander	LCDR
중령 O-5	Lieutenant Colonel	LTC	LtCol	Commander	CDR
대령 O-6	Colonel	COL	Col	Captain	CAPT
준장 O-7	Brigadier General	BG	Brig Gen	Rear Admiral Lower Half	RADM(L)
소장 O-8	Major General	MG	Maj Gen	Rear Admiral Upper Half	RADM(U)

구분	육·해병·공	육군	해병·공	해군	
중장 O-9	Lieutenant General	LTG	LtGen	Vice Admiral	VADM
대장 O-10	General	GEN	Gen	Admiral	ADM

⊙ 부사관 및 사병 계급 체계

미군				한국군
계급명		약칭	계급장	계급명
Private	이등병	PVT		이등병
		PV2	⌃	
Private First Class	일등병	PFC		일등병
Specialist	특등병	SPC		상등병
Corporal	상등병	CPL		
Sergeant	병장	SGT		병장
Staff Sergeant	하사	SSG		하사
Sergeant First Class	중사	SFC		중사
Master Sergeant	상사	MSG		상사
First Sergeant	일등상사	1ST		
Sergeant Major	원사	SGM		원사
Command Sergeant Major	주임원사	CSM		
Sergeant Major of the Army	육군주임원사	SMA		

* 준위: Warrant Officer
* 군무원: a civilian attached to the military

⊙ 진급 관련 주요 용어

- 진급선발위원회: Promotion board
- 인사평정: OER(Officer Evaluation Report)
- 다면평가: Multi-dimension evaluation
- 진급 대상자: Promotion-eligible personnel

  * He is eligible for promotion this year(in a promotion zone).

- 진급 추천: Promotion recommendation
- 임시 진급: Temporary promotion
- 중령(진): MAJ(P) * P : Promotable

⊙ Useful Expressions

1. The Modern military services recognize three broad categories of personnel.
2. These are codified in the Geneva Conventions, which distinguish enlisted men, non-commissioned officers and officers.
3. Enlisted personnel are personnel below commissioned rank.
4. The base of the Non-Commissioned Officer(NCO) ranks, CPLs serve as team leaders of the smallest Army units.
5. NCOs are responsible for the care and direct control of junior military members.
6. Company grade officers also fill staff roles in some units.
7. Typical army and marine field officer ranks include colonel, lieutenant colonel, major.
8. General-officer ranks typically include general, lieutenant general, major general, and brigadier general.

Military Unit(제대)

⊙ Technique of Smart Expression

- The division consists of 5 infantry RGTs, 9 ARTY BNs, 3 ENG BNs, 3 RECON units, and 9 tank companies.

  * RGT(=Regiment): 연대 | ARTY(=Artillery): 포병 | ENG(=Engineer): 공병

- 5 AVN GRPs will be attached and 3 AVN BDEs will be assigned to my command.

  * Attach: 배속하다 | Assign: 예속하다 | AVN GRP: 항공단

⊙ 제대 구분

축약어	영어	한국어
FA	Field Army	야전군
Corps	Corps	군단
DIV	Division	사단
BDE	Brigade	여단
RGT	Regiment	연대

축약어	영어	한국어
BN	Battalion	대대
CO	Company	중대
PLT	Platoon	소대
SQD	Squad	분대
SEC	Section	반

⊙ 사단의 종류

축약어	영어	한국어
ID	Infantry Division	보병사단
MID	Mechanized Infantry Division	기계화보병사단
AD	Armored Division	기갑사단
AD	Air Division	비행사단
CD	Cavalry Division	기병사단

축약어	영어	한국어
HRD	Homeland Reserve Division	향토사단
MRD	Mobilization Reserve Division	동원사단

⊙ Technique of Smart Expression

- 단은 Group, 파견대는 Detachment, 포대는 Battery를 사용
- 통상적으로 2nd나 3rd는 2d, 3d로 표기 가능(예: 2d CAB)
- 일반적으로 부대 명칭 앞에는 정관사 the를 사용하지 않음
- 군단이나 원정기동군(MEF)의 경우 숫자를 로마자로 표기(예: II Corps)
- 숫자 '0'은 O(오)로 읽음(예: 601st BN[Six O First Battalion]).
- 1-2 ATK BN은 'Half Attack'으로, 2-2 BN은 'Two Two BN'으로 읽음

⊙ 군수 분야 용어 해설

약어	영어	한국어
AA	Ammunition Allocation	탄약할당
AD	Ammunition Depot	탄약창
ASP	Ammunition Supply Point	탄약보급소
BDA	Battle Damage Assessment	전투피해평가
CCM	Cross Country Movement	야지기동성 분석도
CSR	Controlled Supply Rate	통제보급률
IROAN	Inspect and Repair Only As Necessary	아이론 정비개념
JPO	Joint Petroleum Office	합동유류사무소
LCA	Logistics Coordinating Agency	군수협조단
LP&P	Logistics Policy&Procedure	군수 방침 및 절차
TMC	Transportation Movement Center	수송이동본부
PME	Preventative Maintenance Equipment	예방정비

약어	영어	한국어
POE	Port of Embarkation	탑재항만
PSP	Prepositioned Stock Point	장벽고
RSO&I	Reception, Staging, Onward Movement & Integration	연합전시 증원(수용, 대기, 전방이동 및 통합)

⊙ Useful Expressions

1. A unit is any organized group that is a subdivision of a larger group.

2. A squad is the smallest military tactical unit.

3. A squad is normally under the command of a squad leader.

4. A platoon is larger than a squad and smaller than a company.

5. A platoon leader is a lieutenant.

6. A battalion is larger than a company and smaller than a brigade or a regiment.

7. A battalion is under the command of a lieutenant colonel.

8. There are two or more battalions in a regiment.

9. A brigade consists of varying numbers of battalions and support troops.

10. The commanding officer of a brigade is a colonel.

11. A division is larger than a brigade and smaller than corps.

12. A corps is under the command of a three-star general or lieutenant general.

13. An army is the largest unit of the forces.

14. Where is the JPO located?

15. The most important factors when storing munitions are to keep a safe distance between magazines, prevent mixed storage, and store by lot-number.

    * magazine: 무기고, 탄창

Unit 4 | 작전실무용어 해설 II (작전 분야)

Organization(편성)

⊙ Technique of Smart Expression

- The unit is mainly manned by aviators.

  * Man: ~에 사람을 배치하다

- The unit is organized to support airlift(공수).

- Operations division at AAOC is seriously understaffed.

  * AAOC: Army Aviation Operation Command
  * Understaffed(short-handed): 인원이 부족한 ⇔ Outnumbered

⊙ 주요 용어

- 조직표: Organizational Chart
- 편성 및 장비표: TO/E(Table of Organization and Equipment)
- 수정 편성표: MTO(Modified Table of Organization)
- 편제장비, 편제화기: Organized Equipment / Organized Weapons
- 병과 필수 보직: Branch qualified job
- 비인가 보직 인원: BMM(Borrowed Military Manpower)
- 승인에 의한 군 인력 초과 운용: DMO(Directed Military Overhire)
- 적절한 인원 수준: Right manning level

◉ 편성표(Table of Organization)

PAR NO	NO	PSNTL	GR	BR	MOS	RQ STR	AU STR
100	1	HHC, ATTACK BN					
101	00	COMMAND SECTION					
	01	COMMNADER	O5	AV	15B00	1	1
	13	VEHICLE DRIVER	E3		93P10	2	2
102	00	S1 SECTION					
	01	SR PERSONNEL SVC SGT	E7	MP	75H40	1	1

– PARNO: 문단 번호(Paragraph Number)
– MOS: 군사주특기(Military Occupational Specialty)
– RQSTR: 전시편제(Required Strength)
– AUSTR: 평시편제(Authorized Strength)
– HHC: 본부 및 본부 중대(HQ & HQ Company)
– SR: 특수정찰(Special Reconnaissance)

– PSNTL: 직책(Position Title)
– BR: 병과(Branch)
– GR: 계급(Grade)
– S1 SECTION: 인사반
– SVC: 근무(Service)
– MP: 군사경찰(Military Police)

◉ Useful Expressions

1. A table of allowance[1] refers to equipment allowance document that prescribes basic allowances of organizational equipment, and provides the control to develop, revise, or change equipment authorization inventory data.

2. On hand means the quantity of an item that is physically available in a storage location and contained in the accountable property book records of an issuing activity.

3. What's the reason for the difference between authorized and assigned personnel?

---

1)   table of allowance: 할당표

4. Can you give me information on the current status of the personnel strength of USFK?

Command Control(지휘통제)

⊙ Technique of Smart Expression

- 작전통제 시키다

  5th DIV will OPCON 103 BN to 6th DIV.

  5사단은 103대대를 6사단에 작전통제시킬 것이다.

- 작전통제를 해제하다

  5th DIV will release OPCON of 103 BN(back to 6th DIV).

  5사단은 103대대의 작전통제를 해제할 것이다.

  * OPCON: operational Control

- 작전통제를 전환하다

  GCC will CHOP[2] 506 BN to 1st corps.

  지구사는 506대대를 1군단으로 작통전환할 것이다.

- 작전통제가 되다

  103 BN was placed under OPCON of 2nd corps.

  103 BN was OPCONed to 2nd corps.

  103대대가 2군단에 작전통제되었다.

---

2) CHOP: Change of Operational Control

- '권한행사'를 하다

At D-2, CDR CFC will exercise OPCON over ROK forces.

D-2에 연합사령관은 한국군에 대해 작전통제 권한을 행사하게 된다.

◉ 韓 · 美 지휘관계 비교

구분	지휘관계 용어
韓側	예속, 배속, 작전지휘, 작전통제, 전술통제, 지원
美側	전투지휘, 작전통제, 전술통제, 지원

韓側: 작전권과 편성권을 미구분, 예 · 배속을 지휘관계로 구분
美側: 예 · 배속을 편성관계로 구분
* 국방부 장관 지시에 의해 할당/전환

◉ 부대 지휘 관계

구분	한국어	영어
COCOM	전투지휘	Combatant Command
OPCOM	작전지휘	Operational Command
OPCON	작전통제	Operational Control
TACON	전술통제	Tactical Control
ADCON	행정통제	Administrative Control
CHOP	작통전환, 작통변경	Change of OPCON

- DS: 직접지원(Direct Support)   - R: 증원(Reinforcement)
- GS: 일반지원(General Support)   - 주 임무 수행부대: Supported Command
- 지원부대: Supporting Command   - 전시작전통제권 전환: Wartime OPCON Transfer

* Directives / Instructions: 지시사항   * Guidance: 지침

Crisis Action(위기조치)

⊙ Technique of Smart Expression

- DEFCON II was declared as of 1300hrs, yesterday.

  데프콘 2는 작일 13:00시부로 선포되었다.

- O/O at DEF-III, action ID ABC001(BPT to move to ALTCP) will be activated.

  조치부호 ABC001(예비지휘소 이동준비)는 데프콘 3에 의명 시행될 것이다.

  * O/O: On Order(의명) | Action ID: 조치부호 | BPT: Be Prepared To |
  ALTCP: Alternate Command Post(예비지휘소) Activate ↔ Deactivate

- Our objective is to get 95% destruction of each brigade by D+2.

  우리의 목표는 D+2일까지 각 여단별 파괴를 95% 달성하는 것이다.

⊙ DEFCON(Defense Readiness Condition/방어준비태세)

실제	DEFCON VI	DEFCON III	DEFCON II	DEFCON I
연습	Double Take	Round House	Fast Pace	Cocked Pistol

⊙ Origin of Word(어원)

- Double Take: 두 번 본다 ⇒ 경계태세 강화
- Round House: 원형의 기관차 정비고 ⇒ 전쟁 대비 정비/준비
- Fast Pace: 빠른 걸음걸이 / 속도 ⇒ 급박히 돌아가는 상황
- Cocked Pistol: Cock(공이치기를 당기다) / Pistol(권총) ⇒ 일촉즉발의 상황

⊙ Words of Operational Action(작전 조치 용어)

M-Day	Mobilization Day	동원 개시일
C-Day	Commencement Day	美증원 전력 전개 개시일
KA-Hour	Korea Alert Hour	한국 비상대기 시간
F-Hour	Fire Hour	Pre-ATO 시행 기준시간
H-Hour	Hostility Hour	전쟁선포 기준시간
D-Day	Date of Attack Day	공격 개시일

Order(명령)

⊙ Technique of Smart Expression

- JCS has issued an order to stand up a crisis action team.

  * JCS(Joint Chiefs of Staff): 합참 | Issue(release): 하달하다

- Finish drafting a force protection plan by 0800 on my desk.

  * Draft: 작성하다 | Force protection: 부대방호

- AAOC acknowledged receipt of the FRAGO from JCS.

  * Acknowledge: (명령수령을) 확인하다 | Receipt: 수령

⊙ Type of Order(명령의 종류)

약어	영어	한국어
FRAGO	Fragmentary Order	단편명령
DEPORD	Deployment Order	전개명령
WARNO	Warning Order	준비명령

약어	영어	한국어
EXORD	Execution Order	시행명령
	Standby order	대기명령
	Alert order	비상대기명령

⊙ Format of Order(명령 작성 양식)

- Situation(상황)
- Mission(임무)
- Execution(실시)
    - Commander Intent(지휘관 의도)
    - CONOP: Concept of Operations(작전개념)
    - Tasks to Subordinate Units(예하부대 과업)
    - Coordinating Instructions(협조지시)
- Combat Service Support(전투근무지원)
- Command and Signal(지휘 및 통신)

⊙ Useful Expressions

1. I would like to brief you on the current status and operational readiness.
2. Reconnaissance of and crossing of MDL by small groups of personnel were recent enemy activities noticed along the front line area.
3. Inspections and ongoing repairs of combat facilities were also observed.
4. In the deep area,[3] the summer command, control and communication exercises were carried out between June and August.

---

3) deep area: 종심지역

5. A national level assessment inspection was completed in November, from which NK achieved the highest combat readiness posture.

6. A recent activity noticed on the West Coast was an infiltration exercise using infiltration vessels and midget submarines.

7. Enemy infiltration and local provocation of disorder[4] always exists as a threat.

8. Are any changes needed to our operation concept, task organization,[5] or mission?

9. Is the current situation radically[6] different from the enemy and the friendly situation portrayed in our higher command's OPLAN?

10. Battle areas are basic consideration to determine locating reinforcements, reserve positions, supply nodes, and tactical airbases.

11. Our objective is to get 80% destruction of each enemy brigade by D+3.

12. All aircraft operating on these routes at night must be fully lit.[7]

---

4) local provocation of disorder: 국지도발

5) task organization: 전투편성

6) radically: 현저하게

7) lit: '불을 밝혔다'의 의미로 light의 과거, 과거 분사형임. 따라서 군사용어로는 등화관제의 의미임.

Unit 5 | 작전실무용어 해설 III (작전/정보 분야)

OPLAN(작전계획)

⊙ Technique of Smart Expression

- Meet operational requirements(expectations, standards).

  * meet: 요구(기대, 표준)에 맞추다 / 부응하다 / 충족시키다

- We wargamed several options.

  * 몇 가지 방안을 가지고 워게임을 했다.

- CDR's guidance is nested in the new OPLAN.

  * Be nested in: ~가 ~에 반영되어 있다

⊙ Words of OPLAN (작전계획 관련 용어)

- OPLAN(Operational Plan): 작전계획
  - CONPLAN(Concept Plan): 개념계획
  - Contingency Plan: 우발계획
  - Branch Plan: 보조계획
  - CONOP(Concept of Operation): 작전개념
- COA(Course of Action): 방책
  - MLCOA(Most Likely COA): 가장 가능성이 높은 방책
  - MDCOA(Most Dangerous COA): 가장 위험한 방책
  - Development of COA: 방책 발전

- Evaluation of COA: 방책 평가
- 수준 'A' 보고: Level A Briefing
  → 계획 발전 과정의 첫 번째 브리핑. Level B, C, D 등으로 구분
- 작전계획 단계: Phase-Stage로 구분(예: Phase III Stage A)
- 문서의 부록
  - 부록 → 별지 → 별첨 → 부첨
  - Annex → Appendix → Tab → Encl. (Enclosed)

Staff(참모부)

⊙ Technique of Smart Expression

- He is assigned as Chief of G3 plans branch.
  * Assign: 보직/예속하다 | Attach: 배속하다 | Plans Branch: 작전계획과
- He will assume the position of operations officer, G3.
- He served as 1st Brigade commander.
  * Serve as: ~의 직책으로 근무하다 | Command: 지휘하다

⊙ 참모 구분

구 분		사용 제대
S	Staff	대대, 연대, 여단 이하
G	General Staff	장관급 이상 부대
J	Joint Staff	합동부대
C	Combined Staff	연합군

구 분		사용 제대
A	Air Force	공군
N	Navy	해군
– G3: 작전처 조직 또는 사람들		
– The G3: 작전참모		

항공작전사령부		합참 합동작전본부		연합군사령부	
G1	인사참모처	J1	인사참모부	C1	인사참모부
G2	정보참모처	J2	정보참모부	C2	정보참모부
G3	작전참모처	J3	작전참모부	C3	작전참모부
G4	군수참모처	J4	군수참모부	C4	군수참모부
– TNG: 교훈참모처 – IG: 감찰참모부 – Finance: 경리, 참모부		J5	작전기획참모부	C5	기획참모부
		J6	지휘통신참모부	C6	통신전자참모부
		J7	공병참모부	CFEN	공병참모부

회의 및 보고

⊙ Technique of Smart Expression

- I'd like to convene a meeting between G1 and G4.

  * convene: 회의를 소집하다

- Today, I will brief you on the restructuring of army aviation units.

  * brief A on B: B에 대하여 A에게 브리핑하다

⊙ 회의의 종류

구분	내용
Meeting	회의를 뜻하는 가장 일반적이고 포괄적인 단어
Conference	특정 문제 연구를 위한 회의. 여러 부서 · 기관 참여
Forum	특정 주제에 대한 상반된 견해를 가진 전문가들이 청중 앞에서 벌이는 공개 토론회
Symposium	포럼에 비해 격식을 갖추고, 청중의 질의 기회도 적음
Workshop	회의의 한 부분으로, 문제 · 과제에 관한 정보교류 · 교육을 위한 소규모 단위 일반회의

구분	내용
Seminar	교육 목적의 회의. 담당자가 맡은 소주제에 대해 발표하고 전 참가자가 함께 토의하여 대주제에 대한 이해 도모

- OPT(Operational Planning Team): 작전계획반(실무계획회의)
- SLS(Senior Leaders Seminar): 주요지휘관회의(교육 목적)
- Working-level meeting: 실무자급 회의
- IPC/MPC/FPC(Initial/Middle/Final Planning Conference): 최초/중간/최종 계획회의

⊙ 보고의 종류

구분	내용
Confirmation Brief	확인보고. 예하부대가 상급부대로부터 작전명령이나 단편명령을 수령하는 즉시 실시
Backbrief	임무수행계획보고. 부여된 임무를 어떻게 수행할 것인가를 상급부대 지휘관에게 보고
Debriefing	결과보고. (전투, 행사, 임무 및 훈련 종료 후) 결과보고

- SITREP(Situation Report): 특정 사건에 대한 상황보고
- Update: 최신화. 정기적으로 실시되는 상황보고. (Ex. Daily Update)
- 현안업무보고: STU(Special Topic Update)
- 중간보고(추진 현황보고): IPR(In-progress review)
- 서면보고: Report in writing
- 대면보고: Face-to-face briefing

⊙ Useful Expressions

1. I will brief at 1700 today, so I need you to send me your data.

2. Could you give me more detailed information on this mission?

3. Who is in charge of writing the CASOP(Crisis Action Standard Operating

Procedures)?[1]

4. Where is US 7th AF HQs located?

5. This tactic is not currently applied but could be used in an emergency.

Military Intelligence(군사정보)

⊙ Technique of Smart Expression

• All-source intelligence indicates that ~

  * indicates that ~: ~를 나타내다

• This image shows indication of ~

  * shows indication of ~: ~의 징후를 보여 주다, 나타내다

• Collected intelligence should be disseminated by the most expeditious means.

  * disseminate: 전파하다 | expeditious: 신속한

⊙ 정보 출처

구분	한국어	영어
IMINT	영상정보	Imagery Intelligence
SIGINT	신호정보	Signal Intelligence
COMINT	통신정보	Communications Intelligence
ELINT	전자정보	Electronic Intelligence
HUMINT	인간정보	Human Intelligence
OPTINT	광학정보	Optical Intelligence

---

1) CASOP: 위기조치예규

OSINT	공개정보	Open-Source Intelligence
TECHINT	기술정보	Technical Intelligence
CI	대정보	Counterintelligence

Security(보안)

⊙ Technique of Smart Expression

- Ensure that all documents remain secured at all times.

  * Ensure: 보장하다 | Secured: 보안 조치가 되다

- Make sure that you do not shred classified materials by mistake.

  * Shred: 세절하다 | Classified materials: 비밀 자료

- Never leave classified material unattended.

  * Leave:(~인 채로) 남겨 두다 | Attend: 보살피다, 돌보다

- RC-800G captured the imagery of key facilities.

  * Capture: 획득하다 | Imagery:(집합적) 영상

- It is capable of providing video feed into HQs.

  * Video Feed: 비디오 자료

⊙ 비밀등급(Classification)

한국어	영어
1급 비밀	Top Secret
2급 비밀	Secret
3급 비밀	Confidential
대외비	FOUO(For Official Use Only)

한국어	영어
평문	Unclassified
한측 단독 비밀	ROK Only Secret
한미 2급 비밀	Secret ROKUS
유엔사 공개가능 비밀	Secret REL UNC (REL: Releasable to)

⊙ 주요 용어

- 비밀취급 인가: Clearance
- 비밀등급을 해제하다: Declassify(n. Declassification)
- 세절기: Shredder
- 비문함: Safe
- 비밀번호: Combination
- 비화기: Secure Phone / STU(Secure Telephone Unit)
- 출입증: Pass
- 출입자 명단: Access Roster
- 차량 출입증(보안 스티커): DECAL(Decalcomania, Automobile Pass)
- 보안 업무 담당관(정): Security Manager
- 보안 업무 담당관(부): Alternate Security Manager
- 물샐틈없는 작전보안: Robust OPSEC(Operation Security)

⊙ Useful Expressions

1. Shredding, burning, or pulping[2] is used to destroy classified information.

---

2) pulp: 분쇄하다 | burning: 소각

2. All personnel must be placed on the exercise site access roster.[3]

3. What is the terrorist and information warfare threat to UNC/CFC personnel and facilities.

4. How many initial CUWTF[4] HUMINT collection teams are employed and what is their rate of survival?

5. Last night at around 1800hrs, SOF[5] activities were sighted at the DMZ.

6. What is the combat strength and disposition of NK residual forces?[6]

---

3) exercise site access roster: 연습장 출입자 명단
4) CUWTF(Combined Unconventional Warfare Task Forces): 연합특전사
5) SOF(Special Operations Forces): 특수작전부대
6) residual forces: 잔여부대 | disposition: 배치

Unit 6 | Military Units

Key Words

be assigned to 배정되다	**theater army** 전구육군, 전구군
artillery 포병	**associated** 조합된, 연합된, 편조된
cavalry 기병대	**affiliated** 가입한, 제휴된, 계열의
heraldic 전령의, 의전의	**combat service support** 전투근무지원
combat support 전투지원	**insignia** 휘장, 표장, 훈장
air assault 강습	**airborne** 공정(부대)
turn in 제출하다	**aviation** 항공, 비행
application 신청, 적용	**TDA(Table of Distribution and Allowances)**
orderly room 중대 행정반	분배 및 배당표
weekend pass 주말 외출(증)	**echelon** 제대, 단계
crackle 군소리, 탁탁거리는 소리	**active army** 상비군, 상비육군
hunt and peck 독수리 타법	**army reserve** 예비군, 예비육군
squadron 기병대대, 비행대대	

Useful Expressions

1. A unit is any organized group that is a subdivision of a larger group.

2. A squad is the smallest military tactical unit.

3. A platoon is larger than a squad and smaller than a company.

4. A battalion is under the command of a lieutenant colonel.

5. There are two or more battalions in a regiment.

6. A brigade consists of varying numbers of battalions and support troops.

7. A division is larger than a brigade and smaller than a corps.

8. A corps is under the command of a three-star general or lieutenant general.

9. An army is the largest unit of the forces.

Reading Text[1)]

⊙ Military Organization from Squad to Theater Army

Squad. The squad is the smallest and basic military unit. The number of soldiers assigned to a squad varies[2)] but may be visualized as from eight to eleven

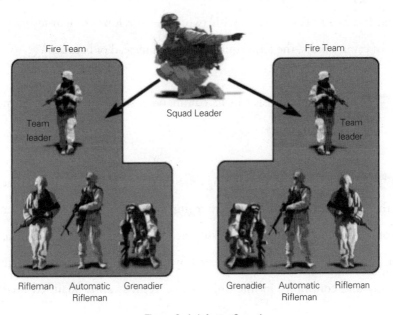

Figure 6-1. Infantry Squad

* Source: FM 3-21.8(FM 7-8), *Infantry Rifle and Squad*(Headquarters Department of the Army, Washington, DC, March 2007), pp. 1-17.

---

1) US Army Homepage, http://www.goarmy.com/about/personnel.html, 검색일: 2015. 7. 29.

2) vary: 여러 가지이다, 다양하다, 바뀌다

soldiers divided[3] into two or more fire teams.

Platoon. The platoon consists of[4] the platoon leader, an officer in grade of lieutenant, and three or more squads.

Company. The company has been the appropriate[5] command for a captain. It includes its headquarters and three or more platoons, and can function for short periods as a separate command. In the artillery, the term battery is used instead of company. In cavalry units, the term troop is used instead of company.

Battalion. Traditionally the battalion has included its commander, his or her staff and headquarters elements, with two, three, or four companies/batteries/troops. In cavalry units, the term squadron is used instead of battalion.

Brigade. The brigade consists of its commander, staff, headquarters elements, and normally three battalions.

Regiment. There are two meanings for the term regiment. In the tactical sense, there are several armored cavalry regiments, which consist of three cavalry squadrons. The term is more closely associated,[6] however with the historical and heraldic[7] meaning. The Army Regimental System is aimed at creating a climate of stability and continuity in line units whose combat arms-qualified members

---

3) divided: 분할된

4) consist of: ~으로 구성되다

5) appropriate: 적당한

6) associated: 조합된, 연합된, 편조된

7) heraldic: 전령의, 의전의

will be affiliated[8] with their regiments throughout their careers. In addition to the combat arms regiments, the various combat support and combat service support branches have been brought under the regimental system. Soldiers affiliated with a regiment wear distinctive[9] unit insignia.[10]

Division. There are currently six types of combat divisions: armored, mechanized, medium, light infantry, airborne, and air assault. The division is the appropriate command of a major general. Each type of division has command & control, combat, combat support, and combat service support elements. The command & control element includes division headquarters and four to five brigade headquarters. The combat element includes varying proportions[11] of combat battalions of different types to make up the division. The mix of units can be further tailored[12] to accomplish a specific task.

Army Corps. An army corps consists of its headquarters, two or more divisions, and such other organizations as its mission may require. The additional units may consist of artillery, aviation, engineer units, medical units, and others.

Field Army. If a field army is required, it will be an organization consisting of a TDA[13] headquarters, two or more army corps, and other organizations of all kinds needed for sustained[14] field operations.

---

8) affiliated: 가입한, 제휴된, 계열의
9) distinctive: 특유의
10) insignia: 휘장, 표장, 훈장
11) proportion: 비율, 크기
12) tailored: 맞춤식으로
13) TDA(Table of Distribution and Allowances): 분배 및 배당표
14) sustained: 지속된

Theater Army.[15] The Army component of the U.S. unified command in theater of operations. An echelon above the corps organization, it provides combat support and combat service support to the U.S. Army combat and combat support forces in the theater. It must be tailored for each theater.

⊙ What Is The U.S. Army Made Of?[16]

The Army is strong because its soldiers are strong. No matter what job a soldier holds, or what rank he or she has earned, each individual plays a role in maintaining our nation's security. More than 675,000 soldiers make up today's Army, which include 488,000 on Active Duty and 189,000 in the Army Reserve.

Structure. Because the Army is made of such a large number of soldiers, it must be organized into units, each with its own leaders and reporting structure. Each unit-whether it's a squad or division-was created to respond to any mission, regardless of size or complexity.

Composition.[17] The Army is made of two major components: Active Duty and Army Reserve. Enlisted Soldiers, noncommissioned Officers(NCOs), Warrant Officers and Commissioned Officers make up both components.[18]

---

15) theater army: 전구육군, 전구군

16) US Army Homepage, http://www.goarmy.com/about/personnel.html, 검색일: 2015. 7. 30.

17) composition: 구성

18) component: 구성원, 구성요소

QUESTIONS —————————————————————

1. What is a unit?

2. What is the rank of the platoon leader?

3. How many men are in a squad?

4. What is a company composed of?

5. Who is in command of a battalion?

6. What unit is larger than the division and smaller than the field army?

7. What types of combat divisions are in the US Army?

Dialogue: A New Assignment

LT Lee   PVT Baker, effective tomorrow you are transferred to Headquarters Company to work in the battalion S-3 Section.

PVT Baker   Yes, sir. Who am I to report to?

LT Lee   To the Sergeant Major. But you'd better do it this afternoon in order to find your way around Headquarters and to familiarize yourself with the organization.

PVT Baker   Sir, I've requested a pass for the coming weekend. Do I have to turn in[19] another application[20] at Headquarters Company?

LT Lee   See SGT Keen at the company orderly room.[21] He'll tell you what to do.

In the company orderly room

PVT Baker   Say, Sarge, how about my weekend pass?[22] Do I have to apply⋯.

SGT Keen   PVT Baker, express yourself in a soldierly manner.[23] What did you want to say?

PVT Baker   Sergeant, I've been told by LT Lee to report to you and ask about my weekend pass. I've been transferred to[24] Headquarters Company, and now⋯.

---

19) turn in: 제출하다

20) application: 신청, 적용

21) orderly room: 중대 사무실, 중대 행정반

22) weekend pass: 주말 외출(증)

23) soldierly manner: 군대예절, 군인다운 용모

24) transferred to: ~으로 전속되다

SGT Keen	Cut the crackle[25] and come down to the point.
PVT Baker	O. K., Sergeant. All I meant to say was that I've been transferred and want to know whether a new application is necessary.
SGT Keen	We can only approve passes for personnel of our company. You'll have to apply again at your new outfit.
PVT Baker	Couldn't you call up the people at Headquarters Company and tell them about the pass?
SGT Keen	Baker, you still have a lot to learn about channels of command in the Army. I wonder how a man like you ever got a transfer to HQ.
PVT Baker	Well, Sergeant, I know how to type···.
SGT Keen	Hunt and peck[26] system?
PVT Baker	No, Sergeant, all ten fingers. I'm also familiar with the filing system, and I'm really good at making strong black coffee.
SGT Keen	Well, that qualifies[27] you.

---

25) crackle: 군소리, 탁탁거리는 소리

26) hunt and peck: 독수리 타법, 검지 타법

27) qualify: 자격이 있다

QUESTIONS

1. What would PVT Baker's assignment be at headquarters Company?

2. Why did LT Lee recommend that PVT Baker report to the Sergeant Major in advance?

3. What did PVT Baker have in mind when he went to see SGT Keen?

4. In what manner did PVT Baker express himself to SGT Keen?

5. What did PVT Baker have to do to get his weekend pass?

Military Terminology

be assigned to 배정되다
active army 상비군, 상비육군
affiliated 가입한, 제휴된, 계열의
air assault 강습
airborne 공정(부대)
application 신청, 적용
appropriate 적당한
army reserve 예비군, 예비육군
artillery 포병
associated 조합된, 연합된, 편조된
aviation 항공, 비행
burning 소각
CASOP 위기조치예규
cavalry 기병대
CHOP(Change of Operational Control)
    작전통제
combat service support 전투근무지원
combat support 전투지원
component 구성원, 구성요소
composition 구성
consist of ~으로 구성되다
crackle 군소리, 탁탁거리는 소리
CUWTF(Combined Unconventional Warfare
    Task Forces) 연합특전사
deep area 종심지역
disposition 배치
distinctive 특유의
divided 분할된

echelon 제대, 단계
exercise site access roster 연습장 출입자
    명단
heraldic 전령의, 의전의
hunt and peck 독수리 타법
insignia 휘장, 표장, 훈장
local provocation of disorder 국지도발
orderly room 중대 사무실, 중대 행정반
proportion 비율, 크기
pulp 분쇄하다
qualify 자격이 있다
radically 현저하게
residual forces 잔여부대
SOF(Special Operations Forces)
    특수작전부대
soldierly manner 군대예절, 군인다운 용모
squadron 기병대대, 비행대대
sustained 지속된
table of allowance 할당표
tailored 맞춤식으로
task organization 전투편성
TDA(Table of Distribution and
    Allowances) 분배 및 배당표
theater army 전구육군, 전구군
transferred to ~으로 전속되다
turn in 제출하다
vary 여러 가지이다, 다양하다
weekend pass 주말 외출(증)

Unit 7 | Rifle Parts & Ammunition

Key Words	
barrel 총열	rear sight 가늠자
butt 개머리판	receiver 총몸
cartridge 탄약(통)	sling 멜빵
corrective action 교정조치	stock 개머리, 재고, 축적
defective parts 결함부품	stoppage 기능고장
front sight 가늠쇠	trigger 방아쇠, 쏘다
hammer 공이치기	cartridge case 탄피
lubrication 주유(윤활유)	ignite 점화하다
maintenance 정비, 지속	wear 마모
malfunction 기능불량(장애)	magazine 탄알집, 잡지
muzzle 총구, 포구	disassembly and assembly 분해결합
projectile 탄두, 탄환, 발사체	bolt 노리쇠
propellant 추진시키는	

Useful Expressions

1. The rifle is designed to fire or shoot rounds of ammunition.

2. A semiautomatic weapon fires one round each time the trigger is squeezed.

3. An automatic rifle continues to fire as long as you maintain pressure on the trigger.

4. The sights are used for aiming directly at the target.

5. The receiver is designed to house the firing mechanism.

6. The trigger guard protects the trigger from being accidently damaged or

pressed.

7. The chamber is the part of the barrel that holds rounds of ammunition.

8. A malfunction is a failure of a weapon to operate satisfactorily.

Reading Text[1]

The rifle is a basic arm of the infantry. It is designed to fire or shoot rounds of ammunition. The M1 is a semiautomatic shoulder weapon. This means that the rifle is fired from the shoulder and that it fires one round each time the trigger is squeezed. The M16, on the other hand, is an automatic rifle. The automatic rifle continues to fire as long as you maintain pressure on the trigger or until the cartridge supply[2] in the receiver is fired.

First, let's describe some parts of the rifle. The barrel is the metal tube in which ammunition is fired. The muzzle is the front end of the barrel where the bullet comes out. Sights project or stick out above the barrel. There are two sights: the rear sight and the front sight. The rear sight is on the rear end and the front sight is on the front end of the barrel. These two sights are used for aiming directly at the target. The stock is used to hold, aim, and fire the rifle: the butt is the rear face of the stock. The removable sling is to assist in carrying and holding the rifle steady.

The receiver is a metal container that is designed to house the firing mechanism.[3] The firing mechanism consists of the trigger, the hammer, and

---

1) 육군사관학교 영어과, 『Military English I』(서울: 도서출판 봉명, 2008), pp. 33-38과 MCRP 3-01A, Rifle Marksmanship, Department of the Navy HQs US Marine Corps Washington D.C., October 2012 참조하여 재구성.

2) cartridge supply: 장전된 탄약

3) house the firing mechanism: 격발장치를 수용하다

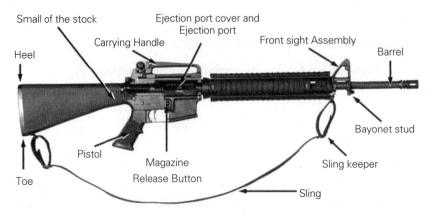

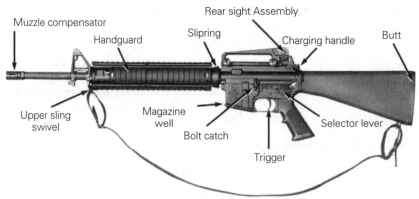

Figure 7-1. Nomenclature, M-16 Series Rifle

* Source: FM 3-21.5, *Drill and Ceremonies*(Department of the Army, Washington, DC, January 2012).

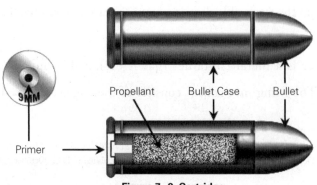

Figure 7-2. Cartridge

* Source: http://www.ibuzzle.com/articles/how-does-a-bullet-work.html, 검색일: 2020.1.24.

the firing pin. The trigger that is operated by squeezing is to release the firing mechanism,[4] the hammer is designed to drive the firing pin, and the firing pin is used to strike the primer.[5] When the rifleman squeezes the trigger, a round or rounds of ammunition are fired. The trigger guard[6] is a detachable metal loop of the trigger housing group.[7] It is used to protect the trigger from being accidentally damaged or pressed.

Next, let's talk about a cartridge. A cartridge is a round of ammunition. A complete round consists of a primer, cartridge case,[8] propellant,[9] and projectile or bullet. The projectile is the part that strikes the target. The propellant or propellant powder provides the energy for propelling the bullet forward, by burning or exploding itself and forming the expanding gas. The cartridge case is the container that holds the primer and the propellant, and to which the projectile may be affixed. The primer is used to ignite the propelling powder.

Finally, let's take a brief look at maintenance. Maintenance prevents any stoppage or malfunction of a weapon. A stoppage is an unintentional break or interruption in the cycle of operation of a weapon. You may have a stoppage, if the firing pin in your rifle is bent or broken. A malfunction is a failure of a weapon to operate satisfactorily. You may, for instance, have a malfunction, if the safety releases when you apply pressure to the trigger. Thus, to keep his rifle in good firing condition, the rifleman always takes all the actions such as normal cleaning, inspection for detective parts, repair, and lubrication.

Most stoppage occur because of dirty, worn, or broken parts, and lack of

---

4) release the firing mechanism: 격발장치를 작동시키다

5) primer: 뇌관

6) trigger guard: 방아쇠울

7) trigger housing group: 방아쇠 뭉치

8) cartridge case: 탄피

9) propellant: 추진장약

lubrication. Dirty parts should be cleaned. Dry parts should be cleaned and lubricated. Dirty, dry parts operate sluggishly or slowly, whereas clean, properly lubricated parts operate smoothly or easily. Therefore, the rifleman always keeps the operating parts of his weapon clean and properly lubricated to prevent the problem of sluggish or slow operation. Worn parts damaged by use or wear should be replaced. Broken parts must be replaced. As stoppages result from these defective parts, the rifleman always watches for these defects and takes corrective action to eliminate or remove them.

QUESTIONS ────────────────────────────────────

1. Is the M16 an automatic or semiautomatic weapon?

2. What is the difference between an automatic rifle and a semiautomatic rifle?

3. What is the muzzle?

4. If the trigger guard is broken, what will happen to the trigger?

5. What part of a rifle is designed for driving the firing pin?

6. What gives the energy for propelling the bullet forward?

7. What are the main parts of a round of ammunition?

8. Why is maintenance necessary?

9. If the safety releases when you squeeze the trigger, is it a stoppage or a malfunction?

10. Do dirty and dry parts operate smoothly or sluggishly?

11. Who is responsible for ensuring that the working parts of a rifle operate satisfactorily?

Dialogue: Immediate Action

John   Well, I often hear the expression 'immediate action' during our firing practice.

Bill   You mean the prompt action taken by the firer to reduce a stoppage?

John   Yes, of course. But what should we do for the immediate action?

Bill   Well, let me explain, taking the M16 for example.

For the immediate actions, S-P-O-R-T-S is very important.

John   Sports? What on earth are you talking about?

Are you making fun of me?

Bill   Come on, John. Take it easy. The S-P-O-R-T-S here is quite different from the sports you have in mind.

John   Well, what kind is it?

Bill   It's from the initial letters of slap, pull, observe, release, tap and shoot.

John   Oh, I see. Your explanation reminds me of the first step of the immediate action; slap upward on the magazine to make sure it's properly seated.

Bill   And the second step is to pull the charging handle[10] all the way back and observe the ejection of the case or cartridge.

John   I don't remember what the 'R' stands for.

Bill   It means to release the charging handle to feed a new round if the cartridge or case is ejected or the chamber is clear.

John   I see. And the letter 'T' means to tap the forward assist, doesn't it?

Bill   Yes, it does. And the final action is to shoot. If the rifle still doesn't fire, then you must look for the trouble and apply remedial action.

John   I think a soldier must do SPORTS well, but I still prefer real sports.

---

10) charging handle: 장전손잡이

QUESTIONS

1. What do you mean by the expression, 'immediate action'?

2. What does the acronym SPORTS stand for?

3. What is the first step of the immediate action?

4. What does the letter 'T' in SPORTS stand for?

5. What are you expected to do when the rifle doesn't fire even after you apply all the steps of the immediate action?

Military Terminology —————————————

barrel   총열

bolt   노리쇠

butt   개머리판

cartridge   탄약

cartridge case   탄피

cartridge supply   장전된 탄약

charging handle   장전손잡이

corrective action   교정조치

defective parts   결함부품

disassembly and assembly   분해결합

front sight   가늠쇠

hammer   공이치기

house the firing mechanism   격발장치를
　　　　수용하다

ignite   점화하다

lubrication   주유(윤활유)

magazine   탄알집, 잡지

maintenance   정비, 지속

malfunction   기능불량(장애)

muzzle   총구, 포구

primer   뇌관

projectile   탄두, 탄환, 발사체

propellant   추진시키는, 추진장약

rear sight   가늠자

receiver   총몸

release the firing mechanism   격발장치를
　　　　작동시키다

sling   멜빵

stock   개머리(재고, 축적)

stoppage   기능고장

trigger   방아쇠, 쏘다

trigger guard   방아쇠울

trigger housing group   방아쇠 뭉치

wear   마모

Unit 8 | Military Branches & Symbols

Key Words	
rectangle 직사각형	mounted mobile 탑승기동
troop unit 부대 단위	armor plate 장갑판
headquarter 본부	track 궤도
triangle 삼각형	self-propelled 자주
observation post 관측소	bullet 탄환
basic branch 기본병과	projectile 발사체
combat arm 전투부대	demolition 파괴, 폭파
adjutant general's corps 부관단, 부관병과	signal corps 통신단
ordnance 병기	smoke and flame 연막 및 화염
quartermaster 병참	ordnance corps 병기단
nucleus 핵심, 중심	transportation corps 수송단
repel 격퇴하다	quartermaster corps 병참단

Useful Expressions

1. A rectangle is the military symbol for a troop unit.

2. A flag for a command post or headquarters; and a triangle for an observation post; dots, vertical lines, and X's are also used to represent unit size.

3. Each branch of the Army is classified as combat, combat support, or combat service support.

4. Combat arms are those branches whose officers and men are directly involved in the conduct of actual fighting.

5. Combat support arms provide operational assistance to the combat arms.

6. Combat service support arms, or the services, are those branches whose officers and men are primarily concerned with providing administrative and/or logistic support to the Army.

7. Infantry units are trained, equipped, and organized to fight on foot.

8. Armor units are trained, equipped, and organized to conduct mounted mobile land warfare.

Reading Text[1]

Each unit has its own military symbol. A rectangle is the military symbol for a troop unit; a flag for a command post or headquarters; and a triangle for an observation post. Dots, vertical lines, and X's are also used to represent unit size. For example, a dot above a rectangle is the military symbol for a squad; two dots for a section; and three dots for a platoon. One vertical line above a rectangle represents the company; two vertical lines the battalion; and three vertical lines the regiment. A rectangle with two X's above it stands for the division. The

Table 8-1. Unit Size Symbols

unit	symbol	unit	symbol
Squad	.	Section	..
Platoon	...	Company	I
Battalion	I I	Regiment	I I I
Brigade	×	Division	× ×
Corps	× × ×	Army	× × × ×

---

1) America's Army Homepage, http://www.tioh.hqda.pentagon.mil/Catalog/HeraldryList.aspx?CategoryId=9362&grp=2&menu=Uniformed%20Services, 검색일: 2015. 7. 30.

military symbol for the corps consists of three X's over a rectangle. And the Army is symbolized by four X's over a rectangle.[2]

There are many basic branches[3] in the Army. Each branch of the Army is classified as combat, combat support, or combat service support. Combat arms are those branches whose officers and men are directly involved in the conduct of actual fighting. They are Air Defence Artillery, Armor, Field Artillery, and Infantry. Combat support arms provide operational assistance to the combat arms. They are the Chemical Corps, Corps of Engineers, Military Police Corps, and the Signal Corps. Combat service support arms, or the services, are those branches whose officers and men are primarily concerned with[4] providing administrative and/or logistic support to the Army. They are the Adjutant General's Corps, the Finance Corps, the Ordnance Corps, the Quartermaster Corps, and the Transportation Corps. Every branch of the Army has its own functions and duties for the overall accomplishment of the Army's mission.

Infantry is a basic branch and arm of the Army. It forms the nucleus of the Army's fighting strength around which the other arms and services are grouped. Infantry units are trained, equipped, and organized to fight on foot. The rifle is the basic infantry weapon, but machine guns, mortars, and grenades[5] are also employed. In offensive operations, infantry units close with the enemy by means of[6] fire and maneuver in order to[7] destroy or capture him. In defensive operations, they repel

---

2) 육군사관학교 영어과, 『Military English I』(서울: 도서출판 봉명, 2008), p. 70.

3) branch는 미국에서 병종으로도 사용됨 예) There are five military branches: The Army, Air Force, Navy, Marine Corps, and Coast Guard.

4) concerned with: ~와 관계된

5) grenade: 수류탄

6) by means of: ~의 수단으로, ~으로

7) in order to: ~하기 위하여

the enemy assault by fire, close combat, and counterattack.[8] The military symbol for Infantry is crossed rifles.

Armor is also a basic branch and arm of the Arms. Armor units are trained, equipped, and organized to conduct mounted mobile land warfare. They are equipped with tanks and other armored vehicles. Tanks are enclosed in armor plate to protect the crew or group of men. They are also mounted on heavy tracks and self-propelled[9] combat vehicles. The primary mission of Armor is to conduct Armor combat operations with enemy forces by employing armor-protected fire power, mobility, and shock effect to gain a decision. The symbol for Armor is a tank track.

Field Artillery and Air Defense Artillery are basic branches and arms of the Army. Field Artillery is trained and organized to provide fire support to infantrymen. Field Artillery units are equipped with both cannon and missiles, placing either nuclear or nonnuclear fires on enemy targets. They provide continuous and timely fire support to the combat forces by destroying or neutralizing[10] the enemy's jeopardizing[11] targets. The symbol for Field Artillery is a bullet or projectile.

Air Defense Artillery is equipped with both guns and missiles, placing either nuclear or nonnuclear fires on enemy targets. The primary mission of Air Defense Artillery is to engage and to destroy hostile airborne aircraft and missiles or nullify[12] or reduce their effectiveness.

The Corps of Engineers is one of the combat support arms of the Army.

---

8) counterattack: 역습
9) self-propelled: 자주
10) neutralize: 무력화하다
11) jeopardize: 위태롭게 하다
12) nullify: 파기하다, 무력화하다

Engineer units take care of construction, demolition, road and bridge building, and camouflage.[13] Demolition is the destruction of things by use of fire, water, or by explosive, mechanical or other means. The Corps of Engineers uses a bridge as its own symbol.

The Signal Corps is both an arm and a service whose officers are concerned with communication, weather, and photographic and range-finding works.[14] Signal units have communications and electronics equipment. The primary function of the Signal Corps is to provide combat support communications essential to the mission of the Army in the field and other communications and electronics support required for all other Army operations, tasks, and objectives. The symbol for the Signal Corps is a lightning flash.

The Chemical Corps is one of the basic branches of the Army. It is in charge of chemical, radiological,[15] smoke and flame operations and biological defense. The Chemical Corps officers must have a basic qualifications in military tactics and be especially qualified in the tactical and strategic employment and defense of men and weapons in CBR activities and environments.

The Military Police Corps performs combat, combat support, and combat service support missions. It is in charge of enforcement[16] of military laws, orders, and regulations as well as prevention and investigation of crime.

The Ordnance Corps is a technical service branch. It is primarily responsible for all weapons and ammunition used in warfare. It is also responsible for equipment or supply used in servicing weapons. The symbol for the Ordnance Corps is a bursting bomb.

---

13) camouflage: 위장하다

14) range-finding works: 거리측정 작업

15) radiological: 방사선의, 방사선 물질에 의한

16) enforcement: 집행, 시행

The Transportation Corps is a technical or supporting military service. It is in charge of the movement of personnel and materiel as required to accomplish the assigned mission of the Army. Materiel is all items necessary for the equipment, maintenance,[17] operation, and supply of military activities. The symbol for a transportation unit is a wheel.

The Quartermaster Corps is a service branch. The primary function of the Quartermaster Corps is to procure,[18] supply and manage Army materiel, and to provide logistical service support to the Army at all echelons.[19] The Quartermaster Corps uses a key as its own symbol.

Branch Symbol of US Army

Acquisition Corps	Adjutant General's Corps	Air Defense Artillery	Armor
Tank and Armor Obsolete	Aviation	Army Security, USAR Obsolete	Army Bands
Cavalry Collar Insignia	Chaplain Candidate	Chaplain Corps	Collar Insignia - Chaplain Assistant

---

17) maintenance: 정비, 지속, 유지

18) procure: 획득

19) echelon: 제대

Chemical Corps

Civil Affairs

Coast Artillery (Obsolete)

Corps of Engineers

Cyber Corps

Electronic Warfare

Field Artillery

Finance Corps

General Staff

Immaterial and Command Sergeant Major

Infantry

Inspector General

Acquisition Corps

Judge Advocate General

Logistics

Military Intelligence

Military Intelligence, USAR (Obsolete)

Military Police Corps

National Guard Bureau

Ordnance Corps

Psychological Operations

Public Affairs

Quartermaster Corps

Signal Corps

Special Forces

Staff Specialist, ARNG/ USAR, Officers

Transportation Corps

Warrant Officer's Collar Insignia (Obsolete)

Insignia of Branch -
Women's Army Corps
(Obsolete)

Army Medical
Department -
Medical Corps

Army Medical
Department -
Dental Corps

Army Medical
Department -
Veterinary Corps

Army Medical
Department -
Nurse Corps

Army Medical
Department -
Specialist Corps

Army Medical
Department -
Service Corps

Figures 8-1. Military Branches and Symbols

* Source: America's Army Homepage, https://www.army.mil/, 검색일: 2020.1.27.

QUESTIONS ──────────────────

1. What arms actually fight in combat?

2. What are some basic infantry weapons?

3. What characteristics do armor units have to conduct combat operations?

4. How do artillery units provide fire support?

5. What's the primary mission of air defense artillery?

6. What do the engineer units take care of?

7. What are signal officers concerned with?

8. What does CBR stand for?

9. What symbol is used to represent the ordnance corps?

10. What is materiel?

Dialogue: Bragging about Branches[20]

Infantry	Hello, gentleman. Did you enjoy your Officer's Basic Course?
Artillery	Enjoyed? Before OBC, I used to have a clear head. But now my head is all stuffed up.[21]
Armor	I think I can understand you. You must have wrestled with numbers during the whole course.
Artillery	That's true. But I also realize the importance of the artillery. Without the firepower of the artillery, one can hardly imagine modern warfare.
Infantry	Don't brag about the artillery. You cannon-cockers are just popping guns far behind the combat area. Did you ever hear of a war without infantrymen? We're the Queen of Battle.
Artillery	The Queen of Battle? What do you infantrymen do in the battle except collect the killed and wounded by our firepower? We're the King of Battle.
Armor	Come on, gentlemen. The rifle is a toy compared to the tank. The gun is just a small heap of iron that lacks mobility. Armor has both firepower and mobility.
Infantry	Armor is just like a blind man. You tankers can't move a step without our help. Besides, remember all the branches are so organized that the infantrymen may accomplish their assigned mission.
Artillery	Stop it. That's enough. We'd better stop arguing. Each branch has its own merit.

---

20) 육군사관학교 영어과(2008), 앞의 책, pp. 79-80.

21) stuff up: ~을 꽉 막다

Armor	That's true. Each branch is organized for one goal, to win the battle.
Infantry	I'm also of the same opinion. We'd better forget about branches and battles. I'm very hungry. Let's go to the dining hall. I'll treat you today.

QUESTIONS ————————————

1. What does OBC stand for?

2. Why is the artillery important in modern warfare?

3. What is the merit of armor?

4. Who helps tankers move forward in the battle?

5. Each branch is organized for one goal. What is it?

6. Which branch is the most attractive to you; the artillery, the infantry, or the armor?

7. What is the nickname for artillerymen?

8. What is the nickname for tankers?

9. What is the nickname for infantrymen?

Military Terminology ────────────────

rectangle 직사각형

armor plate 장갑판

basic branch 기본병과

bullet 탄환

by means of ~의 수단으로, ~으로

camouflage 위장하다

combat arm 전투부대

concerned with ~와 관계된

counterattack 역습

demolition 파괴, 폭파

enforcement 집행, 시행

grenade 수류탄

headquarter 본부

in order to ~하기 위하여

jeopardize 위태롭게 하다

adjutant general's corps 부관단, 부관병과

maintenance 정비, 지속, 유지

mounted mobile 탑승기동

neutralize 무력화하다

nucleus 핵심, 중심

nullify 파기하다, 무력화하다

observation post 관측소

ordnance 병기

ordnance corps 병기단

procure 획득

projectile 발사체

quartermaster 병참

quartermaster corps 병참단

radiological 방사선의, 방사선 물질에 의한

range-finding works 거리측정 작업

repel 격퇴하다

self-propelled 자주

signal corps 통신단

smoke and flame 연막 및 화염

stuff up ~을 꽉 막다

track 궤도

transportation corps 수송단

triangle 삼각형

troop unit 부대 단위

Key Words	
fire and maneuver 사격과 기동	**maneuver** 기동, 책략
assault 습격, 급습	**emplacement** 배치, 위치
counterattack 역습	**assign** 할당하다, 임명하다
aggressive 공격적인	**oversee** 감독하다
inherent 고유의, 본래의	**property** 자산
land warfare 지상전	**end state** 최종상태
METT-TC Mission, Enemy, Troop, Terrain, Time, Civilian	**assess** 평가하다
	accountability 책임, 의무
subordinate 부대원, 하급의	**raid** 습격
initiative 주도권, 선제의	**ration** 식량, 배급량
expertise 전문기술, 전문지식	**consolidate** 강화하다

Useful Expressions

1. The primary mission of the Infantry platoon and squad is to get close to the enemy.

2. Infantry rifle platoons and squads are optimized to conduct offensive, defensive, and stability or defense support of civil authorities' tasks.

3. The Infantry rifle platoon and its squads can be task-organized alone or as a combined arms force based upon METT-TC.

4. The fundamental considerations for employing Infantry units result from the missions, types, equipment, capabilities, limitations, and organization of

units.

5. This centralized authority enables him to maintain unit discipline, unity, and to act decisively.

Reading Text[1]

⊙ Mission of Infantry platoon and squad

The primary mission of the Infantry platoon and squad is to close with the enemy by means of fire and maneuver to destroy, capture, or repel an assault by fire, close combat, and counterattack. In order to succeed, Infantry platoons and squads are aggressive, physically fit,[2] disciplined, and well trained. The inherent strategic mobility of Infantry units dictates[3] a need to be prepared for rapid deployment in response to situations in different operational environment. This chapter provides a brief discussion of operational environments and an operational overview of unified land operations, and the law of land warfare. It focuses on the role and organization, as well as the duties and responsibilities within the Infantry platoon and squad.

Infantry rifle platoons and squads are optimized to conduct offensive, defensive, and stability or defense support of civil authorities' tasks. The Infantry rifle platoon and squad can deploy worldwide and conduct unified land operations.

---

1) US Army Training Publication(ATP) 3-21. 8: The Infantry and Squad(Fort Benning, 2016), http://www. benning.army.mil/infantry/DoctrineSupplement/ATP3-21. 8/, 검색일: 2016. 8. 27. 과 US FM 3-21.8 위의 책(Headquarters Department of the Army Washington, DC, 28 March 2007) 참고.

2) physically fit: 육체적으로 적합한

3) dictate: 구술하다, 지령(명령)하다, 강요하다, 요구하다

⊙ ORGANIZATION

The Infantry rifle platoon and its squads can be task-organized alone or as a combined arms force based upon METT-TC. Its effectiveness increases through the synergy of combined arms including tanks, Bradley fighting vehicles(BFVs) and Stryker Infantry carrier vehicles(ICVs), engineers, and other support elements. The Infantry rifle platoon and squad as a combined arms force can capitalize on[4] the strengths of the team's elements while minimizing their limitations.

Infantry units can operate in all terrain and weather conditions. They might be the dominant force because of rapid strategic deployment. In such cases, they can

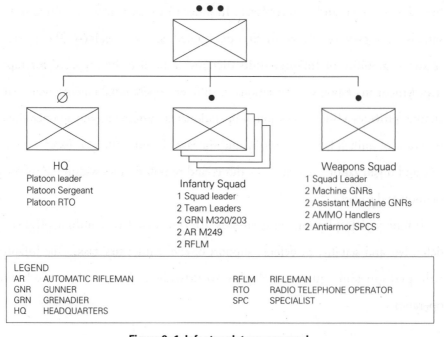

Figure 9-1. Infantry platoon or squad

* Source: US Army Training Publication(ATP) 3-21.8, *The Infantry and Squad*(Fort Benning, 2016).

---

4) capitalize on: ~을 이용하다, ~에 편승하다

Military English I

84

take and gain the initiative early, seize and hold[5] ground, and mass fires to stop the enemy. Infantry units are particularly effective in urban terrain, where they can infiltrate and move rapidly to the rear of enemy positions. The leader can enhance their mobility by using helicopters and airlift.

The fundamental considerations for employing Infantry units result from[6] the missions, types, equipment, capabilities, limitations, and organization of units. Other capabilities result from a unit's training program, leadership, morale, personnel strengths, and many other factors. These other capabilities constantly change based on the current situation.

⊙ DUTIES AND RESPONSIBILITIES

1) PLATOON LEADER

The platoon leader leads his Soldiers by personal example[7] and is responsible for all the platoon does or fails to do, having complete authority over his subordinates. This centralized authority enables him to maintain unit discipline, unity, and to act decisively. He must be prepared to exercise initiative within his company commander's intent and without specific guidance for every situation. The platoon leader knows his Soldiers, how to employ the platoon, its weapons, and its systems. Relying on the expertise of the platoon sergeant, the platoon leader regularly consults with[8] him on all platoon matters. During operations, the platoon leader —

---

5) seize and hold: 탈취 및 확보
6) result from: ~에 기인하다
7) lead by personal example: 몸소 모범을 보여 인도하다
8) consults with ~: ~와 상의하다

- Leads the platoon in supporting the higher headquarters missions. He bases his actions on[9] his assigned mission and intent and concept of his higher commanders.
- Conducts troop leading procedures.
- Maneuvers squads and fighting elements.
- Synchronizes the efforts of squads.
- Looks ahead to the next "move" of the platoon.
- Requests and controls supporting assets.
- Employs mission command systems available to the squads and platoon.
- Checks with squad leaders ensuring 360-degree, three-dimensional security[10] is maintained.
- Checks with weapons squad leader controlling the emplacement of key weapon systems.
- Issues accurate and timely reports.
- Places himself where he is most needed to accomplish the mission.
- Assigns clear tasks and purposes to the squads.
- Understands the mission and commander's intent two levels up(company and battalion).
- Receives on-hand status reports from the platoon sergeant and squad leaders during planning.
- Coordinates and assists in the development of the obstacle plan.
- Oversees and is responsible for property management.

The platoon leader works to develop and maintain situational

---

9) base on ~: ~에 기초하다, 바탕을 두다

10) three-dimensional security: 3차원 경계, 보안

understanding. This is a product of four elements. First, the platoon leader attempts to know what is happening in present terms[11] of friendly, enemy, neutral, and terrain situations. Second, he knows the end state representing mission accomplishment. Third, he determines the critical actions and events occurring to move his unit from the present to the end state. Finally, he assesses the risk throughout.

2) PLATOON SERGEANT

The platoon sergeant is the platoon's most experienced NCO and second-in-charge, accountable to the platoon leader for leadership, discipline, training, and welfare of the platoon's Soldiers. He sets the example in everything. He assists the platoon leader by upholding standards and platoon discipline. His expertise includes tactical maneuver, employment of weapons and systems, sustainment, administration, security, accountability, protection warfighting functions, and Soldier care. As the second-in-charge, the platoon sergeant assumes no formal duties except those prescribed by the platoon leader. However, the platoon sergeant traditionally —

- Ensures the platoon is prepared to accomplish its mission, which includes supervising precombat checks and inspections.
- Updates the platoon leader on appropriate reports and forwards reports needed by higher headquarters.
- Prepares to assume the role and responsibilities of the platoon leader.
- Takes charge of task-organized elements in the platoon during tactical operations, which may include but are not limited to, quartering

---

11) present term: 현재의 조건

parties, support elements in raids or attacks, and security patrols.[12]

- Monitors the morale, discipline, and health of the platoon.
- Positions where best needed to help the engagement(either in the base of fire or with the assault element).
- Receives squad leaders' administrative, logistical, and maintenance reports, and requests rations, water, fuel, and ammunition.
- Requests logistical support from the higher headquarters, and usually coordinates with the company's first sergeant or executive officer.
- Ensures Soldiers maintain all equipment.
- Ensures ammunition and supplies are properly and evenly distributed after the platoon consolidates on the objective and while the platoon reorganizes.
- Manages the unit's combat load[13] prior to operations, and monitors logistical status during operations.
- Establishes and operates the unit's casualty collection point(CCP).[14] This includes directing the platoon medic and aid/litter teams in moving casualties, maintaining platoon strength level information, consolidating and forwarding the platoon's casualty reports, and receiving and arranging replacements.
- Employs the available digital mission command systems to the squads and platoon.
- Ensures Soldiers distribute supplies according to the platoon leader's guidance and direction.
- Accounts for Soldiers, equipment, and supplies.

---

12) security patrol: 경계 정찰
13) combat load: 전투 휴대량
14) casualty collection point: 전사상자 수집소

- Coaches, counsels, and mentors Soldiers.

- Upholds standards and platoon discipline.

- Understands the mission and commander's intent two levels up(company and battalion).

QUESTIONS

1. What is the primary mission of the Infantry platoon and squad?

2. What do the fundamental considerations for employing Infantry units result from?

3. Can the Infantry rifle platoon and squad deploy worldwide and conduct unified land operations?

4. What does the Infantry rifle platoon and the effectiveness of its squad increase through the synergy of combined arms?

5. What must the platoon leader synchronize?

6. What does the platoon sergeant traditionally prepare to assume?

Dialogue: Marksmanship Practice

Bob   Well, what do you think about the lesson we had today?

Bill   Frankly, I enjoyed the lecture part, but hated the practical part.

Bob   Why? What do you mean?

Bill   When the instructor was lecturing on sighting and aiming, I was sure I could knock down any enemy with one shot.

Bob   You mean you could 'theoretically' kill your enemy with one shot?

Bill   Don't make fun of me. I'm serious.

Bob   Oh, I'm sorry. Go ahead.

Bill   When the instructor was talking about the firing positions, I thought I could hit any target by making the best use of the proper firing position.

Bob   What about practice?

Bill   The only impression I got during practice was that the instructor took great delight in punishing us instead of putting the theory into practice.

Bob   Now I think I know what you mean.

Bill   Speaking of practice, I'm sick of[15] it.

Bob   Don't get so upset. Why don't you just practice marksmanship by yourself on a Sunday afternoon?

---

15) sick of ~: ~에 신물이 나다, ~에 질리다

QUESTIONS

1. What kind of lesson did Bill have today?

2. How did Bill feel at the end of the lecture?

3. Did he also enjoy the practice part? If not, why?

4. What did Bob suggest to Bill?

Military Terminology ────────────────

accountability 책임, 의무

aggressive 공격적인

assault 습격, 급습

assess 평가하다

assign 할당하다, 임명하다

base on ~ ~에 기초하다, 바탕을 두다

capitalize on ~을 이용하다, ~에 편승하다

casualty collection point 전사상자 수집소

combat load 전투 휴대량

consolidate 강화하다

consults with ~ ~와 상의하다

counterattack 역습

dictate 구술하다, 지령(명령)하다

emplacement 배치, 위치

end state 최종상태

expertise 전문기술, 전문지식

fire and maneuver 사격과 기동

initiative 주도권, 선제의

land warfare 지상전

lead by personal example 몸소 모범을 보여 인도하다

maneuver 기동, 책략

METT-TC Mission, Enemy, Troop, Terrain, Time, Civilian

oversee 감독하다

physically fit 육체적으로 적합한

present term 현재의 조건

property 자산

raid 습격

ration 식량, 배급량

result from ~에 기인하다

security patrol 경계 정찰

seize and hold 탈취 및 확보

sick of ~ ~에 신물이 나다, ~에 질리다

subordinate 부대원, 하급의

three-dimensional security 3차원 경계, 보안

Unit 10 | Company Organization

Key Words

night vision device 야시장비	sniper team 저격팀
surveillance 감시, 정찰	Stryker brigade combat team(SBCT)
dominant 지배적인, 우세한	스트라이커 여단 전투팀
fast-breaking operation 신속 돌파 작전	mobile gun system(MGS) 기동포체제
deployability 전개 능력	primary maneuver force 주요기동 부대
initiative 주도권	Infantry carrier vehicle(ICV) 보병 수송차량
seize and hold 탈취 및 확보하다	restricted terrain 제한된 지형
urban terrain 도심지역	capability and limitation 능력과 제한사항
conventional Infantry unit 재래식 보병부대	breach 돌파하다
combined arms element 연합부대요소	reconnoiter 정찰하다
capstone manual 기본교범	conjunction 연결
Heavy Infantry 중보병	amphibious operation 상륙작전
Heavy brigade combat team(HBCT)	sustainment assets 지속능력자산
중여단 전투팀	decontamination 해독

Useful Expressions

1. Infantry, Heavy, Stryker, and Ranger comprise the four types of Infantry rifle companies.

2. Most of the combat power of the Infantry rifle company lies in its highly trained squads and platoons.

3. Infantry units can operate effectively in most terrain and weather conditions.

4. They might be the dominant arm in fast-breaking operations because of

their rapid strategic deployability.

5. Ranger units are rapidly deployable, airborne-capable, and trained to conduct joint strike operations with(or in support of) special operations units of all services in any environment.

6. Heavy Infantry units are mounted on Bradley fighting vehicles.

7. The battalions of the Stryker brigade combat team(SBCT) serve as its primary maneuver force.

Reading Text[1)]

Types and Characteristics of Infantry Rifle Companies

Infantry, Heavy, Stryker, and Ranger comprise[2)] the four types of Infantry rifle companies. Some of these have specialized capabilities such as airborne and air assault. Though differences exist between them, they share some similarities in organization, tactics, and employment. The main differences lie in the means of transportation to and on the battlefield, and in the organic supporting assets available to them.

Most of the combat power of the Infantry rifle company lies in its highly trained squads and platoons. The company maneuvers in all types of terrain and in climatic and visibility conditions and capitalizes[3)] on all forms of mobility. It

---

1) FM 3-21. 10(FM 7-10) *The Infantry Rifle Company*(Headquarters Department of the Army, Washington, DC, July 2006), pp. 1-8~1-12.

2) comprise: 구성하다

3) capitalize: 이용하다

also uses night vision devices and surveillance equipment.

⊙ INFANTRY

Infantry units can operate effectively in most terrain and weather conditions. They might be the dominant arm in fast-breaking operations because of their rapid strategic deployability. In such cases, they can wrest[4] the initiative early, seize and hold ground, and mass fires to stop the enemy. They are particularly effective in urban terrain, where they can infiltrate and move rapidly to the rear of enemy positions. The commander can enhance their tactical mobility by using helicopters and tactical airlift.

⊙ RANGER

Ranger units are rapidly deployable, airborne-capable, and trained to conduct joint strike operations with(or in support of) special operations units of all services in any environment. They plan and conduct special military operations to support national policies and objectives. They also conduct direct-action missions to support the geographic combatant commanders and operate as conventional Infantry units when integrated with other combined arms elements. (FM 7-85 is the capstone manual for Ranger operations.)

⊙ HEAVY

Heavy Infantry units are mounted on Bradley fighting vehicles. These units are

---

4) wrest: 쟁취하다, 빼앗다(비틀다)

task organized with M1 Abrams tanks in combined arms battalions of the Heavy brigade combat team(HBCT). These heavy units are highly mobile with tremendous combined arms firepower. They are best suited to less restrictive terrain and combat against an armored enemy.

⊙ STRYKER

The battalions of the Stryker brigade combat team(SBCT) serve as its primary maneuver force. The battalion is organized three-by-three: three rifle companies, with three rifle platoons each. Companies fight as combined arms teams with a section of organic[5] 60-mm and strap-on 81-mm mortars, mobile gun system(MGS) platoon, and sniper team. The SBCT units are equipped with the Stryker Infantry carrier vehicle(ICV). The SBCT battalion retains most of the capabilities of the other Infantry plus the additional mobility of Stryker vehicles. Stryker companies operate across the full spectrum of modern combat operations. They are organized to maintain tactical flexibility within restricted and severely restricted terrain.

⊙ Additional Capabilities and Limitations

The following shows the capabilities and limitations of the Infantry rifle company.

1) Capabilities

- Conduct offensive and defensive operations in all types of environments, primarily at night.

---

5) organic: 편제의

- Seize, secure, occupy, and retain terrain.
- Destroy, neutralize, suppress,[6] interdict, disrupt, block, canalize,[7] and fix enemy forces.
- Breach enemy obstacles.
- Feint and demonstrate to deceive[8] the enemy.
- Screen and guard friendly units.
- Reconnoiter, deny, bypass, clear, contain, and isolate. (These tasks might be oriented on both terrain and enemy.)
- Conduct small-unit operations.
- Participate in air assault operations.
- Participate in airborne operations(airborne and Ranger companies).
- Operate in conjunction with mounted or special operations forces.
- Participate in amphibious operations.

2) Limitations

- Limited combat support(CS) and sustainment assets.
- Limited vehicle mobility.
- Vulnerable to enemy armor, artillery, and air assets when employed in open terrain.
- Vulnerable to enemy chemical, biological, radiological, nuclear, and high yield explosive(CBRNE)[9] attacks with limited decontamination capability.

---

6) suppress: 강압

7) canalize: 유도하다

8) deceive: 기만하다

9) high yield explosive(CBRNE): 고성능 폭발(CBRNE: chemical, biological, radiological, nuclear Explosive)

⊙ Organization

With the exception of Ranger units, all Infantry rifle company organizations have the same TOE.[10] Air assault and airborne-trained companies require some special equipment associated with[11] unique capabilities. However, despite these

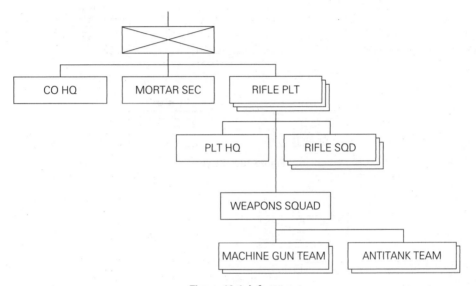

Figure 10-1. Infantry

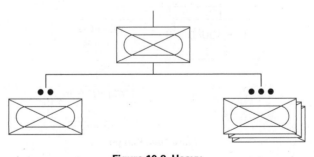

Figure 10-2. Heavy

---

10) TOE(Table of Equipment): 장비표

11) associated with: 관련된

few differences, the mission and employment considerations and tactics are nearly the same.

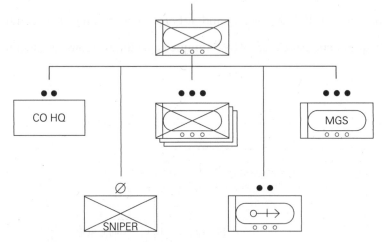

Figure 10-3. Stryker

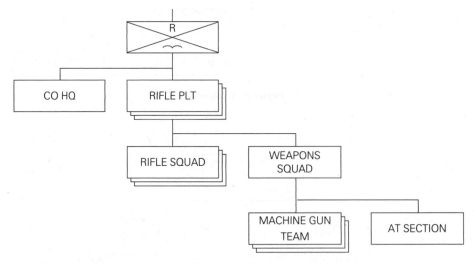

Figure 10-4. Ranger

QUESTIONS

1. What is the characteristic of the Infantry company?

2. What is the characteristic of the Ranger company?

3. What is the characteristic of the Heavy company?

4. What is the characteristic of the Stryker company?

5. What are the capabilities and limitations of the Infantry company?

6. What are the capabilities and limitations of the Ranger company?

7. What are the capabilities and limitations of the Heavy company?

8. What are the capabilities and limitations of the Stryker company?

Dialogue 1: I haven't seen you for a long time[12)]

LTC Kim   MAJ Brown, I haven't seen you for a long time.[13)] Where have you been lately?

MAJ Brown   I have been to the 1st corps headquarters for two weeks for the KR(Key Resolve) exercise.

LTC Kim   Is that so? How was your trip? Did you have difficult time?

MAJ Brown   Yes, sir. There was a lot of work and the place was crowded. However, I really learned a lot.

LTC Kim   Of course, since this was your first KR exercise.

MAJ Brown   Yes, sir. I guess you are right. I'll need to prepare well before the next exercise.

* TROKA: Third Republic of Korea Army

Dialogue 2: Do you have any good news?

MAJ Lee   Captain Thomas, you look happy. Do you have any good news?

CPT Thomas   Yes, Major Lee. I will be receiving a letter of commendation[14)] this morning during the staff meeting.

MAJ Lee   Congratulations! You must be getting it for setting up the

---

12) 이후 예문으로 제시한 dialogue는 필자가 연합사에서 사용했던 『Practical Military English II』(비매품)의 내용을 인용하여 재구성한 것이 많음을 밝혀 둔다.

13) I haven't seen you for a long time. 만난 지 정말 오래되었습니다.
How have you been(doing)? 어떻게 지냈습니까?
It's been quite a while, hasn't it? 오랜만이지 않습니까?

14) a letter of commendation: 표창장

	Deep Area Operation Plan.[15]
CPT Thomas	Yes, sir. Actually the Branch Chief should get the letter of commendation but instead I'm getting the credit.
MAJ Lee	You've been working hard and have made a lot of improvements compared to the last plan, so you deserve it.[16]
CPT Thomas	Well, thank you, sir. But I couldn't have it without the help of him and my co-workers.

* You've come a long way. 정말 큰일을 해내셨군요.
* Great! 훌륭합니다.
* Good job! 잘했습니다.
* I'm really proud of you. 당신이 정말 자랑스러워요.

---

15) Deep Area Operation Plan: 종심지역 작전 계획

16) you deserve it: 당신은 자격이 있습니다

QUESTIONS

1. According to dialogue 1, where has MAJ Brown been lately?

2. Why does MAJ Brown say he learned a lot?

3. What good news does CPT Thomas reveal in dialogue 2?

4. Explain the Deep Area Operation Plan in Korean.

Military Terminology ———

amphibious operation   상륙작전
associated with   관련된
breach   돌파하다
canalize   유도하다
capability and limitation   능력과 제한사항
capitalize   이용하다
capstone manual   기본교범
CBRNE   chemical, biological, radiological,
       nuclear Explosive
combined arms element   연합부대요소
comprise   구성하다
conjunction   연결
conventional Infantry unit   재래식 보병부대
deceive   기만하다
decontamination   해독
deep area operation plan   종심지역 작전 계획
deployability   전개 능력
dominant   지배적인, 우세한
fast-breaking operation   신속 돌파작전
heavy brigade combat team   중여단 전투팀
       (HBCT)

heavy infantry   중보병
high yield explosive   고성능 폭발
infantry carrier vehicle(ICV)   보병수송차량
initiative   주도권
letter of commendation   표창장
mobile gun system(MGS)   기동포체제
night vision device   야시장비
organic   편제의
primary maneuver force   주요기동부대
reconnoiter   정찰하다
restricted terrain   제한된 지형
seize and hold   탈취 및 확보하다
sniper team   저격팀
stryker brigade combat team
       스트라이커 여단 전투팀(SBCT)
suppress   강압
surveillance   감시, 정찰
sustainment assets   지속능력자산
TOE: Table of Equipment   장비표
urban terrain   도심지역
wrest   쟁취하다, 빼앗다(비틀다)

Unit 11 | Map Reading

Key Words	

graphic 그림의, 도표의, 시각	**topographic symbol** 지형부호
representation 표현, 설명	**installation** 시설물
scale 척도	**contour line** 등고선
label 부호	**topographic crest** 지형적 정상
variation 변화	**military crest** 군사적 정상
extent 넓이, 범위	**ridge** 능선
vegetation 초목	**saddle** 안부
cultural feature 인공물, 문화적 특징	**grid system** 방안 좌표법
geographic feature 지형물, 지리적 특징	**crosswise** (십자형의) 가로로
swamp 늪	**grid square** 격자방안
orchard 과수원	**coordinate** 좌표
relief feature 기복지형	

Useful Expressions

1. A map is a graphic representation of a portion of the earth's surface drawn to scale.

2. A map is a line drawing of the earth's surface.

3. Cultural features are those made by man.

4. Geographic features are those by nature.

5. The grid system is used to locate points on a map.

6. Coordinates are used to identify points within grid squares.

7. A saddle is a ridge between two hilltops.

8. The topographic crest is the highest elevation on top of a hill.

9. The military map can spot your exact location by means of a grid system.

10. You are lucky to be away from this place.

Reading Text[1]

A map is a graphic representation of a portion of the earth's surface drawn to scale. It uses colors, symbols, and labels to represent features found on the ground. A map provides information on the existence of, the location of, and the distance between ground features such as populated places and routes of travel and communication. It also indicates variations in terrain, heights of natural features, and the extent of vegetation cover.

A map is a line drawing of all or part of the earth's surface. On a map are shown cultural and geographic surface features. Cultural features are those made by man. Buildings, schools, and telegraph wires belong to cultural features. Geographic features are those made by nature. Mountains, swamps, and lakes are geographic features. These natural and man-made features are shown by symbols on a map. Therefore, the key to map reading is to know how to identify the ground features by symbols.

Colors sometimes play an important role in reading a map. If you know what class of features the colors represent on your map, you can read it with ease. Cultural or man-made features usually appear in black, but red is also used to classify man-made features as to[2] their types or use, e.g., main roads, built-up

---

1) 육군사관학교 영어과(2008), 앞의 책, pp. 96-102와 U.S. FM 3-25. 26, *Map Reading and Land Navigation* (Headquarters Department of the Army, 30 August 2006)을 참조하여 재구성.

2) as to: ~에 대하여

areas, and special features. Geographic features appear in other colors such as blue, green, and brown. Blue is used to indicate water features such as lakes, rivers, and swamps. Green is used to identify vegetation such as woods, orchards, vine-yards, etc. Brown, or sometimes gray, is used to depict relief features such as contour lines.

Military maps use military symbols and topographic symbols. Military symbols are used to identify a particular military unit, activity, or installation. Topographic symbols are used to identify the surface of a region, including hills, valleys, rivers, lakes, canals, bridges, roads, cities, etc. In other words, topographic symbols are used to show cultural as well as geographic features.

Geographic features are depicted contour lines[3] on military maps. For example, a hilltop is drawn in closed contour lines on map. On the ground, it is the top of a hill. When you are on a hilltop, the ground slopes down in all directions. It has a topographic crest or military crest. The topographic crest is the highest elevation on top of a hill; but the military crest is a line of the forward slope of a hill from which you can observe the slope to the foot of the hill. A valley is drawn in U- or V-shaped contour lines with the base of the U or V pointing toward higher ground. A valley is a wide area of low land between hills or mountains. It usually has a river or stream. When you are in a valley, the ground slopes up in three directions and down in one direction.

As you can see, a ridge is a long, narrow elevation of ground. In other words, it's a long narrow raised formation that extends along the top of a hill or mountains. When you are standing on a ridge, the ground will go uphill in one direction and downhill in the other three directions. On a map, it is drawn in U- or V- shaped contour lines with the base of the U or V pointing away from higher

---

3)　contour line: 등고선(closed contour line: 폐쇄등고선)

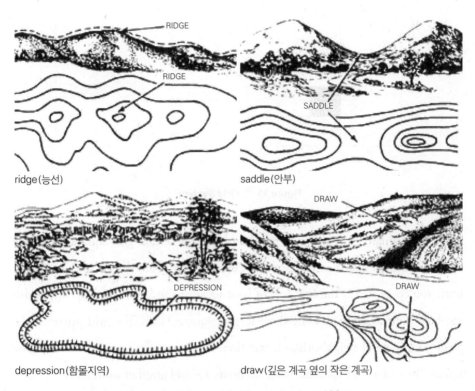

RIDGE

RIDGE

SADDLE

ridge(능선)

saddle(안부)

DEPRESSION

DRAW

DRAW

depression(함몰지역)

draw(깊은 계곡 옆의 작은 계곡)

Figure 11-1. Features of Topographic and Map

ground. A saddle is a ridge between two hilltops or mountain tops. In other words, it is located between two peaks or summits. When you are in a saddle, there is higher ground in two opposing directions and lower ground in two opposing directions. On a map, it is indicated in the figure-eight shaped contour lines.

To keep from getting lost in a combat area or on a map, we have to know how to find the exact location or address. There are no street addresses in the combat, but the military map can spot your exact location by means of a grid system. The military map has black parallel lines running up and down(north and south) and crosswise(east and west). These lines from small squares called grids. The lines are numbered along the outside edge of the map picture. Using the numbers we can

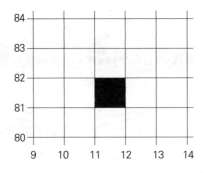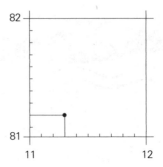

Figure 11-2. Grid System

name each square. To get the correct number for a certain grid square, first read from left to right and then read up. For example, start from the left and read right until you come to 11, the first half of your location, and then read up to 81, the last half. Your location is somewhere in grid square 1181. The grid square 1181 gives your general neighborhood, but there are a lot of points inside that grid square. To make your location more accurate, we add another number to the first half and another to the last half--so your address has six numbers instead of four. These six numbers are called your coordinates. If you always know what your exact coordinates are, you can never be lost.

QUESTIONS

1. What are cultural features?

2. What are geographic features?

3. In what colors do the cultural features appear on a map?

4. What color is used to represent vegetarian?

5. What features are depicted by brown or grey?

6. What are military symbols used for?

7. What are topographic symbols used for?

8. How is a hilltop drown on a map?

9. Explain the difference between the topographic crest and the military crest.

Dialogue 1: The way to the OP

Jack   Where have you been? I have been looking for you all afternoon.

Bill   Why, is there anything that I can do for you?

Jack   Yes, I'm going to the OP on Hill 347.

Bill   What are you talking about? You've only been assigned to our battery[4] for a week. Anyway, you are lucky to be away from this place.

Jack   What do you mean by that?

Bill   Our battery commander is a notorious guy in the battalion.

Jack   Be that as it may,[5] I still don't know how to get to the OP.

Bill   No sweat.[6] The OP has many prominent features around it.

Jack   They say that you've been there many times. Can you direct me to the OP?

Bill   Of course. Do you see the big tree over there? Turn left and walk for about 30 minutes. Then you'll come to a marsh and two trails[7] around it. Take the right trail and⋯.

Jack   Wait a minute. You've got me all confused.

Bill   Well, then, you'd better follow the small creek over there.
It runs to the lake near the OP. That's a prominent feature that will lead you there safely.

Jack   And it seems more simple. However, can I still get someone who will escort me all the way to the OP?

Bill   Sure! Why don't you ask the battery commander?

---

4) battery:(포병)포대

5) be that as it may: 어쨌든(anyway)

6) no sweat: 괜찮아, 걱정 마

7) trail: 오솔길

QUESTIONS ————————————————

1. Why has Jack been looking for Bill?

2. Where is Jack going?

3. Where is the OP?

4. What do they think of their commander?

5. Why do they want to be away from their battery?

Dialogue 2: Terrain and Weather

John   Hey, Bill. Give me a hand here.

Bill   Sure, what do you need?

John   The old man[8] asked me to prepare a template[9] of radiological effects of a nuclear blast. I'm trying to work up[10] some numbers showing the radius of fall out.[11]

Bill   Wow! Sounds pretty technical to me. What's this 'Radius of Fallout' stuff?

John   You know. That's how far the nuclear fall out will travel after a blast occurs. It's important that we plot that on a map so our troops won't stumble into[12] a contaminated area.

Bill   Contaminated! That sounds like getting poisoned!

John   That's right. That's what happens to troops that wander into a radiologically contaminated area. They pick up the radiation[13] and get sick. That's what we call 'the effects of fall out.'

Bill   If we have all that to worry about, isn't there a better way to deny an area besides a nuclear attack?

John   There sure is. You can also use chemical agents to block the passage of troops. But that can be overcome if the troops are well prepared.

Bill   How do you prepare for something like chemical weapons?

---

8) old man: 직속상관 등을 칭하는 속어

9) template: 형판, 상황판

10) work up: 연구하다, 정리하다, 계산하다

11) radius of fall out: 낙진 반경

12) stumble into: 모르고 들어가다

13) pick up the radiation: 방사능에 오염되다

John   Well, it's not easy, but you can also use chemical decontamination[14] to offset the impact of chemical agents on the troops. But this is tough to manage as it requires special training and materials.

Bill   Is that what all those funny looking clothes and protective masks are about?

John   Yes, that's part of it. But the rest has to do with spraying your vehicles and equipment with special chemical compounds and water to knock off[15] the chemical agents.

Bill   That sounds awfully complicated. Isn't there an easy way to block off an area?

John   Well, now that you mention it, there is other method. That's old fashioned smoke.[16] Been around for years and is still in use. The old soviet army really used this to its advantage! While it doesn't exactly deny the area. it does prevent someone from looking into it.

---

14) decontamination: 제독제
15) knock off: 제거하다
16) that's old fashioned smoke: 그것은 구식의 연막차장 방법이다

QUESTIONS

1. What was John preparing for his commander?

2. What are John's idea of an easier way of denying an area?

3. Was John working on something very technical?

4. Is the use of chemical agents as effective as a nuclear attack in denying an area?

Military Terminology ——————————————

as to ~ ~에 대하여
battery (포병)포대
be that as it may 어쨌든(anyway)
closed contour line 폐쇄등고선
contour line 등고선
coordinate 좌표
crosswise (십자형의) 가로로
cultural feature 인공물, 문화적 특징
decontamination 제독제
extent 넓이, 범위
geographic feature 지형물, 지리적 특징
graphic 그림의, 도표의, 시각
grid square 격자방안
grid system 방안 좌표법
installation 시설물
knock off 제거하다
label 부호
military crest 군사적 정상
no sweat 괜찮아, 걱정 마

old man 직속상관 등을 칭하는 속어
orchard 과수원
pick up the radiation 방사능에 오염되다
radius of fall out 낙진 반경
relief feature 기복지형
representation 표현, 설명
ridge 능선
saddle 안부
scale 척도
stumble into 모르고 들어가다
swamp 늪
template 형판, 상황판
topographic crest 지형적 정상
topographic symbol 지형부호
trail 오솔길
variation 변화
vegetation 초목
work up 연구하다, 정리하다, 계산하다

Unit 12 | Communication

Key Words	
transmit 송신하다	correction 정정
wire 유선	out 교신 끝
radio 무선	over 이상
audible 가청의	radio check 감도점검
signal interference 신호에 의한 통신간섭	read back 복창하라
jamming 전파방해	roger 수신양호
radio station 무선통신소	say again 재송하라
phonetic alphabet 음성문자	silence 무선침묵
procedure words(prowords) 통화약어	transmitting station 송신소
acknowledge 수신여부	receiving station 수신소

Useful Expressions

1. A message is a report, order or other information sent from one person to another.

2. A concise message is brief and does not contain any unnecessary words.

3. A transmission must be audibly delivered.

4. Wire and radio are the main means of transmitting messages.

5. Jamming is deliberate interference intended to prevent reception of transmission.

6. The phonetic alphabet is used to avoid confusion and errors during voice transmission.

7. Numbers are spoken digit by digit.

8. Hold on a minute, please, I'll get him.

9. If you have any question, please call me at TANGO 4129.

Reading Text[1]

A message is a report, order, or other information sent from one person to another. Most messages are transmitted by either wire or radio. Wire is used to connect one telephone with another. Radio waves are used to connect one radio set with another. A well-prepared message must meet three requirements: clear, complete, and concise. A clear message is easily understood. A complete message answers the questions what, when, and where. A concise message is brief. In other words, it does not contain any unnecessary words.

A message has no value unless it can be heard. That is, a transmission must be delivered well and must be audible. However, transmission may not be audible be-

Phonetic Alphabet Chart

Letter	Word	Letter	Word	Letter	Word
A	Alfa	J	Juliett	S	Sierra
B	Bravo	K	Kilo	T	Tango
C	Charlie	L	Lima	U	Uniform
D	Delta	M	Mike	V	Victor
E	Echo	N	November	W	Whiskey
F	Foxtrot	O	Oscar	X	X-Ray
G	Golf	P	Papa	Y	Yankee
H	Hotel	Q	Quebec	Z	Zulu
I	India	R	Romeo		

1) 육군사관학교 영어과(2008), 앞의 책, pp. 104-109와 U.S. FM 6-02. 53, *Tactical Radio Operations*(Headquarters Department of the Army, Washington, DC, 5 August 2009)를 참고하여 재구성.

cause of sound or signal interference. Interference is undesirable natural or man-made noise or signals that cause difficulty in reception of transmission. Jamming is deliberate interference intended to prevent reception of transmission. In other words, jamming is intentional interference with reception of signals. Enemy jamming must be reported in detail to the supervisor of the radio station.

The phonetic alphabet is used to avoid confusion and errors during voice transmission. This alphabet is used to spell a difficult word or words that might be misunderstood.

Numbers are spoken digit by digit, but even hundreds and thousands are spoken this way: 2,500 is "tu faif hʌndrəd"; 15,000 is "wʌn faif θáuzənd." As you will remember, map coordinates are spoken digit by digit.

Radio operators use procedure word(proword) to take the place of long sentences. They use prowords to keep voice transmission as short and clear as possible. Here are prowords commonly used in voice transmission.

ACKNOWLEDGE	Let me know that you have received and understood this message.
CORRECTION	I made an error in this transmission. The correct information is···
FIGURES[2]	Numbers or numerals follow.
I READ BACK[3]	The following is my response to your instruction to read back.
I SAY AGAIN[4]	I am repeating transmission(or portion) indicated.
I SPELL[5]	I will spell the next word phonetically.
I VERIFY[6]	The following message(or portion) has been verified at your request and is repeated. (To verify is to check for correctness.) Used only as a reply to VERIFY.

---

2) figure: 숫자로 부르겠다

3) I read back: 복창한다

4) I say again: 재송한다

5) I spell: 음성문자로 송신한다

6) I verify: 확인한다

OUT	This is the end of my transmission to you and no answer is required or expected.
OVER	This is the end of my transmission to you and a response is necessary. Go ahead ; transmit.
RADIO CHECK	What is my signal strength and readability, i.e., how do you hear me?
READ BACK	Repeat the entire transmission back to me exactly as you received it.
ROGER	I have received your last transmission back to me exactly as you received it.
SAY AGAIN	Repeat all of your transmission.
SILENCE	Close(stop) transmission immediately.
SILENCE LIFTED[7]	Resume(start) normal transmission.
SPEAK SLOWER[8]	Reduce speed of transmission.
WILCO[9]	I have received your signal, understand it, and will comply. To be used only by the addressee. Since the meaning of ROGER is included in that of WILCO, the prowords are never used together.

The AN/PRC-150 I radio, refer to Figure 12-1, provides units with state of the art HF[10] radio capabilities in support of fast moving, wide area operations. HF signals travel longer distances over the ground than the VHF[11](SINCGARS)[12] or UHF[13](EPLRS)[14] signals do because they are less affected by factors such as terrain or vegetation. The AN/PRC-150 I and AN/VRC-104(V) 1 and(V) 3 vehicular radio systems, provide units with BLOS[15] communications without having to rely on satellite availability on a crowded communications battlefield. The systems'

---

7) silence lifted: 무선침묵대기 해제

8) speak slower: 천천히 송신하라

9) wilco(will comply): 정확히 수신했으며 지시대로 시행하겠다

10) HF(High Frequency): 고주파

11) VHF(Very High Frequency): 초단파

12) SINCGARS(Single Channel Ground and Airborne Radio System): 단일 채널 지상 및 공중무선 체계

13) UHF(Ultra High Frequencies): 극초단파

14) EPLRS(the Enhanced Position Location Reporting System): 강화된 진지 위치 보고 시스템

15) BLOS(beyond line-of-sight): 초과 가시선

Figure 12-1. AN/PRC-150 I

* source: FM 6-02.53, *Tactical Radio Operations*(Headquarters, Department of the Army, Washington, DC, 5 August 2009).

manpack and vehicular configurations ensure units have reliable communications while on the move, and allow for rapid transmission of data and imagery.

QUESTIONS ─────────────────────────

1. What are the main means of communication?

2. What are the three requirements of a well-prepared message?

3. What is a concise message?

4. What kind of message answers the question what, when, and where?

5. When does a message have no value?

6. What causes difficulty in reception of transmission?

7. What is interference?

8. What is jamming?

9. What is the proword for the sentence, "I've received your last transmission"?

10. What is the proword for the sentence, "Let me know that you have received and understood this message"?

11. What should you use for the sentence, "Repeat all of your last transmission"?

Dialogue 1: Telephone Communication

CPT Wood	Hello. Is this ROKA 4525?
Miss Kim	Yes, it is.
CPT Wood	May I speak to Major Kang, please?
Miss Kim	Hold on a minute, please. I'll get him.
MAJ Kang	This is MAJ Kang speaking.
CPT Wood	This is Captain Wood, Protocol and Liaison Branch,[16] CFC. Did you get message CFC B-P?
MAJ Kang	Yes, I got it yesterday.
CPT Wood	I just called to inform you that LTC Forest, Assistant G-3, CFC, will also escort General Eastland.
MAJ Kang	I see. How do you spell Forest?
CPT Wood	F-O-R-E-S-T-Forest.
MAJ Kang	Is he going to get back to his headquarters immediately after his visit?
CPT Wood	Yes, he is. By the way, is there a heliport near the briefing site at Hill 560?
MAJ Kang	Yes, there is. It'll take about three minutes to get there on foot.
CPT Wood	That'll be fine. Thank you very much. if you have any question, please call me at TANGO 4129. Good-bye.
MAJ Kang	Good-bye.

---

16) Protocol and Liaison Branch: 의전 및 연락

Dialogue 2: Radio Communication

General Information:

1. Message: ROAD 38 TO TILLEPS WILL BE FLOODED BY 1800 HRS. INITIATE PLAN B.

2. Transmitting Station Call sign: Z8C28.

3. Receiving Station Call sign: U4H07.

4. Transmitting Radio Operator: Bill.

5. Receiving Radio Operator: Bob.

Bill	UNIFORM FOUR HOTEL ZERO SEVEN-THIS IS ZULU EIGHT CHARLIE TWO EIGHT-MESSAGE-OVER.
Bob	UNIFORM FOUR HOTEL ZERO SEVEN-OVER.
Bill	ROAD-FIGURES-THREE EIGHT TO-TILLEPS-I SPELL-TANGO INDIA LIMA LIMA ECHO PAPA SIERRA-TILLEPS-WILL BE FLOODED BY ONE EIGHT ZERO ZERO HOTEL ROMEO SIERRA-PERIOD[17]-INITIATE PLAN BRAVO-PERIOD- ACKNOWLEDGE-OVER.
Bob	SAY AGAIN-OVER.
Bill	I SAY AGAIN. ROAD-FIGURES-THREE EIGHT-TO TILLEPS-I SPELL-TANGO INDIA LIMA LIMA ECHO PAPA SIERRA-TILLEPS-WILL BE FLOODED BY ONE EIGHT ZERO ZERO HOTEL ROMEO SIERRA-PERIOD-INITIATE PLAN BRAVO-PERIOD-READ BACK-OVER.
Bob	I READ BACK. ROAD-FIGURES-THREE EIGHT-TO

---

17) period: 끝, 마침표

TILLEPS-I SPELL-TANGO INDIA LIMA LIMA ECHO PAPA
SIERRA-TILLEPS-WILL BE FLOODED BY ONE EIGHT
ZERO ZERO HOTEL ROMEO SIERRA-PERIOD-INITIATE
PLAN BRAVO - PERIOD - READ BACK-OVER.

| Bill | OUT. |
| Bob | OUT. |

QUESTIONS ————————————

1. Why did Captain Wood call Major Kang?

2. What branch does Captain Wood represent?

3. If Major Kang want to contact Captain Wood, what number should he use?

Military Terminology

acknowledge 수신여부

audible 가청의

BLOS(beyond line-of-sight) 초과 가시선

correction 정정

EPLRS(Enhanced Position Location
       Reporting System) 강화된 진지
       위치보고 시스템

figure 숫자로 부르겠다

HF(High Frequency) 고주파

I read back 복창한다

I say again 재송한다

I spell 음성문자로 송신한다

I verify 확인한다

jamming 전파방해

out 교신 끝

over 이상

phonetic alphabet 음성문자

procedure words(prowords) 통화 약어

protocol and liaison branch 의전 및 연락

radio 무선

radio check 감도점검

radio station 무선통신소

read back 복창하라

receiving station 수신소

roger 수신양호

say again 재송하라

signal interference 신호에 의한 통신간섭

silence 무선침묵

silence lifted 무선침묵대기 해제

SINCGARS 단일 채널 지상 및 공중무선 체계

speak slower 천천히 송신하라

transmit 송신하다

transmitting station 송신소

UHF(Ultra High requencies) 극초단파

VHF(Very High Frequency) 초단파

wilco(will comply) 정확히 수신했으며
       지시대로 시행하겠다

wire 유선

Unit 13 | Combat Training

Key Words

equip 장비하다	**assault position** 돌격진지
resist 저항하다	**in reserve** 예비로, 예비대로
agile 기민한	**meadow** 초원, 목초지
thorough 철저한	**in single file** 일렬종대로
noncombatant 비전투원	**open space** 개활지
chain of hills 연달은 고지들	**casualty** 사상자
assembly area 집결지	**cover and concealment** 엄폐와 은폐
reconnaissance patrol 수색정찰대	**machine gun nest** 기관총좌
be attached to ～에 배속되다	**by surprise** 기습으로
hold down 고착시키다	**bayonet** 총검, 대검
foxhole 개인호	

Useful Expressions

1. One platoon is entrenched on the top of Hill 505.

2. 'A' Company is forming up in a plain south of the hills.

3. The weakest point of the enemy's defense is on the western slope.

4. The objective is the enemy position blocking the approach.

5. The task is to pin the enemy down with fire power.

6. A mortar section has been attached to the company.

7. The 3rd platoon is in reserve.

8. Under cover of the mist they reach the foot of the hill.

9. The point of resistance has to be wiped out.

10. That's what's meant by "finish him."

Reading Text[1]

⊙ Preparation of War

Infantry companies are organized and equipped to close with and kill the enemy, to destroy his equipment, and to shatter his will to resist. This close personal fight requires combat-ready units with skilled Soldiers and leaders. These units are developed into agile combat forces by tough, thorough, and demanding training. This takes leaders who understand the effective employment of Infantry forces in a complex OE.[2] All units receive extensive training in reconnaissance techniques. This ensures a thorough situational understanding, which allows the Infantry company commanders to employ overwhelming, precise force within the enemy's decision cycle. This precise application of combat power and agility helps reduce collateral damage[3] to facilities and noncombatants.

⊙ Soldier

The successful resolution of ground combat depends on the Infantry. Individual Soldiers, molded[4] into a disciplined and well-led team, create a

---

1) US Army Training Publication(ATP) 3-21.8, The Infantry and Squad(Fort Benning, 2016)과 육군사관학교 영어과(2008), 앞의 책, pp. 88-93을 참고하여 재구성.

2) OE(Operational Environment) : 작전환경

3) collateral damage: 부수적인 손해, 피해

4) mold: 형성하다, ~을 틀로 만들다

combat-ready force. No Soldier must master a more diverse set of skills than the Infantry Soldier. He is an authority on the employment of weapons from the basic bayonet to high-tech mortars and multipurpose missiles. As needed, he can simultaneously function as an engineer, doctor, air defender, senior radio operator, diplomat, computer expert, mechanic, and construction expert. He is a survivor, because he can conduct operations and attain victory against steep odds[5] in any conditions. Furthermore, Every Soldier as a Sensor means that Soldiers are trained to actively observe for details related to CCIR[6] while in an AO,[7] and they are competent, concise,[8] and accurate in their reporting. Their leaders understand how to optimize the collection, processing, and dissemination of information in their unit to enable generation[9] of timely intelligence. The individual Soldier is the Infantry's most precious[10] resource.

⊙ Combat Training

It's a cool morning. 'A' and 'B' Companies are in the field for combat training. 'A' Company is the attacker, 'B' Company the defender. One platoon of 'B' Company is entrenched[11] on the top of Hill 505. The other two platoons are holding a village which is situated in a valley beyond a chain of hills. 'A' Company is forming up on a plain south of the hills. The assembly area is hidden in mist.

In spite of bad weather conditions, a reconnaissance patrol of the 1st platoon

---

5) steep odds: 어려운 가능성

6) CCIR(Commander's Critical Information Requirement) : 지휘관 주요첩보 요구

7) AO(Area of Operation): 작전지역

8) concise: 간결한, 명료한

9) generation: 생산

10) precious: 소중한, 귀중한

11) is entrenched: 참호진지를 구축하여 방어편성을 하다

was sent out earlier to locate the enemy. They have found out that he is occupying Hill 505, and that the weakest point of his defense is on the western slope.

The platoon leaders have just received the attack order. The objective is the enemy position which is just outside the village and blocking the approach.

The next task is to pin the enemy down[12] with firepower. For this purpose, an additional mortar section has been attached to the company.

While the machine guns of the 1st Platoon and the fire of the mortar sections are holding down the enemy in his foxholes, the 2nd Platoon is approaching the assault position. The 3rd Platoon is in reserve. At the moment, the men of the 2nd Platoon are crossing a meadow in single file. They can hardly see one another because of the thick mist. On the other hand, this mist is an advantage because the enemy is prevented from aiming accurately. At the assault position the men are ordered to deploy. They are crossing the open space in skirmish line.[13] Under cover of the mist they reach the foot of the hill without suffering any casualties. There, they stop short. The hardest part of the mission, however, hasn't yet been accomplished. Shortly, they will have to climb the hill and take the enemy position.

Now they are halfway up the slope. They are clear of[14] the protecting layer of mist which is now below them, so that they can only advance by taking full advantage of[15] all the possible cover and concealment. The enemy on top of the hill is still kept down by heavy mortar fire; but there is still a machine gun nest above the attacking platoon, which opens fire on them from the left side of the northern

---

12) pin ～ down: ～을 고착시키다

13) skirmish line: 산개대형

14) be clear of: ～에서 벗어나다

15) take advantage of: ～을 최대한 이용하다

slope. This point of resistance has to be wiped out[16] first. Three men of the platoon succeed in approaching it from the rear and taking the crew by surprise.

Meanwhile, the mortar fire has been shifted. In a last assault the men have reached the edge of the trench. They are finally taking and destroying the enemy position in close combat[17] by using hand grenades[18] and bayonets.

The combat mission has been accomplished. The companies are reassembling at the edge of a wood near the hill. There, a mobile field mess[19] was waiting for them. The men are tired and hungry; but when they smell the food, they feel a little happier. They are served a hot meal, which in the open air tastes very good. It has been a hard day, but useful practice for the maneuvers that will take place in the early fall.

---

16) wipe out: 소탕하다
17) close combat: 근접전투
18) hand grenade: 수류탄
19) mobile field mess: 야전 이동 취사반

QUESTIONS

1. Which companies are in the field for combat training?

2. Why was the reconnaissance patrol sent out?

3. Where is the enemy position?

4. Which platoon of 'A' Company is in reserve?

5. Why couldn't the men of the 2nd platoon see one another?

6. Where are the men ordered to deploy?

7. Did they suffer casualties?

8. What did the attacking platoon prevent from advancing?

9. How did they destroy the enemy position?

10. What is waiting for the men at the edge of a wood near the hill?

11. Can you distinguish the difference between cover and concealment? If you
    can, what do you call them in Korean, respectively?

Dialogue 1: A Lesson on Combat Principles

SGT Keen	(to LT lee, who has just entered the classroom) 2nd Platoon, attention!
SGT Keen	sir⋯.
LT Lee	O.K., Sergeant. What are you doing?
SGT Keen	Combat principles, sir.
LT Lee	Right. Carry on, Sergeant.
SGT Keen	At ease![20] Right. Let's review what we've discussed lately. What are the basic combat principles? Can anyone tell me? Yes, Private[21] Brown.
PVT Brown	You must find the enemy, fix him, and finish him.
SGT Keen	How do you finish him?
PVT Brown	By fighting him until he surrenders.
SGT Keen	Exactly. Private Harvey, repeat the four main principles.
PVT Bob	The four main principles are find, fix, fight, and finish the enemy.
SGT Keen	Very good! What are these principles also called? Private Baker.
PVT Baker	They're also called 'The Four F's of Fighting.'
SGT Keen	That's it. Now let's hear what the four F's stand for. First: Find the enemy. Private Miller.
PVT Miller	We have to find out by reconnaissance where and how strong the enemy is.
SGT Keen	O.K. What comes next? Private Fisher.
PVT Fisher	We have to pin down the enemy in his position with firepower.
SGT Keen	Right. That's what "fix him" means. Now the third step. Private

---

20) at ease!: 쉬어!

21) private: 이병

Blank.

PVT Blank	We must attack the enemy.
SGT Keen	Yes. But before we can attack him, what must we do?
PVT Blank	We must move forward.
LT Lee	Just a minute. What do you understand by "move forward" just moving forward?
PVT Blank	No, we have to move forward and fight.
LT Lee	That's better. Carry on, Sergeant.
SGT Keen	Thank you, sir. O.K. In other words "fight him with firepower and maneuver". And what then? Private Jackson.
PVT Bill	We have to knock him out.
SGT Keen	How?
PVT Bill	By capturing him or killing him.
SGT Keen	Yes, that's what's meant by "finish him".
PVT Bob	(aside)[22] He'll finish me too, if he doesn't shut up.

---

22) aside: 방백으로(혼자 중얼거리는 소리로)

QUESTIONS

1. What was the 2nd Platoon doing?

2. What do you call the four main combat principles?

3. What does "the Four F's of Fighting" stand for?

4. What does "fix the enemy" mean?

5. How can you pin down the enemy?

6. What does "move forward" mean?

7. How can you knock down the enemy?

Military Terminology

agile 기민한

AO(Area of Operation) 작전지역

aside 방백으로(혼자 중얼거리는 소리로)

assault position 돌격진지

assembly area 집결지

at ease! 쉬어!

bayonet 총검, 대검

be attached to ∼ ∼에 배속되다

be clear of ∼에서 벗어나다

by surprise 기습으로

casualty 사상자

CCIR(Commander's Critical Information
    Requirement) 지휘관 주요첩보 요구

chain of hills 연달은 고지들

close combat 근접전투

collateral damage 부수적인 손해, 피해

concise 간결한, 명료한

cover and concealment 엄폐와 은폐

equip 장비하다

foxhole 개인호

generation 생산

hand grenade 수류탄

hold down 고착시키다

in reserve 예비로, 예비대로

in single file 일렬종대로

is entrenched 참호진지를 구축하여 방어편성을
    하다

machine gun nest 기관총좌

meadow 초원, 목초지

mobile field mess 야전 이동 취사반

mold 형성하다, ∼을 틀로 만들다

noncombatant 비전투원

OE: Operational Environment 작전환경

open space 개활지

pin ∼ down ∼을 고착시키다

precious 소중한, 귀중한

private 이병

reconnaissance patrol 수색정찰대

resist 저항하다

skirmish line 산개대형

steep odds 어려운 가능성

take advantage of ∼을 최대한 이용하다

thorough 철저한

wipe out 소탕하다

Unit 14 | Tactical Control Measures

Key Words

lateral maneuver 측방기동	NLT(not later than) 늦어도
all-round defense 사주방어	contact point 접촉점
axis of advance 전진축	phase line 통제선
line of contact 접촉선	defeat in detail 각개격파
assault phase 돌격단계	tactical unit 전술단위부대
main effort 주공	direction of attack 공격방향
assembly area 집결지	zone of action 전투지역, 전투지대
dispersion 소산	hand-to-hand fighting 백병전
suitable route forward 적절한 전진로	attack position 공격대기지점
effective range 유효사거리	attack formation 공격 대형
retrograde operations 후퇴작전	key terrain feature 중요지형지물
cf.) delay 지연전	degree of surprise 기습의 정도
withdrawal 철수	time of attack 공격 개시 시간
retirement 철퇴	line of departure(LD) 공격 개시선
seizure 탈취	line of contact(LC) 접촉선
consolidation 진지강화	boundary 전투지경선
scheme of maneuver 기동계획	area of responsibility 책임지역
check point 확인점	Area of Operations(AO) 작전지역
shift (사격 방향을) 전환하다	Area of Interest(AI) 관심지역
cf.) lift (사격을) 연신하다	final coordination line 최종 협조선
ridgeline north to ~로 향하는 북쪽 능선	link-up 연결하다
End of Evening Nautical	Beginning of Morning Nautical
Twilight(EENT) 해상박명종	Twilight(BMNT) 해상박명초
maneuver unit 기동부대	

Useful Expressions

1. The commander controls the maneuver units and supporting fires by means of tactical control measures.

2. The tactical control measures insure teamwork and coordination between and within maneuver units and supporting fires.

3. An assembly area is an area in which a command assembles to prepare for further action.

4. The line of departure should be an easily recognized feature on the ground and under control of friendly units.

5. Time of attack is always specified in the combat order to control both the maneuver and fire support element.

6. Boundaries are lines to control the fires and lateral maneuver of advancing and adjacent units.

7. The commander is responsible for locating and destroying all enemy forces in his zone of action.

8. The terrain around check point 30 provides the cover and concealment.

Reading Text[1]

Tactical Control Measures are used for control and coordination of military operations, usually a prominent terrain feature extending across the zone of action.

The commander controls the maneuver units and supporting fires by means

---

1) US Army Training Publication(ATP) 3-21.8, *The Infantry and Squad*(Fort Benning, 2016)와 육군사관학교 영어과(2008), 앞의 책, pp. 112-117을 참고하여 재구성.

of tactical control measures. The tactical control measures insure teamwork and coordination between and within maneuver units and supporting fires. They not only minimize the possibility of defeat in detail by insuring the controlled application of combat power, but they also permit the commander maximum freedom of action within prescribed limits.[2] Normally, tactical control measures include: time of attack, assembly area, attack position, line of departure, boundary, zone of action, axis of advance, direction of attack, check point, contact point, phase line, final coordination line, intermediate objective, and objective.

An assembly area is an area in which a command assembles to prepare for further action. The assembly areas are normally designated by the next higher command.[3] For example, the company commander designates his dispersed platoon assembly areas. In the assembly area, the attack orders are issued, maintenance and supply are accomplished, and the organization for combat[4] is completed. The assembly areas should be positioned and prepared for all-round defense to the extent the situation and time permit. They should also provide concealment, room for dispersion,[5] suitable routes forward, and security from ground and air. When possible, they should be beyond the effective range of most enemy indirect fire weapons.

An attack position is the last position short of[6] the line of departure(LD) where rifle elements deploy into the initial attack formation, and accomplish the final coordination. It should offer cover and concealment[7] from enemy observation and direct fire, be easily recognized on the ground, and be large enough to accom-

---

2) prescribed limit: 정해진 한계, 범위
3) next higher command: 차상급부대
4) organization for combat: 전투편성
5) room for dispersion: 소산 공간
6) short of: 못 미쳐서
7) cover and concealment: 엄폐와 은폐

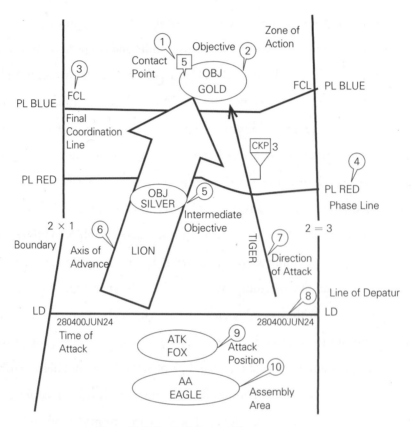

Figure 14-1. Tactical Control Measures

modate the attacking elements in the initial attack formation. Attack positions should be designated even if they are not used.

A halt in the attack position is made only when final preparations cannot be completed in the assembly area or on the move.[8] Any unnecessary delay at the attack position needlessly exposes the unit to enemy fires and reduces the degree of surprise which could otherwise be achieved. The company commander normally designates the exact location of the attack position for his attack platoons.

---

8)   on the move: 이동 중에

Time of attack is the time when the leading rifle elements[9] of the attacking force cross the line of departure. Time of attack is always specified in the combat order to control both the maneuver and fire support elements.

A line of departure is designated to coordinate the beginning of an attack. A line of departure should be an easily recognized feature on the ground, generally perpendicular[10] to the direction of attack, under control of friendly units, as close as possible to the enemy, and not under enemy direct fire or observation. When the LD specified by the company commander may be unsuitable for the elements of the company, the company commander selects and uses a company LD short of the battalion LD; however, it is imperative that the elements of the company cross the battalion LD at the time specified in the battalion order. When the LD cannot be fixed on the terrain, the line of contact(LC) may be designated as the LD. The line of contact is the front line along which our units are in contact with the enemy. If the line of contact is used as a line of departure, it will be marked 'LD/ LC' at each end of the arced line.

Boundaries are lines to delineate areas of responsibility for units, and to control the fires and lateral maneuver of advancing and adjacent units. In the offense, boundaries are referred to as[11] zones of action. In the defense and retrograde operations, they are referred to as sectors of responsibility. Boundaries are normally placed along terrain features easily recognized on the ground such as rivers, valleys, roads, or woodless. Whenever possible, key terrain features and avenues of approach are included wholly in one unit's zone of action so as not to split the responsibility for their control. A boundary should extend beyond the objective at least to the depth necessary for coordination of fires in the seizure and consolida-

---

9) leading rifle element: 선도 소총부대

10) perpendicular: 수직의, 수직선 상의

11) be referred to as: ~라고 불리다

tion of the objective. Boundaries are not normally used at the platoon level except when visual coordination between platoons cannot be accomplished or when, for other reasons, intermingling of platoons is likely. Units may move and fire temporarily across boundaries, but only after coordination with the adjacent commander[12] and after notifying the next higher commander.

A zone of action is a tactical subdivision of a larger offensive area. Normally, it is the terrain between two boundaries, with the forward and rearward limits of the boundaries specifying the forward and rearward limits of the zone. A zone of action for a unit provides adequate maneuver space for the subordinate elements of that unit and is commensurate in size with[13] the unit's capabilities. Zones of action are assigned when close coordination between adjacent units is required, or when the missions of units require a clear delineation of areas of responsibility, such as when the area must be cleared of the enemy as the attacking progresses. When assigned a zone, the commander is responsible for all military operations conducted within the zone except those specifically assumed by the higher headquarters. He is free to maneuver his elements within the zone to accomplish his mission. He is responsible for locating and destroying all enemy forces in his zone, consistent with the accomplishment of his mission and the security of his command.

---

12) adjacent commander: 인접 부대장

13) be commensurate in size with: 규모상 ~에 상응하다

QUESTIONS

1. What does the commander control by means of tactical control measure?

2. What do tactical control measures insure between and within maneuver units and supporting fires?

3. In what way do tactical control measures minimize the possibility of defeat in detail?

4. What is done in assembly area?

5. What should be taken into consideration when choosing the attack position?

6. Why is the time of attack always specified in the combat order?

7. When the LD can not be fixed on the terrain, what may be designated as the LD?

8. In the offense, what are boundaries referred to as?

9. When are platoon boundaries used?

10. What is the commander responsible for in his zone of action?

Dialogue 1: A Burst of Questions[14)]

PVT Blank   What's the subject to be discussed this morning?

PVT Jones   I think it's on the tactical control measures.

PVT Blank   That's great. I'm pretty good in that area.

PVT Jones   Then maybe you could help me. I didn't have time to prepare for today's class. Pvt. Blank: What's your problem?

PVT Blank   What your problem?

PVT Jones   The terms such as assembly area, zone of action, assault phase, and final coordination line confuse me.

PVT Blank   You'll never be a good infantry man unless you learn them. Anyway, the assembly area is an area where troops are prepared for further action.

PVT Jones   O.K. What's the zone of action, then?

PVT Blank   It's a tactical division of a larger area. A tactical unit is in charge of it.

PVT Jones   Oh, I see. But the term assault phase is most puzzling to me.

PVT Blank   It's rather difficult. It's a phase of an attack where forces close with the enemy to engage him in hand-to-hand fighting. Do you intend to knock me down with a burst of questions?

PVT Jones   Maybe not a burst, but there is one more question. What's the final coordination line?

PVT Blank   I'll leave it unanswered. You'd better ask it to your instructor.

---

14) a burst of question: 연속적인 질문

QUESTIONS

1. What is the military expression which includes terms such as assembly area, zone of action, and assault phase?

2. What does 'assault phase' mean?

3. In what way, according to PVT Blank, can PVT be a good infantry man?

4. Who is in charge of the zone of action?

5. What does the expression 'a burst of questions' mean?

Military Terminology

a burst of question 연속적인 질문
adjacent commander 인접 부대장
all-round defense 사주방어
area of interest(AI) 관심지역
area of operations(AO) 작전지역
area of responsibility 책임지역
assault phase 돌격단계
assembly area 집결지
attack formation 공격 대형
attack position 공격대기지점
axis of advance 전진축
be commensurate in size with 규모상 ~에
    상응하다
be referred to as ~라고 불리다
Beginning of Morning Nautical
    Twilight(BMNT) 해상박명초
boundary 전투지경선
check point 확인점
consolidation 진지강화
contact point 접촉점
cover and concealment 엄폐와 은폐
defeat in detail 각개격파
degree of surprise 기습의 정도
delay 지연전
direction of attack 공격방향
dispersion 소산
effective range 유효사거리
End of Evening Nautical Twilight(EENT)
    해상박명종
final coordination line 최종 협조선

hand-to-hand fighting 백병전
key terrain feature 중요지형지물
lateral maneuver 측방기동
leading rifle element 선도 소총부대
lift (사격을) 연신하다
line of contact(LC) 접촉선
line of departure(LD) 공격 개시선
link-up 연결하다
main effort 주공
maneuver unit 기동부대
next higher command 차상급부대
NLT(not later than) 늦어도
on the move 이동 중에
organization for combat 전투편성
perpendicular 수직의, 수직선 상의
phase line 통제선
prescribed limit 정해진 한계, 범위
retirement 철퇴
retrograde operations 후퇴작전
ridgeline north to ~로 향하는 북쪽 능선
room for dispersion 소산 공간
scheme of maneuver 기동계획
seizure 탈취
shift (사격 방향을) 전환하다
short of 못 미쳐서
suitable route forward 적절한 전진로
tactical unit 전술단위부대
time of attack 공격 개시 시간
withdrawal 철수
zone of action 전투지역

Unit 15 | Close Air Support Request

Key Words

close air support 근접항공지원

preplanned mission 기계획 임무

ground tactical plan 지상전술계획

preassault bombardment 공격준비 폭격

air interdiction 항공차단

standpoint 견지, 입장, 관점

munition 군수품, 탄약

fire support coordination center(FSCC)
화력지원협조본부

tactical operations centers(TOC)
전술작전본부

airspace 공역

priority/precedence 우선권

tactical air control parties(TACP)
전술항공통제반

tactical air support element(TASE)
전술항공지원반

clock reference 시계 방향

field army tactical operations center
(FATOC) 야전군 전술작전본부

tactical air control center(TACC)
전술항공통제본부

contingency 우발상황

warning order 준비명령

point or area target 점 또는 지역 표적

neutralize 무력화하다

harass 교란

time on target(TOT) 표적공격시간

direct air support center(DASC)
직접항공지원본부

air liaison officer(ALO) 공군연락 장교

forward air controller(FAC) 전방 항공통제관

fire support team(FIST) 화력 지원반

Useful Expressions

1. Requests for close air support(CAS) missions are categorized as preplanned or immediate.

2. Typical preplanned missions are pre-assault bombardment and air interdiction of key bridges or lines of communication.

* Definition of CAS: Close air support is Air action by fixed – and rotary-wing aircraft against hostile targets that are in close proximity to friendly forces.

3. The TACC assigns sorties[1] in accordance with priorities / precedence established by the Army.

4. Immediate missions are executed in response to requests from supported ground commanders to fulfill urgent requirements.

5. In all situations, the supported ground commander or his representative approves or disapproves all immediate air requests.

6. Corrections to the target must be complete but concise and fast.

7. Cardinal directions are preferred over clock reference corrections.

8. Division has given us priority of close air support.

9. Your platoon is in the most forward position.

Reading Text[2]

Close air support is Air action by fixed - and rotary-wing aircraft against hostile

---

1) sortie:(전투기의) 출격

2) Joint Publication 1-02, *Department of Defense Dictionary of Military and Associated Terms* (15 January 2012)과 육군사관학교 영어과(2008), 앞의 책, pp. 130-136을 참고하여 재구성.

targets that are in close proximity to friendly forces and that require detailed integration of each air mission with the fire and movement of those forces. Also called CAS. See also air interdiction; immediate mission request; preplanned mission request. (JP 3-0)

Requests for close air support(CAS) missions are categorized as preplanned or immediate.[3] Preplanned missions are those for which a requirement can be foreseen. They permit detailed planning, integration, and coordination with the ground tactical plan. Typical preplanned missions are preassault bombardment and air interdiction of key bridges or lines of communication. Preplanned missions are most desirable from the standpoint[4] of efficient utilization because munitions can be tailored[5] precisely to the target and complete mission planning can be accomplished.

Preplanned requests for the close air support are forwarded through operations channels to the fire support coordination center(FSCC) or to tactical operations centers(TOC). The commander at each echelon evaluates the report ; coordinates such requirements as airspace, fires, and intelligence ; consolidates ; and, if approved, assigns a priority/precedence to the request. He then forwards approved requests by existing voice circuits[6] or radio nets to the next higher echelon. During this process, the Air Force tactical air control parties(TACP) provide advice and assistance to the Army command level where located.

The tactical air support element(TASE) of the field army tactical operations center(FATOC) makes the final consolidation and approves preplanned requests for

---

3) immediate: 긴급의
4) standpoint: 견지, 입장, 관점
5) tailor: 맞게 선택하다, 맞추다
6) voice circuit: 음성회로

close air support. The request then is submitted to the Air Force tactical air control center(TACC). Here the Army liaison element consolidates the theaterwide[7] requests and passes them as Army requirements to the TACC. The TACC assigns sorties[8] in accordance with priorities/precedence established by the Army.

Immediate missions are executed in response to requests from supported ground commanders to fulfill urgent requirements that could not be foreseen.[9] To meet unforeseen contingencies during ground operations, the Air Force commander normally retains a portion of his air support in reserve. Details of the immediate mission generally are coordinated while aircrafts are airborne.[10]

Immediate requests may be initiated at any level and must include the following elements:

a. observer identification

b. warning order(request close air support)

c. target location

d. type and number of targets

e. activity or movement of targets

f. point or area target

g. results desired(neutralize, destroy, or harass)

h. desired time on target(TOT)

Immediate requests initiated below battalion level are forwarded to the battalion command post by the most rapid means available. If approved here, the re-

---

7) theaterwide: 전(全) 전역(戰域)에 걸친

8) sortie: (전투기의) 출격

9) foresee: 예감하다, 미리 알다

10) airborne: 비행 중인

quest is passed to the TACP. The TACP transmits the request directly to the direct air support center(DASC) collocated[11] with the tactical air support element of the corps. The TACP may include the air liaison officer(ALO) and the forward air controller(FAC). These members of the air element, however, act in an advisory capacity[12] only; in all situations, the supported ground commander or his representative approves or disapproves all immediate air requests. The ALO, the fire support coordinator, and the unit commander are normally collocated, enabling them to travel together during operations.

When requesting the immediate CAS mission, the supported ground unit communicates the target location and friendly positions to the FAC, who communicates them to the strike flight. FACs control airstrikes from either ground or airborne positions. In the absence of a FAC, ground personnel, usually the fire support team(FIST) chief, directs strike flights on target. Corrections to the target must be complete but concise and fast because of enemy jamming potential. Cardinal directions[13] are preferred over clock reference or attack heading[14] corrections. The observer-target method of correcting artillery or mortar fires could be dangerously confusing in a fast-moving airstrikes.

---

11) collocate: 인접배치하다

12) in an advisory capacity: 자문관 자격으로

13) cardinal direction: 기본방위방향

14) attack heading: 항공기의 공격방향

QUESTIONS

1. What are the two types of close air support request?

2. What are typical preplanned CAS missions?

3. Who assigns the priority or precedence of the preplanned CAS requests?

4. What is the TACP's function with respect to requests for CAS?

5. Who makes the final consolidation of preplanned requests?

6. When is the immediate CAS mission requested?

7. When are the details of the immediate mission coordinated?

8. Where does the TACP transmit the immediate request?

9. Who controls airstrikes normally?

10. Why is the observer-target method of correction dangerously confusing in airstrikes?

11. Why must corrections to the target be concise and fast?

Dialogue 1: Immediate CAS Request

Enemy situation: Enemy's five T-62s are located at CT 123,567, north of the Imjin River. According to the intelligence, when enemy forces are reorganized completely, they intend to cross the Imjin River, setting an armor unit in front of them.

Friendly situation: 72nd Infantry Regiment completed construction of their bunkers to delay the enemy force's river crossing at the Imjin River. Especially, in order to delay the river crossing of the enemy armor, a tactical air strike is necessary because artillery support is expected to be difficult.

NOTE	DASC call sign[15]: RB36, FAC call sign: pintail

Pintail	RB36, this is pintail. Radio check.[16] How do you hear me? Over.
RB36	Your radio loud and clear. Go ahead, over.
Pintail	I will request immediate CAS, ready to copy?[17]
RB36	Go ahead, over.
Pintail	Target information is as follows. This is pintail request number 1-PN-007,[18] immediate mission, priority is two. Target is five tanks, location is CT 123567. Time on target is as soon as possible, not later than 11:00. Desired result is destroy. Have you copied? Over.
RB36	Roger, out.

---

15) call sign: 호출부호

16) radio check: 감도 점검

17) ready to copy?: 받아쓸 준비 되었나?

18) 1-PN-007: 1은 지원요청번호(1: CAS, 2: air reconnaissance, 3: airlift), PN은 SOP에 의한 요청부대부호, 007은 요청 일련번호

QUESTIONS

1. What is the call sign of the DASC?

2. What is the request number?

3. What is the priority of the mission?

4. What is the desired result of the airstrike?

5. Where is the location of the tanks?

6. What intention do you think the enemy force has?

7. Why did 72nd infantry Regiment construct bunkers?

Dialogue 2: CAS

> **NOTE** You are the platoon leader of a light infantry company. You presently occupy a hasty defensive position[19] on the south side of the Imjin River. Your company just defeated an enemy mechanized infantry regiment attempting to conduct a hasty river-crossing operation in front of your defensive positions. There is a lull[20] in combat and your company commander has called you to his position.

CPT   LT. What is the status of your platoon?

LT   Sir, we are in good shape. Two personnel received minor wound, but are already back to duty. We continue to improve our defensive positions and have received additional ammunition.

CPT   Good. The S2 reports that there is an additional enemy mechanized regiment along with an engineer river-crossing company that is expected to attempt to conduct a deliberate crossing[21] at the same location. Division has given us priority of Close Air Support(CAS). Because your platoon is in the most forward position,[22] you will direct the CAS against the enemy's next attempt to cross the river.

LT   Yes Sir. But I do have some questions.

CPT   Ask.

LT   Do we have artillery available?

CPT   The artillery is still moving into position. It will take about four hours.

---

19) hasty defensive position: 급조 방어 진지

20) lull: 일시적인 전투 중지, 소강상태

21) deliberate crossing: 정밀 도하

22) forward position: 전방진지

LT	When will the CAS be available?
CPT	CAS will be available in about 90 minutes. Do you have some proposed targets?
LT	Yes sir. I have an enemy assembly area about 2 kilometers away from the last enemy river crossing attempt, a concentration of engineer river crossing equipment just inside the tree line, and a concentration of enemy APCs[23] and T-55 tanks. I believe that the best possible target for the CAS will be the engineer equipment.
CPT	Why is that?
LT	Well sir, if we stop the enemy from crossing the river by destroying his bridging equipment,[24] we stop them cold![25] Then we destroy the enemy forces across the river at our leisure.

---

23) APC(Armored Personnel Carrier) : 병력 수송 장갑차

24) bridging equipment: 가교 장비

25) cold: 완전히

QUESTIONS ───────────────────

1. What is the present combat situation?

2. How does the LT respond to the CO's question about the status of the platoon?

3. Who is expected to attempt to conduct a deliberate crossing at the same location?

4. What are some proposed targets?

5. What is the best possible target for the CAS?

6. Why is the engineer equipment selected to be the best possible target for the CAS?

Military Terminology

air interdiction　항공차단
air liaison officer(ALO)　공군연락장교
airspace　공역
APC: Armored Personnel Carrier
　　　병력 수송 장갑차
attack heading　항공기의 공격방향
bridging equipment　가교 장비
call sign　호출부호
cardinal direction　기본방위방향
clock reference　시계방향
close air support　근접항공지원
cold　완전히
collocate　인접배치하다
contingency　우발상황
deliberate crossing　정밀 도하
direct air support center(DASC)
　　　직접항공지원본부
field army tactical operations center
　　　(FATOC)　야전군 전술작전본부
fire support coordination center
　　　(FSCC)　화력지원협조본부
fire support team(FIST)　화력 지원반
forward air controller(FAC)
　　　전방항공통제관
forward position　전방진지
ground tactical plan　지상전술계획
harass　교란

hasty defensive position　급조 방어 진지
immediate　긴급의
in an advisory capacity　자문관 자격으로
lull　일시적인 전투 중지, 소강 상태
munition　군수품, 탄약
neutralize　무력화하다
point or area target　점 또는 지역표적
preassault bombardment　공격준비폭격
preplanned mission　기계획 임무
priority/precedence　우선권
radio check　감도 점검
ready to copy?　받아쓸 준비 되었나?
sortie　(전투기의) 출격
standpoint　견지, 입장, 관점
tactical air control center(TACC)
　　　전술항공통제본부
tactical air control party(TACP)
　　　전술항공통제반
tactical air support element(TASE)
　　　전술항공지원반
tactical operations centers(TOC)
　　　전술작전본부
theaterwide　전(全) 전역(戰域)에 걸친
time on target(TOT)　표적공격시간
voice circuit　음성회로
warning order　준비명령

Military English

II

Unit 1 | Staff Organization and Operation

Key Words		
resisting enemy 저항하는 적		**scope** 범위
competent 유능한, 능력이 있는		**complexity** 복잡성
lateral 측면의, 옆의		**in isolation** 별개로, 홀로
recommendation 건의, 장점, 추천		**flawlessly** 흠 없는, 완벽한
initiative 주도권, 선제의		**allocation** 할당, 배당
size up 판단하다		**commitment** 의무, 책임, 투입
reasoning 추리, 논리		**engagement** 교전, 개입
alternative 대안		**constraint** 범위, 제약
adherence 집착, 견지, 충실		**C2 system** command and control 시스템
adage 속담, 격언		**cohesive** 응집력 있는
adversary 적, 적의		

Useful Expressions

1. Staffs exist to help the commander make and implement decisions.

2. Every staff officer has to be competent in all aspects of his position and know his specific duties and responsibilities better than anyone else.

3. A staff officer must have the initiative to anticipate requirements.

4. A commander is always looking for new and innovative solutions to problems.

5. A staff officer must have the maturity and presence of mind to keep from becoming overwhelmed or frustrated by changing requirements and

priorities.

6. Adherence to loyalty will help the staff officer tell the commander the right information rather than what he thinks the commander wants to hear.

7. The staff officer must never forget how his recommendation will affect the soldier.

8. The first is situational awareness information, which creates an understanding of the situation as the basis for making a decision.

Reading Text[1)]

Staffs exist to help the commander make and implement decisions. No command decision is more important, or more difficult to make, than that which risks the lives of soldiers to impose the nation's will over a resisting enemy. Staff organizations and procedures are structured to meet the commander's critical information requirements. Therefore, to understand the staff and its organization, responsibilities, and procedures, it is first necessary to understand how commanders command. Since the Army exists to successfully fight and win the nation's wars, understanding command begins with understanding how the Army fights. The skills, procedures, and techniques associated with command in war also may apply to managing Army organizations in peacetime; however, our doctrine must focus on war fighting.

The coordinating staff consists of the following positions:

- Assistant chief of staff(ACOS), G-1(S-1)-personnel.

---

1) US Army FM 101-5, *Staff Organization and Operation*(July 4th 2009).

- ACOS, G-2(S-2)-intelligence.

- ACOS, G-3(S-3)-operations.

- ACOS, G-4(S-4)-logistics.

- ACOS, G-5-plans.

- ACOS, G-6(S-6)-signal.

- ACOS, G-8-financial management.

- ACOS, G-9(S-9)-civil affairs operations.

- Chief of fires.

- Chief of protection.

- Chief of sustainment.

A chief of fires, a chief of protection, and a chief of sustainment are authorized at division and corps levels. They coordinate their respective warfighting functions for the commander through functional cells within the main command post.[2]

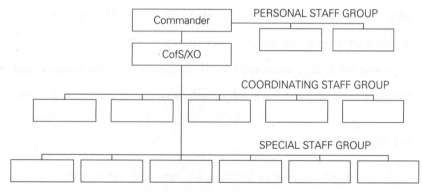

Figure 1-1. Staff Structure Model

* Source: ATTP 5-0.1, *Commander and Staff Officer Guide*(Headquarters Department of the Army, September 2011), pp. 2-4.

---

2) US Army FM 6-0, *Commander and Staff Organization and Operations*(Headquarters, Department of the Army, May 2014), pp. 2-6.

⊙ Characteristics of a Staff Officer

1) COMPETENCE

Every staff officer has to be competent in all aspects of his position and know his specific duties and responsibilities better than anyone else. He also must be familiar with[3] the duties of other staff members to accomplish vertical and lateral coordination to reach the best recommendation for the commander. The commander expects the staff officer to properly analyze each problem and know, not guess at, the correct answer to make a recommendation. The staff officer must have the moral courage to admit when he does not know the correct answer to any question.

2) INITIATIVE AND JUDGMENT

A staff officer must have the initiative to anticipate requirements. He must also use good judgment to size up a situation quickly, determine what is important, and do what needs to be done. He cannot wait for the commander to give specific guidance on when and where to act. He must anticipate what the commander needs to accomplish the mission and the questions the commander will ask in order to make an informed decision.

3) CREATIVITY

A commander is always looking for new and innovative solutions to problems. The staff officer must be creative in researching solutions to difficult and unique situations. Creative thinking and critical reasoning are skills that aid the staff officer in developing and analyzing, respectively,

---

3) be familiar with: ~에 익숙하다

courses of action. If he cannot recommend a course of action in one direction or area, he must find an alternative.

4) FLEXIBILITY

A staff officer must have the maturity[4] and presence of mind[5] to keep from becoming overwhelmed or frustrated by changing requirements and priorities. A commander will frequently change his mind or direction after receiving additional information or a new requirement from his commander. More frequently than not, the commander will not share with the staff officer why he suddenly changed his mind. The staff officer must remain flexible and adjust to the needs and desires of the commander.

5) CONFIDENCE

A staff officer must have the mental discipline and confidence to understand that all staff work serves the commander, even though the commander may reject the resulting recommendation. The staff officer must not put in a "half effort" because he thinks the commander will disagree with the recommendation. The work of the staff officer has assisted the commander in making the best possible decision.

6) LOYALTY

The staff officer must be loyal to the commander. Adherence to loyalty will help the staff officer tell the commander the right information rather than what he thinks the commander wants to hear. The staff officer must have the moral courage to tell the commander the "good" and "bad" news.

---

4)   maturity: 성숙, 원숙

5)   presence of mind: 침착성

The old adage "bad news never gets better with age"[6] is appropriate for every staff officer.

The staff officer must also be loyal to the soldier. Any staff work, whether it is an operation plan(OPLAN) or a training event, will eventually affect the soldier. The soldier will have to execute the recommendation of the staff officer if the commander approves the recommendation. The staff officer must never forget how his recommendation will affect the soldier.

7) TEAM PLAYER

The staff officer must be a team player. He cannot complete staff actions and staff work in a vacuum; he must advise, consult, and cooperate with others. He must be prepared to represent another's decisions as if they were his own. A wise staff officer should also maintain a pleasant disposition because it will help achieve results which he could not otherwise obtain.

8) EFFECTIVE COMMUNICATOR

The staff officer must be an effective communicator. Effective communication is crucial for the staff officer. The staff officer must clearly articulate[7] orally, in writing, and visually(with charts and graphs) the commander's intent and decisions.

⊙ The Staff's Roll

The commander and his staff focus on recognizing and anticipating battlefield activities in order to decide and act faster than the enemy. All staff organizations

---

6) bad news never gets better with age: 나쁜 소식은 나이가 들수록 좋아지지 않는다

7) articulate: 똑똑히 발음하다

and procedures exist to make the organization, analysis, and presentation of vast amounts of information manageable for the commander. The commander relies on his staff to get from battlefield information to battlefield understanding or situational awareness, quicker than his adversary. Once a decision is made, the commander depends on his staff to communicate the decision to subordinates in a manner that quickly focuses the necessary capabilities within the command to achieve the commander's vision or will over the enemy at the right place and time.

The primary product the staff produces for the commander, and for subordinate commanders, is understanding, or situational awareness. True understanding should be the basis for information provided to commanders to make decisions. Formal staff processes provide two types of information associated with understanding and decision making. All other staff activities are secondary. The first is situational awareness information, which creates an understanding of the situation as the basis for making a decision. Simply, it is understanding oneself, the enemy, and the terrain or environment.

The second type of information, execution information, communicates a clearly understood vision of the operation and desired outcome after a decision is made. Examples of execution information are conclusions, recommendations, guidance, intent, concept statements, and orders.

Every commander must make decisions concerning the allocation, commitment, and engagement of troops and resources. In turn, the commander must give his staff the authority to make routine decisions,[8] within the constraints of the commander's intent, while conducting operations. The C2 system is the tool by which the commander quickly distributes his decisions to his subordinate commanders.

---

8) routine decisions: 일상적인 결심사항들

The commander rigorously[9] trains his staff, shaping them into a cohesive group that can work together to understand what information he deems[10] important. Staff officers must be able to anticipate the outcome of current operations to develop concepts for follow-on missions. They must also understand and be able to apply commonly understood doctrine in executing their missions.

---

9) rigorously: 엄격한, 엄밀한
10) deem: 생각하다, 의견을 갖다

QUESTIONS

1. When must the staff officer have the moral courage to admit something?

2. Why doesn't the staff officer have to put in a 'half effort' to his recommendation?

3. Give the examples of execution information.

4. How does the staff officer become an effective communicator?

5. What are included to the situational awareness information?

6. Why does the commander rigorously train his staff?

Dialogue 1: I was wondering if you could ~

MAJ Cho   What is the purpose of your visit?

MAJ Brown   Well, I was wondering if you could help us with a little problem at my branch.

MAJ Cho   We would······ if only we had the time.

MAJ Brown   But it won't take long.

MAJ Cho   I'm sorry, I'm tied up till this Wednesday.

MAJ Brown   Well, thanks anyway. This should be done as soon as possible, so I'll see if there is an alternative.

MAJ Cho   I'm awfully sorry I couldn't help you.

* I was wondering if you could ~ : ~을 해주실 수 있는지요.
* I have no time to spare. 시간의 여유가 없습니다.
* I am pressed for time. 시간이 촉박합니다.

Dialogue 2: You always helped me out

MAJ Hong   Lieutenant Colonel Burn, have you ever been to a Korean home?

LTC Burn   No, not yet.

MAJ Hong   Then, if you don't have any plans for this Thursday, would you like to come to my house for dinner? Since you always help me out my work.

LTC Burn   Thank you. Well, I just did my job.

MAJ Hong   Even though you think you just did your job, it surely was a great help to me.

LTC Burn   You're welcome, Major Hong. I was glad to help.

* You always help me out. 당신은 항상 저를 도와주셨습니다.

Military Terminology

adage 속담, 격언

adherence 집착, 견지, 충실

adversary 적, 적의

allocation 할당, 배당

alternative 대안

articulate 똑똑히 발음하다

be familiar with ~에 익숙하다

C2 system command and control 시스템

cohesive 응집력 있는

commitment 의무, 책임, 투입

competent 유능한, 능력이 있는

complexity 복잡성

constraint 범위, 제약

deem 생각하다, 의견을 갖다

engagement 교전, 개입

flawlessly 흠 없는, 완벽한

in isolation 별개로, 홀로

initiative 주도권, 선제의

lateral 측면의, 옆의

maturity 성숙, 원숙

presence 존재, 영향력

reasoning 추리, 논리

recommendation 건의, 장점, 추천

resisting enemy 저항하는 적

rigorously 엄격한, 엄밀한

routine decisions 일상적인 결심사항들

scope 범위

size up 판단하다

Unit 2 | ACOS, G1(S1), Personnel

Key Words

principal staff 주요 참모	**line-of-duty** 임무계선
human resource 인적자원	**reenlistment** 재입대, 재모집
headquarters management 본부 관리	**prisoner of war** 포로
Personnel readiness management 인사준비태세 관리	**civilian personnel officer** 민간인 인사장교
personnel strength 인력	**personnel service support** 인사 근무지원
cohesion 단결	**band operation** 군악대 운용
replacement management 보충 관리	**internal arrangement** 내부배치
commitment 헌신, 구금, 투입	**space allocation** 공간배치
non battle losses 비전투손실	**augmentee** 증강요원
notification 통지	**leave** 휴가

Useful Expressions

1. The G1(S1) is the principal staff officer for all matters concerning human resources(military and civilian).

2. Personnel readiness management includes analyzing personnel strength data to determine current combat capabilities.

3. Health and personnel service support includes staff planning and supervising such as morale support activities, including recreational and fitness activities.

4. Headquarters management includes coordinating and supervising such as movement, internal arrangement, space allocation, administrative support.

5. One of the G1 or S1 duties is staff planning and supervision over administrative support for military and civilian personnel, to include leaves, passes, counseling, and personal affairs.

Reading Text[1]

The G1(S1) is the principal staff officer for all matters concerning human resources(military and civilian), which include personnel readiness, personnel services, and headquarters management. A personnel officer is located at every echelon from battalion through corps. The common staff duties and responsibilities were listed in the previous section.[2] Following are the areas and activities that are the specific responsibility of the G1(S1).

Manning, which involves -
- Personnel readiness management, which includes
  - Analyzing personnel strength data to determine current combat capabilities.
  - Projecting[3] future requirements.
- Unit strength maintenance, including monitoring, collecting, and analyzing data affecting soldier readiness(such as morale, organizational climate, commitment, and cohesion).
- Monitoring of unit strength status.
- Development of plans to maintain strength.

---

1) US Army FM 101-5, *Staff Organization and Operation*(May 31 1997, July 4th 2009). pp. 4-9~4-10.
2) Unit 1을 참조할 것
3) project: 전망하다

- Personnel replacement management, which includes
  - Receiving, accounting, processing, and delivering personnel.
  - Advising the commander and staff on matters concerning individual replacements and the operation of the replacement system.
  - Preparing estimates for personnel replacement requirements based on estimated casualties, non battle losses, and foreseeable administrative losses.
  - Preparing plans and policies to govern assignment of replacement personnel.
  - Requesting and allocating individual replacements according to G3 priorities.
  - Integrating the personnel replacement plan from the G1 with the equipment replacement plan from the G4 and with the training plan from the G3.
  - Coordinating and monitoring readiness processing, movement support, and the positioning of replacement-processing units.
  - Planning and coordinating policies for personnel determined unfit for combat duty(for example, medical reasons).
- Casualty operations management, which involves casualty reporting, notification, and assistance; line-of-duty determination; reporting of status of remains; and casualty mail coordination.
- Retention(reenlistment).
- Assessing and documenting of enemy prisoner of war(EPW) injury, sick, and wound rates.
- Deployment of civilian personnel.
- Use of civilian labor in coordination with the civilian personnel officer(CPO).

- Monitoring of the deployability of military personnel.

Health and personnel service support, which involves -
- Staff planning and supervising, which includes
  - Morale support activities, including recreational and fitness activities.
  - Community and family support activities and programs.
  - Quality-of-life programs.
  - Postal operations(operational and technical control), including EPW mail services.
  - Band operations.
  - Awards programs.[4]
  - Administration of discipline.
- Personnel service support, including finance, record keeping, Servicemen's Group Life Insurance(SGLI),[5] religious support, legal services, and command information.
- Assessment of the status of morale and recommendation of programs to enhance low morale.
- Coordination of interaction with
  - Army and Air Force Exchange Service(AAFES), for example, for movies.
  - Nonmilitary agencies servicing the command, such as the American Red Cross.

Headquarters management, which includes -
- Managing the organization and administration of the headquarters.

---

4) awards program: 수상계획
5) Servicemen's Group Life Insurance(SGLI): 군인생명보험

- Recommending manpower allocation.
- Coordinating and supervising.
  - Movement.
  - Internal arrangement.
  - Space allocation.
  - Administrative support.

Staff planning and supervision over -

- Administrative support for military and civilian personnel, to include leaves, passes, counseling, and personal affairs.
- Administrative support for augmentees(non-US forces, foreign nationals, civilian internees[6]).
- Administration of discipline, and law and order(in coordination with the G3(PM)), including absence without leave(AWOL),[7] desertion,[8] court martial offenses,[9] requests for transfers, rewards and punishments,[10] and disposition of stragglers.[11]
- Recommending of intelligence requirements(IR) to the G2.

Coordination of staff responsibility for the following special staff officers:

- Adjutant general(AG). (부관)
- Civilian personnel officer(CPO). (민간인 인사장교)
- Dental surgeon. (치과 진료)

---

6) civilian internee: 민간인 피수용자
7) absence without leave(AWOL): 탈영, 무단이탈
8) desertion: 탈영, 도망
9) court martial offense: 군사법정위반
10) rewards and punishments: 상벌
11) disposition of straggler: 낙오자 처리

- Equal opportunity advisor(EOA). (기회균등 상담관)

- Finance officer. (경리장교)

- Surgeon. (외과 군의관)

- Veterinary officer. (수의장교)

> **NOTE** The duties and responsibilities of these special staff officers can be found under the special staff officer section, page 4-17(FM 101-5).

Coordination of staff responsibility for the following special and personal staff officers (when coordination is necessary):

- Chaplain. (목사)

- Inspector general. (감찰)

- Public affairs officer. (공무장교)

- Staff judge advocate. (법무참모)

> **NOTE** When these personal staff officers are performing duties as special staff officers, the G1 is responsible for staff coordination. See the personal staff officer section, page 4-29(FM 101-5), for the duties and responsibilities of the chaplain, IG, PAO, and SJA.

QUESTIONS

1. Which assistant chief of staff does perform tasks concerning human resources?

2. Is the task of personnel replacement management included in health and personnel service support?

3. Give some examples of the assistant chief of staff, G1 including headquarters management.

4. Who is responsible for coordinating staff responsibility with special and personal staff officers such as chaplain, inspector general and public affairs officer?

5. Say about the S1's tasks including personnel readiness management.

Dialogue 1: Let me introduce you to my family

MAJ Cortez   Major Kim, let me introduce you to my family. This is my wife, Alice. Alice, this is major Kim.

MAJ Kim   I'm glad to meet you, Alice.

Alice   The pleasure is all mine. I've heard so much about you. Steve says you helped him a lot during the past months.

MAJ Kim   It wasn't much. But thank you, anyway.

MAJ Cortez   And sir, the kid playing with the dog over there is my son, Max.

MAJ Kim   He has the good looks of his father.

MAJ Cortez   Oh, thank you.

Dialogue 2: You always helped me out

MAJ Lee   Major Smith! It's such a nice day, and it's good to get out and spend time with good friends.

MAJ Smith   Yes, Major Lee, It's been a really long time since I had such a comfortable time.[12] Anyway, what about getting together at my place next time?

MAJ Lee   At your place? Wouldn't it be too much trouble for your wife if we get together at your house?

MAJ Smith   No, we can have a barbecue in the back yeard. Our wives just need to prepare some salad.

CAP Johnson   Sounds good, but what wives try to avoid isn't the cooking, it's

---

12) comfortable time: 여유 있는 시간

the cleaning. So we're done, don't you think we should clean up?

MAJ Smith   Captain Johnson is right. Besides, each of us can prepare a dish at home and bring it to the BBQ.[13)]

Job Specific Expression of Personnels

Do you have a regulation regarding duty assignment and promotion?
보직과 진급 관련 규정이 있습니까?

Who reports a change of record, and how is done?
기록 변경보고는 누가 어떻게 하나요?

Replacement priorities will based primarily on the tactical situation and personnel readiness evaluation.
병력보충의 우선순위는 전술상황 및 병력준비태세평가에 근거를 둡니다.

The change of current task organization must be reflected to make personnel summary reports more accurate.
정확한 병력요약보고는 현재의 전투편성 변경이 반영되어야 합니다.

The five types of CFC Personnel reports are Personnel summary, Mass Casualty, Critical personnel shortage, Remarks, and EPW facility.
연합사 인사병력보고의 5가지는 병력요약, 대량사상자, 주요보직자 소요, 비고, 적 포로수용 시설 보고입니다.

---

13) BBQ(barbecue): 바비큐

Military Terminology ───────────────

absence without leave(AWOL) 탈영,
    무단이탈
adjutant general(AG) 부관
augmentee 증강요원
awards program 수상계획
band operation 군악대 운용
BBQ(barbecue) 바비큐
chaplain 목사
civilian internee 민간인 피수용자
civilian personnel officer(CPO)
    민간인 인사장교
cohesion 단결
comfortable time 여유 있는 시간
commitment 헌신, 구금, 투입
court martial offense 군사법정위반
dental surgeon 치과 진료
desertion 탈영, 도망
disposition of straggler 낙오자 처리
equal opportunity advisor(EOA)
    기회균등 상담관
finance officer 경리장교
headquarters management 본부관리
human resource 인적자원

inspector general 감찰
internal arrangement 내부배치
leave 휴가
line-of-duty 임무계선
non battle losses 비전투손실
notification 통지
Personnel readiness management
    인사준비태세관리
personnel service support 인사근무지원
personnel strength 인력
principal staff 주요 참모
prisoner of war 포로
project 전망하다
public affairs officer 공무장교, 공공장교
reenlistment 재입대, 재모집
replacement management 보충관리
rewards and punishments 상벌
Servicemen's Group Life
    Insurance(SGLI) 군인생명보험
space allocation 공간배치
staff judge advocate 법무참모
surgeon 외과 군의관
veterinary officer 수의장교

Unit 3 | ACOS, G2(S2), Intelligence

Useful Expressions

1. The G2(S2) is the principal staff officer for all matters concerning military intelligence(MI), counterintelligence, security operations, and military intelligence training.

2. Military intelligence(MI) involves disseminating intelligence to commanders and other users in a timely manner.

3. Military intelligence(MI) involves assisting the G3(deception officer) in preparing deception plans by recommending the target and objective based on assessed enemy collection capability and susceptibility to deception.

4. Counterintelligence(CI) involves identifying enemy intelligence collection capabilities, such as human intelligence(HUMINT), signals intelligence(SIGINT), imagery intelligence(IMINT), and efforts targeted against the unit.

5. Security operations involve supervising the command and personnel security program.

6. Intelligence training involves preparing the command intelligence training plan and integrating intelligence, counterintelligence, operational security, enemy(organization, equipment, and operations), and intelligence preparation of the battlefield considerations into other training plans.

Reading Text[1]

The G2(S2) is the principal staff officer for all matters concerning military intelligence(MI), counterintelligence, security operations, and military intelligence training. An intelligence officer is located at every echelon from battalion through corps. The common staff duties and responsibilities were listed in the previous section. Following are the areas and activities that are the specific responsibility of the G2(S2).

Military intelligence(MI), which involves -
- Disseminating intelligence to commanders and other users in a timely manner.
- Collecting, processing, producing, and disseminating intelligence.
- Conducting and coordinating intelligence preparation of the

---

1) US Army FM 101-5, *Staff Organization and Operation*(May 31 1997, July 4th 2009). pp. 4-10~4-12.

battlefield(IPB).

- Recommending unit area of interest and assisting the staff in defining unit battle space.
- Describing the effects of the battlefield environment on friendly and enemy capabilities.
- Evaluating the threat(their doctrine, order of battle factors, high-value targets(HVTs), capabilities, and weaknesses).
- Determining enemy most probable and most dangerous courses of action and key events.
- Coordinating with the entire staff and recommending PIR for the commander's critical information requirements.
- Integrating staff input to IPB products for staff planning, decision making, and targeting.
- Coordinating with the G3(PM)[2] for processing(for intelligence purposes) materials taken from EPWs[3] and civilian internees.
- Coordinating ground and aerial reconnaissance and surveillance operations with other collection assets.
- Participating in targeting meeting.
- Debriefing personnel returning from enemy control.
- Analyzing, in coordination with the G3(engineer coordinator(ENCOORD)), enemy capability to use environmental manipulation[4] as a means to impede friendly forces or jeopardize long-term objectives.
- Coordinating technical intelligence activities and disseminating information.

---

2) PM(Program Manager): 사업관리관, 주무참모의 의미일 것으로 추정
3) EPWs(Enemy Prisoner of War): 적 포로
4) environmental manipulation: 환경 조성

- Assisting the G3 in planning target acquisition activities for collection of target information.
- Coordination with the chemical officer to analyze the enemy's capability and predictability of using nuclear, biological, and chemical(NBC) weapons.
- Coordinating with the G1 the enemy situation that may affect evacuation or hospitalization plans.[5]
- Coordinating with the G4 the enemy situation that may affect logistics operations.
- Coordinating with the G5 the enemy situation that may affect civil-military operations.
- Assisting the G3(deception officer) in preparing deception plans by recommending the target and objective based on assessed enemy collection capability and susceptibility to deception.
- Assisting the G3 in information operations, to include command and control warfare(C2W).
- Planning and managing intelligence collection operations in coordination with the G3 and fire support planners.
- Recording, evaluating, and analyzing collected information to produce all-source intelligence that answers the commander's priority intelligence requirements and information requirements.
- Maintaining the current situation regarding the enemy and environmental factors and updating IPB and the intelligence estimate.
- Determining map requirements and managing the acquisition and distribution of map and terrain products in coordination with the

---

5) evacuation or hospitalization plans: 후송 및 의무계획

G3(ENCOORD), who is responsible for map and terrain product production.

Counterintelligence(CI), which involves -

- Identifying enemy intelligence collection capabilities, such as human intelligence(HUMINT), signals intelligence(SIGINT), imagery intelligence(IMINT), and efforts targeted against the unit.
- Evaluating enemy intelligence capabilities as they affect the areas of OPSEC,[6] countersurveillance, signals security(SIGSEC),[7] security operations, deceptions planning, psychological operations(PSYOP),[8] rear area operations, and force protection.
- Conducting counterintelligence liaison for security and force protection.
- Conducting counterintelligence force protection source operations.

Security operations, which involve -

- Supervising the command and personnel security program.
- Evaluating physical security vulnerabilities to support the G3.
- Coordinating security checks for indigenous personnel.[9]

Staff planning and supervision over the special security office

Intelligence training, which involves -

- Preparing the command intelligence training plan and integrating

---

6) OPSEC(Operations Security): 작전보안
7) signals security(SIGSEC): 통신보안, 신호보안
8) psychological operations(PSYOP): 심리전
9) indigenous personnel: 토착민

intelligence, counterintelligence, operational security, enemy(organization, equipment, and operations), and intelligence preparation of the battlefield considerations into other training plans.

• Exercising staff supervision of MI[10] support to the command's intelligence training program.

Coordination of staff responsibility for the special staff officer, the staff weather officer(SWO). (The duties and responsibilities of the SWO can be found under the special staff officer section.)

---

10) MI: Military Intelligence(군사정보)

QUESTIONS

1. Which assistant chief of staff does perform concerning 'military intelligence'?

2. Does it determine that the enemy's most probable and most dangerous course of action are included in the counterintelligence work of the G2?

3. Give some examples of the duties of the assistant chief of staff, G2 including security operations.

4. Who is responsible for coordinating staff responsibility with the staff weather officer?

Dialogue 1: You got it all wrong

COL Kim	Welcome to my house, Colonel Smith.
COL Smith	Thank you for inviting me, Colonel Kim.
COL Kim	My wife has prepared some traditional Korean food for you. We have Bulgogi, Japche, Kimchi and many other foods.
COL Smith	Wait! Is Kimchi a traditional Korean food? I thought it was a Japanese food because I heard Japanese call it Ki-mu-chi while I was in Japan.
COL Kim	No, you've got it all wrong. Kimchi is originally from Korea, and it was taken over to Japan. The Japanese imitated it because it tasted good and healthful.

* You've got it all wrong. 당신은 잘못 알고 계십니다.

* I'm afraid I can't agree with you. 유감이지만 당신에게 동의할 수 없습니다.

Dialogue 2: get better

LTC Kim	What a lovely house you have, Colonel Wilson.
COL Wilson	Thanks. We just moved in.
LTC Kim	The good thing is that your house is near the base.
COL Wilson	Yes, it only take about five minutes by car and it give me more time with family.
LTC Kim	How is your family adjusting to their new life in Korea?
COL Wilson	Well, at first we had a hard time setting in, but now we have a beautiful house and got to know many friends, so life in Korea is getting better.

* What a fabulous house you have! 아주 멋진 집을 가지고 계시군요!

* getting better: 나아지다 | greatly improved: 많이 나아졌다

Job Specific Expression of Intelligences

Shredding, burning, or pulping is used for destroying classified information.

비밀정보 파기 시에는 세절, 소각, 또는 분쇄합니다.

Last night around 1800hrs., SOF[11] activities were sighted at the DMZ.

어제 저녁 18시경 DMZ에서 북한 특수부대의 활동이 있었습니다.

What is the ability of the KPA[12] to sustain combat?

북한 인민군 전투지속능력은 어떠합니까?

What are the main targets of the enemy's Special Forces and what kind of preparation do we have against them?

적 특작부대의 주요타격목표는 무엇이며, 이에 대한 아군 측의 대비태세는 무엇입니까?

What is the combat strength and disposition of NK residual forces?

북한 잔여부대의 전투력 및 배치는 어떠합니까?

Are there any known environmentally hazardous(Chem/Bio) locations?

알려진 환경적 위험(화학/생물학)지역이 있습니까?

What is the terrorist and information warfare threat to UNC/CFC personnel and facilities?

유엔사/연합사 요원 및 시설에 대한 테러 및 정보전 위협은 무엇입니까?

How many levels does WATCHCON[13] have? What activity/events will cause a change in the WATCHCON status?

정보감시태세는 몇 단계이며 단계별 상태와 감시활동수준은 어떻게 됩니까?

---

11) SOF(Special Operation Forces): 특수작전부대

12) KPA(Korean People's Army): 북한 인민군

13) WATCHCON(Watch Condition): 감시태세

What is the relationship between DEFCON and WATCHCON?

데프콘과 워치콘의 관계는 어떻게 됩니까?

What are information gathering means and how are they applied?

첩보수집자산은 무엇이며 어떻게 운용됩니까?

What is the role of the G2 section at this initial planing meeting?

이번 최초계획회의에서 정부참모부가 수행해야 하는 역할은 무엇입니까?

How often do you update a TSAR[14] of NK?

북한표적체계분석보고는 몇 년마다 최신화되고 있습니까?

---

14) TSAR(Theater System Analysis Report): 표적분석체계보고

Military Terminology

civilian internees 민간인 피억류자

command and control warfare(C2W)
　　지휘통제전

commander's priority intelligence
　　requirement 지휘관 우선 정보요구

counterintelligence 대정보

debrief 임무수행계획보고

deception plan 기만계획

disseminate 전파하다

environmental manipulation 환경 조성

EPWs(Enemy Prisoner of War) 적 포로

evacuation or hospitalization plans
　　후송 및 의무 계획

high-value targets(HVTs) 고가치표적

human intelligence(HUMINT) 인간정보

imagery intelligence 영상정보

indigenous personnel 토착민

information requirement 정보요구

intelligence preparation of the battlefield
　　(IPB) 전장정보준비

KPA(Korean People's Army) 북한 인민군

map requirement 지도 소요

MI(Military Intelligence) 군사정보

OPSEC(Operations Security) 작전보안

PM(Program Manager) 사업관리관

Priority Intelligence Requirement(PIR)
　　우선 정보요구

psychological operations(PSYOP) 심리전

rear area operation 후방지역작전

signals intelligence(SIGINT) 신호정보

signals security(SIGSEC) 통신보안, 신호보안

SOF(Special Operation Forces)
　　특수작전부대

susceptibility 민감성

TSAR(Theater System Analysis Report)
　　표적분석체계보고

vulnerability 취약점

WATCHCON(Watch Condition) 감시태세

Unit 4 | ACOS, G3(S3), Operations

Key Words

command 지휘, 통수, 명령, 구령, 사령부

training guidance 훈련지침

mission-essential task list(METL)
   임무과제목록

quotas 정원, 물량

SOP(Standing Operating Procedure)
   예규, 내규

OPORD(Operation Order) 작전명령

combat support 전투지원

annex 부록

appendix 별지

quartering 숙영지 할당

staging 대기(지역)

ammunition basic load 탄약 기본 휴대량

controlled supply rate(CSR) 통제 보급률

required supply rate(RSR) 소요 보급률

requisition 획득, 징발, 청구

combat service support(CSS) 전투 근무지원

decision support template(DST)
   결심지원형판

FSCOORD(Fire Support coordinator)
   화력지원협조관

ENCOORD(Environmental coordinator)
   환경문제협조관

attaching 배속

detaching unit 파견부대

Force development 전력개발

unit activation 부대신설

workload 작업량, 업무량

OPSEC(Operation Security) 작전 보안

Useful Expressions

1. The G3(S3) is the principal staff officer for all matters concerning training, operations and plans, as well as force development and modernization.

2. Training duties of G3's involves assisting the commander in developing and training the unit's mission-essential task list(METL).

3. Tasks related to operations and plans among G3's involves preparing, coor-dinating, authenticating, publishing, and distributing the command

SOP, OPLANs, OPORDs, fragmentary orders(FRAGOs), and warning orders(WARNOs) to which other staff sections contribute.

4. Operations and plans involves developing ammunition required supply rate(RSR) in coordination with the G2 and G4.

5. Force development and modernization involves processing procedures for unit activation, inactivation, establishment, discontinuance, and reorganization(force accounting).

Reading Text[1]

The G3(S3) is the principal staff officer for all matters concerning training, operations and plans, and force development and modernization. An operations officer is located at every echelon from battalion through corps. The common staff duties and responsibilities were listed in the previous section. The areas and activities that are the specific responsibility of the G3(S3) follow.

Training, which involves -
- Supervising the command training program.
- Preparing and supervising the execution of training within the command.
- Preparing the training guidance for the commander's approval and signature.
- Assisting the commander in developing and training the unit's mission-essential task list(METL).

---

1)   US Army FM 101-5, *Staff Organization and Operation*(May 31 1997, July 4th 2009). pp. 4-12~4-14.

- Identifying training requirements, based on the unit's METL and training status.
- Ensuring that training requirements orient on conditions and standards of combat.
- Determining requirements for and allocation of training resources.
- Organizing and conducting internal schools and obtaining and allocating quotas for external schools.
- Planning and conducting training inspections, tests, and evaluations.
- Maintaining the unit-readiness status of each unit in the command.
- Compiling[2] training records and reports as appropriate.

Operations and plans, which involves -
- Preparing, coordinating, authenticating,[3] publishing, and distributing the command SOP, OPLANs, OPORDs, fragmentary orders(FRAGOs), and warning orders(WARNOs) to which other staff sections contribute.
- Planning, coordinating, and supervising exercises.
- Participating in targeting meetings.
- Reviewing plans and orders of subordinate units.
- Synchronizing[4] tactical operations with all staff sections.
- Reviewing entire OPLANs and OPORDs for synchronization and completeness.[5]
- Monitoring the battle.
- Ensuring necessary combat support(CS) requirements are provided when

---

2) compile: 편집하다, 만들다, ~을 축적하다
3) authenticate: 인증하다, 입증하다
4) synchronize: 동시화하다
5) completeness: 완성, 완벽화

and where required.

- Coordinating with the G5 on using tactical forces to establish civil government.
- Coordinating with the G2 to write the reconnaissance and surveillance annex, which includes tasking units with available assets, to collect the commander's priority intelligence requirements.
- Recommending IR to the G2.
- Integrating fire support into all operations.
- Planning troop movement, including route selection, priority of movement, timing, providing of security, bivouacking,[6] quartering, staging, and preparing of movement order.
- Recommending priorities for allocating critical command resources, such as, but not limited to
  - Time(available planning time).
  - Ammunition basic loads and the controlled supply rate(CSR) of ammunition.
  - Personnel and equipment replacements.
  - Electronic frequencies and secure key lists.
- Developing ammunition required supply rate(RSR) in coordination with the G2 and G4.
- Requisitioning replacement units through operational channels.
- Establishing criteria[7] for reconstitution operations.
- Recommending use of resources to accomplish both maneuver and support, including resources required for deception purposes.
- Coordinating and directing terrain management(overall ground manager).

---

6) bivouacking: 야외 숙영지(bivouac로도 표기)

7) criteria: 조건, 평가기준, 기준

- Determining combat service support(CSS) resource requirements in coordination with the G1 and G4.
- Participating in course of action and decision support template(DST) development with G2 and FSCOORD.
- Coordinating with ENCOORD, G2, G5, and surgeon to establish environmental vulnerability protection levels.
- Furnishing[8] priorities for allocation of personnel and critical weapon systems replacement to combat units.
- Recommending the general locations of command posts.
- Recommending task organization and assigning missions to subordinate elements, which includes -
  - Developing, maintaining, and revising the troop list.
  - Organizing and equipping units, including estimating the numbers and types of units to be organized and the priority for phasing in or replacing personnel and equipment.
  - Assigning, attaching, and detaching units, detachments, or teams.
  - Receiving units, detachments, or teams, including orienting,[9] training, and reorganizing them as necessary.
- Coordinating with the G1(CPO)[10] civilian personnel involvement in tactical operations.

Force development and modernization, which involves -
- Reviewing, analyzing, and recommending a planned or programmed force structure.

---

8) furnishing: 비품, 장비의 설치, 공급하다, 비치해주다
9) orienting: 적응시키기
10) CPO(Civilian Personnel Office): 민간인 인사처

- Processing procedures for unit activation, inactivation, establishment, discontinuance, and reorganization(force accounting).
- Fielding[11] new weapons and equipment systems(force modernization).
- Evaluating the organizational structure, functions, and workload of military and civilian personnel to ensure their proper use and requirements(manpower utilization and requirements).
- Allocating manpower resources to subordinate commands within established ceilings and guidance[12](manpower allocation).
- Developing and revising unit force data for documenting any changes to the MTOE[13] and modification table of distribution and allowances(MTDA).[14]
- Planning and conducting formal, on-site manpower and equipment surveys.[15]
- Recording and reporting data for information, planning and programming, allocation, and justification(manpower reports).
- Ensuring MTDA and MTOE documents reflect the minimum-essential and most-economical equipment needed to accomplish the assigned mission.

The G3 determines qualitative and quantitative personnel requirements for new equipment and systems.

---

11) fielding: 배치
12) ceilings and guidance: 한도와 지침
13) MTOE(Modified Table of Organization and Equipment): 수정 편제장비표
14) modification table of distribution and allowances(MTDA): 수정 분배 및 할당표
15) on-site manpower and equipment surveys: 현지 인력 및 장비조사

Staff planning and supervision over -

- OPSEC, including analyzing the OPSEC posture of the command, determining essential elements of friendly information(EEFI)[16] and OPSEC vulnerabilities, evaluating and planning countersurveillance operations and countermeasures, coordinating SIGSEC measures with the G6(S6), conducting OPSEC surveys, and evaluating effectiveness of forceprotection measures.
- Force protection.
- Airspace command and control(AC2).[17]
- Information operations, to include C2W.
- Area damage control.
- Rear operations(G3 prepares the rear operations annex).
- Discipline, and law and order(coordinates with the G1 on administrative procedures dealing with discipline, law and order).
- Activation and deactivation of units.[18]
- Mobilization and demobilization.
- Operations concerning EPWs and civilian internees, in coordination with the provost marshal.[19]

Coordination of staff responsibility for the following special staff officers:

- Air defense coordinator(ADCOORD). (방공협조관)
- Air liaison officer(ALO). (공군연락장교)
- Air/naval gunfire liaison company(ANGLICO) commander. (항공/함포연락중대

---

16) essential elements of friendly information(EEFI): 우군첩보기본요소
17) Airspace command and control(AC2): 공역지휘 및 통제
18) Activation and deactivation of units: 부대창설 및 해체
19) provost marshal: 헌병사령관(장교), 법무장교

지휘관)

- Aviation coordinator(AVCOORD). (육군항공협조관)

- Chemical officer(CHEMO). (화학장교)

- Deception officer. (기만작전 장교)

- Electronic warfare officer(EWO). (전자전 장교)

- Engineer coordinator(ENCOORD). (공병협조 장교)

- Explosive ordnance disposal(EOD) officer. (폭발물 처리 장교)

- Fire support coordinator(FSCOORD). (화력지원 협조장교)

- Historian. (역사담당관)

- Liaison officer(LNO). (연락장교)

- Provost marshal(PM). (군사경찰대장)

- Psychological operations(PSYOP) officer. (심리전 장교)

- Safety officer. (안전장교)

- Special operations coordinator(SOCOORD). (특수작전 협조관)

- Theater airlift liaison officer(TALO). (전구공수연락장교)

NOTE The duties and responsibilities of these special staff officers can be found under the special staff officer section.

QUESTIONS

1. Which assistant chief of staff is in charge of staff planning and supervision over force protection?

2. Give some examples of the assistant chief of staff, G3 including the task of training.

3. What does the G3 determine for new weapons and equipment systems?

4. Does the G3 develop ammunition required supply rate(RSR) with whom he has to coordinate?

5. Who is responsible for coordinating staff responsibility with psychological operations(PSYOP) officer?

Dialogue 1: Can you be more specific?

CAP Kim Major Wheeler, when did you say you were going to have the staff picnic?

MAJ Wheeler Sometime next month.

CAP Kim Can you be more specific? I've got to make some plans.

MAJ Wheeler I was thinking of having it on the first or second Saturday of next month.

CAP Kim That may fit right into my schedule. By the way, can I bring my kids along?

MAJ Wheeler Be my guest.

* Can you be more specific? 조금 더 자세히 말씀해 주시겠습니까?
* Be my guest. 편할 대로 하세요(As you wish / If you want to).

Dialogue 2: The weather is great today

MAJ Black Captain Lee, the weather is beautiful today.

CAP Lee Yes, sir, Major Black. It rained all day yesterday, the weather is great today.

MAJ Black I thought the ROK/US friendship event would be canceled due to rain, but fortunately the weather is getting better. By the way, do you have any good idea for friendship event?

CAP Lee I heard we were playing soccer as scheduled.

MAJ Black The ground must be slippery because of yesterday's rain. Someone might fall and get hurt. Wouldn't playing volleyball indoors be better?

CAP Lee   The ground will be dry by the afternoon. So we only need to make up the teems by then.

* What a beautiful day! / What a nice day! 날씨가 정말 좋군요!

* It's sweltering. 찌는 듯이 덥습니다. | It's nippy. 살을 에는 듯이 춥습니다.

Job Specific Expression of Operations

This tactic is not currently applied but could be used in an emergency.

이 전술은 현재 적용되지 않으나 비상시에는 사용될 수 있습니다.

Who is in charge of writing the CASOP?[20]

위기조치예규임무를 누가 담당하고 있습니까?

Could you correct the grammar of my English script and rewrite it?

제가 작성한 영문 스크립트를 문법에 맞게 재작성해 주시겠습니까?

Do you have any reference related to this document?

당신은 이 문서와 관련된 참고문헌을 가지고 있습니까?

The CACC is responsible for providing ASOCSs[21] to GCC field armies and ACPs to ground maneuver units.

* CACC: CFC Air Component Command | GCC: Ground Component Command

공구사사령관은 지구사 야전군에게 항공지원작전본부를 그리고 지상군 기동부대에 전술항공통제반을 제공할 책임이 있습니다.

I will brief at 1700 today, so I need you to send me your data.

금일 17시에 보고 예정이니 보고 관련 자료를 주십시오.

Which areas need to be improved for the exercise?

금번 연습을 통해 개선될 사항은 무엇입니까?

---

20) CASOP(Crisis Action Standard Operating Procedure): 위기조치예규

21) ASOCS(Air Support Operation Center): 항공지원작전본부

Will NK continue to employ chemical weapons?

북한은 화학무기 사용을 계속할 것입니까?

I want an overall assessment of each functional area with emphasis on current and future operational impacts.

현재 및 장차 작전에 영향을 주는 전반적인 기능별 평가사항을 알고 싶습니다.

We'll continue to monitor this activity.

우리는 이 활동을 계속 추적 감시하겠습니다.

What additional or new information has been obtained?

획득된 추가 또는 새로운 첩보는 무엇입니까?

In the future wars, why is Biological warfare emphasized, and what is the expected biological defense doctrine?

장차전에서 생물학전을 강조하는 배경은 어떠하며 예상 생물학 방어 교리는 무엇입니까?

Military Terminology

activation and deactivation of units
부대 창설 및 해체

air defense coordinator(ADCOORD)
방공협조관

air liaison officer(ALO) 공군연락장교

air/naval gunfire liaison company
(ANGLICO) commander
항공/함포연락중대 지휘관

airspace command and control(AC2)
공역지휘 및 통제

ammunition basic load 탄약기본휴대량

annex 첨부, 붙임

appendix 부록

ASOCS(Air Support Operation Center)
항공지원작전본부

attaching 배속

authenticate 인증하다, 입증하다

aviation coordinator(AVCOORD)
육군항공협조관

bivouacking 야외 숙영지(bivouac로도 표기)

CASOP(Crisis Action Standard Operating
Procedure) 위기조치예규

ceilings and guidance 한도와 지침

chemical officer(CHEMO) 화학장교

combat support 전투지원

command 지휘, 통수, 명령, 구령, 사령부

compile 편집하다, ~을 축적하다

completeness 완성화, 완벽화

controlled supply rate(CSR) 통제보급률

CPO(Civilian Personnel Office)
민간인 인사처

criteria 조건, 평가기준, 기준

deception officer 기만작전 장교

decision support template(DST)
결심지원형판

detaching unit 파견부대

electronic warfare officer(EWO) 전자전 장교

ENCOORD(Environmental Coordinator)
환경문제협조관

engineer coordinator(ENCOORD)
공병협조 장교

essential elements of friendly information
(EEFI) 우군첩보기본요소

explosive ordnance disposal(EOD) officer
폭발물 처리 장교

fielding 배치

fire support coordinator(FSCOORD)
화력지원 협조장교

force development 전력개발

FSCOORD(Fire Support Coordinator)
화력지원협조관

furnishing 비품, 장비의 설치

historian 역사담당관

liaison officer(LNO) 연락장교

mission-essential task list(METL)
임무과제목록

modification table of distribution and
allowances(MTDA) 수정 분배 및 할당표

MTOE(Modified Table of Organization and
Equipment) 수정 편제 장비표

on-site manpower and equipment surveys
현지 인력 및 장비조사

orienting 적응시키기

provost marshal 헌병사령관(장교), 법무장교

provost marshal(PM) 헌병대장

psychological operations(PSYOP) officer
심리전 장교

quartering 숙영지 활당

quotas 정원, 물량

required supply rate(RSR) 소요보급률

requisition 획득, 징발, 청구

safety officer 안전장교

SOP(Standing Operating Procedure)
예규, 내규

special operations coordinator(SOCOORD)
특수작전 협조관

staging 대기(지역)

synchronize 동시화하다

theater airlift liaison officer(TALO)
전구공수연락장교

training guidance 훈련지침

unit activation 부대 신설

workload 작업량, 업무량

Unit 5 | ACOS, G4(S4), Logistics

Key Words	
supply 보급	mode 방법
maintenance 정비	terminal operation 종결작전
transportation 수송	troop movement 부대이동
service 근무	facility 시설
visibility 가시성	installation 설비
IPB(Intelligence Preparation of the battlefield) 전장정보분석	fortification 축성
	field sanitation 야전 위생
main supply route(MSR) 주 보급로	organizational clothing 조직 의류
excess property 잉여자산	water purification 정수
salvage 구조, 구난	mortuary affair 시신처리
prescribed load 규정 휴대량	hazardous material 위험물자
disposal 처리, 처분	identification 확인
petroleum product 석유제품	detainee 구류자
host nation 주둔국	procurement and contracting 획득 및 계약
equipment recovery 장비복구	

Useful Expressions

1. The G4(S4) is the principal staff officer for coordinating the logistics integration of supply, maintenance, transportation, and services for the command.

2. Tasks related to the logistics operations and plans for the G4 involves providing information on enemy logistics operations to the G2(S2) for inclusion to IPB.

3. Supply tasks for the G4 involves coordinating all classes of supply, except Class VIII(medical), according to commander's priorities. Class VIII is coordinated through medical supply channels.

4. One of maintenance fields of the G4 involves monitoring and analyzing the equipment-readiness status.

5. One of transportation tasks of the ACOS, G4 involves conducting operational and tactical planning to support movement control and mode as well as terminal operations.

6. The ACOS, G4 has to carry out staff planning and supervision over identification of requirements and restrictions for using local civilians, EPWs, and civilian internees and detainees in logistics support operations.

Reading Text[1]

The G4(S4) is the principal staff officer for coordinating the logistics integration of supply, maintenance, transportation, and services for the command. The G4(S4) is the link between the support unit and his commander plus the rest of the staff. The G4(S4) assists the support unit commander in maintaining logistics visibility with the commander and the rest of the staff. The G4(S4) must also maintain close and continuous coordination with the G3(S3). A logistics officer is located at every echelon of command from battalion through corps. At brigade and battalion levels, the S4 not only coordinates activities but also executes requirements for the commander and unit. The common staff duties and responsibilities were listed in the previous section. The areas and activities that are the specific responsibility of

---

1) US Army FM 101-5, *Staff Organization and Operation*(May 31 1997, July 4th 2009), pp. 4-14~4-15.

the G4(S4) follow.

Logistics operations and plans(general), which involves -

- Providing information on enemy logistics operations to the G2(S2) for inclusion to IPB.
- Developing with the G3 the logistics plan to support operations.
- Coordinating with the G3 and G1 on equipping replacement personnel and units.
- Coordinating with supporting unit commander on the current and future support capability of that unit.
- Coordinating the selection and recommending of main supply routes(MSRs) and logistics support areas, in coordination with the ENCOORD, to the G3.
- Performing logistics preparation of the battlefield in coordination with support command.
- Recommending IR[2] to the G2.
- Recommending command policy for collection and disposal of excess property and salvage.
- Participating in targeting meetings.

Supply, which involves -

- Determining supply requirements(except for medical requirements). This function is shared with the support unit commander and the G3.
- Recommending support and supply priorities and controlled supply rates for publication in OPLANs and OPORDs.

---

2) IR(information Requirement): 첩보요구

- Coordinating all classes of supply, except Class VIII(medical), according to commander's priorities. Class VIII is coordinated through medical supply channels.
- Coordinating the requisition, acquisition, and storage of supplies and equipment, and the maintenance of materiel records.
- Ensuring, in coordination with the provost marshall, that accountability and security of supplies and equipment are adequate.[3]
- Calculating and recommending to the G3 basic and prescribed loads and assisting the G3 in determining the required supply rates.
- Coordinating and monitoring the collection and distribution of excess, surplus, and salvage supplies and equipment.
- Directing the disposal of captured enemy supplies and equipment after coordination with the G2.
- Coordinating the allocation of petroleum products to subordinate units.
- Coordinating with the G5(S5) to support foreign nation and host nation support requirements.

Maintenance, which involves -
- Monitoring and analyzing the equipment-readiness status.
- Determining, with the support command, maintenance workload requirements(less medical).
- Coordinating, with the support command, equipment recovery and evacuation operations.
- Determining maintenance time lines.

---

3) adequate: 적절한

Transportation, which involves -

- Conducting operational and tactical planning to support movement control and mode and terminal operations.
- Coordinating transportation assets for other services.
- Coordinating with G5(S5) for host nation support.
- Coordinating with the G1 and the G3(PM) on transporting replacement personnel and EPWs.
- Coordinating special transport requirements to move the command post.
- Coordinating with the G3 for logistics planning of tactical troop movement.

Services, which involves -

- Coordinating the construction of facilities and installations, except for fortifications and signal systems.
- Coordinating field sanitation.
- Coordinating actions for establishing an organizational clothing and individual equipment operation for exchange and for replacing personal field(TA-50) equipment.
- Coordinating or providing food preparation, water purification, mortuary affairs, aerial delivery, laundry, shower, and clothing and light textile repair.
- Coordinating the transportation, storage, handling, and disposal of hazardous material or hazardous waste.
- Coordinating unit spill prevention plans.

- Identification of requirements and restrictions for using local civilians, EPWs, and civilian internees and detainees in logistics support operations.
- Battlefield procurement and contracting.
- Coordination with SJA[4] on legal aspects of contracting.
- Coordination with the RM[5] officer and the finance officer on the financial aspects of contracting.
- Real property control.[6]
- Food service.
- Fire protection.
- Bath and laundry services, and clothing exchange.
- Mortuary affairs.

Coordination of staff responsibility for the special staff officer:

Transportation officer. (The duties and responsibilities of the transportation officer can be found under the special staff officer section, page 4-29(FM 101-5).)

---

4) SJA(staff Judge Advocate): 법무참모
5) RM(Road Management): 도로관리, Radiant Mercury: 보안장비
6) Real property control: 부동산 통제

QUESTIONS

1. Which assistant chief of staff is in charge of coordinating the requisition, acquisition, and storage of supplies and equipment, and the maintenance of material records?

2. Give some examples of the duties of assistant chief of staff, G4 including the task of logistics operations and plans.

3. What are the typical task that the G4 provides to the G2(S2) for inclusion to IPB?

4. Who does the G4 coordinate transportation with for host nation support?

5. Which assistant chief of staff is responsible for mortuary affairs?

Dialogue 1: Mountain Hiking

LTC Harrison — Wow! This is a tough mountain to climb, Major Kim.

MAJ Kim — Have you ever climbed a mountain, Lieutenant Colonel Harrison?

LTC Harrison — Yes, I've been up mountains almost every time during the training. But Mt. Pukhan's slop is much steeper.

MAJ Kim — You know, Lieutenant Colonel Harrison, although it is hard to reach the mountain top, the feeling after getting there is beyond words.[7]

LTC Harrison — Yes, I guess so, but I'm already short of breath.[8] Could we take the safe, easy course?

MAJ Kim — Come on, you can do it! We are almost near the top of the mountain.

* catch one's breath: 한차례 쉬다
* get one's breath back: (운동 따위를 한 후) 호흡이 제 상태로 돌아오다

Dialogue 2: Language and Culture

CPT Nixon — Major Kim, from hearing you speak, I think you speak English very well.

MAJ Kim — Thank you, Captain Nixon. Actually, counting Korean, Japanese, and French, I speak four languages. What language other than English do you speak?

---

7) beyond words: 말로 이루 다 표현할 수 없는(beyond expression)

8) be short of breath: 숨이 차다

CPT Nixon	I know only English, But, English is a global language and generally with speaking English alone, there is little difficulty[9] living in foreign countries.
MAJ Kim	That's true. So there is no need to learn a foreign language.
CPT Nixon	But even though language is not a problem, often Americans have difficulty adapting to foreign cultures.
MAJ Kim	I understand what you are saying. I believe learning to speak the native language[10] is a way to gain a better understanding of another culture.

Job Specific Expression of Logistics

The FACDAM[11] report can help us to verify the status of the infrastructure.
시설피해 보고서는 기반시설 상태를 확인하는 데 많은 도움을 줄 수 있습니다.

The purpose of the IPC is to establish exercise planing and to develop the exercise concept of operations and supporting requirements.
최초계획회의의 목적은 연습계획을 수립하며 요구되는 지원과 작전연습개념을 발전시키는 것입니다.

Each functional division has to submit bilingual MSELs[12] to P&O branch.[13]
각 기능처는 한 · 영으로 작성된 주요사태목록 입력자료를 계획운영과로 제출해야 합니다.

---

9) there is little difficulty: 거의 어려움이 없다

10) native language: 현지 언어

11) FACDAM(Facilities Damage): 시설피해

12) MSEL(Master Scenario Event List): 주요사태목록

13) P&O branch(Plans and Operations branch): 계획운영과

Operations and Exercise branch chairs a SLS[14] workshop at the Walker Center.

운영과는 워커센터에서 주요지휘관세미나 실무회의를 주관합니다.

Where possible, exercise scenarios have to give all levels of the training audiences with incorporated logistics - related matters.

가능한 한 연습각본은 훈련 참가자 각 제대가 군수와 관련된 훈련을 할 수 있도록 계획해야 합니다.

I want to know the characteristics and specifications of main USFK equipment and materials.

미군이 사용 중인 주요장비와 물자의 특성과 제원을 알고 싶습니다.

Please confirm that CRDL[15] items are included in the TPFDD(Time Phased Forces Deployment Data).

긴급소요부족품목록이 시차별 부대 전개 제원에 포함되어 있는지 확인하여 주십시오.

Please explain USFK's food, POL,[16] and supply support system.

주한 미군의 급식, 유류, 보급지원체제에 대하여 설명해 주십시오.

Where are the major US depots providing support to USFK? Also, how many major depots are there in the US?

주한미군을 지원하기 위한 미국 내 주요 보급창이 어디에 있으며, 몇 개나 있습니까?

Who is the POC[17] for POLCAP?[18]

유류능력 보고서는 누가 담당합니까?

Any maintenance requiring ROK-US mutual support must be coordinated through ROK-US Logistics Coordination Group.

한미 상호정비지원 사항은 한미 군수협조단을 통하여 이루어져야 됩니다.

---

14) SLS(Senior Leader's Seminar) : 주요지휘관 세미나
15) CRDL(Critical Requirements Deficiency List) : 긴급소요부족품목록
16) POL(Petroleum, Oils and Lubricants) : 유류(석유, 오일, 윤활유)
17) POC(Point of Contact) : 담당자, 연락처
18) POLCAP(POL Capabilities Report) : 유류능력보고

What's the basis of making the AA/CSR?[19)

탄약할당/통제보급률을 작성하기 위한 기준은 무엇입니까?

Which ASP[20)] will be in charge of the X divisional direct support for munitions?

X 사단에 대한 탄약직접지원은 어느 탄약보급소가 담당합니까?

How many container cranes does this port have?

이 항에는 컨테이너 크레인이 몇 대나 있습니까?

---

19) AA/CSR(Ammunition Allocation/Controled Supply Rate) : 탄약할당/통제보급률
20) ASP(Ammunition Supply Point) : 탄약보급소

Military Terminology —————————

AA/CSR(Ammunition Allocation/Controled
    Supply Rate) 탄약할당/통제보급률
adequate 적절한
ASP(Ammunition Supply Point) 탄약보급소
be short of breath 숨이 차다
beyond words 말로 이루 다 표현할 수 없는
CRDL(Critical Requirements Deficiency
    List) 긴급소요부족품 목록
detainee 구류자
disposal 처리, 처분
equipment recovery 장비복구
excess property 잉여자산
FACDAM(Facilities Damage) 시설피해
facility 시설
field sanitation 야전 위생
fortification 축성
hazardous material 위험물자
host nation 주둔국
identification 확인
installation 설비
IPB(Intelligence Preparation of the
    Battlefield) 전장정보분석
IR(Information Requirement) 첩보요구
Main Supply Route(MSR) 주 보급로
maintenance 정비
mode 방법
mortuary affair 시신처리
MSEL(Master Scenario Event List)
    주요사태목록

native language 현지 언어
organizational clothing 조직 의류
P&O branch(Plans and Operations branch)
    계획운영과
petroleum product 석유제품
POC(Point of Contact) 담당자, 연락처
POL(Petroleum, Oils and Lubricants)
    유류(석유, 오일, 윤활유)
POLCAP(POL Capabilities Report)
    유류능력보고
prescribed load 규정 휴대량
procurement and contracting 획득 및 계약
radiant mercury 보안장비
Real property control 부동산 통제
RM(Road Management) 도로관리
salvage 구조, 구난
service 근무
SJA(Staff Judge Advocate) 법무참모
SLS(Senior Leader's Seminar) 주요지휘관
    세미나
supply 보급
terminal operation 종결작전
there is little difficulty 거의 어려움이 없다
transportation 수송
troop movement 부대이동
visibility 가시성
water purification 정수

Unit 6 | Military Decision-Making Process

Key Words

consequence 결과	courses of action 방책
end state 최종상태	doctrine 교리
quantifiable 계량화할 수 있는	guidance 지침
military decision-making	preference 선호도
process(MDMP) 군사적 결심수립절차	technical competence 기술적 능력
thoroughness 완전, 철저함	CofS(Chief of Staff) 참모장
sound judgment 건전한 판단	XO Executive Officer(보좌관, 행정장교, 선임장교)
deliberate 신중한	interaction 상호작용

Useful Expressions

1. Decisions are the means by which the commander translates his vision of the end state into action.

2. The military decision-making process(MDMP) is a single, established, and proven analytical process.

3. The MDMP helps the commander and his staff examine a battlefield situation and reach logical decisions.

4. The advantages of using the complete MDMP instead of abbreviating the process are that it analyzes and compares multiple friendly and enemy COAs in an attempt to identify the best possible friendly COA.

5. The commander is in charge of the military decision-making process and

decides what procedures to use in each situation.

6. The commander uses the entire staff during the MDMP to explore the full range of probable and likely enemy and friendly COAs, and to analyze and compare his own organization's capabilities with the enemy's.

7. The CofS(XO) manages, coordinates, and disciplines the staff and provides quality control.

8. Estimates are revised when important new information is received or when the situation changes significantly.

Reading Text[1)]

Decision making is knowing if to decide, then when and what to decide. It includes understanding the consequence of decisions. Decisions are the means by which the commander translates his vision of the end state into action. Decision making is both science and art. Many aspects of military operations - movement rates, fuel consumption, weapons effects - are quantifiable and, therefore, part of the science of war. Other aspects - the impact of leadership, complexity of operations, and uncertainty regarding enemy intentions - belong to the art of war.

The military decision-making process(MDMP) is a single, established, and proven analytical process. (see Figure 6-1) The MDMP is an adaptation of the Army's analytical approach to problem solving. The MDMP is a tool that assists the commander and staff in developing estimates and a plan. While the formal problem-solving process described in this chapter may start with the receipt of a mission, and has as its goal the production of an order, the analytical aspects of

---

1)   US Army FM 101-5, *Staff Organization and Operation*(May 31 1997, July 4th 2009), pp. 5-1~5-3.

the MDMP continue at all levels during operations.

The MDMP helps the commander and his staff examine a battlefield situation and reach logical decisions. The process helps them apply thoroughness, clarity, sound judgment, logic, and professional knowledge to reach a decision. The full MDMP is a detailed, deliberate, sequential, and time-consuming process used when adequate planning time and sufficient staff support are available to thoroughly examine numerous friendly and enemy courses of action(COAs). This typically occurs when developing the commander's estimate and operation plans(OPLANs), when planning for an entirely new mission, during extended operations, and during staff training designed specifically to teach the MDMP.

The MDMP is the foundation on which planning in a time-constrained[2] environment is based. The products created during the full MDMP can and should be used during subsequent planning sessions when time may not be available for a thorough relook, but where existing METT-T factors have not changed substantially. (See FM 101-5, page 5-27 for a discussion of decision making in a time-constrained environment.)

The MDMP relies on doctrine, especially the terms and symbols(graphics) found in FM 101-5-1. The use of approved terms and symbols facilitates the rapid and consistent assessment of the situation and creation and implementation of plans and orders by minimizing confusion over the meanings of terms and symbols used in the process.

The advantages of using the complete MDMP instead of abbreviating[3] the process are that -

---

2) time-constrained: 시간이 제한된

3) abbreviating: 축약하는

- It analyzes and compares multiple friendly and enemy COAs in an attempt to identify the best possible friendly COA.
- It produces the greatest integration, coordination, and synchronization for an operation and minimizes the risk of overlooking[4] a critical aspect of the operation.
- It results in a detailed operation order or operation plan.

The disadvantage of using the complete MDMP is that it is a time-consuming process.

⊙ ROLES OF THE COMMANDER AND STAFF

The commander is in charge of the military decision-making process and decides what procedures to use in each situation. The planning process hinges on a clear articulation[5] of his battlefield visualization. He is personally responsible for planning, preparing for, and executing operations. From start to finish, the commander's personal role is central: his participation in the process provides focus and guidance to the staff. However, there are responsibilities and decisions that are the commander's alone(Figure 6-1). The amount of his direct involvement is driven by the time available, his personal preferences, and the experience and accessibility of the staff. The less time available, the less experienced the staff,[6] and the less accessible the staff, generally the greater the commander involvement. Examples for discussion of increased commander involvement are found in Decision Making in a Time-Constrained Environment.

---

4) overlooking: 모르고 지나치는
5) clear articulation: 명확한 표현
6) The less time available, the less experienced the staff: 가용시간이 적으면 적을수록 참모들의 숙련도도 떨어진다

The commander uses the entire staff during the MDMP to explore the full range of probable and likely enemy and friendly COAs, and to analyze and compare his own organization's capabilities with the enemy's. This staff effort has one objective - to collectively integrate information with sound doctrine and

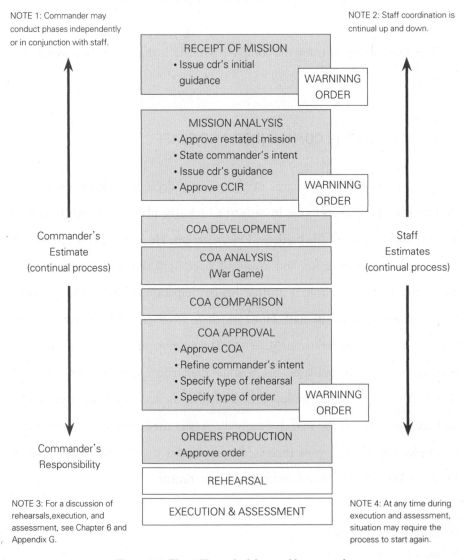

Figure 6-1. The military decision making procedure

- Step 1. Receipt of Mission.
- Step 2. Mission Analysis.
- Step 3. Course of Action Development.
- Step 4. Course of Action Analysis.
- Step 5. Course of Action Comparison.
- Step 6. Course of Action Approval.
- Step 7. Orders Production.

Figure 6-2. Seven steps for decision-making process

technical competence to assist the commander in his decisions, leading ultimately to effective plans.

The CofS(XO) manages, coordinates, and disciplines the staff's work and provides quality control. He must understand the commander's guidance because he supervises the entire process. He ensures the staff has the information, guidance, and facilities it needs. He provides time lines to the staff, establishes briefback times and locations, and provides any unique instructions.

By issuing guidance and participating in formal and informal briefings, the commander and CofS(XO) guide the staff through the decision-making process. Such interaction helps the staff resolve questions and involves the entire staff in the total process. The selected course of action and its implementing operation order are directly linked to how well both the commander and staff accomplish each phase of the MDMP.

The military decision-making process has seven steps(Figure 6-2). Each step of the process begins with certain input that builds upon the previous steps. Each step, in turn, has its own output that drives subsequent steps. Errors committed early in the process will impact on later steps.

Estimates go on continuously to provide important inputs for the MDMP. The commander and each staff section do estimates. Estimates are revised when important new information is received or when the situation changes significantly. They are conducted not only to support the planning process but also during mission execution.

QUESTIONS ——————————————————————————

1. What does the acronym MDMP stand for?

2. How does the MDMP help the commander and his staff?

3. What are the advantages of using the complete MDMP?

4. Who manages, coordinates, and disciplines the staff and provides quality control when using the MDMP?

5. Explain the seven steps for the decision-making process.

Dialogue 1: Drinking Culture

MAJ Lee   I'm planing on having a drink with Major Andrews at the Navy club after work today. Would you like to join us?

CAP John   Sure.

MAJ Lee   What kind of drink do you like? Let's have what you like.

CAP John   I like whiskey. How about you, MAJ Lee?

MAJ Lee   Whiskey sounds good. So, how much can you normally drink?

CAP John   I'm not sure. I always try to drink as little as possible. But l drank with Koreans once, and I remember having a hard time saying no to their hospitality.[7]

MAJ Lee   But these days it's gotten a little better, and it is accepted when one says he doesn't drink or he has enough.

* Party의 종류

- Tea Party	영국에서 유래했으며 가정집에서 친구들 간에 대화를 즐기기 위하여 또는 직장에서 사무적인 목적이나 피로를 풀기 위한 목적으로 실시
- Cocktail Party	많은 사람이 동시에 즐길 수 있는 모임으로 친구들 간에 실시하며 때로는 음식도 함께 준비됨
- Reception	공식적 또는 준공식적인 목적으로 열리며 통상 주 행사 후 2부 행사의 성격을 갖는다.
- Cookie Party	가정주부들이 친구들의 모임을 위해 주선하며 참석자들 또한 소량의 과자나 파이 등을 가져와서 함께 대화를 나누는 것을 목적으로 하는 파티
- Potluck	각자 음식을 가져와서 함께 나눠 먹는 형태의 파티
- Cookouts	바비큐 파티라고도 하며 이동용 석쇠에 돼지갈비, 소고기 스테이크, 닭고기, 햄버거 고기, 햄 등을 구워서 맥주와 함께 먹는 야외 모임(집 정원에서 많이 이루어짐)
- BYOB	각자 음료수 또는 술 등을 가져와서 마시는 파티(Bring Your Own Bottle)

---

7) hospitality: 친절, 환대

Dialogue 2: Korean Ceramics

MAJ Jack   Major Jang, I heard a few days ago that there was a ceramics festival somewhere. Do you happen to know anything about it?

MAJ Jang   Yes, of course. Fortunately, these days a ceramics festival is being held in Ichon. I was there last year and there was a variety of inexpensive ceramics, so I bought a few.

MAJ Jack   Really? Do you know by any chance the difference between the blue celadon and the white porcelain? Somebody explained it to me last time, but I already forgot.

MAJ Jang   The blue stands for[8] nobility, elegance, and dignity,[9] so the blue celadon was loved by the upper class people. The white stands for peace, calmness, and simplicity,[10] so it was loved by ordinary people.

MAJ Jack   Oh, I see. By the way, are only ceramics displayed at the ceramics festival?

MAJ Jang   No. A place has been set up so that you can make your own pottery, and the whole manufacturing process of pottery is on display; so, you can learn how ceramic and porcelain articles are made.

---

8) stands for: 나타내다(represent)

9) nobility, elegance, and dignity: 고결, 우아, 위엄

10) peace, calmness, and simplicity: 평화, 고요, 소박함

Military Terminology

abbreviating 축약하는

clear articulation 명확한 표현

CofS(Chief of Staff) 참모장

consequence 결과

courses of action 방책

deliberate 신중한

doctrine 교리

end state 최종상태

guidance 지침

hospitality 친절, 환대

interaction 상호작용

military decision-making process(MDMP)
  군사적 결심수립절차

nobility, elegance, and dignity 고결, 우아,
  위엄

overlooking 모르고 지나치는

peace, calmness, and simplicity 평화, 고요,
  소박함

preference 선호도

quantifiable 계량화할 수 있는

sound judgment 건전한 판단

stands for 나타내다(represent)

technical competence 기술적 능력

thoroughness 완전, 철저함

time-constrained 시간이 제한된

XO: Executive Officer 보좌관, 행정장교,
  선임장교

Unit 7 | Troop Leading Procedure

Key Words

Troop-leading procedure 부대지휘절차(작전수행과정)	**order format** 명령양식
logic 논리	**nature of the operation** 작전 성격
receive the mission 명령수령	**timeline** 진행계획
warning order 준비명령	**rehearsal** 예행연습
tentative plan 잠정계획	**COA** Course of Action(방책)
initiate movement 최초 이동	**COA development** 방책개발
supervise and assess 감독 및 평가	**COA comparison** 방책비교
operation order 작전명령	**battle position** 전투진지
preclude 배제하다	**attack position** 공격진지
fragmentary order 단편명령	**guide** 선도
confirmation briefing 확인보고	**quartering party** 분할된 일부분
intent (지휘관) 의도	**circumstance** 상황, 환경
concept of the operation 작전개념	**substitute** 대신하다

Useful Expressions

1. Troop-leading procedures(TLP) provide leaders a framework for decision making during the plan and preparation phases of an operation.

2. However, the tempo of operations often precludes this ideal sequence, particularly at the lower levels.

3. Upon receiving the mission, leaders perform an initial assessment of the situation.

4. In the process they allocate roughly one-third of available planning and preparation time to themselves.

5. Leaders issue the initial WARNO as quickly as possible to give subordinates maximum time to plan and prepare.

6. Leaders initiate any movement necessary to continue mission preparation or position the unit for execution.

7. Whenever time and circumstances allow, leaders personally conduct reconnaissance of critical mission aspects.

8. Infantry platoon and squad leaders normally issue verbal combat orders supplemented by graphics and other control measures.

9. Normally unit SOPs state individual responsibilities and the sequence of preparation activities.

Reading Text[1)]

Troop-leading procedures(TLP) provide leaders a framework for decisionmaking during the plan and prepare phases of an operation. This eight-step procedure applies the logic of visualize, describe, and direct to the plan and prepare functions of the operations process. Steps in the TLP include:

- Receive the mission.
- Issue a warning order(WARNO).
- Make a tentative plan.
- Initiate movement.

---

1) FM 3-21.8, *Infantry Rifle Platoon and Squad*(Headquarters Department of the Army, March 2007), pp. 1-29~1-32.

- Conduct reconnaissance.
- Complete the plan.
- Issue the order.
- Supervise and assess.

For a complete discussion on making a tentative plan, see Chapter 6(FM 3-21.8).

⊙ Receive the Mission

Leaders receive their missions in several ways — ideally through a series of warning orders(WARNOs), operation orders(OPORD)s, and briefings from their leader/commander. However, the tempo of operations often precludes this ideal sequence, particularly at the lower levels. This means that leaders may often receive only a WARNO or a fragmentary order(FRAGO), but the process is the same.

After receiving an order, leaders are normally required to give a confirmation briefing to their higher commander. This is done to clarify their understanding of the commander's mission, intent, and concept of the operation, as well as their role within the operation. The leader obtains clarification on any portions[2] of the higher headquarters' plan as required.

Upon receiving the mission, leaders perform an initial assessment of the situation(mission, enemy, terrain, troops-time, civil [METT-TC] analysis), focusing on the mission, the unit's role in the larger operation, and allocating time for planning and preparing. The two most important products from this initial assessment should be at least a partial restated mission, and a timeline. Leaders issue their initial WARNO on this first assessment and time allocation.

---

2)   portion: 일부, 분할

Based on their knowledge, leaders estimate the time available to plan and prepare for the mission. They issue a tentative timeline that is as detailed as possible. In the process they allocate roughly one-third of available planning and preparation time to themselves, allowing their subordinates the remaining two-thirds. During fast-paced operations, planning and preparation time might be extremely limited. Knowing this in advance enables leaders to emplace[3] SOPs to assist them in these situations.

⊙ Issue a Warning Order

Leaders issue the initial WARNO as quickly as possible to give subordinates maximum time to plan and prepare. They do not wait for additional information. The WARNO, following the five-paragraph field order format, contains as much detail as available. At a minimum, subordinates need to know critical times like the earliest time of movement, and when they must be ready to conduct operations. Leaders do not delay in issuing the initial WARNO. As more information becomes available, leaders can — and should — issue additional WARNOs. At a minimum the WARNO normally includes:

- Mission or nature of the operation.
- Time and place for issuing the OPORD.[4]
- Units or elements participating in the operation.
- Specific tasks not addressed by unit SOP.
- Timeline for the operation.
- Rehearsal guidance.

---

3) emplace: 적용하다

4) OPORD(Operation Order): 작전명령

⊙ Make a Tentative Plan

Once he has issued the initial WARNO, the leader continues to develop a tentative plan. Making a tentative plan follows the basic decisionmaking method of visualize, describe, direct, and the Army standard planning process. This step combines steps 2 through 6 of the military decisionmaking process: mission analysis, COA development, COA analysis, COA comparison, and COA selection. At the Infantry platoon level, these steps are often performed mentally.[5] The platoon leader and squad leaders may include their principal subordinates — especially during COA development, analysis, and comparison.

To frame the tentative plan, Army leaders perform mission analysis. This mission analysis follows the METT-TC format, continuing the initial assessment performed in TLP step 1. This step is covered in detail in Chapter 6(FM 3-21.8).

⊙ Initiate Movement

Movement of the unit may occur simultaneously with the TLPs. Leaders initiate any movement necessary to continue mission preparation or position the unit for execution. They do this as soon as they have enough information to do so, or when the unit is required to move to position itself for the upcoming mission. Movements may be to an assembly area, a battle position, a new AO, or an attack position. They may include movement of reconnaissance elements, guides, or quartering parties. Infantry leaders can initiate movement based on their tentative plan and issue the order to subordinates in the new location.

---

5) mentally: 염두로, 머릿속으로

⊙ Conduct Reconnaissance

Whenever time and circumstances allow, leaders personally conduct reconnaissance of critical mission aspects.[6] No amount of planning can substitute for firsthand[7] assessment of the situation. Unfortunately, many factors can keep leaders from performing a personal reconnaissance. However, there are several means available to the leader to develop and confirm his visualization. They include: internal reconnaissance and surveillance elements, unmanned sensors, the higher unit's intelligence, surveillance, reconnaissance(ISR) elements, adjacent units,[8] map reconnaissance, imagery,[9] and intelligence products. One of the most difficult aspects of conducting reconnaissance is the process of identifying what the leader needs to know(the information requirements [IR]).[10]

⊙ Complete the Plan

During this step, leaders incorporate[11] the result of reconnaissance into their selected course of action(COA) to complete the plan and order. This includes preparing overlays,[12] refining[13] the indirect fire target list, coordinating sustainment and C2 requirements, and updating the tentative plan as a result of the reconnaissance. At the platoon and squad levels, this step normally involves

---

6) aspect: 지점, 관점, 양상
7) firsthand: 직접, 직접의
8) adjacent unit: 인접부대
9) imagery: 모형, 모형 상황판
10) information requirement: 첩보요구
11) incorporate: 통합하다
12) overlay: 투명도
13) refine: 정교화하다

only confirming or updating information contained in the tentative plan. If time allows, leaders make final coordination with adjacent units and higher headquarters before issuing the order.

⊙ Issue the Order

Infantry platoon and squad leaders normally issue verbal combat orders[14] supplemented[15] by graphics and other control measures. The order follows the standard five-paragraph field order format. Infantry leaders use many different techniques to convey their orders(see Chapter 6). Typically, platoon and squad leaders do not issue a commander's intent. They reiterate[16] the intent of their company and battalion commanders.

The ideal location for issuing the order is a point in the AO with a view of the objective and other aspects of the terrain. The leader may perform reconnaissance, complete the order, and then summon subordinates to a specified location to receive it. At times, security or other constraints[17] make it infeasible[18] to issue the order on the terrain. In such cases, leaders use a sand table,[19] detailed sketch, maps, aerial photos and images, and other products to depict the AO and situation.

---

14) verbal combat order: 구두전투명령

15) supplement: 보충하다, 추가

16) reiterate: 되풀이하다, 반복하다

17) constraint: 제한사항

18) infeasible: 실행 불가능한

19) sand table: 사판, 모래를 이용한 모형판

⊙ Supervise and assess

This final step of the TLP is crucial. Normally unit SOPs state individual responsibilities and the sequence of preparation activities. After issuing the OPORD, the platoon leader and his subordinate leaders must ensure the required activities and tasks are completed in a timely manner prior to mission execution. It is imperative[20] that both officers and NCOs check everything that is important for successful mission accomplishment. The process should include:

- Ensuring the second in command of each element is prepared to execute in their leader's absence.[21]
- Listening to subordinate operation orders.
- Checking load plans to ensure Soldiers are carrying only what is necessary for the mission and or what was specified[22] in the OPORD.
- Checking the status and serviceability of weapons.
- Checking on maintenance activities of subordinate units.
- Ensuring local security is maintained.
- Conducting rehearsals.

Platoons and squads use five types of rehearsals:

(1) Confirmation brief.[23]
(2) Backbrief.

---

20) imperative: 필수의, 반드시 실행해야 하는
21) leader's absence: 지휘자 부재
22) specify: 명시하다, 열거하다
23) confirmation brief: 임무확인 보고

(3) Combined arms rehearsal.[24]

(4) Support rehearsal.

(5) Battle drill or SOP rehearsal.

---

24) combined arms rehearsal: 연합부대 예행연습

QUESTIONS

1. Why does the tempo of operations often preclude the ideal sequence?

2. What portion of time does the leader/commander allow their subordinates among available time remaining?

3. What is the acronym for fragmentary order?

4. What does the METT-TC stand for?

5. Explain the military decision making process from 2 to 6 steps based on Army standard planning process.

6. Do platoon and squad leaders typically issue a commander's intent?

7. How do the leaders supervise the preparation of the unit?

Dialogue 1: Take time to adapt

MAJ Kang   Hello? I'm Major Kang and PCSed[25] in to the office next door, the Rear Area Plans Branch.

MAJ McGill   Congratulations on your assignment. I am Major McGill, Operations Officer, Operations Branch. What was your last duty assignment?

MAJ Kang   I worked as a Unit Training Officer at the Operations Division, CDC.[26]

MAJ McGill   Then, Rear Area Operations is nothing new to you?

MAJ Kang   That's right. I am familiar with Rear Area Operations, but it's going to take me some time to adapt, because it's the first time I have served in a combined unit.

MAJ McGill   As I see it, you will have no problem adapting with your outstanding ability to speak English.

Dialogue 2: Would you mind waiting for a moment?

LTC White   Hello? I'm LTC White, C-1, Plans and Operations. I believe LTC Lee is expecting me.[27]

MAJ McGill   I'm terribly sorry, but LTC Lee was called suddenly. Would you mind waiting for a moment?

LTC White   Not at all. I will wait for him.

---

25) PCS(Permanent Change of Station) in: 전입, PCS out: 전출

26) CDC(Capital Defense Command): 수도방위사령부

27) expect me: 나를 기다리다

(After a while)

LTC Lee　　　How are you doing, LTC White? Please come in. I'm sorry I've kept you waiting for such a long time.

LTC White　　Not a problem! It was my pleasure.[28]

* called away: 불려가다

---

28) It was my pleasure: 괜찮습니다(My pleasure)

Military Terminology

adjacent unit 인접부대

aspect 지점, 관점, 양상

attack position 공격진지

battle position 전투진지

CDC(Capital Defense Command)
　　　수도방위사령부

circumstance 상황, 환경

COA(Course of Action) 방책

COA comparison 방책비교

COA development 방책개발

combined arms rehearsal 연합부대 예행연습

concept of the operation 작전개념

confirmation brief 임무확인 보고

constraint 제한사항

emplace 적용하다

expect me 나를 기다리다

firsthand 직접, 직접의

fragmentary order 단편명령

guide 선도

imagery 모형, 모형 상황판

imperative 필수의, 반드시 실행해야 하는

incorporate 통합하다

infeasible 실행 불가능한

information requirement 첩보요구

initiate movement 최초 이동

intent (지휘관) 의도

It was my pleasure 괜찮습니다(My pleasure)

leader's absence 지휘자 부재

logic 논리

mentally 염두로, 머릿속으로

nature of the operation 작전 성격

OPORD(Operation Order) 작전명령

order format 명령양식

overlay 투명도

PCS(Permanent Change of Station) in 전입

PCS out 전출

portion 일부, 분할

preclude 배제하다

quartering party 분할된 일부분

receive the mission 명령수령

refine 정교화하다

rehearsal 예행연습

reiterate 되풀이하다, 반복하다

sand table 사판, 모래를 이용한 모형판

specify 명시하다, 열거하다

substitute 대신하다

supervise and assess 감독 및 평가

supplement 보충하다, 추가

tentative plan 잠정계획

timeline 진행계획

troop-leading procedure
　　　부대지휘절차(작전수행과정)

verbal combat order 구두전투명령

warning order 준비명령

Unit 8 | Warfighting Functions

Key Words

warfighting function 전투수행기능	**shock** 충격
protection 방호	**momentum** 기세
sustainment 작전지속지원	**dominance** 우세
facilitate 용이하게 하다	**indirect fire** 간접화력
surveillance 감시	**offensive information operation** 공세적
reconnaissance 정찰	정보작전
architecture 구조, 구성	**preserve** 보존하다
civil populace 시민 대중	**combatant** 전투원
movement and maneuver 이동 및 기동	**fratricide avoidance** 우군 간 피해 회피
advantage 우위, 유리, 이점	**counterproliferation** 확산방지
direct fire 직접화력	**field service** 야전 근무
force projection 전투력 투사	**subordinate** 하급부대, 부하
countermobility 대기동	

Useful Expressions

1. A warfighting function is a group of tasks and systems(people, organization, information, and processes) united by a common purpose that commanders use to accomplish missions and training objectives.

2. Commanders visualize, describe, direct, and lead operations and training in terms of the warfighting functions.

3. The intelligence warfighting function involves the related tasks and systems that facilitate understanding of the enemy, terrain, weather, and civil

considerations.

4. Movement and maneuver are the means through which commanders concentrate combat power to achieve surprise, shock, momentum, and dominance.

5. The protection warfighting function involves the related tasks and systems that preserve the force so the commander can apply maximum combat power.

6. Sustainment includes those tasks associated with maintenance, transportation, supply and so on.

7. Command and control has two parts: the commander; and the command and control system.

8. At the core of a unit's ability to fight are three time-tested components of close combat: firepower, mobility, protection/security.

Reading Text[1]

A warfighting function is a group of tasks and systems(people, organization, information, and processes) united by a common purpose that commanders use to accomplish missions and training objectives. The warfighting functions are intelligence, movement and maneuver, fire support, protection, sustainment, and command and control. These warfighting functions replace[2] the battlefield operating systems.

Commanders visualize, describe, direct, and lead operations and training in terms of the warfighting functions. Decisive, shaping, and sustaining operations

---

1) FM 3-21.8, *Infantry Rifle Platoon and Squad*(Headquarters Department of the Army, March 2007), pp. 1-3~1-6.
2) replace: 대신하다, 대체하다

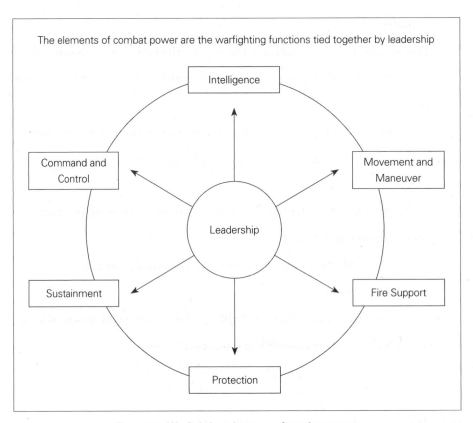

The elements of combat power are the warfighting functions tied together by leadership

Intelligence

Command and Control

Movement and Maneuver

Leadership

Sustainment

Fire Support

Protection

Figure 8-1. Warfighting elements of combat power

* Source: FM 3-21.8, *Infantry Rifle Platoon and Squad*(Headquarters Department of the Army, March 2007), pp.1-4.

combine[3] all the warfighting functions. No function is exclusively decisive, shaping, or sustaining. Figure 8-1 illustrates the warfighting elements of combat power.

⊙ INTELLIGENCE

The intelligence warfighting function involves the related tasks and

---

3) combine: 결합하다, 연합하다

systems that facilitate understanding of the enemy, terrain, weather, and civil considerations. It includes those tasks associated with[4] intelligence, surveillance, and reconnaissance. The intelligence warfighting function combines a flexible and adjustable architecture of procedures, personnel, organizations, and equipment to provide commanders with relevant information and products relating to an area's threat, civil populace, and environment.

⊙ MOVEMENT AND MANEUVER

The movement and maneuver warfighting function involves the related tasks and systems that move forces to achieve a position of advantage in relation to[5] the enemy. It includes those tasks associated with employing forces in combination with[6] direct fire or fire potential(maneuver), force projection(movement), and mobility and countermobility. Movement and maneuver are the means through which commanders concentrate combat power to achieve surprise, shock, momentum, and dominance.

⊙ FIRE SUPPORT

The fire support warfighting function involves the related tasks and systems that provide collective and coordinated use of Army indirect fires, joint fires, and offensive information operations. It includes those tasks associated with integrating and synchronizing the effects[7] of these types of fires with the other

---

4) associated with: ~와 관련된, 연관된

5) in relation to: ~와 비교하여, ~에 관하여

6) in combination with: ~와 결합하여, 짝지어

7) integrating and synchronizing the effects: 통합되고 동시적인 효과

warfighting functions to accomplish operational and tactical objectives.

⊙ PROTECTION

The protection warfighting function involves the related tasks and systems that preserve the force so the commander can apply maximum combat power. Preserving the force includes protecting personnel(combatant and noncombatant), physical assets, and information of the United States and multinational partners.[8] The following tasks are included in the protection warfighting function:

- Safety.
- Fratricide avoidance.
- Survivability.
- Air and missile defense.
- Antiterrorism.
- Counterproliferation and consequence management actions[9] associated with chemical, biological, radiological, nuclear, and high-yield explosive weapons.
- Defensive information operations.
- Force health protection.[10]

⊙ SUSTAINMENT

The sustainment warfighting function involves the related tasks and systems

---

8) multinational partner: 다국적 파트너
9) consequence management action: 주요 관리 행위
10) Force health protection: 부대 건강 방호

that provide support and services to ensure freedom of action, extend operational reach,[11] and prolong endurance.[12] Sustainment includes those tasks associated with -

- Maintenance.
- Transportation.
- Supply.
- Field services.
- Explosive ordnance disposal.[13]
- Human resources support.[14]
- Financial management.
- Health service support.
- Religious support.
- Band support.[15]
- Related general engineering.[16]

Sustainment allows uninterrupted operations[17] through adequate and continuous logistical support such as supply systems, maintenance, and other services.

---

11) extend operational reach: 확장된 작전 범위

12) prolong endurance: 신장된 내구력

13) Explosive ordnance disposal: 폭발성 무기류 처치

14) Human resources support: 인적자원 지원(보충)

15) Band support: (군)악대 지원

16) Related general engineering: 일반 공병과 관련된 것

17) uninterrupted operation: 지속작전, 단절 없는 작전

⊙ COMMAND AND CONTROL

The command and control warfighting function involves the related tasks and systems that support commanders in exercising authority and direction. It includes the tasks of acquiring friendly information, managing relevant information, and directing and leading subordinates.

Command and control has two parts: the commander; and the command and control system. Information systems - including communications systems, intelligence-support systems, and computer networks - back the command and control systems. They let the commander lead from anywhere in their area of operations(AO)[18] subordinate. Through command and control, the commander initiates and integrates all warfighting functions.

⊙ Combat Power

Combat power is a unit's ability to fight. The primary challenge of leadership at the tactical level is mastering the art of generating and applying combat power[19] at a decisive point to accomplish a mission. Leaders use the operations process(plan, prepare, execute, and assess) to generate combat power. They conduct operations following the Find, Fix, Finish, and Follow-through model to apply combat power.

At the core of a unit's ability to fight are three time-tested[20] components of close combat:

---

18) area of operations(AO): 작전지역

19) generating and applying combat power: 전투력의 창출 및 적용

20) time-tested: 유효성이 증명된

(1) Firepower.

(2) Mobility.

(3) Protection/Security.

These components appear throughout military history under various names as the central elements required to fight and win against the enemy. Firepower consists of the weapons used to inflict[21] casualties upon the enemy. Firepower alone is indecisive without movement. Mobility is the ability to move on the battlefield, dictating[22] the speed, tempo, and tactical positioning of forces. Inherent[23] in both firepower and mobility is the need for protection from the enemy's firepower and mobility. Leaders employ protection and security measures to preserve their unit's ability to fight. They deny[24] the enemy protection through creative combinations of unit firepower and mobility.

⊙ Situation

Every combat situation is unique. Leaders do their best to accurately assess the situation[25] and make good decisions about employing their units. The environment of combat, the application of military principles, and the desired end state of Army operations culminate[26] with the close fight of Infantry platoons and squads. The leader should understand the larger military purpose and how his actions and decisions might affect the outcome of the larger operation.

---

21) inflict: 주다, 가하다, 입히다

22) dictate: 좌우하다, 결정하다

23) Inherent: 본질, 필연성

24) deny: 거부하다

25) accurately assess the situation: 정확히 상황을 평가하다

26) culminate: 최고점에 달하다, 완결하다

QUESTIONS

1. What are included in a group of tasks and systems for warfighting function?

2. Explain the warfighting elements of combat power.

3. The intelligence warfighting function involves the related tasks and systems that facilitate understanding of the enemy and terrain. What are the others?

4. What are the means that commanders use to concentrate combat power in order to achieve surprise, shock, momentum, and dominance?

5. What is the purpose of unit protection?

6. Why do you think sustainment is important in the operation?

7. Command and control has two parts. One is the commander. What is the other?

8. What is the core of a unit's ability to fight in close combat?

9. Explain the operations process.

Dialogue 1: What' wrong?

MAJ Park   MAJ Fox, what's wrong ? You don't look well.

MAJ Fox   No, it's just that I've had a headache since last night. I took some aspirin this morning, but it doesn't do any good.

MAJ Park   Then, why don't you go to the hospital for sick call?[27]

MAJ Fox   I've already made an appointment for 10:00.

MAJ Park   I hope it's nothing serious.

MAJ Fox   Me, too. I want to get rid of[28] this headache, otherwise I will have to go home and lie down.

Dialogue 2: Thank you for your help

LTC John   Hello? Major Lee. Thank you for all your help.

MAJ Lee   Are you going somewhere, Lieutenant Colonel? You are talking as if you are being transferred.

LTC John   That's right. I'll be going back to CONUS[29] next Tuesday.

MAJ Lee   Why are you leaving so soon? When I asked you about your transfer at the end of last year. you said you'd be working until the end of this year.

LTC John   I was supposed to[30] leave in November, but something came up and I have to leave early.

---

27) sick call: 군인들이 몸이 불편하여 병원에 갈 경우

28) get rid of: ~에서 벗어나다, ~을 없애다

29) CONUS(Continental United States): 미 본토

30) be supposed to ~: ~하기로 되어 있다

MAJ Lee   Well, I'm sorry that you are leaving so soon, but I hope you won't

forget the good times you had here in Korea.

* Thank you for the tip. 알려 주셔서 감사합니다.
* I can't thank you enough. 어떻게 감사를 드려야 할지 모르겠군요.

Military Terminology

accurately assess the situation   정확히
상황을 평가하다

advantage   우위, 유리, 이점

architecture   구조, 구성

associated with   ~와 관련된, 연관된

band support   (군)악대 지원

be supposed to ~   ~하기로 되어 있다

civil populace   시민 대중

combatant   전투원

combine   결합하다, 연합하다

consequence management action   주요
관리 행위

CONUS(Continental United States)   미 본토

countermobility   대기동

counterproliferation   확산방지

culminate   최고점에 달하다, 완결하다

deny   거부하다

dictate   좌우하다, 결정하다

direct fire   직접화력

dominance   우세

explosive ordnance disposal   폭발성 무기류
처치

extend operational reach   확장된 작전 범위

facilitate   용이하게 하다

Field service   야전 근무

force health protection   부대 건강 방호

force projection   전투력 투사

fratricide avoidance   우군 간 피해 회피

generating and applying combat power
전투력의 창출 및 적용

get rid of   ~에서 벗어나다, ~을 없애다

human resources support   인적자원 지원
(보충)

in combination with   ~와 결합하여, 짝지어

in relation to   ~와 비교하여, ~에 관하여

indirect fire   간접화력

inflict   주다, 가하다, 입히다

inherent   본질, 필연성

integrating and synchronizing the
effects   통합되고 동시적인 효과

momentum   기세

movement and maneuver   이동 및 기동

multinational partner   다국적 파트너

offensive information operation   공세적
정보작전

preserve   보존하다

prolong endurance   신장된 내구력

protection   방호

reconnaissance   정찰

related general engineering   일반 공병과
관련된 것

replace   대신하다, 대체하다

shock   충격

sick call   군인들이 병원에 가는 것

subordinate   하급부대, 부하

surveillance   감시

sustainment   작전지속지원

time-tested   유효성이 증명된

uninterrupted operation   지속작전, 단절
없는 작전

warfighting function   전투수행기능

Unit 9 | Offensive Operations

Key Words

movement to contact 접적 이동	guard 보초, 경계
search and attack 수색 및 공격	area security(including route and convey)
approach march 접적 전진	지역경계(통로, 수송로 포함)
attack 공격	combined arms breach operation
special purpose attacks 특수목적 공격	연합군 돌파 작전
ambush 매복	passage of lines 초월전진
demonstration 양동, 시위	relief in place 진지교대
feint 양공	troop movement(road march) 부대 이동
spoiling attack 파쇄공격	(도로 행군)
forms of maneuver 기동형태	area defense 지역방어
envelopment 포위	retrograde operations 후퇴작전
frontal attack 정면공격	delay 지연
infiltration 침투	withdrawal 철수
penetration 돌파	retirement 철퇴, 전역, 하기식
turning Movement 우회공격	patrols 정찰, 순찰
reconnaissance operation 수색작전	combat patrols 전투정찰
area 지역	reconnaissance patrols 수색정찰
route 통로	security patrols 경계정찰
zone 지대	tactical movement 전술적 이동
reconnaissance in force 위력수색	battle drills 전투훈련
security operation 경계작전	crew drills 승무원 훈련
screen 차장	

Useful Expressions

1. Figure 9-1 shows the doctrinal hierarchy and the relationship between the
   types and subordinate forms of operations.

2. In fact, many of these types of operations are only conducted at the battalion, brigade, or division level.

3. Offensive operations aim to destroy or defeat an enemy.

4. Effective offensive operations require accurate intelligence on enemy forces, weather, and terrain.

5. Destruction results in an enemy unit(Soldiers and their equipment) that is no longer able to fight.

6. At the platoon and squad level, these offensive operations are basically planned, prepared for, and executed the same.

7. The four types of offensive operations include movement to contact, attack, exploitation and pursuit.

Reading Text[1]

⊙ Doctrinal Hierarchy of Operations

Figure 9-1 shows the doctrinal hierarchy[2] and the relationship between the types and subordinate forms of operations. While an operation's predominant[3] characteristic labels[4] it as an offensive, defensive, stability,[5] or civil support operation, different units involved in that operation may be conducting different types and subordinate[6] forms of operations. These units often transition rapidly

---

1) FM 3-21.8, *Infantry Rifle Platoon and Squad*(Headquarters Department of the Army, March 2007), pp. 1-37~1-39.

2) doctrinal hierarchy: 교리 체계

3) predominant: 지배적

4) label: 구분하다

5) stability operation: 안정화 작전

6) subordinate: 하위의, 종속의

from one type or subordinate form to another. While positioning his forces for maximum effectiveness, the commander rapidly shifts from one type or form of operation to another to continually keep the enemy off balance. Flexibility in transitioning contributes to a successful operation.

Offensive Operations	

• Movement to contact
  – Search and attack
  – Approach march
 	
• Attack
 	
• Special purpose attacks
  – Amush
  – Demonstraion
  – Feint
  – Spoiling attack
 	
• Forms of maneuver
  – Envelopment
  – Frontal attack
  – Infiltration
  – Penetration
  – Turning Movement
	• Reconnaissance operation
	  – Area
	  – Route
	  – Zone
	  – Reconnaissance in force
	
	• Security operation
	  – Screen
	  – Guard
	  – Area security(including route and convey)
	
	• Combined arms breach operation
	
	• Passage of lines
	
	• Relief in place
	
	• Troop movement(road march)

Defensive Operations	

• Area Defense
 	
• Retrograde Operations
  – Delay
  – Withdrawal
  – Retirement
	• Patrols
	  – Combat patrols
	  – Reconnaissance patrols
	  – Security patrols
	
	• Tactical movement
	
	• Battle drills
	
	• Crew drills

Figure 9-1. Doctrinal hierarchy of operations

* Source: FM 3-21.8, *Infantry Rifle Platoon and Squad*(Headquarters Department of the Army, March 2007), pp.1-38.

Infantry platoons and squads conduct all the types of operations listed in the doctrinal hierarchy. However, the Infantry platoon and squad will almost always conduct these operations and their subordinate forms and types as part of a larger unit. In fact, many of these types of operations are only conducted at the battalion, brigade, or division level. Only the types of operations applicable to Infantry platoons and squads are further covered in this manual.

⊙ Offensive Operations

Offensive operations aim to destroy or defeat an enemy. Their purpose is to impose U.S. will on the enemy and achieve decisive victory(FM 3-0, Operations). Dominance of the offense is a basic tenet[7] of U.S. Army operations doctrine. While the defense is the stronger form of military action, the offense is the decisive form. Tactical considerations may call for Army forces to execute defensive operations for a period of time. However, leaders are constantly looking for ways to shift to the offense. Offensive operations do not exist in a vacuum[8] — they exist side by side with defense, and tactical enabling operations.[9] Leaders analyze the mission two levels up to determine how their unit's mission nests within the overall concept. For example, an Infantry platoon leader would analyze company and battalion missions.

Effective offensive operations require accurate intelligence on enemy forces, weather, and terrain. Leaders then maneuver their forces to advantageous positions before contact. Contact with enemy forces before the decisive action is deliberate and designed to shape the optimum situation for the decisive action. The decisive

---

7) tenet: 교리, 견해

8) vacuum: 공백

9) tactical enabling operations: 전술적 운용 가능 작전들

action is sudden and violent, capitalizing on subordinate initiative. Infantry platoon and squad leaders therefore execute offensive operations and attack with surprise, concentration, tempo, and audacity.

There is a subtle difference between attacking and conducting an attack. Attacking in everyday usage generally means the close combat action of fire and movement on an enemy or position. Attacking occurs frequently on the battlefield in all types of operations. Conducting an attack is one of the four types of offensive operations with specific doctrine meanings and requirements.

⊙ Offensive Purposes

How a unit conducts its offensive operations is determined by the mission's purpose and overall intent. There are four general purposes for the offense: throw the enemy off balance; overwhelm the enemy's capabilities; disrupt the enemy's defense; and ensure their defeat or destruction. In practice, each of these purposes has orientation on both the enemy force and the terrain. The labels merely describe the dominant characteristic of the operation.

⊙ Enemy-Oriented

Leaders employ enemy-oriented attacks[10] to destroy enemy formations and their capabilities. Destruction results in an enemy unit(Soldiers and their equipment) that is no longer able to fight. Not everything has to be destroyed for the force-oriented attack offense to be successful. It is usually enough to focus on an enemy capability or unit cohesion. These attacks are best employed against an enemy vulnerability.

---

10) enemy-oriented attack: 적 지향 공격

Once destruction occurs, a window of opportunity opens. It is up to the leader to take advantage of an unbalanced enemy through local and general exploitations and pursuit.

⊙ Terrain-Oriented

Leaders employ terrain-oriented attacks to seize control of terrain or facilities. Units conducting terrain-oriented attacks have less freedom of action to take advantage of a window of opportunity. The unit's first priority is the terrain or facility. Exploiting an enemy vulnerability can occur only when the security of the terrain or facility is no longer in question.

⊙ Tactical Enabling and Infantry Platoon Actions

Although friendly forces always remain enemy focused, there are many actions friendly forces conduct that are offensive in nature and are designed to shape or sustain other operations. Leaders employ tactical enabling operations to support the overall purpose of an operation.

⊙ Types of Offensive Operations

Types of offensive operations are described by the context surrounding an operation(terrain or force oriented). At the platoon and squad level, these offensive operations are basically planned, prepared for, and executed the same. The four types of offensive operations include:

(1) Movement to Contact – undertaken to gain or regain contact with the

enemy(force-oriented).

(2) Attack – undertaken to achieve a decisive outcome(terrain-oriented or force-oriented).

(3) Exploitation[11] – undertaken to take advantage of a successful attack(force-oriented).

(4) Pursuit[12] – undertaken to destroy an escaping enemy(force-oriented).

This order of offensive operations is deliberate because they are listed in order of their normal occurrence. Generally, leaders conduct a movement to contact to find the enemy. When the leader has enough information about the enemy to be successful, he conducts an attack. Following a successful attack, the leader takes advantage of the enemy's disorganization and exploits the attack's success. After exploiting his success, the leader executes a pursuit to catch or cut off a fleeing enemy to complete its destruction. Although Infantry platoons and squads participate in exploit and pursuit operations, they do not plan them.

---

11) exploitation: 전과확대

12) pursuit: 추격

QUESTIONS

1. What are the purposes of an offensive operation?

2. Mention some requirements for effective offensive operations?

3. Why do leaders employ enemy-oriented attacks?

4. Why do leaders employ terrain-oriented attacks?

5. Explain the four types of offensive operations.

Dialogue 1: What to ask about ~

MAJ Williams	Plans Branch, Major Williams speaking.
MAJ Kim	Hello? Major Williams? This is Major Kim, Policy Branch.
MAJ Williams	Well, how do you do, Major Kim? How have you been?
MAJ Kim	I'm fine. I just wanted to ask you about the current status of the US personnel participating in this exercise.
MAJ Williams	That's not a problem. Do you need the current personnel status by rank or unit?
MAJ Kim	I need both.
MAJ Williams	I got it. I'll send it through GCCS-K right away.[13]

* GCCS-K: Global Command and Control System Korea(주한 범세계 지휘통제체계)

Dialogue 2: Pass the message

MAJ Johnson	Plans Division, Major Johnson speaking.
LTC Jung	Hello? this is the XO for the deputy chief of Staff, Lieutenant Colonel Jung. May I speak with the chief of Plans Division, Colonel Gilmore?
MAJ Johnson	Oh! I'm sorry. He's not here. He's in a meeting right now.
LTC Jung	Then please pass the message that he has to go with the Deputy Chief of Staff tomorrow at 14:00 to inspect the preparations for the UFG exercise.
MAJ Johnson	All right. I'll give him the message.

---

13) right away: 바로

LTC Jung   This is a just a reminder. We sent the official message last week, so Colonel Gilmore already knows about it.

* XO(Executive Officer): 보좌관, 행정장교
* UFG(Ulchi-Freedom Guardian): 을지 프리덤 가디언
* May I leave a message? 메모를 남겨도 되겠습니까?
* Would you take a message? 메모를 좀 받아 주시겠습니까?
* Please remind him to call me. 그에게 전화해 달라고 일러 주세요.
* Could you ask him to call me back when he returns? 그분이 돌아오시면 저한테 전화해 달라고 해 주시겠어요?
* I'll make sure that he gets the message. 꼭 전해 드리겠습니다.
* Can I get some information about ~? ~에 대한 정보 좀 얻을 수 있습니까?
* I need your help. 당신의 도움이 필요해요.
* I will let you know what was decided. 제가 결정된 일을 알려 드리지요.
* May I ask who is calling? 전화하는 분이 누구이신지 여쭤 봐도 되겠습니까?
* He's tied up now. 그는 지금 바쁘십니다.

Military Terminology

ambush   매복

approach march   접적 전진

area   지역

area defense   지역방어

area security(including route and convey)
    지역경계(통로, 수송로 포함)

attack   공격

battle drills   전투훈련

combat patrols   전투정찰

combined arms breach operation   연합군
    돌파 작전

crew drills   승무원 훈련

delay   지연

demonstration   양동, 시위

doctrinal hierarchy   교리 체계

enemy-oriented attack   적 지향 공격

envelopment   포위

exploitation   전과확대

feint   양공

forms of maneuver   기동형태

frontal attack   정면공격

guard   보초, 경계

infiltration   침투

label   구분하다

movement to contact   접적이동

passage of lines   초월전진

patrols   정찰, 순찰

penetration   돌파

predominant   지배적

pursuit   추격

reconnaissance in force   위력수색

reconnaissance operation   수색작전

reconnaissance patrols   수색정찰

relief in place   진지교대

retirement   철퇴, 전역, 하기식

retrograde operations   후퇴작전

right away   바로

route   통로

screen   차장

search and attack   수색 및 공격

security operation   경계 작전

security patrols   경계 정찰

special purpose attacks   특수목적 공격

spoiling attack   파쇄공격

stability operation   안정화 작전

subordinate   하위의, 종속의

tactical enabling operations   전술적 운용
    가능 작전들

tactical movement   전술적 이동

tenet   교리, 견해

troop movement(road march)   부대이동
    (도로 행군)

turning Movement   우회공격

vacuum   공백

withdrawal   철수

zone   지대

Unit 10 | Defensive Operations

Key Words

overarching 아주 중요한

counteroffensive 반격

ingredient 성분, 구성요소

blow 타격, 공격

deflect 빗나가게 하다, 비끼다

immediately 즉시, 곧장

rapid 신속

window of opportunity 기회의 창

counterattack 역습

economy of force 병력의 절약

allocate 할당하다

secondary effort 조공, 부차적 노력

buy time 시간을 절약하다

sustaining actions
　지탱하는 행동, 작전지속지원을 위한 행동

consolidation and reorganization
　진지강화 및 재편성

resupply 재보급

LOGPAC(Logistics Package) 군수 패키지

pickup zone 회수지점, 탑승지점

landing zone 착륙지점, 상륙지점

CASEVAC(Casualty Evacuation) 사상자 후송

MEDEVAC(Medical Evacuation) 의무후송

assembly area 집결지

lodgment 숙영

mobile defense 기동방어

Useful Expressions

1. Defensive operations defeat an enemy attack, buy time, economize forces, or develop conditions favorable for offensive operations.

2. How a unit establishes its defenses is determined by the mission's purpose and intent.

3. Commanders seldom have all the combat forces they desire to conduct operations without accepting risk.

4. As a result, commanders arrange forces in space and time to create favorable

conditions for a mobile defense and offensive operations in other areas.

5. Defenses to preserve friendly combat power are designed to protect the friendly force and prevent the destruction of key friendly assets.

6. Exploiting the vulnerability of an enemy can occur only when the security of the terrain or facility is no longer in question.

7. Retrograde is a technique used by higher-level commanders to maintain or break contact with the enemy.

8. Retrograde is the defensive counterpart to an offensive exploitation or pursuit. There are three techniques used to retrograde.

Reading Text[1)]

⊙ Defensive Operations

Defensive operations defeat an enemy attack, buy time, economize forces, or develop conditions favorable for offensive operations. Defensive operations alone normally cannot achieve a decision. Their overarching purpose is to create conditions for a counteroffensive that allows Army forces to regain the initiative(FM 1-02). Defensive operations do not exist in a vacuum — they exist side by side with[2)] offense, tactical enabling operations, and Infantry platoon actions. Leaders analyze the mission two levels up to determine how their unit's mission nests[3)] within the overall concept.

---

1) FM 3-21.8, *Infantry Rifle Platoon and Squad*(Headquarters Department of the Army, March 2007), pp. 1-39~1-41.

2) side by side with: ~와 나란히, 밀접한 관계를 가지고

3) nest: 기여하다, 차곡차곡 포개 넣다, ~을 보금자리에 깃들게 하다

The principles of tactical maneuver also apply to the defense. To be decisive, defensive tactics must have both ingredients. Ensuring mobility remains a part of the defense is one of the leader's greatest challenges. While it is true that defending forces await the attacker's blow and defeat the attack by successfully deflecting it, this does not mean that defending is a passive activity. Leaders always look for ways to integrate movement into their defensive activities.

During the conduct of operations, regardless of type, friendly forces make many transitions requiring the unit to stop and restart movement. Infantry platoons and squads that are not moving are defending. Units that stop moving(attacking), immediately transition to defending. This transition is rapid and should be second nature to all Soldiers and their units. This is particularly relevant at the Infantry platoon and squad levels where the tactical situation can quickly shift to one where the unit is outnumbered[4] and fighting for its survival.

⊙ Defensive Purposes

How a unit establishes its defenses is determined by the mission's purpose and intent. There are four general purposes for conducting a defense: defeat an attacking enemy; economize friendly forces in one area so they can be concentrated in another area; buy time; and develop conditions favorable for resuming offensive operations. In practice, each of these stated purposes for conducting a defense is considered in all defenses; the categories just describe the dominant purpose. Infantry platoons and squads can also be tasked to defend specific locations such as key terrain or facilities.

---

4)　outnumber: 압도하다, ~보다 수적으로 우세하다

⊙ Defeat an Attacking Enemy and Develop Conditions for Offensive Operations

Defenses are designed to defeat enemy attack while preserving friendly forces. Defeating the enemy's attack requires him to transition to his own defensive actions. While this occurs, a window of opportunity for friendly forces may also occur. It is up to the leader to take advantage of an unbalanced enemy through local and general counterattacks.

⊙ Economy of Force to Concentrate in Another Area

Commanders seldom have all the combat forces they desire to conduct operations without accepting risk. Economy of force is defined as allocating minimum essential combat power to secondary efforts(FM 1-02). It requires accepting prudent[5] risk in selected areas to achieve superiority — overwhelming effects — in the decisive operation. As a result, commanders arrange forces in space and time to create favorable conditions for a mobile defense and offensive operations in other areas.

⊙ Buy Time

Defenses to preserve friendly combat power are designed to protect the friendly force and prevent the destruction of key friendly assets. There are times when the unit establishes defenses to protect itself. Although friendly forces always remain enemy focused, there are many actions friendly forces conduct to sustain

---

5) prudent: 신중한

the unit. These sustaining actions typically require the unit to establish a defensive posture while the activity is conducted. Examples include: consolidation and reorganization, resupply/LOGPAC, pickup zone/landing zone, and CASEVAC/ MEDEVAC. This type of defense can also be associated with assembly area activities, establishing lodgments for building up combat power, and facing a numerically-superior enemy force.

⊙ Develop Conditions Favorable for Resuming Offensive Operations

The enemy may have the advantage over friendly forces in areas such as combat power or position. This often occurs during forced entry operations[6] where friendly forces defend in order to build up combat power.

⊙ Key Terrain or Facilities

Defenses for denying enemy access to an area are designed to protect specific location, key terrain, or facilities. Infantry platoons can be assigned missions to defend sites that range from hill tops - to key infrastructure - to religious sites. Because the defense is terrain oriented, leaders have less freedom of action when it comes to taking advantage of a window of opportunity. The unit's first priority is the terrain or facility. Exploiting an enemy vulnerability can occur only when the security of the terrain or facility is no longer in question.

---

6) forced entry operation: 강압 진입 작전

⊙ Types of Defensive Operations

Defensive operations fall into one of the following three categories:

(1) Area defense – focuses on retaining terrain for a specified period of time(terrain-oriented).

(2) Mobile defense – stops an enemy attack with a fixing force and destroys it with a strike force(division level and higher operations [force-oriented]).

(3) Retrograde – a type of defensive operation that involves an organized movement away from the enemy. The three types of retrograde operations are: delay; withdrawal; and retirement.

⊙ Area Defense

The area defense is the most common defensive operation undertaken at the tactical level(brigade and below). This is discussed in Chapter 9(FM 3-21.8).

⊙ Mobile Defense

The mobile defense is usually a corps-level operation. A mobile defense has three categories of forces: a fixing force, a strike force, or a reserve force. The decisive operation of a mobile defense is the strike force. Those units designated as the fixing force are essentially performing an area defense. Units designated as the strike force are essentially performing an attack. (For more information on the mobile defense, see FM 3-90, Tactics.)

⊙ Retrograde

The retrograde is a technique used by higher-level commanders to maintain or break contact with the enemy. This is done as part of a larger scheme of maneuver to create conditions to regain the initiative and defeat the enemy. Retrogrades improve the current situation or prevent a situation from deteriorating.[7] These operations are a means to an end; not an end in itself. The Infantry platoon's fight in the higher commander's retrograde operation uses one of two techniques: fighting the enemy, or moving to the new location. Leaders must be aware of the potentially catastrophic impact[8] a retrograde has on friendly troop's morale. The retrograde is the defensive counterpart to an offensive exploitation or pursuit. There are three techniques used to retrograde:

- Delay – trades space for time(attempting to slow the enemy's momentum).
- Withdrawal – trades time for space(breaking contact as far from the enemy as possible).
- Retirement – movement that is not in contact with the enemy.

---

7) deteriorate: 악화되다

8) catastrophic impact: 비극적 영향(충격)

QUESTIONS

1. Define defensive operation.

2. What is the overarching purpose of a defensive operation?

3. Which operation is usually a corps-level among types of defensive operation?

4. Which operation is a technique used by higher-level commanders to maintain or break contact with the enemy among types of defensive operation?

5. The Infantry platoon's fight in the higher commander's retrograde operation uses one of two techniques. What are the two techniques?

6. Explain three techniques used to retrograde.

Dialogue 1: Come by

MAJ Park   Good morning? This is Major Park, C-3 Plans Division.

I'd like to know about the transportation support plan for KR this year. When can I stop by[9] your office?

CAP Miller   Hello? Major Park. I have been looking forward to[10] meeting you. Would 11:00 hours be convenient for you?

MAJ Park   Sure. I'll come by with Major Kim from Aviation Division, if that's okay with you.

CAP Miller   Good idea. I was about to ask you to bring him with you.

MAJ Park   Fine. I'll see you then.

* Major Kim came over to my house after work. 김 소령은 일과 후에 우리 집에 왔습니다.

Dialogue 2: Return a call

COL Smith   C-5 Plans Division, Corporal Smith speaking.

MAJ Lee   This is Major Lee, C-3 Exercise Division. I'm returning a call from the Chief of Plans Division.

COL McBurn   Colonel McBurn speaking.

MAJ Lee   Sir, this is UFG Exercise officer, Major Lee, C-3. I'm returning your call.

COL McBurn   Yes, I called you to discuss the UFG this year initial planing conference. Do you have a few minutes right now?

---

9) stop by, drop by, visit, come over to: 들르다

10) look forward to(anticipate): 기다리다, 기대하다

MAJ Lee   Sure, sir.

* Please tell him to call me back. 전화를 다시 해달라고 전해 주십시오.
* I got a message to call you. 전화해 달라는 메모를 받았습니다.
* I heard that you tried to call me earlier. 저한테 전화를 거셨다면서요.
* Can you spare a second(some time)? 시간 좀 내주시겠습니까?
* Are you free now? / Are you available now? 지금 시간 있습니까?
* When do you have time / When will you be available? 언제 시간이 있습니까?

Military Terminology ———————————————

allocate 할당하다

assembly area 집결지

blow 타격, 공격

buy time 시간을 절약하다

CASEVAC(Casualty Evacuation) 사상자 후송

catastrophic impact 비극적 영향(충격)

consolidation and reorganization 진지강화 및 재편성

counterattack 역습

counteroffensive 반격

deflect 빗나가게 하다, 비끼다

deteriorate 악화되다

economy of force 병력의 절약

forced entry operation 강압 진입 작전

immediately 즉시, 곧장

ingredient 성분, 구성요소

landing zone 착륙지점, 상륙지점

lodgment 숙영

LOGPAC(Logistics Package) 군수 패키지

look forward to(anticipate) 기다리다, 기대하다

MEDEVAC(Medical Evacuation) 의무후송

mobile defense 기동방어

nest 기여하다, 차곡차곡 포개 넣다

outnumber 압도하다, ~보다 수적으로 우세하다

overarching 아주 중요한

pickup zone 회수지점, 탑승지점

prudent 신중한

rapid 신속

resupply 재보급

secondary effort 조공, 부차적 노력

side by side with ~와 나란히, 밀접한 관계를 가지고

stop by, drop by, visit, come over to 들르다

sustaining actions 지탱하는 행동, 작전지속지원을 위한 행동

window of opportunity 기회의 창

Unit 11 | Operation Order Format

Key Words	
no change 변동 없음	**execution** 실시
overlay or sketch 투명도 또는 요도	**concept of operation** 작전개념
assumption 가정	**coordinating instruction** 협조지시
disposition (부대의) 배치	**rules of engagement** 교전규칙
composition (부대의) 구성	**SOI(Signal Operation Instructions)**
reinforce 증강하다	통신운용지시
attachment 배속	**index** 색인
detachment 파견	**code word** 암구어
annex 부록	**challenge and password** 수하 및 암호

Useful Expressions

1. Task Organization explains how the unit is organized for the operation. If there is no change to previous task organization, indicate 'no change.'

2. Situation provides information essential to the subordinate leader's understanding of the situation.

3. Mission provides a clear, concise statement of the task to be accomplished and the purpose for doing it.

4. Execution consists of the following: commander's intent, concept of operations, scheme of movement and maneuver, scheme of fires, casualty evacuation, tasks to subordinate units, tasks to combat support.

5. Sustainment includes logistics, personnel services support and army health

system support.

6. Command and Control consists of command, control and signal.

Reading Text[1]

An order is a communication — verbal, written, or signaled — which conveys instructions from a superior to a subordinate. Commanders issue orders verbally or in writing. The five-paragraph format(situation, mission, execution, sustainment, and command and signal) remains the standard for issuing orders. The technique used to issue orders(verbal or written) is at the discretion of the commander; each technique depends on time and the situation. Army organizations use three types of orders: Operation order(OPORD), Fragmentary order(FRAGO), Warning order(WARNO).

Operation Order Format

(Classification)

(Change from oral orders, if any)(Optional)

Copy of copies

Issuing headquarters

Place of issue

Date-time group of signature

Message reference number

---

1) FM 3-21.8, *Infantry Rifle Platoon and Squad*(Headquarters Department of the Army, March 2007), pp. 5-20~5-21. ATTP 5-0.1, *Commander and Staff Officer Guide*(Headquarters, Department of the Army, September, 2011), pp. 12-3~12-4.

Task Organization: Explain how the unit is organized for the operation. If there is no change to previous task organization, indicate "no change."

1. SITUATION

Provide information essential to the subordinate leader's understanding of the situation.

- Area of Interest.
- Area of Operations.
    (1) Terrain.
    (2) Weather.

a. **Enemy forces.** Refer to the overlay or sketch. Include pertinent[2] intelligence provided by higher HQ and other facts and assumption about the enemy. This analysis is stated as conclusions and addressed —

    (1) Disposition, composition, and strength.
    (2) Recent Activities.
    (3) Locations and Capabilities.
    (4) Most probable course of action.

b. **Friendly Forces.** Provide information that subordinates need to accomplish their tasks.

    (1) Higher HQ Mission and Intent. A verbatim[3] statement of the higher unit commender's mission statement from paragraph 2 and concept of operation statement from paragraph 3a.
    (2) Left unit's mission
    (3) Right unit's mission
    (4) forward unit's mission

---

2) pertinent: 관계있는, 적절한
3) verbatim: 말 그대로의, 축어적인

(5) Mission of unit in reserve or following.

(6) Units in support or reinforcing the higher unit.

c. **Attachments and Detachments.** When not shown under task organization, list here or in annex, units attached or detached from the platoon, together with the effective time.

2. MISSION

Provide a clear, concise statement of the task to be accomplished and the purpose for doing it(Who, What, When, Where, and Why). The leader derives the mission from his mission analysis.

3. EXECUTION

Intent. Give the stated vision that defines the purpose of the operation and the relationship among the force, the enemy, and the terrain.

a. **Commander's Intent**

b. **Concept of operations.**

(1) Maneuver.

(2) Fires.

(3) Reconnaissance and Surveillance.

(4) Intelligence.

(5) Engineer.

(6) Air Defense.

(7) Information Operations.

c. **Scheme of Movement and Maneuver.**

d. **Scheme of Fires.**

e. **Casualty Evacuation.**

f. **Tasks to Subordinate Units**

g. Tasks to Combat Support.

   (1) Intelligence.

   (2) Engineer.

   (3) Fire Support.

   (4) Air Defense.

   (5) Signal.

   (6) CBRNE(Chemical, Biological, Radiological, Nuclear, and Explosive weapons)

   (7) Provost Marshal.

   (8) MISO(Military Information Support Operations, formerly Psychological Operations or PSYOP)

   (9) Civil Military.

h. Coordinating Instructions.

   (1) Time or condition when the plan or order becomes effective.

   (2) CCIR(Commander's Critical Information Requirements)

   (3) EEFI(Essential Elements of Friendly Information)

   (4) Risk Reduction Control Measures.[4]

   (5) Rules of Engagement.

   (6) Environmental Considerations.

   (7) Force Protection.

4. SUSTAINMENT

a. Logistics.

   (1) Sustainment Overlay.

   (2) Maintenance.

   (3) Transportation.

---

4)   risk reduction control measures: 위험감소 통제수단

(4) Supply.

(5) Field Services.

b. Personnel Services Support.[5]

(1) Method of marking and handling EPWs.

(2) Religious Services.

c. Army Health System Support.

(1) Medical Command and Control.

(2) Medical Treatment.

(3) Medical Evacuation.

(4) Preventive Medicine.

5. COMMAND AND CONTROL

a. Command.

(1) Location of Commander.

(2) Succession of Command.[6]

b. Control.

(1) Command Posts.

(2) Reports.

c. Signal.

(1) SOI index in effect.

(2) Methods of communication by priority.

(3) Pyrotechnics and Signals.[7]

(4) Code Words.

(5) Challenge and Password.

---

5) personnel services support: 인사근무지원

6) succession of command: 지휘권 승계

7) Pyrotechnic and Signal: 불꽃 신호, 섬광 신호탄, 신호탄 및 신호

(6) Number Combination.[8]

(7) Running Password.[9]

(8) Recognition Signals.

ACKNOWLEDGE: (Mandatory)[10]

NAME(Commander's last name)

RANK(Commander's rank)

OFFICIAL:(Optional)

ANNEXES: List annexes by letter and title in the sequence:

Annex A(Task Organization)

Annex B(Intelligence)

Annex C(Operation Overlay)

Annex D(Fire Support)

Annex E(Rules of Engagement)

Annex F(Engineer)

Annex G(Air Defense)

Annex H(Signal)

Annex I(Service Support)

Annex J(Nuclear, Biological)

Annex K(Provost Marshal)

Annex L(Reconnaissance and Surveillance)

Annex M(Deep Operations)

Annex N(Rear Operations)

---

8) Number Combination: 숫자 조합

9) running password: 일상(상비) 암구어

10) ACKNOWLEDGE(Mandatory): 수신여부(필수)

Annex O(Airspace Command and Control)

Annex P(Command and Control Warfare)

Annex Q(Operations Security(OPSEC))

Annex R(Psychological Operations(PSYOP))

Annex S(Deception) instruction

Annex T(Electronic Warfare) instruction

Annex U(Civil-Military Operations)

Annex V(Public Affairs)

(If a particular annex is not used, place a "not used" beside that annex letter.)

Warning Order Format and Content

(Classification)

(Change from oral orders, if any)(Optional)

A WARNING ORDER DOES NOT AUTHORIZE EXECUTION UNLESS SPECIFICALLY STATED

Copy of copies

Issuing headquarters

Place of issue

Date-time group of signature

Message reference number

WARNING ORDER ____

References: Refer to higher headquarters OPLAN/OPORD, and identify map sheet for operation. (Optional.)

Time Zone Used Throughout the Order:(Optional)

Task Organization: (Optional)

1. SITUATION

a. Enemy forces. Include significant changes in enemy composition dispositions and courses of action. Information not available for inclusion in the initial WARNO can be included in subsequent warning orders.

b. Friendly forces. (Optional) Only address if essential to the WARNO.

(1) Higher commander's mission.

(2) Higher commander's intent.

c. Attachments and detachments. Initial task organization, only address major unit changes.

2. MISSION

Issuing headquarters' mission at the time of the WARNO. This is nothing more than higher headquarters' restated mission or commander's decisions during MDMP.

3. EXECUTION

Intent:

a. **Concept of operations.** Provide as much information as available, this may be done during the initial WARNO.

b. **Tasks to maneuver units.** Any information on tasks to units for execution, movement to initiate, reconnaissance to initiate, or security to emplace.

c. **Tasks to combat support units.** See paragraph 3b.

d. **Coordinating instructions.** Include any information available at the time of the issuance of the WARNO. It may include the following:

• Risk guidance.

- Specific priorities, in order of completion.
- Time line.
- Guidance on orders and rehearsals.
- Orders group meeting(attendees, location, and time).
- Earliest movement time and degree of notice.

4. SERVICE SUPPORT(Optional)

Include any known logistics preparation for the operation.

a. **Special equipment.** Identifying requirements, and coordinating transfer to using units.

b. **Transportation.** Identifying requirements, and coordinating for pre-position of assets.

5. COMMAND AND SIGNAL(Optional)

a. **Command.** State the chain of command if different from unit SOP.

b. **Signal.** Identify current SOI edition, and pre-position signal assets to support operation.

ACKNOWLEDGE: (Mandatory)
NAME(Commander's last name)
RANK(Commander's rank)
OFFICIAL:(Optional)

Fragmentary Order(FRAGO) Format and Content

두문 부분: 생략(Warning Order와 동일)

1. SITUATION

(Mandatory) Include any changes to the existing order.

2. MISSION

(Mandatory) List the new mission.

3. EXECUTION

Intent: (Optional)

a. **Concept of operations.** (Mandatory)

b. **Tasks to subordinate units.** (Mandatory)

c. **Coordinating instructions.** (Mandatory) Include statement, "Current overlay remains in effect" or "See change 1 to Annex C, Operations Overlay." Mark changes to control measures on overlay or issue a new overlay.

4. SERVICE SUPPORT.

Include any changes to existing order or the statement, "No change to OPORD xx."

5. COMMAND AND SIGNAL.

Include any changes to existing order or "No change to OPORD xx."

미문 생략(Warning Order와 동일)

Military Terminology

ACKNOWLEDGE(Mandatory) 수신여부
      (필수)
annex 부록
assumption 가정
attachment 배속
challenge and password 수하 및 암호
code word 암구어
composition (부대의) 구성
concept of operation 작전개념
coordinating instruction 협조지시
detachment 파견
disposition (부대의) 배치
execution 실시
index 색인
no change 변동 없음

number combination 숫자 조합
overlay or sketch 투명도 또는 요도
personnel services support 인사근무지원
pertinent 관계 있는, 적절한
pyrotechnic and signal 불꽃신호,
      섬광신호탄, 신호탄 및 신호
reinforce 증강하다
risk reduction control measures 위험감소
      통제수단
rules of engagement 교전규칙
running password 일상(상비) 암구어
SOI(Signal Operation Instructions)
      통신운용지시
succession of command 지휘권 승계
verbatim 말 그대로의, 축어적인

Unit 12 | Future Operational Environment

Key Words

diverse enemy 다양한 적	**diffusion** 확산, 전파
unconventional 비정규적	**amplify** 확대하다
vital interest 핵심이익	**narrative** 이야기, 서술
insurgent 반란, 폭도	**overmatch** 능가, 강적
precision strike 정밀타격	**malware** 악성코드, 악성소프트웨어
intermingle 혼합되다, 섞이다	**proliferation** 확산
domain 영토, 영역, 범위	**incite** 자극하다, 유발하다
dominance 우월, 지배	**contest** 경쟁, 논쟁, 다투다
subvert 전복시키다	**raid** 습격, 침입
disinformation 허위정보	**demographics** 실태적 인구통계
paradoxically 역설적으로	**employment** 고용, 일자리
velocity 속도	**disaffection** 불만, 불평, 혐오
diffuse 퍼트리다	**governance** 지배, 지배권, 통치, 관리
via ~을 경유해서, ~에 의하여	**cohesive** 응집력의, 결합시키는

Useful Expressions

1. Diverse enemies will employ traditional, unconventional, and hybrid strategies to threaten U.S. security and vital interests.

2. State and non-state actors apply technology to disrupt U.S. advantages in communications, long-range precision fires, and surveillance.

3. The diffusion of information via the Internet and social media amplifies and accelerates interaction between people, governments, militaries, and threats.

4. Overmatch is the application of capabilities or use of tactics in a way that renders an adversary unable to respond effectively.

5. A broad array of actors challenges the Joint Force's freedom of action in space and cyberspace.

6. Internal migration and higher birth rates contribute to increase urbanization.

Reading Text

⊙ Anticipated threats and the future operational environment[1]

Diverse enemies will employ traditional, unconventional, and hybrid strategies to threaten U.S. security and vital interests. Threats may emanate from[2] nation states or non-state actors such as transnational terrorists, insurgents, and criminal organizations. Enemies will continue to apply advanced as well as simple and dual-use technologies(such as improvised explosive devices). Enemies avoid U.S. strengths(such as long-range surveillance and precision strike) through traditional countermeasures(such as dispersion, concealment, and intermingling with civilian populations). As new military technologies are more easily transferred, potential threats emulate[3] U.S. military capabilities to counter U.S. power projection and limit U.S. freedom of action. These capabilities include precision-guided rockets, artillery, mortars, and missiles that target traditional U.S. strengths in the air and maritime domains. Hostile nation states may attempt to overwhelm defense systems and impose a high cost on the

---

1) US TRADOC Pamphlet 525-3-1, *The US Army Operating Concept*(October 2014), pp. 10-12.

2) emanate from: ~에서 나오다, 발산하다

3) emulate: 경쟁하다, 다투다, 모방하다

United States to intervene in a contingency or crisis.

State and non-state actors apply technology to disrupt U.S. advantages in communications, long-range precision fires, and surveillance. Enemy actions reduce U.S. ability to achieve dominance in the land, air, maritime, space, and cyberspace domains. Additionally, to accomplish political objectives, enemy organizations expand operations to the U.S. homeland. Enemies and adversaries will operate beyond physical battlegrounds and enemies will subvert efforts through infiltration of U.S. and partner forces(e.g., insider threat) while using propaganda and disinformation to effect public perception. Paradoxically, the connectedness of networked devices within the U.S. presents adversaries with exploitable vulnerabilities.

The following five characteristics of the future operational environment are likely to have significant impact on land force operations.

1) Increased velocity and momentum of human interaction and events

The speed at which information diffuses globally through multiple means increases the velocity, momentum, and degree of interaction among people. The diffusion of information via the Internet and social media amplifies and accelerates interaction between people, governments, militaries, and threats. Access to information allows organizations to mobilize people and resources locally, regionally, and globally. Disinformation and propaganda drive violence in support of political objectives. The compression of events in time requires forces capable of responding rapidly in sufficient scale to seize the initiative, control the narrative, and consolidate order.

2) Potential for overmatch

Overmatch is the application of capabilities or use of tactics in a way that renders[4] an adversary unable to respond effectively. Potential enemies invest in technologies to obtain a differential advantage and undermine U.S. ability to achieve overmatch.

These technologies include long-range precision fires, air defense systems, electric fires, and unmanned aerial systems(UAS). Anti-access and area denial capabilities challenge the Joint Force's ability to achieve air dominance and sea control as well as its ability to project power onto land from the air and maritime domains.

Potential enemies develop cyberspace capabilities such as disruptive and destructive malware and space capabilities such as anti-satellite weapons to disrupt U.S. communications and freedom of maneuver. To prevent enemy overmatch, the Army must develop new capabilities while anticipating enemy efforts to emulate or disrupt those capabilities. To retain overmatch, the Joint Force will have to combine technologies and integrate efforts across multiple domains to present enemies with multiple dilemmas.

3) Proliferation of weapons of mass destruction

WMD proliferation to diverse state and nonstate actors in the form of chemical, biological, radiological, nuclear, and high-yield explosive(CBRNE) weapons poses an increased threat to U.S. and international security.

Adversaries share CBRNE knowledge, technology, and materiel. The risk of a nation losing control over nuclear assets increases as extremist organizations incite civil wars and establish control of territories, populations, and weapons.

---

4) render: 제공하다, 표현하다, ~이 되게 하다

Moreover, directed energy and sophisticated CBRNE weapons could give adversaries unprecedented[5] capabilities to threaten U.S. forces and civilian populations with mass casualties. Coping with CBRNE threats requires specially trained, equipped, and organized Army forces that have the ability to operate in inhospitable conditions,[6] conduct reconnaissance to confirm or deny the presence of weapons, destroy enemy forces that possess those weapons, and secure territory to contain those weapons until CBRNE units reduce or neutralize them.

4) Spread of advanced cyberspace and counter-space capabilities

The cyberspace and space domains grow in importance as global and regional competitors as well as nonstate actors invest in capabilities to protect their access and disrupt or deny access to others.

A broad array of actors challenges the Joint Force's freedom of action in space and cyberspace. Enemies and adversaries collaborate as contests in space and cyberspace extend to and affect tactical operations. For example, enemy global positioning satellite jamming capabilities could render precision fires inaccurate.[7] Army commanders must protect their own systems and disrupt the enemy's ability to operate. Army units will have to operate with degraded communications and reduced access to cyber and space capabilities. Army forces will have to support joint operations through reconnaissance, offensive operations or raids to destroy land-based enemy space and cyberspace capabilities.

---

5) unprecedented: 전례가 없는

6) inhospitable condition: 비우호적인 조건, 황폐한 조건

7) render precision fires inaccurate: 정확한 사격(타격)을 부정확하게 만든다

5) Demographics and operations among populations, in cities, and in complex terrain

The percentage of the world's population in urban areas will rise to sixty percent by 2030. Internal migration and higher birth rates contribute to increasing urbanization.

Adversaries operate among the people in these urban areas and other complex terrain to avoid U.S. military advantages and they operate in cities because war, as a political phenomenon, is inherently[8] about people. As cities grow, many governments fail to provide adequate security, employment, infrastructure, and services. Armed groups will exploit popular disaffection and weak governance. Urban areas become safe havens[9] and support bases for terrorists, insurgents, or criminal organizations. Urban areas are potential scenes for mass atrocities.[10] Enemies may use cities as launching platforms for long-range missiles that threaten allied as well as U.S. populations. Because urban environments degrade the ability to target threats with precision, joint operations will require land forces capable of operating in congested and restricted urban terrain(to include subsurface, surface, supersurface) to defeat those threats.

Understanding the technological, geographic, political, and military challenges of the urban environment will require innovative, adaptive leaders and cohesive teams who thrive[11] in complex and uncertain environments. Operating in urban environments will require decentralized combined arms and joint capabilities.

---

8) inherently: 본래의, 고유의

9) safe haven: 안전한 피난처

10) atrocity: 포악, 잔학행위, 잔인성

11) thrive: 성장하다, 무성하다, 성공하다

QUESTIONS

1. What diverse strategies will enemies employ to threaten U.S. security and vital interests?

2. Why do adversaries diffuse and increase information globally through multiple means?

3. What kinds of technologies do adversaries use to achieve overmatch?

4. What does the acronym CBRNE stand for?

5. How do enemies and adversaries collaborate as contests in space and cyberspace extend to and affect tactical operations?

6. What will adversaries or armed groups exploit to operate urban areas and other complex terrain?

Military Terminology ────────────────────

amplify 확대하다

atrocity 포악, 잔학행위, 잔인성

cohesive 응집력의, 결합시키는

contest 경쟁, 논쟁, 다투다

demographics 실태적 인구통계

diffuse 퍼트리다

diffusion 확산, 전파

disaffection 불만, 불평, 혐오

disinformation 허위정보

diverse enemy 다양한 적

domain 영토, 영역, 범위

dominance 우월, 지배

emanate from ~에서 나오다, 발산하다

employment 고용, 일자리

emulate 경쟁하다, 다투다, 모방하다

governance 지배, 지배권, 통치, 관리

incite 자극하다, 유발하다

inherently 본래의, 고유의

inhospitable condition 비우호적인 조건,
    황폐한 조건

insurgent 반란, 폭도

intermingle 혼합되다, 섞이다

malware 악성코드, 악성소프트웨어

narrative 이야기, 서술

overmatch 능가, 강적

paradoxically 역설적으로

precision strike 정밀타격

proliferation 확산

raid 습격, 침입

render 제공하다, 표현하다, ~이 되게 하다

render precision fires inaccurate
    정확한 사격(타격)을 부정확하게 만들다

safe haven 안전한 피난처

subvert 전복시키다

thrive 성장하다, 무성하다, 성공하다

unconventional 비정규적

unprecedented 전례가 없는

velocity 속도

via ~을 경유해서, ~에 의하여

vital interest 핵심이익

Unit 13 | Military Leadership

Key Words	
mission command 임무형 지휘	**embody** 구현하다, 구체화하다
confident 확신하는, 자신 있는	**character** 성격, 인격, 특성
bystander 방관자	**empathy** 공감, 감정이입
populace 대중	**ethos** 기풍, 기질, 도덕적 특질
entail 수반하다	**discipline** 사기, 훈련, 규율
follower 추종자	**obligation** 의무, 책무
modify 수정하다, 변경하다	**integrity** 고결, 청렴, 진실성
initiative 주도권, 선제의	**sympathy** 동정, 연민
reassurance 안도, 안심시키는 것	**adversity** 역경, 불행
drive 동력, 추동력	**interact** 상호 작용하다
stewardship 책무	**suffuse** 채우다, 가득 차게 하다
after action reviews 사후강평	**permeate** 퍼지다, 스며들다, 보급되다
regardless of~ ~에 구애 없이, 상관없이	**willingly** 자진해서
consequence 결과	**propensity** 성향, 기호, 경향
consistent 일관된, 고정된	**constitute** 구성하다, ~에 해당하다

Useful Expressions

1. Leadership is the process of influencing people by providing purpose, direction, and motivation to accomplish the mission and improve the organization.

2. This includes leadership presence at night, weekends, and in any conditions or location where subordinates are working.

3. Two proven techniques that involve subordinates in assessing for improvement are in-progress reviews and after action reviews(AAR).

4. Character, comprised of a person's moral and ethical qualities, helps determine what is right and gives a leader motivation to do what is appropriate, regardless of the circumstances or consequences.

5. Character determines who people are, how they act, helps determine right from wrong, and choose what is right.

6. By taking an oath to serve the nation and the institution, one agrees to live and act by a new set of values - Army Values.

7. When read in sequence, the first letters of the Army Values form the acronym 'LDRSHIP.'

8. Army leaders show empathy when they genuinely relate to another person's situation, motives, and feelings.

9. Discipline at the individual level is primarily self-discipline, the ability to control one's own behavior.

Reading Text[1)]

⊙ LEADERSHIP DEFINED

Leadership is the process of influencing people by providing purpose, direction, and motivation to accomplish the mission and improve the organization. As an element of combat power, leadership unifies the other elements of combat power(information, mission command, movement and maneuver, intelligence, fires, sustainment and protection). Confident, competent, and informed leadership intensifies the effectiveness of the other elements of combat power.

---

1) ADRP 6-22(FM 6-22), *Army Leadership*(HQ Department of the Army, Washington, DC, 2012), pp. 1-1~ 1-2와 pp. 3-1~3-5 참조하여 재구성.

INFLUENCING. Influencing is getting people — military and civilian, governmental and non-governmental partners, or even bystanders such as a local populace — to do what is required. Influencing entails more than simply passing along orders. Through words and personal example, leaders communicate purpose, direction, and motivation.

PURPOSE. Purpose gives subordinates the reason to achieve a desired outcome. Leaders should provide clear purpose for their followers. Leaders can use direct means of conveying purpose through requests or orders.

DIRECTION. Providing clear direction involves communicating what to do to accomplish a mission: prioritizing tasks, assigning responsibility for completion, and ensuring subordinates understand the standard. Although subordinates want and need direction, they expect challenging tasks, quality training, and adequate resources. They should have appropriate freedom of action. Providing clear direction allows followers to adapt to changing circumstances through modifying plans and orders through disciplined initiative within the commander's intent.

MOTIVATION. Motivation supplies the will and initiative to do what is necessary to accomplish a mission. Motivation comes from within, but others' actions and words affect it. A leader's role in motivation is to understand the needs and desires of others, to align and elevate individual desires into team goals, and to inspire others to accomplish those larger goals. Some people have high levels of internal motivation to get a job done, while others need more reassurance, positive reinforcement, and feedback.

Indirect approaches[2] to motivation can be as successful as direct approaches. Setting a personal example can sustain the drive in others. This becomes apparent when leaders share the hardships. When a unit prepares for a deployment, all key leaders should share in the hard work. This includes leadership presence at night, weekends, and in any conditions or location where subordinates are working.

IMPROVE THE ORGANIZATION. Improving for the future means capturing and acting on important lessons of ongoing and completed projects and missions. Improving is an act of stewardship, striving to create effective, efficient organizations. Developmental counseling is crucial for helping subordinates improve performance and prepare for future responsibilities. Counseling should address strong areas as well as weak ones. Part Three provides information on counseling. Two proven techniques that involve subordinates in assessing for improvement are in-progress reviews and after action reviews(AAR).

FOUNDATIONS OF ARMY LEADER CHARACTER. Character, comprised of a person's moral and ethical qualities,[3] helps determine what is right and gives a leader motivation to do what is appropriate, regardless of the circumstances or consequences. An informed ethical conscience consistent with the Army Values strengthens leaders to make the right choices when faced with[4] tough issues. Army leaders must embody these values and inspire others to do the same.

Character is essential to successful leadership. It determines who people are, how they act, helps determine right from wrong, and choose what is right. Elements internal and central to a leader's core are -

---

2) indirect approach: 간접 접근

3) moral and ethical qualities: 도덕적 및 윤리적 품성들

4) faced with ~: ~에 직면한

- Army Values.
- Empathy.
- Warrior Ethos and Service Ethos.
- Discipline.

ARMY VALUES. Soldiers and Army Civilians enter the Army with personal values developed in childhood and nurtured over years of personal experience. By taking an oath to serve the nation and the institution, one agrees to live and act by a new set of values - Army Values. The Army Values consist of the principles, standards, and qualities considered essential for successful Army leaders. They are fundamental to helping Soldiers and Army Civilians make the right decision in any situation. Teaching values is an important leader responsibility by creating a common understanding of the Army Values and expected standards.

The Army recognizes seven values that all Army members must develop. When read in sequence, the first letters of the Army Values form the acronym "LDRSHIP":

- Loyalty: Bear true faith and allegiance to the U.S. constitution, the Army, your unit, and other soldiers.
- Duty: Fulfill your obligations.
- Respect: Treat people as they should be treated.
- Selfless service:[5] Put the welfare of the nation, the Army and your subordinates before your own.
- Honor: Live up to Army values.
- Integrity: Do what is right, legally and morally.

---

5) *selfless service*: 사심 없는 근무

• Personal courage: Face fear, danger, or adversity(Physical and Moral)

⊙ EMPATHY

Army leaders show empathy when they genuinely relate to another person's situation, motives, and feelings. Empathy does not necessarily mean sympathy for another, but identification that leads to a deeper understanding. Empathy allows the leader to anticipate what others are experiencing and to try to envision[6] how decisions or actions affect them. Leaders with a strong tendency for empathy can apply it to understand Army Civilians, Soldiers and their Families, local populations, and enemy combatants. The ability to see something from another person's point of view, to identify with, and enter into another person's feelings and emotions, enables the Army leader to better interact with others.

Leaders take care of Soldiers and Army Civilians by giving them the training, equipment, and support needed to accomplish the mission. During operations, empathetic Army leaders share hardships to gauge if their plans and decisions are realistic. They recognize the need to provide Soldiers and Army Civilians with reasonable comforts and rest periods to maintain good morale and mission effectiveness.

⊙ THE WARRIOR ETHOS AND SERVICE ETHOS

The Warrior Ethos refers to the professional attitudes and beliefs that characterize the American Soldier. It reflects a Soldier's selfless commitment to the nation, mission, unit, and fellow Soldiers. Army Civilians, while not warfighters,

---

6) envision: 상상하다, 계획하다

I am an American Soldier.

I am a Warrior and a Member of a team.

I serve the people of the United States, and live the Army Values.

I will always place the mission first.

I will never accept defeat.

Warrior Ethos

I will never quit.

I will never leave a fallen comrade.

I am disciplined, physically and mentally tough, trained and proficient in my warrior tasks and drills.

I always maintain my arms, my equipment and myself.

I am an expert and professional.

I stand ready to deploy, engage and destroy, the enemies of the United States of America in close combat.

I am a guardian of freedom and the American way of life.

I am an American Soldier.

Figure 13-1. The Soldier's Creed

embody the principles of the Warrior Ethos through a service ethos that suffuses their conduct of duty with the same attitudes, beliefs, and commitment. The Warrior Ethos is developed and sustained through discipline, commitment to the Army Values, and pride in the Army's heritage. Lived by Soldiers and supported by Army Civilians, the Warrior Ethos is the foundation for the winning spirit that permeates the institution.

⊙ DISCIPLINE

Discipline at the individual level is primarily self-discipline, the ability to control one's own behavior. Discipline expresses what the Army Values require -

Table 13-1. Summary of the attributes associated with Character

	Factors internal and central to a leader that constitute an individual's core
Army Values	• Values are principles, standards, or qualities considered essential for successful leaders. • Values are fundamental to help people discern[7] right from wrong in any situation. • The Army has seven values to develop in all Army individuals: loyalty, duty, respect, selfless service, honor, integrity, and personal courage.
Empathy	• The propensity to experience something from another person's point of view. • The ability to identify with and enter into another person's feelings and emotions. • The desire to care for and take care of Soldiers and others.
Warrior Ethos/ Service Ethos	• The internal shared attitudes and beliefs that embody the spirit of the Army profession for Soldiers and Army Civilians alike.
Discipline	• Control of one's own behavior according to Army Values; mindset to obey and enforce good orderly practices in administrative, organizational, training, and operational duties.

willingly doing what is right.

Discipline is a mindset for a unit or an organization to practice sustained, systematic actions to reach and sustain a capability to perform its military function. Often this involves attending to the details of organization and administration, which are less urgent than an organization's key tasks, but necessary for efficiency and long-term effectiveness. Examples include an effective Command Supply Discipline Program, Organizational Inspection Programs, and training management.

---

7) discern: 분별하다, 식별하다

QUESTIONS

1. How does leadership influence people?

2. What elements are internal and central to a leader's core?

3. What does purpose give subordinates a reason to achieve in military leadership?

4. What is a leader's role in motivation of military leadership?

5. What does the acronym LDRSHIP represent?

6. What principles in the Soldier's Creed are considered the foundation for the winning spirit that permeates the Army?

Military Terminology

adversity 역경, 불행

after action reviews 사후강평

bystander 방관자

character 성격, 인격, 특성

confident 확신하는, 자신 있는

consequence 결과

consistent 일관된, 고정된

constitute 구성하다, ~에 해당하다

discern 분별하다, 식별하다

discipline 사기, 훈련, 규율

drive 동력, 추동력

embody 구현하다, 구체화하다

empathy 공감, 감정이입

entail 수반하다

envision 상상하다, 계획하다

ethos 기풍, 기질, 도덕적 특질

faced with ~ ~에 직면한

follower 추종자

indirect approach 간접 접근

initiative 주도권, 선제의

integrity 고결, 청렴, 진실성

interact 상호 작용하다

mission command 임무형 지휘

modify 수정하다, 변경하다

moral and ethical qualities 도덕적 및 윤리적 품성들

obligation 의무, 책무

permeate 퍼지다, 스며들다, 보급되다

populace 대중

propensity 성향, 기호, 경향

reassurance 안도, 안심시키는 것

regardless of~ ~에 구애 없이, 상관없이

selfless service 사심 없는 근무

stewardship 책무

suffuse 채우다, 가득 차게 하다

sympathy 동정, 연민

willingly 자진해서

Unit 14 | NK's Threat and Combat Strength
(Example of Briefing)

Key Words	
honor 영광, 명예	**submarine** 잠수함
monolithic 획일적이고 자유가 없는	**amphibious warfare** 상륙전
sanction 제재	**torpedo boat** 어뢰정
WMD(Weapons of Mass destruction) 대량살상무기	**coastal patrol boat** 해안경비정
	mine sweeper 소해함
ballistic missile 탄도미사일	**inventory** 보유, 비축, 재고
conventional forces 재래식 전력	**biological agent** 생물학 작용제
UAV(Unmanned Aerial Vehicle) 무인 항공기	**anthrax** 탄저균
active duty 현역	**smallpox** 천연두
reserve 예비역	**miniaturize** 소형화하다
ADA(Air Defense Artillery) 방공포	**strategic Force** 전략군
recon 정찰, 정찰대	**asymmetric forces** 비대칭 전력
second front 제2전선	**armaments factory** 군수공장
maritime sniper brigade 해상저격여단	**stockpile** 비축

Briefing Text[1]

Good morning, I consider it an honor to have the opportunity of brief you on NK's threat and combat strength.

As you know well, North Korea has focused its energy on consolidating its

---

1) 필자가 연합사에서 사용했던 『Practical Military English II』(비매품)와 『국방백서 2016』을 참조하여 재구성한 것임.

monolithic rule and stabilizing its regime since Kim Jong-un took over.[2] It has constantly used provocation-dialogue tactics in order to take the initiative in inter-Korean relations and escape from international sanctions and isolation. North Korea continues to pose a serious threat to the ROK and the international community by developing WMD such as nuclear weapons and ballistic missiles, reinforcing its conventional forces, conducting armed provocations in enemy contact areas, and continuously carrying out[3] provocations such as cyber-attacks and infiltration of small UAVs.

First of all, I will discuss NK's combat strength. To begin with, 70% of NK's soldiers are located south of Pyongyang-Wonsan line, and its ground troops are estimated at 1,100,000 personnel on active duty and 7,620,000 reserves. Other NK's Army weapon assets are 4,300 tanks, 2,500 APCs, 5,500 MRLs, 8,600 artillery pieces, and 5,500 ADA guns.[4]

Of these troops, about 200,000 are Special Operation Forces, whose mission is to recon, to support conventional operations, to establish a second front in enemy's rear area, to counter[5] enemy SOF in NK, and to maintain internal security.

Next is the combat strength of NK's Navy and Air Forces. First the location and strength of NK's Naval Organization. The Navy, organized under the Naval Command, is composed of two fleet commands on the East and West Seas, 13 naval squadrons and two maritime sniper brigades. Of the North Korean Navy, 60% is forward deployed to the south of the Pyongyang- Wonsan line, allowing it to maintain surprise attack capability.

---

2) took over: 인수하다, 넘겨받다

3) carry out: 수행하다

4) 국방부, 『국방백서 2016』(국방부, 2016. 12. 31.), p. 238 및 pp. 24-29 참조

5) counter: 대항하다

Fleet Command Headquarters are located at Toejo-dong and Nampo, and Naval bases are located Najin, Wansan, and Pipagot. There are 60,000 personnel and 810 plus vessels, including submarines, amphibious warfare, torpedo boats, coastal patrol boats, and mine sweepers. These are all threat to sea lines of communication.[6]

Following is information regarding NK's Air Forces. The North Korean Air Force Command has changed its name to the Air and Anti-Air Command.[7] Under the command there are four flight divisions, two tactical transport brigades, two air force sniper brigades[8] and air defense units.

The North Korean Air Force has positioned its forces in four different zones. Most North Korean Air Force aircraft are outdated models. About 40% of the 820 combat aircraft are forward deployed south of the Pyongyang-Wonsan line. There are about 110,000 personnel and 1,340 aircraft, including 810 tactical fighters, bombers, transports, and helicopters in the NK Air Force inventory.

The Air Force is capable of launching surprise attacks against the ROK's control and command facilities, air defense assets and industrial facilities without further deployment or adjustment of aircraft. AN-2 aircraft and helicopters can transport large-scale special operation forces for infiltration. The Air Force has recently produced and deployed UAVs for reconnaissance and strikes.

Other than NK's Army, Navy, and Air Force, there are theater ballistic missiles, chemical weapons, and nuclear capabilities which would leave a great number of casualties, if war broke out. There are three kinds of theater ballistic missiles. SCUD missiles have a range of 500km, NO Dong missiles which can reach as far as 1,300km, and lately Musudan missiles which can strike a target at 3,000 plus

---

6) sea lines of communication: 해상병참선

7) Air and Anti-Air Command: 항공 및 반항공 사령부

8) two air force sniper brigades: 2개의 항공저격여단

kilometers. Following these deployments, North Korea has gained direct strike capabilities against South Korea, Japan, Guam, and other surrounding countries. Taepodong Missiles have a rang of 10,000 plus kilometer which is estimated that North Korea has the ability to threaten the continental United States.

North Korea began producing chemical weapons in the 1980s and it is estimated that it has about 2,500 to 5,000 tons in stock. It appears that North Korea is also capable of cultivating various types of biological agents such as anthrax, smallpox, and pest on its own and producing them into biological weapons.

North Korea conducted several nuclear tests. It is estimated that North Korea possesses about 00 kg of plutonium that can be used to produce nuclear weapons after several rounds of reprocessing spent fuel rods,[9] and it is also assessed that a highly enriched uranium(HEU)[10] program is underway. North Korea's ability to miniaturize nuclear weapons also seems to have reached a considerable level.[11]

The Strategic Rocket Command has changed its name to the Strategic Force, being promoted to the military command at the same level as the Ground Force, Navy, and Air and Anti-Air Command. The Strategic Force is likely to carry out similar functions as those of the 2nd Artillery Force of China and the Strategic Missile Troops of Russia. It is expected that their effort toward increasing asymmetric forces will continue in the future.

Next I will brief you about NK's War Sustainment Capability. Despite its economic difficulties, North Korea places a top priority on developing its defense industry in order to maintain a war sustainment capability.[12] It possesses about

---

9) reprocessing spent fuel rods: 폐연료봉 재처리 과정

10) highly enriched uranium(HEU): 고농축 우라늄

11) considerable level: 상당한 수준

12) war sustainment capability: 전쟁지속능력

300 armaments factories, while civilian factories designated for the transition to armaments production in wartime are capable of making such a transition in a short period of time.

The majority of North Korea's wartime material is stored in underground storage facilities, and the stockpile of these materials is estimated to last one to three months. However, it seems that North Korea's ability to sustain a prolonged war will be limited without additional purchases or external assistance.

Now, if we consider all the factors discussed today, Seoul, with a population of 10 million, 1/5 of the entire South Korean population, has some vulnerabilities. Being a historical and cultural center of gravity, it is only 22 miles from the DMZ, it's within range of artillery close, and is vulnerable[13] to sea infiltration. This is why we have to keep our state of readiness high at all times with the cooperation of US Forces in Korea.

---

13) vulnerable: 취약한

QUESTIONS

1. Where has North Korea focused its energy on since Kim Jong-un took over?

2. How does North Korea continue to pose a serious threat to the ROK and the international community?

3. How much strength does North Korea have and how much ground forces are deployed south of Pyongyang-Wonsan line?

4. Explain the location and strength of NK's Naval Organization.

5. Explain the location and strength of NK's Air Force Organization.

6. In terms of asymmetric weapons, what capabilities does North Korea have to strike South Korea?

7. By your estimations, how much plutonium does North Korea possess?

Military Terminology

active duty 현역

ADA(Air Defense Artillery) 방공포

air and anti-air command 항공 및 반항공
    사령부

amphibious warfare 상륙전

anthrax 탄저균

armaments factory 군수공장

asymmetric forces 비대칭 전력

ballistic missile 탄도미사일

biological agent 생물학 작용제

carry out 수행하다

coastal patrol boat 해안경비정

considerable level 상당한 수준

conventional forces 재래식 전력

counter 대항하다

highly enriched uranium(HEU)
    고농축 우라늄

honor 영광, 명예

inventory 보유, 비축, 재고

maritime sniper brigade 해상저격여단

mine sweeper 소해함

miniaturize 소형화하다

monolithic 획일적이고 자유가 없는

recon 정찰, 정찰대

reprocessing spent fuel rods 폐연료봉
    재처리 과정

reserve 예비역

sanction 제재

sea lines of communication 해상병참선

second front 제2전선

smallpox 천연두

stockpile 비축

strategic force 전략군

submarine 잠수함

took over 인수하다, 넘겨받다

torpedo boat 어뢰정

two air force sniper brigades 2개의
    항공저격여단

UAV(Unmanned Aerial Vehicle) 무인 항공기

vulnerable 취약한

war sustainment capability 전쟁지속능력

WMD(Weapons of Mass Destruction)
    대량살상무기

Unit **15** | Oral Terrain Briefing
(Dora Observation Post, 암기용)

Key Words

frontal area 전방지역	**unpaved road** 비포장도로
observation post(OP) 관측소	**chimney smoke** 굴뚝 연기
southern boundary 남방한계선	**freedom village** 자유마을
DMZ(Demilitarized Zone) 비무장 지대	**inhabited village** 사람이 거주하는 마을
military demarcation line 군사 분계선	**comprise** 구성하다, 포함되다
propaganda slogan 선전문구	**exempt** 면제된, 면제하다
fence 울타리	**Joint Security Area** 공동경비구역
disarmament 무장해제	**binocular** 쌍안경
front line 전방전선	

Briefing Text[1]

Good morning, Ladies and Gentleman. I am Second Lieutenant Kim. It's nice to see all of you. From now on, I am going to brief you on the situation of the frontal area.

You are now at the Dora Observation Post, which is on the Southern Boundary of DMZ. Our 10th Division opens to civilians the front area, Myolgong Museum, the 3rd invasion tunnel[2] including this OP to help them understand the military tension between two Koreas. Seoul is located 43km to the south, and Kaesung, one

---

1) 필자가 연합사에서 사용했던 『Practical Military English II』(비매품)와 『국방백서 2016』을 참조하여 재구성한 것임.
2) 3rd invasion tunnel: 제3침투 땅굴

of the North Korea(NK) cities, located 8km to the North.

First of all, I'd like to explain the Military Demarcation Line. Please give your attention to your front. You can see the small hill with the NK propaganda slogan. The MDL passes the base of the hill, which divides our peninsula, the South and NK. There is no fence for the MDL; yellow signposts just stand every 200 meters.

The origin of the MDL was divided by US and Russian forces at the 38th parallel after World War II. It was set to facilitate the Japanese disarmament. It has been almost ○ ○ years since the Korean War and we are the only remaining divided country in the world as the result of Cold War. Although Cold War between the East and the West does not exist any more, NK never gives up its intention to unify Korea by force.

About 35 km to the front from here is the Southern Boundary Line. That is our front line. Please look to your right side. You can see the wire fence along the unpaved road. To the direction of 2 o'clock you can see the NK red flag, or 'In Gong Ki' over a high tower. The flag is 15 meters in width and 30 meters in length. The NK propaganda village, or Gi Jung Dong is located there.

None of the buildings have windows. All the lights are of the same color and are switched on and off at the same time. Chimney smokes and laundries are not visible and they built a number of tall buildings just for us to see. Only soldiers and keepers of the village live there to protect the village.

Please look at about 3 km to the right side of it. There is our freedom village, Dae Sung Dong, which is only inhabited village within the DMZ. You can see another high tower with the South Korean national flag, 'Tae Keuk Ki' on the top of it. About ○ ○ people comprising about ○ ○ families live there and they are exempt from military services and taxes.

Look at about 2km to the right side of the flag. You can see a white building in the forest. That is 'the Peace Hall' of Panmujom, otherwise known as the Joint

Security Area.

To the left side, there is an old rusted locomotive[3] in the forest that ran between NK and South Korea before the Korean War. But now it stands there as the symbol of people's desire for peaceful unification. It has been almost ○ ○ years since the Korean War.

This concludes my briefing. Thank you. Now you are free to look around front area through these binoculars on both sides.

---

3) old rusted locomotive: 오래된 녹슨 기관차

Military Terminology ——————————

3rd invasion tunnel 제3침투 땅굴
binocular 쌍안경
chimney smoke 굴뚝 연기
comprise 구성하다, 포함되다
disarmament 무장해제
DMZ(Demilitarized Zone) 비무장지대
exempt 면제된, 면제하다
fence 울타리
freedom village 자유마을
front line 전방전선

frontal area 전방지역
inhabited village 사람이 거주하는 마을
joint security area 공동경비구역
military demarcation line 군사분계선
observation post OP 관측소
old rusted locomotive
            오래된 녹슨 기관차
propaganda slogan 선전문구
southern boundary 남방한계선
unpaved road 비포장도로

Appendix

Appendix 1 | History of the U.S. Army

⊙ FROM THE REVOLUTIONARY WAR TO TODAY[1]

From the first skirmishes at Lexington and Concord to the Civil War to the liberation of Nazi-controlled Europe, American Soldiers are celebrated for their vigor and bravery in combat.

⊙ AN ARMY FOR FREEDOM

On 14 June 1775, The Second Continental Congress formed the Continental Army as a means for the 13 unified American colonies to fight the forces of Britain. George Washington was unanimously elected Commander-In-Chief of

---

1) US Army Careers: Ways to Serve in the Army 홈페이지, http://www.goarmy.com/about/what-is-the-army/history.html, 검색일: 2017. 2. 3.

the fledgling Army, and he would lead the colonies to victory and independence.

⊙ LEWIS AND CLARK TO THE WAR OF 1812

Following the acquisition of the Louisiana territories in 1804, Army Officers Capt. Meriwether Lewis and Lt. William Clark lead an expedition into the western frontier. Lewis and Clark arrived at the Pacific Ocean about two years later.

In 1812, still suffering under British-enforced trade restrictions and other unsettled disputes from the American Revolution, the United States declared war on Britain for the second time. The war was a back and forth struggle that is perhaps most notable for the shelling of Baltimore harbor, which became Francis Scott Key's inspiration for the Star Spangled Banner.

⊙ THE MEXICAN WAR

In 1846, the United States and Mexico went to war following a period of border tensions. This conflict featured several Army Officers who would go on to become important figures in American history, including Gen. Zachary Taylor, Robert E. Lee, Ulysses S. Grant, Thomas Jonathan "Stonewall" Jackson, and Winfield Scott.

⊙ THE CIVIL WAR

In 1860, after a long-standing dispute over states' rights to allow their citizens to own slaves, southern states began seceding from the Union. The war that followed would become one of the most important conflicts in American history.

During the secession, almost one-third of regular Army Officers resigned to join the Confederacy, and more than three million American Soldiers would serve by the time the war ended in 1865.

⊙ THE WORLD WARS

As the United States rebuilt in the aftermath of the Civil War, total Army strength grew relatively slowly until the mid 1900s. The World War I era saw the creation of several important Army branches, including the Veterinarian Corps, the Chemical Corps, and the Aviation Section within the Army Signal Corps, the precursor to the Air Force.

World War II led to several more milestones in Army history, including the creation of the Office of Strategic Services, which became the CIA, and Franklin Delano Roosevelt's introduction of the G.I. Bill. Two years after the war, the Army established the Medical Service Corps, later renamed the Army Medical Department(AMEDD).

⊙ AFTER WORLD WAR II

Following World War II, the United States entered a standoff period with Soviet Russia, known as the Cold War, leading to conflicts in Korea and Vietnam. During the 1980's, the Army began to reorganize to focus on training and technology. By the end of the decade, the Pentagon introduced plans to reduce total Army strength. In 1989, the fall of the Berlin Wall signaled the end to the Cold War.

In 1991, American and allied forces responded to Saddam Hussein's invasion of Kuwait. The ground campaign lasted just 100 hours before a ceasefire was declared. After the attacks of September 11, 2001, American and coalition forces would again enter into a conflict in the Middle East against terrorist forces in Iraq and Afghanistan.

⊙ TODAY'S ARMY

Today, the Army is made up of more than 700,000 Soldiers, including active duty and Army Reserve personnel.

Army Soldiers fill many roles. They are doctors, lawyers, and engineers; they are electricians, computer programmers and helicopter pilots; they are police officers, logistics experts and civil affairs representatives. The Army's constant need for a diverse range of individual Soldiers, each with his or her own expertise is what sets it apart from other military branches.

Appendix 2 | Oaths, Codes, and Creeds[1]

⊙ Oath of Enlistedman(미 육군 병사 입대 선서)

I, _____, do solemnly swear(or affirm) that I will support and defend the Constitution of the United States against all enemies, foreign and domestic; that I will bear true faith and allegiance to the same; and that I will obey the orders of the President of the United States and the orders of the officers appointed over me, according to regulations and the Uniform Code of Military Justice. So help me God.

⊙ Oath of Commissioned Officers(미 육군 장교 임관 선서)

I, _____, having been appointed an officer in the Army of the United States, as indicated above in the grade of _____ do solemnly swear(or affirm) that I will support and defend the Constitution of the United States against all enemies, foreign and domestic, that I will bear true faith and allegiance to the same; that I take this obligation freely, without any mental reservations or purpose of evasion; and that I will well and faithfully discharge the duties of the office upon which I am about to enter; So help me God.

---

1) US Army Value 홈페이지, https://www.army.mil/values/oath.html, 검색일: 2017. 2. 3

⊙ The Code of Conduct(행동 수칙)

1. I am an American fighting man. I serve in the forces which guard my country and our way of life. I am prepared to give my life in their defense.

2. I will never surrender of my own free will. If in command I will never surrender my men while they still have the means to resist.

3. If I am captured I will continue to resist by all means available. I will make every effort to escape and aid others to escape. I will accept neither parole nor special favors from the enemy.

4. If I become a prisoner of war, I will keep faith with my fellow prisoners. I will give no information or take part in any action which might be harmful to my comrades. If I am senior, I will take command. If not I will obey the lawful orders of those appointed over me and will back them up in every way.

5. When questioned, should I become a prisoner of war, I am required to give name, rank, service number, and date of birth. I will evade answering further questions to the utmost of my ability. I will make no written statements disloyal to my country and its allies or harmful to their cause.

6. I will never forget that I am an American fighting man, responsible for my actions, and dedicated to the principles which made my country free. I will trust in my God and in the United States of America.

⊙ Code of an Officer(장교 복무 수칙)

I am an officer of the Army of the United States and I am proud of this fact. I recognize the rich heritage behind the corps of officers, of which I am part, that has been built up by those who have marched before me at Saratoga, at

Chapaltpec, at Gettysburg, at the Meuse-Argonne, at St. Lo and on the Naktong.

This rich heritage has been built on a code--the code of an officer. This code is simple and easy to remember··· Duty··· Honor··· Country. But it is not so simple to execute and requires a lifetime devoted to work, self discipline, and courage.

DUTY

The word duty means to me that···

When I am assigned a mission, I accomplish it thoroughly, efficiently, and quickly. I accept all of my responsibilities even when not assigned them. Within my field, I hold myself responsible to be aware of everything that occurs and to take positive action to correct what is wrong or improve that which is merely possible. I do my job regardless of danger to me personally.

HONOR

Honor to me means that···

As an officer of the Army of the United States my personal integrity is irreproachable. I will never degrade myself by lying, cheating or stealing. I hold myself personally and unequivocally responsible to ensure the preservation of the honor of the officer corps of the United States Army.

COUNTRY

Country means to me that···

In addition to being an officer of the Army, I am an American citizen. I am an official representative of my country and will so comport myself. I will endure any hardship, any sacrifice, for the welfare of these my United States.

This is the code I will live by··· Duty··· Honor··· Country··· all of these I put above myself whatever the cost.

⊙ Soldier's Creed(미육군 병사 복무 신조)

I am an American Soldier. I am a member of the United States Army--a protector of the greatest nation on earth. Because I am proud of the uniform I wear, I will always act in ways creditable to the military service and the nation it is sworn to guard.

I am proud of my own organization. I will do all I can to make it the finest unit in the Army. I will be loyal to those under whom I serve. I will do my full part to carry out orders and instructions given to me or my unit.

As a soldier, I realize that I am a member of a time-honored profession--that I am doing my share to keep alive the principles of freedom for which my country stands. No matter what the situation I am in, I will never do anything, for pleasure, profit, or personal safety, which will disgrace my uniform, my unit, or my country. I will use every means I have, even beyond the line of duty, to restrain my Army comrades from actions disgraceful to themselves and to the uniform.

I am proud of my country and its flag. I will try to make the people of this nation proud of the service I represent, for I am an American Soldier.

⊙ Creed of the Noncommissioned Officer(부사관 복무 신조)

No man is more professional than I. I am a Noncommissioned Officer, a leader of soldiers, as a Noncommissioned Officer, I realize that I am a member of a time honored Corps, which is known as "The Backbone of the Army." I am proud of the Corps of Noncommissioned Officers and will at all times conduct myself so as to bring credit upon the Corps, the military service, and my country regardless of the situation I find myself. I will not use my grade or position to attain pleasure, profit, or personal safety.

Competence is my watch-word. My two basic responsibilities will always be uppermost in my mind -accomplishment of my mission and the welfare of my Soldiers. I will strive to remain tactically and technically proficient. I am aware of my role as a Noncommissioned Officer. I will fulfill my responsibilities inherent in that role. All Soldiers are entitled to outstanding leadership; I will provide that leadership. I know my Soldiers, and I will always place their needs above my own. I will communicate consistently with my Soldiers and never leave them uninformed. I will be fair and impartial when recommending both rewards and punishment.

Officers of my unit will have maximum time to accomplish their duties; they will not have to accomplish mine. I will earn their respect and confidence as well as that of my Soldiers. I will be loyal to those with whom I serve; seniors, peers and subordinates alike. I will exercise initiative by taking appropriate action in the absence of orders. I will not compromise my integrity, nor my moral courage. I will not forget, nor will I allow my comrades to forget that we are professionals, Noncommissioned Officers, Leaders of Soldiers!

⦿ Cadet Creed (사관생도 신조)

I am an Army Cadet. Soon I will take an oath and become an Army Officer committed to defending the values which make this Nation great. Honor is my touchstone. I understand mission first and people always.

I am the past: the spirit of those warriors who have made the final sacrifice.

I am the present: the scholar and apprentice soldier enhancing my skills in the science of warfare and the art of leadership.

But above all, I am the future: the future warrior leader of the United States Army. May God give me the compassion and judgement to lead and the gallantry in battle to win.

I will do my duty.

⊙ Officer Creed(장교 복무 신조)

I will give the selfless performance of my duty and my mission the best that effort, thought, and dedication can provide.

To this end, I will not only seek continually to improve my knowledge and practice of my profession, but also I will exercise the authority entrusted to me by the President and the Congress with fairness, justice, patience, and restraint, respecting the dignity and human rights of others and devoting myself to the welfare of those placed under my command.

In justifying and fulfilling the trust placed in me, I will conduct my private life as well as my public service so as to be free both from impropriety and the appearance of impropriety, acting with candor and integrity to earn the unquestioning trust of my fellow soldiers — juniors, senior, and associates — and employing my rank and position not to serve myself but to serve my country and my unit.

By practicing physical and moral courage, I will endeavor to inspire these qualities in others by my example.

In all my actions, I will put loyalty to the highest moral principles and the United States of America above loyalty to organizations, persons, and my personal interest.

Appendix 3 | 일상 언어 영어로 표현하기

Here you go again.   또 시작이군.

Snap out of it.   꿈 깨.

Don't make a fuss.   수다 떨지 마라.

I'm stuck speechless.   기가 막혀 말이 안 나온다.

You are as quiet as a mouse.   쥐 죽은 듯이 조용하다.

That's a rip off!   바가지 쓰셨군요!

That's a steal!   공짜나 다름없군요!

I'm worried sick.   걱정되어 죽겠다.

I did well on my test.   시험 잘 보았어요.

In this day and age, ~   요즘 같은 세상에, ~

I'd like to make withdraw.   (은행에서) 돈을 찾으려고 한다.

How would you like that?   저거 어때?

That's money down the drain.   그건 돈 낭비다.

Old habits die hard.   세 살 버릇 여든까지 간다.

I'm sorry to hear that.   그거 안됐군.

It's out of the question.   말도 안 돼.

He will get back on his feet in no time.   그는 곧 회복할 거야. (in no time: 곧)

My car stalled.   차가 고장이 나서 섰다.

You're gonna have to junk it.   그 차를 폐기 처분해라.

They cooked up a scheme.   그들이 계략을 꾸몄다.

I know a thing or two.   나는 조금 안다.

What's wrong?   무슨 일이니?

Let me take a look at it.   어디 보자.

We can't afford it.   그거 살 수 없다.

Have you lost weight?   너 살 빠졌니?

It wouldn't hurt to go look?   가서 보는 것 정도야 괜찮겠지?

I'd look great behind the wheel.   운전하는 내 모습은 멋져 보일 거야.

It's a token of my appreciation.   작은 성의이다.

You got what you pay for.   비싸면 비싼 대로 좋다. / 싼 것이 비지떡이다.

You name it, you get it.   말만 하세요, 다 있습니다.

I'd like give it a try.   내가 한번 해볼게.

Fools rush in.   서둘러서 좋을 건 없다.

I want a rush service.   빠른 서비스를 원한다.

A.S.A.P.   가능한 빨리(As soon as possible)

D.U.I.   음주운전(driving under influence)

Where are you calling from?   어디 전화하는 거니?

He is dying to see you.   그는 네가 보고 싶어 죽을 지경이다.

Something came up.   무슨 일이 생겼어.

Don't count your chickens before they are hatched.   김칫국부터 마시지 마라.

What kind of business are you in?   무슨 일 하세요?

What's gotten into her?   저 여자 왜 저래?

You still have feeling for him.   너는 여전히 그를 좋아한다.

I pulled my muscles on my back. 허리를 삐끗했다.

He is making a big deal out of it. 별거 아닌 거 가지고 수선 떤다.

While you are at it, could you refill my coffee? 이왕 하는 김에 커피를 더 주실래요?

You always stick up for him. 항상 그의 편만 든다.

The pie is on the house. 파이는 서비스입니다.

Get out of face. 꺼져. / 나가!

Let's drink night away. 밤새도록 한잔하자.

I'm managing in there. 그럭저럭 지낸다.

Drop me a line. 편지 좀 하세요.

Spill it. 비밀을 다 털어놓다.

So, sue me! 그래, 어쩔래!

I get up with the chickens. 새벽에 일찍 일어나다.

Jump the gun. 서둘러 결론을 내리다.

Poor thing! 불쌍해라!

You look familiar. 얼굴이 낯익다.

I think you've got the wrong person. 사람을 잘못 보신 것 같군요.

Can I try this on? 이것 입어 봐도 됩니까?

How does it fit? 사이즈가 잘 맞나요?

The boss makes a face at me. 사장이 나에게 인상을 썼다.

I break up with her. / I'm through with her. 그녀와 깨졌다.

I'm looking for a tie to go well with this shirt.

이 셔츠에 어울릴 넥타이를 찾고 있습니다.

I'll ring it up for you.   계산하겠다.

Is this on sale?   세일하는 것입니까?

It's 30 percent off.   30% 세일이다.

The price was recently marked down.   가격이 인하되었습니다.

How much do I owe you?   얼마입니까?

That's a good buy(good deal, real bargain)!   싸게 사셨군요.

I'm 3 dollar's short.   3달러 부족합니다.

alumni meeting.   동창회

We have a lot in common.   우린 공통점이 많아.

arranged marriage   중매결혼

I'd like to open an account.   계좌를 개설하고 싶어요.

bankbook   통장

I heard it through the grape vine.   소문을 통해 들었다.

Just leave it there.   그냥 놔두세요.

I'm all thumb.   잘 못해요.

I'm out of shape.   몸매가 엉망이에요.

I went on a fool's errand.   헛걸음했다.

You're just like I thought you'd be.   내가 생각한 대로군요.

Get off me.   저리 비켜.

Some parents you are!   대단한 부모군요.

You're getting off the subject.   주제에서 벗어난 얘기를 하고 있어요.

I'm all for it.   동감이야.

Would you move over a little?   조금만 비켜 주시겠어요?

This is a small gift from me.   약소하지만 받아 주시겠어요?

How brave of you!   배짱도 좋다.

Let's put it a vote.   표결에 부칩시다.

You're not making sense.   말이 앞뒤가 안 맞는다.

maternal side / paternal side 외가 / 친가

I don't get it.   이해가 안 돼.

I have mixed feeling./It's bitter sweet.   시원섭섭하다.

You pinhead!   이 돌머리야.

Look who's talking.   사돈 남 말 하네.

It can't be helped.   어쩔 수 없었어.

I'm gonna go for it?   내가 해볼까?

You look great dressed up.   차려입으니 멋지군요.

paper, scissors, rock 가위, 바위, 보

You're making a scene here.   다들 너를 쳐다보고 있어.

What a windfall!   웬 떡이야.

Enjoy your meal.   맛있게 드세요.

It makes my mouth water. / This food makes me drool.
이 음식이 군침 돌게 하는군요.

No pain, no gain.   고생 끝에 낙이 온다.

come to think of it.   가만히 생각해 보니,

I'm just browsing. / I'm just looking around.   그냥 구경하는 중이에요.

Cash or charge?   현금인가요, 카드인가요?

Take your time.   천천히 하십시오.

It's up to you.　당신에게 달려 있습니다.

So far so good.　지금까지는 좋습니다.

Drop me off at this store.　이 가게에서 내려 주세요.

I can't think of it off hand.　금방 생각이 떠오르지 않네요.

It's a pain in the neck.　정말 지겨운 일이네요.

It's up to my ears in work.　일이 산더미처럼 쌓여 있어요.

The cokes are on me.　콜라는 내가 사겠어요.

That's a close call.　큰일 날 뻔했어요.

My chances are slim.　가망이 없어요.

You name it.　말만 하세요.

Not on your life.　어림없는 소리.

I'll keep my fingers crossed.　행운을 빌겠어요.

He's gone for the day.　그는 퇴근했어요.

After you, please.　먼저 하세요.

We are in the same boat.　같은 처지군요.

What a small world!　참 좁은 세상이군요.

It doesn't make any difference to me.　제겐 아무거나 상관없어요.

It's not myself today.　오늘 제정신이 아니군요.

Let's get to the point.　본론으로 들어갑시다.

Who's in charge?　책임자가 누구입니까?

Don't get me wrong.　나를 오해하지 마세요.

If I were in your shoes　당신 입장이라면

Are you pulling my leg?　날 놀리는 겁니까?

Three more hours to go.　세 시간이 더 남았다.

Neck and Neck   막상막하

It's Greek to me.   무슨 뜻인지 모르겠습니다.

Stick around.   기다려 봐요.

Take you pick.   하나 골라 보세요.

Things are looking up.   점점 나아지고 있어요.

Not bad for an amateur.   아마추어치고는 괜찮은데.

I ache all over.   온몸이 쑤신다.

I'm returning your call.   저에게 전화하셨다면서요.

What's the best time for you? / When is convenient time for you?
언제가 가장 좋으세요?

Let's meet halfway.   조금씩 서로 양보합시다.

We'll have to wait and see.   두고 봐야 합니다.

He had it coming.   혼날 만한 짓을 했군요.

All is well that ends well.   끝이 좋아야 다 좋다.

We made it.   해냈다.

Couldn't it cause side effects?   부작용은 없을까요?

He's driving me up the wall.   그 남자 때문에 미치겠어요.

I don't touch the liquor.   나는 술 안 마신다.

I'm social drinker.   분위기에 맞추어서 한잔한다.

How about a drink after work?   근무 끝나고 한잔 어때?

You up for it?   그러고 싶은 마음이 드니?

You twisted my arms.   네가 억지로 시켰다.

We don't have money to burn.   우리는 낭비할 돈이 없다.

I did well to marry her.   그녀와 결혼하길 잘했다.

Quit singing you own praises.   자랑 좀 그만해라.

I gave him a talking to.   그에게 한 소리 했다.

in a dog's age   오랫동안

Mr. (Miss.) right   이상형

I hear you.   동감이야.

That's a good point.   바로 그거야.

You've learned to pay lip service.   아부할 줄도 아는군요.

I hear you loud and clear.   정말 그래요.

He's a little edgy.   그는 신경이 날카로워요.

I have to cram for the finals.   나는 기말시험 벼락치기 공부 해야 돼.

The price is out of line.   너무 비싸요.

The night's still young.   아직 초저녁이다.

I locked out of my room.   열쇠를 방 안에 두고 나왔다.

It made a good impression on me.   그것은 나에게 좋은 인상을 주었다.

It's a hot item.   그건 아주 잘 팔리는 제품입니다.

It's settled.   자 그럼 결정됐다.

If my memory serves me right   제 기억이 맞는다면

My mouth is watering.   군침 도는군요.

I'll buy the second round.   두 번째 잔은 내가 살게요.

It really works.   정말 효과가 있었어요.

How was it?   어땠어요?

First come, first served.   선착순

I can't pinpoint it.   딱 꼬집어 말할 수 없어요.

I tossed and turned all night. 밤새 뒤척였어요.

I have a runny nose. 콧물이 난다.

The end doesn't justify the means. 목적이 수단을 정당화할 수 없다.

Grow up. 철 좀 들어라.

It runs in the family. 집안 내력이다.

I wan't born yesterday. 나는 철부지가 아니다.

We will have him paged. 그를 찾는 방송을 할 것입니다.

I live right above you. 바로 위층에 삽니다.

Welcome to the neighbor. 이웃이 되어 반갑습니다.

What time do you get to work(get off work)? 몇 시에 출근(퇴근)합니까?

My offer still stands. 제안이 여전히 유효하다.

All good things must come to an end. 좋은 것도 끝이 있다.

Don't cut me off. 끼어들지 마.

You're back safe and sound. 무사히 돌아왔구나.

I'll pass the exam with flying colors. 수석으로 합격할 것이다.

Try your hand at business. 사업을 한번 해봐라.

In for a penny, in for a pound. 끝까지 견뎌라.

Every little bit helps. 백지장도 맞들면 낫다.

He's only in his early fifties. 그는 겨우 50대 초반이다.

Wake up and smell the coffee. 빨리 일어나요.

I don't have the slightest idea. 전혀 모르겠습니다.

They've gone too far. 그 사람들 도가 지나쳤군요.

I get the picture. 알았어요.

Would you like seconds?　한 잔 더 드릴까요?

That's the way life goes.　인생이란 다 그런 거야.

Will this do?　이거면 충분하니?

He has a deep pocket.　그는 돈이 많다.

My car is acting up again.　내 차가 또 이상해요.

I'm on cloud nine today. / I'm walking on air.　나는 오늘 기분이 최고다.

You have to hear me out.　끝까지 들으세요.

What do you have in mind?　무슨 생각 하고 있니?

That's cool.　그거 멋지다.

It's sheer luck.　순전히 운이다.

Don't rush me.　재촉하지 마.

Two can play at that game.　나도 할 수 있다. / 나에게도 방법이 있다.

You shamed of me.　내가 창피하지.

You are all grand.　너희 모두 대단하구나.

My heart aches.　내 마음이 아프다.

You are couch potato.　너는 TV만 보는 사람이다.

I'm off now.　지금 간다.

The price is right.　가격이 적당하다.

I drive like a little old lady.　나는 조심스럽게 운전한다.

I stole the show.　내가 가장 인기가 있었다.

He became an instant celebrity.　그는 금방 스타가 되었다.

I ran into a friend of mine.　우연히 친구를 만났다.

She became much classier.　더 멋있어졌다.

Anyone would fall for her.　누구라도 그녀에게 반할 거야.

Business is slow. 경기가 좋지 않다.

I left my umbrella behind. 우산을 두고 왔다.

You have to pitch in. 너희들 도와줘야 해.

I had a field day today. 즐거운 하루였다.

Don't hit below the belt. 약점 건드리지 마.

Seven year itch 권태기

I am wrapped up in my work. 일에 매여 있다.

heart-to-heart talk 마음을 털어놓는 이야기

We are just plugging along as usual. 그럭저럭 지낸다.

Is that it? 그게 다야?

heavy eater / light eater 대식가 / 소식가

We live on a shoestring. 쥐꼬리만 한 월급으로 산다.

You are an apple of my eyes. 너는 눈에 넣어도 안 아플 정도로 사랑스럽다.

He is a baby face. 그는 동안이다.

He looks young for his age. 나이에 비해 어려 보인다.

Don't order me around. 나에게 이래라 저래라 하지 마라.

When it comes down to it 결론적으로 말하자면

You are shaking like a leaf. 너는 나뭇잎처럼 떨고 있다.

I'm worrying for nothing. 괜한 걱정을 했다.

That's an understatement. 그것은 과소평가다.

I'm almost felt like throwing up. 토할 뻔했다.

He'll make it big. 그는 크게 될 것이야.

He was a child prodigy. 그는 신동이었다.

I'll see you to the door. 문까지 바래다줄게.

Don't belittle your husband.　남편 우습게 보지 마라.

I've got cold feet.　바짝 얼었다.

I'll be back in a flash.　금방 돌아올게.

This is all going to blow over.　모든 것은 잊힐 것이다.

It's water under the bridge.　엎질러진 물이야.

Just drop it.　그만해.

No one dies of cold.　감기 때문에 죽지는 않는다.

I'm counting the minutes.　눈 빠지게 기다리고 있다.

Appendix 4 | 영어 명언 모음

Think like a man of action and act like man of thought.

행동하는 사람처럼 생각하고, 생각하는 사람처럼 행동하라.

Courage is very important. Like a muscle, it is strengthened by use.

용기는 대단히 중요하다. 근육과 같이 사용함으로써 강해진다.

Life is the art of drawing sufficient conclusions from insufficient premises.

인생이란 불충분한 전제로부터 충분한 결론을 끌어내는 기술이다.

By doubting we come at the truth.

의심함으로써 우리는 진리에 도달한다.

A man that has no virtue in himself, ever envies virtue in others.

자기에게 덕이 없는 자는 타인의 덕을 시기한다.

When money speaks, the truth keeps silent.

돈이 말할 때는 진실은 입을 다문다.

Better the last smile than the first laughter.

처음의 큰 웃음보다 마지막의 미소가 더 좋다.

In the morning of life, work; in the midday, give counsel; in the evening, pray.

인생의 아침에는 일을 하고, 낮에는 충고하며, 저녁에는 기도하라.

Painless poverty is better than embittered wealth.

고통 없는 빈곤이 괴로운 부보다 낫다.

A poet is the painter of the soul.

시인은 영혼의 화가이다.

Error is the discipline through which we advance.

잘못은 그것을 통하여 우리가 발전할 수 있는 훈련이다.

Faith without deeds is useless.

행함이 없는 믿음은 쓸모가 없다.

Weak things united become strong.

약한 것도 합치면 강해진다.

We give advice, but we cannot give conduct.

충고는 해줄 수 있으나, 행동하게 할 수는 없다.

Nature never deceives us; it is always we who deceive ourselves.

자연은 인간을 결코 속이지 않는다. 우리를 속이는 것은 항상 우리 자신이다.

Forgiveness is better than revenge.

용서는 복수보다 낫다.

We never know the worth of water till the well is dry.

우물이 마르기까지는 물의 가치를 모른다.

Pain past is pleasure.

지나간 고통은 쾌락이다.

Books are ships which pass through the vast seas of time.

책이란 넓고 넓은 시간의 바다를 지나가는 배다.

Who begins too much accomplishes little.

너무 많이 시작하는 사람은 성취하는 것이 별로 없다.

Faith is a higher faculty than reason.

믿음은 이성보다 더 고상한 능력이다.

Until the day of his death, no man can be sure of his courage.

죽는 날까지는, 자기의 용기를 확신할 수 있는 사람은 아무도 없다.

Great art is an instant arrested in eternity.

위대한 예술은 영원 속에서 잡은 한순간이다.

Faith without deeds is useless.

행함이 없는 믿음은 쓸모가 없다.

The world is a beautiful book, but of little use to him who cannot read it.

세상은 한 권의 아름다운 책이다. 그러나 그 책을 읽을 수 없는 사람에게는 별 소용이 없다.

Heaven gives its favorites-early death.

하늘은, 그가 사랑하는 자에게 이른 죽음을 준다.

I never think of the future. It comes soon enough.

나는 미래에 대해서는 결코 생각하지 않는다. 미래는 곧 오고 말 것이므로.

Suspicion follows close on mistrust.

의혹은 불신을 뒤따른다.

He who spares the rod hates his son, but he who loves him is careful to discipline him.

매를 아끼는 것은 자식을 사랑하지 않는 것이다. 자식을 사랑하는 사람은 훈계를 게을리하지 않는다.

All good things which exist are the fruits of originality.

현존하는 모든 훌륭한 것들은 독창력의 결실이다.

The will of a man is his happiness.

인간의 마음가짐이 곧 행복이다.

He that has no shame has no conscience.

수치심이 없는 사람은 양심이 없다.

Weak things united become strong.

약한 것도 합치면 강해진다.

A minute's success pays the failure of years.

단 1분의 성공은 몇 년 동안의 실패를 보상한다.

United we stand, divided we fall.

뭉치면 서고, 흩어지면 쓰러진다.

To doubt is safer than to be secure.

의심하는 것이 확인하는 것보다 더 안전하다.

Time is but the stream I go a-fishing in.

시간은 내가 그 속에서 낚시질을 하는 흐름이다.

A full belly is the mother of all evil.

배부른 것이 모든 악의 어머니이다.

Love your neighbor as yourself.

네 이웃을 네 몸처럼 사랑하여라.

It is a wise father that knows his own child.

자기 자식을 아는 아버지는 현명한 아버지이다.

Absence makes the heart grow fonder.

떨어져 있으면 정이 더 깊어진다.

Habit is second nature.

습관은 제2의 천성이다.

Who knows much believes the less.

많이 아는 사람일수록 조금 믿는다.

Only the just man enjoys peace of mind.

정의로운 사람만이 마음의 평화를 누린다.

Waste not fresh tears over old griefs.

지나간 슬픔에 새 눈물을 낭비하지 말라.

Life itself is a quotation.

인생 그 자체가 하나의 인용이다.

He is greatest who is most often in men's good thoughts.

사람들의 좋은 회상 속에 자주 있는 자가 가장 위대하다.

Envy and wrath shorten the life.

시기와 분노는 수명을 단축한다.

Where there is no desire, there will be no industry.

욕망이 없는 곳에는 근면도 없다.

To be trusted is a greater compliment than to be loved.

신뢰받는 것은 사랑받는 것보다 더 큰 영광이다.

Education is the best provision for old age.

교육은 노년기를 위한 가장 훌륭한 대책이다.

To jaw-jaw is better than to war-war.

전쟁보다 협상이 낫다.

Music is a beautiful opiate, if you don't take it too seriously.

음악은 너무 심하게 취하지만 않는다면 일종의 아름다운 마취제이다.

Appearances are deceptive.

외모는 속임수이다.

Let thy speech be short, comprehending much in few words.

몇 마디 말에 많은 뜻을 담고, 말은 간단히 하라.

Things are always at their best in the beginning.

사물은 항상 시작이 가장 좋다.

A gift in season is a double favor to the needy.

필요할 때 주는 것은 필요한 자에게 두 배의 은혜가 된다.

In giving advice, seek to help, not to please, your friend.

친구에게 충고할 때는 즐겁게 하지 말고, 도움이 되도록 하라.

The difficulty in life is the choice.

인생에 있어서 어려운 것은 선택이다.

The most beautiful thing in the world is, of course, the world itself.

세상에서 가장 아름다운 것은 물론 세상 그 자체이다.

All fortune is to be conquered by bearing it.

모든 운명은 그것을 인내함으로써 극복해야 한다.

Better is to bow than break.

부러지는 것보다 굽는 것이 낫다.

Good fences makes good neighbors.

좋은 울타리는 선한 이웃을 만든다.

Give me liberty, or give me death.

자유가 아니면 죽음을 달라.

Appendix 5 | Glossary 1: English–Korean

A

a burst of question 연속적인 질문

AA/CSR(Ammunition Allocation/
  Controled Supply Rate)
  탄약할당/통제보급률

abbreviating 축약하는

absence without leave(AWOL)
  탈영, 무단이탈

accountability 책임, 의무

accurately assess the situation
  정확히 상황을 평가하다

acknowledge 수신여부

ACKNOWLEDGE(Mandatory)
  수신여부(필수)

activation and deactivation of units
  부대창설 및 해체

active army 상비군, 상비육군

active duty 현역

ADA(Air Defense Artillery) 방공포

adage 속담, 격언

adequate 적절한

adherence 집착, 견지, 충실

adjacent commander 인접 부대장

adjacent unit 인접부대

adjutant general(AG) 부관

adjutant general's Corps 부관단, 부관병과

advantage 우위, 유리, 이점

adversary 적, 적의

adversity 역경, 불행

affiliated 가입한, 제휴된, 계열의

after action reviews 사후강평

aggressive 공격적인

agile 기민한

air and anti-air command
  항공 및 반항공 사령부

air assault 강습

air defense coordinator(ADCOORD)
  방공협조관

air interdiction 항공차단

air liaison officer(ALO) 공군연락장교

air/naval gunfire liaison
  company(ANGLICO) commander
  항공/함포연락중대 지휘관

airborne 공정(부대)

airspace 공역

airspace command and control(AC2)
  공역지휘 및 통제

allocate 할당하다

allocation 할당, 배당

all-round defense 사주방어

alternative 대안

ambush 매복

ammunition basic load 탄약기본휴대량

amphibious operation 상륙작전

amphibious warfare 상륙전

amplify 확대하다

annex   첨부, 붙임

anthrax   탄저균

AO(Area of Operation)   작전지역

APC(Armored Personnel Carrier)
    병력 수송 장갑차

appendix   부록

application   신청, 적용

approach march   접적 전진

appropriate   적당한

architecture   구조, 구성

area   지역

area defense   지역방어

area of interest(AI)   관심지역

area of operations(AO)   작전지역

area of responsibility   책임지역

area security(including route and convey)
    지역경계(통로, 수송로 포함)

armaments factory   군수공장

armor plate   장갑판

army reserve   예비군, 예비육군

articulate   똑똑히 발음하다

artillery   포병

as to ~   ~에 대하여

aside   방백으로(혼자 중얼거리는 소리로)

ASOCS(Air Support Operation Center)
    항공지원작전본부

ASP(Ammunition Supply Point)
    탄약보급소

aspect   지점, 관점, 양상

assault   습격, 급습

assault phase   돌격단계

assault position   돌격진지

assembly area   집결지

assess   평가하다

assign   할당하다, 임명하다

associated   조합된, 연합된, 편조된

associated with   ~와 관련된, 연관된

assumption   가정

asymmetric forces   비대칭 전력

at ease!   쉬어!

atrocity   포악, 잔학행위, 잔인성

attaching   배속

attack   공격

attack formation   공격 대형

attack heading   항공기의 공격방향

attack position   공격대기지점, 공격진지

audible   가청의

augmentee   증강요원

authenticate   인증하다, 입증하다

aviation   항공, 비행

aviation coordinator(AVCOORD)
    육군항공협조관

awards program   수상계획

axis of advance   전진축

B

ballistic missile   탄도미사일

band operation   군악대 운용

band support   (군)악대 지원

barrel   총열

base on ~   ~에 기초하다, 바탕을 두다

basic branch   기본병과

battery   (포병)포대

battle drills   전투훈련

battle position   전투진지

bayonet   총검, 대검

BBQ(barbecue)   바비큐

be assigned to   배정되다

be attached to ~   ~에 배속되다

be clear of ~에서 벗어나다

be commensurate in size with 규모상 ~에 상응하다

be familiar with ~에 익숙하다

be referred to as ~라고 불리다

be short of breath 숨이 차다

be supposed to ~ ~하기로 되어 있다

be that as it may 어쨌든(anyway)

Beginning of Morning Nautical Twilight (BMNT) 해상박명초

beyond words 말로 이루 다 표현할 수 없는

binocular 쌍안경

biological agent 생물학 작용제

bivouacking 야외 숙영지(bivouac로도 표기)

BLOS 초과 가시선(beyond line-of-sight)

blow 타격, 공격

bolt 노리쇠

boundary 전투지경선

breach 돌파하다

bridging equipment 가교 장비

bullet 탄환

burning 소각

butt 개머리판

buy time 시간을 절약하다

by means of ~의 수단으로, ~으로

by surprise 기습으로

bystander 방관자

C

C2(command and control) system 지휘통제 시스템

call sign 호출부호

camouflage 위장하다

canalize 유도하다

capability and limitation 능력과 제한사항

capitalize 이용하다

capitalize on ~을 이용하다, ~에 편승하다

capstone manual 기본교범

cardinal direction 기본방위방향

carry out 수행하다

cartridge 탄약

cartridge case 탄피

cartridge supply 장전된 탄약

CASEVAC(Casualty Evacuation) 사상자 후송

CASOP(Crisis Action Standard Operating Procedure) 위기조치예규

casualty 사상자

casualty collection point 전사상자 수집소

catastrophic impact 비극적 영향(충격)

cavalry 기병대

CBRNE(chemical, biological, radiological, nuclear explosive) 화생방 및 핵폭발

CCIR(Commander's Critical Information Requirement) 지휘관 주요첩보 요구

CDC(Capital Defense Command) 수도방위사령부

ceilings and guidance 한도와 지침

chain of hills 연달은 고지들

challenge and password 수하 및 암호

chaplain 목사

character 성격, 인격, 특성

charging handle 장전손잡이

check point 확인점

chemical officer(CHEMO) 화학장교

chimney smoke 굴뚝 연기

CHOP(change of operational control) 작전통제

circumstance 상황, 환경

civil populace   시민 대중

civilian internee
　　민간인 피수용자, 민간인 피억류자

civilian personnel officer(CPO)
　　민간인 인사장교

clear articulation   명확한 표현

clock reference   시계 방향

close air support   근접항공지원

close combat   근접전투

closed contour line   폐쇄등고선

COA(Course of Action)   방책

COA development   방책개발

coastal patrol boat   해안경비정

code word   암구어

CofS(Chief of Staff)   참모장

cohesion   단결

cohesive   응집력의, 결합시키는

cold   완전히

collateral damage   부수적인 손해, 피해

collocate   인접배치하다

combat arm   전투부대

combat load   전투 휴대량

combat patrols   전투정찰

combat service support   전투근무지원

combat support   전투지원

combatant   전투원

combine   결합하다, 연합하다

combined arms breach operation
　　연합군 돌파 작전

combined arms element   연합부대요소

combined arms rehearsal
　　연합부대 예행연습

comfortable time   여유 있는 시간

command   지휘, 통수, 명령, 구령, 사령부

command and control warfare(C2W)
　　지휘통제전

commander's priority intelligence
　　requirement   지휘관 우선 정보요구

commitment   의무, 책임, 투입, 헌신, 구금

competent   유능한, 능력이 있는

compile   편집하다, ~을 축적하다

completeness   완성, 완벽화

complexity   복잡성

component   구성원, 구성요소

composition   (부대의) 구성

comprise   구성하다, 포함되다

concept of operation   작전개념

concerned with   ~와 관계된

concise   간결한, 명료한

confident   확신하는, 자신 있는

confirmation brief   임무확인 보고

conjunction   연결

consequence   결과

consequence management action
　　주요 관리 행위

considerable level   상당한 수준

consist of   ~으로 구성되다

consistent   일관된, 고정된

consolidate   강화하다

consolidation   진지강화

consolidation and reorganization
　　진지강화 및 재편성

constitute   구성하다, ~에 해당하다

constraint   범위, 제약, 제한사항

consults with ~   ~와 상의하다

contact point   접촉점

contest   경쟁, 논쟁, 다투다

contingency   우발상황

contour line   등고선

controlled supply rate(CSR) 통제보급률

CONUS(Continental United States)
　　미 본토

conventional forces 재래식 전력

conventional Infantry unit 재래식 보병부대

coordinate 좌표

coordinating instruction 협조지시

correction 정정

corrective action 교정조치

counter 대항하다

counterattack 역습

counterintelligence 대정보

countermobility 대기동

counteroffensive 반격

counterproliferation 확산방지

courses of action 방책

court martial offense 군사법정위반

cover and concealment 엄폐와 은폐

CPO(Civilian Personnel Office)
　　민간인 인사처

crackle 군소리, 탁탁거리는 소리

CRDL(Critical Requirements Deficiency
　　List) 긴급소요부족품 목록

crew drills 승무원 훈련

criteria 조건, 평가기준, 기준

crosswise (십자형의) 가로로

culminate 최고점에 달하다, 완결하다

cultural feature 인공물

CUWTF(Combined Unconventional
　　Warfare Task Forces) 연합특전사

D

debrief 임무수행계획보고

deceive 기만하다

deception officer 기만작전 장교

deception plan 기만계획

decision support template(DST)
　　결심지원형판

decontamination 해독, 제독제

deem 생각하다, 의견을 갖다

deep area 종심지역

deep area operation plan
　　종심지역 작전 계획

defeat in detail 각개격파

defective parts 결함부품

deflect 빗나가게 하다, 비끼다

degree of surprise 기습의 정도

delay 지연, 지연전

deliberate 신중한

deliberate crossing 정밀 도하

demographics 실태적 인구통계

demolition 파괴, 폭파

demonstration 양동, 시위

dental surgeon 치과 진료

deny 거부하다

deployability 전개 능력

desertion 탈영, 도망

detaching unit 파견부대

detachment 파견

detainee 구류자

deteriorate 악화되다

dictate 구술하다, 지령(명령)하다, 결정하다

diffuse 퍼트리다

diffusion 확산, 전파

direct air support center(DASC)
　　직접항공지원본부

direct fire 직접화력

direction of attack 공격방향

disaffection 불만, 불평, 혐오

disarmament　무장해제

disassembly and assembly　분해결합

discern　분별하다, 식별하다

discipline　사기, 훈련, 규율

disinformation　허위정보

dispersion　소산

disposal　처리, 처분

disposition　(부대의) 배치

disposition of straggler　낙오자 처리

disseminate　전파하다

distinctive　특유의

diverse enemy　다양한 적

divided　분할된

DMZ(Demilitarized Zone)　비무장지대

doctrinal hierarchy　교리 체계

doctrine　교리

domain　영토, 영역, 범위

dominance　우세, 우월, 지배

dominant　지배적인, 우세한

drive　동력, 추동력

E

echelon　제대, 단계

economy of force　병력의 절약

effective range　유효사거리

electronic warfare officer(EWO)
　　전자전 장교

emanate from　~에서 나오다, 발산하다

embody　구현하다, 구체화하다

empathy　공감, 감정이입

emplace　적용하다

emplacement　배치, 위치

employment　고용, 일자리

emulate　경쟁하다, 다투다

ENCOORD(Environmental Coordinator)
　　환경문제협조관

End of Evening Nautical Twilight
　　(EENT)　해상박명종

end state　최종상태

enemy-oriented attack　적 지향 공격

enforcement　집행, 시행

engagement　교전, 개입

engineer coordinator(ENCOORD)
　　공병협조 장교

entail　수반하다

envelopment　포위

environmental manipulation　환경 조성

envision　상상하다, 계획하다

EPLRS(Enhanced Position Location
　　Reporting System)
　　강화된 진지 위치보고 시스템

EPWs(Enemy Prisoner of War)　적 포로

equal opportunity advisor(EOA)
　　기회균등 상담관

equip　장비하다

equipment recovery　장비복구

essential elements of friendly
　　information(EEFI)　우군첩보기본요소

ethos　기풍, 기질, 도덕적 특질

evacuation or hospitalization plans
　　후송 및 의무계획

excess property　잉여자산

execution　실시

exempt　면제된, 면제하다

exercise site access roster
　　연습장 출입자 명단

expect me　나를 기다리다

expertise　전문기술, 전문지식

exploitation　전과확대

explosive ordnance disposal

폭발성 무기류 처치

explosive ordnance disposal(EOD) officer
　　폭발물 처리 장교

extend operational reach　　확장된 작전 범위

extent　　넓이, 범위

F

FACDAM(Facilities Damage)　　시설피해

faced with ~　　~에 직면한

facilitate　　용이하게 하다

facility　　시설

fast-breaking operation　　신속 돌파작전

feint　　양공

fence　　울타리

field army tactical operations center
　　(FATOC)　　야전군 전술작전본부

field sanitation　　야전 위생

field service　　야전 근무

fielding　　배치

figure　　숫자로 부르겠다

final coordination line　　최종 협조선

finance officer　　경리 장교

fire and maneuver　　사격과 기동

fire support coordination center(FSCC)
　　화력지원 협조본부

fire support coordinator(FSCOORD)
　　화력지원 협조장교

fire support team(FIST)　　화력지원반

firsthand　　직접, 직접의

flawlessly　　흠 없는, 완벽한

follower　　추종자

force development　　전력개발

Force health protection　　부대 건강 방호

force projection　　전투력 투사

forced entry operation　　강압 진입 작전

forms of maneuver　　기동형태

fortification　　축성

forward air controller(FAC)　　전방항공통제관

forward position　　전방진지

foxhole　　개인호

fragmentary order　　단편명령

fratricide avoidance　　우군 간 피해 회피

freedom village　　자유마을

front line　　전방전선

front sight　　가늠쇠

frontal area　　전방지역

frontal attack　　정면공격

furnishing　　비품, 장비의 설치

G

generating and applying combat power
　　전투력의 창출 및 적용

generation　　생산

geographic feature　　지형물

get rid of　　~에서 벗어나다, ~을 없애다

governance　　지배, 지배권, 통치, 관리

graphic　　그림의, 도표의, 시각

grenade　　수류탄

grid square　　격자방안

grid system　　방안 좌표법

ground tactical plan　　지상전술계획

guard　　보초, 경계

guidance　　지침

guide　　선도

H

hammer　　공이치기

hand grenade　수류탄

hand-to-hand fighting　백병전

harass　교란

hasty defensive position　급조 방어 진지

hazardous material　위험물자

headquarter　본부

headquarters management　본부관리

heavy brigade combat team(HBCT)
　　중여단 전투팀

heavy infantry　중보병

heraldic　전령의, 의전의

HF(High Frequency)　고주파

high yield explosive(CBRNE)　고성능 폭발

highly enriched uranium(HEU)
　　고농축 우라늄

high-value targets(HVTs)　고가치표적

historian　역사담당관

hold down　고착시키다

honor　영광, 명예

hospitality　친절, 환대

host nation　주둔국

house the firing mechanism
　　격발장치를 수용하다

human intelligence(HUMINT)　인간정보

human resource　인적자원

human resources support
　　인적자원 지원(보충)

hunt and peck　독수리 타법

I

I read back　복창한다

I say again　재송한다

I spell　음성문자로 송신한다

I verify　확인한다

identification　확인

ignite　점화시키다

imagery　모형, 모형 상황판

imagery intelligence　영상정보

immediate　긴급의

immediately　즉시, 곧장

imperative　필수의, 반드시 실행해야 하는

in an advisory capacity　자문관 자격으로

in combination with　~와 결합하여, 짝지어

in isolation　별개로, 홀로

in order to　~ 하기 위하여

in relation to　~와 비교하여, ~에 관하여

in reserve　예비로, 예비대로

in single file　일렬종대로

incite　자극하다, 유발하다

incorporate　통합하다

index　색인

indigenous personnel　토착민

Indirect approach　간접 접근

indirect fire　간접화력

infantry carrier vehicle(ICV)　보병수송차량

infeasible　실행 불가능한

infiltration　침투

inflict　주다, 가하다, 입히다

information requirement
　　첩보요구, 정보요구

ingredient　성분, 구성요소

inhabited village　사람이 거주하는 마을

inherent　고유의, 본래의, 본질, 필연성

inherently　본래의, 고유의

inhospitable condition
　　비우호적인 조건, 황폐한 조건

Initiate movement　최초 이동

initiative　주도권, 선제의

insignia   휘장, 표장, 훈장

Inspector general   감찰

installation   시설물, 설비

insurgent   반란, 폭도

integrating and synchronizing the effects
    통합되고 동시적인 효과

integrity
    고결, 청렴, 진실성, 완전한 상태, 무결성

intent   (지휘관)의도

interact   상호 작용하다

interaction   상호작용

intermingle   혼합되다, 섞이다

internal arrangement   내부배치

inventory   보유, 비축, 재고

IPB(Intelligence Preparation of the
    Battlefield)   전장정보분석

IR(information Requirement)   첩보요구

is entrenched
    참호진지를 구축하여 방어편성을 하다

It was my pleasure
    괜찮습니다(My pleasure)

J

jamming   전파방해

jeopardize   위태롭게 하다

JSA(Joint Security Area)   공동경비구역

K

key terrain feature   중요지형지물

knock off   제거하다

KPA(Korean People's Army)   북한 인민군

L

label   부호, 구분하다

land warfare   지상전

landing zone   착륙지점, 상륙지점

lateral   측면의, 옆의

lateral maneuver   측방기동

lead by personal example   몸소 모범을
    보여 인도하다

leader's absence   지휘자 부재

leading rifle element   선도 소총부대

leave   휴가

letter of commendation   표창장

liaison officer(LNO)   연락장교

lift   (사격을) 연신하다

line of contact(LC)   접촉선

line of departure(LD)   공격 개시선

line-of-duty   임무계선

link-up   연결하다

local provocation of disorder   국지도발

lodgment   숙영

logic   논리

LOGPAC(Logistics Package)   군수 패키지

look forward to(anticipate)
    기다리다, 기대하다

lubrication   주유(윤활유)

lull   일시적인 전투 중지, 소강상태

M

machine gun nest   기관총좌

magazine   탄알집, 잡지

main effort   주공

main supply route(MSR)   주보급로

maintenance   정비, 지속, 유지

malfunction   기능불량(장애)

malware   악성코드, 악성소프트웨어

maneuver   기동, 책략

maneuver unit　기동부대

map requirement　지도 소요

maritime sniper brigade　해상저격여단

maturity　성숙, 원숙

meadow　초원, 목초지

MEDEVAC(Medical Evacuation)
　의무후송

mentally　염두로, 머릿속으로

METT-TC(Mission, Enemy, Troop,
　Terrain, Time, Civilian)
　임무, 적, 부대, 지형, 시간, 민간인

MI(Military Intelligence)　군사정보

military crest　군사적 정상

military decision-making process(MDMP)
　군사적 결심수립절차

military demarcation line　군사분계선

mine sweeper　소해함

miniaturize　소형화하다

mission command　임무형 지휘

mission-essential task list(METL)
　임무과제목록

mobile defense　기동방어

mobile field mess　야전 이동 취사반

mobile gun system(MGS)　기동포 체제

mode　방법

modification table of distribution and
　allowances(MTDA)　수정 분배 및 할당표

modify　수정하다, 변경하다

mold　형성하다, ~을 틀로 만들다

momentum　기세

monolithic　획일적이고 자유가 없는

moral and ethical qualities
　도덕적 및 윤리적 품성들

mortuary affair　시신처리

mounted mobile　탑승 기동

movement and maneuver　이동 및 기동

movement to contact　접적이동

MSEL(Master Scenario Event List)
　주요사태목록

MTOE(Modified Table of Organization
　and Equipment)　수정 편제 장비표

multinational partner　다국적 파트너

munition　군수품, 탄약

muzzle　총구, 포구

N

narrative　이야기, 서술

native language　현지 언어

nature of the operation　작전 성격

nest　기여하다, 차곡차곡 포개 넣다

neutralize　무력화하다

next higher command　차상급부대

night vision device　야시장비

NLT(not later than)　늦어도

no change　변동 없음

no sweat　괜찮아, 걱정 마

nobility, elegance, and dignity
　고결, 우아, 위엄

non battle losses　비전투손실

noncombatant　비전투원

notification　통지

nucleus　핵심, 중심

nullify　파기하다, 무력화하다

number combination　숫자 조합

O

obligation　의무, 책무

observation post(OP)　관측소

OE(Operational Environment)　작전환경

offensive information operation
공세적 정보작전

old man   직속상관 등을 칭하는 속어

old rusted locomotive   오래된 녹슨 기관차

on the move   이동 중에

on-site manpower and equipment
surveys   현지 인력 및 장비조사

open space   개활지

OPORD(Operation Order)   작전명령

OPSEC(Operations Security)   작전보안

orchard   과수원

order format   명령양식

orderly room   중대 행정반, 중대 사무실

ordnance   병기

ordnance corps   병기단

organic   편제의

organization for combat   전투편성

organizational clothing   조직 의류

orienting   적응시키기

out   교신 끝

outnumber
압도하다, ~보다 수적으로 우세하다

over   이상

overarching   아주 중요한

overlay   투명도

overlay or sketch   투명도 또는 요도

overlooking   모르고 지나치는

overmatch   능가, 강적

oversee   감독하다

P

P&O branch(Plans and Operations branch)
계획운영과

paradoxically   역설적으로

passage of lines   초월전진

patrols   정찰, 순찰

Permanent Change of Station(PCS)
전속

PCS in   전입

PCS out   전출

peace, calmness and simplicity
평화, 고요, 소박함

penetration   돌파

permeate   퍼지다, 스며들다, 보급되다

perpendicular   수직의, 수직선 상의

personnel readiness
management   인사준비태세관리

personnel service support   인사근무지원

personnel strength   인력

pertinent   관계 있는, 적절한

petroleum product   석유제품

phase line   통제선

phonetic alphabet   음성문자

physically fit   육체적으로 적합한

pick up the radiation   방사능에 오염되다

pickup zone   회수지점, 탑승지점

pin down ~   ~을 고착시키다

PM(Program Manager)   사업관리관

POC(Point of Contact)   담당자, 연락처

point or area target   점 또는 지역표적

POL(Petroleum, Oils and Lubricants)
유류(석유, 오일, 윤활유)

POLCAP(POL Capabilities Report)
유류능력보고

populace   대중

portion   일부, 분할

preassault bombardment   공격준비폭격

precious   소중한, 귀중한

precision strike   정밀타격

preclude   배제하다

predominant   지배적

preference   선호도

preplanned mission   기계획 임무

prescribed limit   정해진 한계, 범위

prescribed load   규정 휴대량

presence   존재, 영향력

present term   현재의 조건

preserve   보존하다

primary maneuver force   주요기동부대

primer   뇌관

principal staff   주요 참모

Priority Intelligence Requirement
    우선정보요구(PIR)

priority/precedence   우선권

prisoner of war   포로

private   이병

procedure words(prowords)   통화 약어

procure   획득

procurement and contracting
    획득 및 계약

project   전망하다

projectile   탄두, 탄환, 발사체

proliferation   확산

prolong endurance   신장된 내구력

propaganda slogan   선전문구

propellant   추진시키는, 추진장약

propensity   성향, 기호, 경향

property   자산

proportion   비율, 크기

protection   방호

protocol and liaison branch   의전 및 연락

provost marshal   헌병사령관(장교), 법무장교

prudent   신중한

psychological operations(PSYOP)   심리전

PSYOP officer   심리전 장교

public affairs officer   공무장교, 공공장교

pulp   분쇄하다

pursuit   추격

pyrotechnic and signal
    불꽃신호, 섬광신호탄, 신호탄 및 신호

Q

qualify   자격이 있다

quantifiable   계량화할 수 있는

quartering   숙영지 할당

quartering party   분할된 일부분

quartermaster   병참

quartermaster corps   병참단

quotas   정원, 물량

R

radiant mercury   보안장비

radically   현저하게

radio   무선

radio check   감도 점검

radio station   무선통신소

radiological   방사선의, 방사선 물질에 의한

radius of fall out   낙진반경

raid   습격, 침입

range-finding works   거리측정 작업

rapid   신속

ration   식량, 배급량

read back   복창하라

ready to copy?   받아쓸 준비 되었나?

real property control   부동산 통제

rear area operation   후방지역작전

rear sight　가늠자

reasoning　추리, 논리

reassurance　안도, 안심시키는 것

receive the mission　명령수령

receiver　총몸

receiving station　수신소

recommendation　건의, 장점, 추천

recon　정찰, 정찰대

reconnaissance　정찰

reconnaissance in force　위력수색

reconnaissance operation　수색작전

reconnaissance patrol　수색정찰대

reconnoiter　정찰하다

rectangle　직사각형

reenlistment　재입대, 재모집

refine　정교화하다

regardless of ~　~구애 없이, 상관없이

rehearsal　예행연습

reinforce　증강하다

reiterate　되풀이하다, 반복하다

related general engineering
　일반 공병과 관련된 것

release the firing mechanism
　격발장치를 작동시키다

relief feature　기복지형

relief in place　진지교대

render　제공하다, 표현하다, ~이 되게 하다

render precision fires inaccurate
　정확한 사격(타격)을 부정확하게 만든다

repel　격퇴하다

replace　대신하다, 대체하다

replacement management　보충관리

representation　표현, 설명

reprocessing spent fuel rods
　폐연료봉 재처리 과정

required supply rate(RSR)　소요보급률

requisition　획득, 징발, 청구

reserve　예비역

residual forces　잔여부대

resist　저항하다

resisting enemy　저항하는 적

restricted terrain　제한된 지형

result from　~에 기인하다

resupply　재보급

retirement　철퇴, 전역, 하기식

retrograde operation　후퇴작전

rewards and punishments　상벌

ridge　능선

ridgeline north to　~로 향하는 북쪽 능선

right away　바로

rigorously　엄격한, 엄밀한

risk reduction control measures
　위험감소 통제수단

RM(Road Management)　도로관리

roger　수신양호

room for dispersion　소산 공간

route　통로

routine decisions　일상적인 결심사항들

rules of engagement　교전규칙

running password　일상(상비) 암구어

S

saddle　안부

safe haven　안전한 피난처

safety officer　안전장교

salvage　구조, 구난

sanction　제재

sand table　사판, 모래를 이용한 모형판

say again　재송하라

scale 척도

scheme of maneuver 기동계획

scope 범위

screen 차장

sea lines of communication 해상병참선

search and attack 수색 및 공격

second front 제2전선

secondary effort 조공, 부차적 노력

security operation 경계작전

security patrol 경계 정찰

seize and hold 탈취 및 확보하다

seizure 탈취

selfless service 사심 없는 근무

self-propelled 자주

service 근무

servicemen's group life insurance(SGLI)
　　군인생명보험

shift (사격 방향을) 전환하다

shock 충격

short of 못 미쳐서

sick call 군인들이 병원에 가는 것

sick of ~ ~에 신물이 나다, ~에 질리다

side by side with
　　~와 나란히, 밀접한 관계를 가지고

signal corps 통신단

signal interference 신호에 의한 통신간섭

signals intelligence(SIGINT) 신호정보

signals security(SIGSEC)
　　통신보안, 신호보안

silence 무선침묵

silence lifted 무선침묵대기 해제

SINCGARS 단일 채널 지상 및 공중무선 체계

size up 판단하다

SJA(Staff Judge Advocate) 법무참모

skirmish line 산개대형

sling 멜빵

SLS(Senior Leader's Seminar)
　　주요지휘관 세미나

smallpox 천연두

smoke and flame 연막 및 화염

sniper team 저격팀

SOF(Special Operation Forces)
　　특수작전부대

SOI(Signal Operation
　　Instructions) 통신운용지시

soldierly manner 군대예절, 군인다운 용모

SOP(Standing Operating Procedure)
　　예규, 내규

sortie (전투기의) 출격

sound judgment 건전한 판단

southern boundary 남방한계선

space allocation 공간배치

speak slower 천천히 송신하라

special operations coordinator(SOCOORD)
　　특수작전 협조관

special purpose attacks 특수목적 공격

specify 명시하다, 열거하다

spoiling attack 파쇄공격

squadron 기병대대, 비행대대

stability operation 안정화 작전

staff judge advocate 법무참모

staging 대기(지역)

standpoint 견지, 입장, 관점

stands for 나타내다(represent)

steep odds 어려운 가능성

stewardship 책무

stock 개머리(재고, 축적)

stockpile 비축

stop by, drop by, visit, come over to
　　들르다

stoppage 기능고장

strategic force 전략군

stryker brigade combat team(SBCT) 스트라이커 여단 전투팀

stuff up ~을 꽉 막다

stumble into 모르고 들어가다

submarine 잠수함

subordinate 부대원, 하급의, 부하, 하급부대, 종속의

substitute 대신하다

subvert 전복시키다

succession of command 지휘권 승계

suffuse 채우다, 가득 차게 하다

suitable route forward 적절한 전진로

supervise and assess 감독 및 평가

supplement 보충하다, 추가

supply 보급

suppress 강압

surgeon 외과 군의관

surveillance 감시, 정찰

susceptibility 민감성

sustained 지속된

sustaining actions 지탱하는 행동, 작전지속지원을 위한 행동

sustainment 작전지속지원

sustainment assets 지속능력 유지 자산

swamp 늪

sympathy 동정, 연민

synchronize 동시화하다

T

table of allowance 할당표

tactical air control center(TACC) 전술항공통제본부

tactical air control party(TACP) 전술항공통제반

tactical air support element(TASE) 전술항공지원반

tactical enabling operations 전술적 운용 가능 작전들

tactical movement 전술적 이동

tactical operations centers(TOC) 전술작전본부

tactical unit 전술단위부대

tailored 맞춤식으로

take advantage of ~을 최대한 이용하다

task organization 전투편성

TDA(Table of Distribution and Allowances) 분배 및 배당표

technical competence 기술적 능력

template 형판, 상황판

tenet 교리, 견해

tentative plan 잠정계획

terminal operation 종결작전

theater airlift liaison officer(TALO) 전구공수연락장교

theater army 전구육군, 전구군

theaterwide 전(全) 전역(戰域)에 걸친

there is little difficulty 거의 어려움이 없다

3rd invasion tunnel 제3침투 땅굴

thorough 철저한

thoroughness 완전, 철저함

three-dimensional security 3차원 경계, 보안

thrive 성장하다, 무성하다, 성공하다

time of attack 공격 개시 시간

time on target(TOT) 표적공격시간

time-constrained 시간이 제한된

timeline 진행계획

time-tested 유효성이 증명된

TOE(Table of Equipment) 장비표

took over 인수하다, 넘겨받다

topographic crest 지형적 정상

topographic symbol 지형부호

torpedo boat 어뢰정

track 궤도

trail 오솔길

training guidance 훈련지침

transferred to ~ 으로 전속되다

transmit 송신하다

transmitting Station 송신소

transportation 수송

transportation corps 수송단

triangle 삼각형

trigger 방아쇠, 쏘다

trigger guard 방아쇠 울

trigger housing group 방아쇠 뭉치

troop movement 부대이동

troop movement(road march)
　　부대이동(도로 행군)

troop unit 부대 단위

troop-leading procedure 부대지휘절차

TSAR(Theater System Analysis Report)
　　표적분석체계보고

turn in 제출하다

turning Movement 우회공격

two air force sniper brigades
　　2개의 항공저격여단

U

UAV(Unmanned Aerial Vehicle)
　　무인 항공기

UHF(Ultra High Frequencies) 극초단파

unconventional 비정규적

uninterrupted operation
　　지속작전, 단절 없는 작전

unit activation 부대신설

unpaved road 비포장 도로

unprecedented 전례가 없는

urban terrain 도심지역

V

vacuum 공백

variation 변화

vary 여러 가지이다, 다양하다

vegetation 초목

velocity 속도

verbal combat order 구두전투명령

verbatim 말 그대로의, 축어적인

Veterinary officer 수의장교

VHF(Very High Frequency) 초단파

via ~을 경유해서, ~에 의하여

visibility 가시성

vital interest 핵심이익

voice circuit 음성회로

vulnerability 취약점

vulnerable 취약한

W

war sustainment capability 전쟁지속능력

warfighting function 전투수행기능

warning order 준비명령

WATCHCON(Watch Condition) 감시태세

water purification 정수

wear 마모

weekend pass 주말 외출(증)

wilco(will comply)
정확히 수신했으며 지시대로 시행하겠다

willingly   자진해서

window of opportunity   기회의 창

wipe out   소탕하다

wire   유선

withdrawal   철수

WMD(Weapons of Mass Destruction)
대량살상무기

work up   연구하다, 정리하다, 계산하다

workload   작업량, 업무량

wrest   쟁취하다, 빼앗다(비틀다)

XO(Executive Officer)
보좌관, 행정장교, 선임장교

zone   지대

zone of action   전투지역

Appendix 6 | Glossary 2: Korean–English

ㄱ

가교 장비　bridging equipment

가늠쇠　front sight

가늠자　rear sight

가시성　visibility

가입한, 제휴된, 계열의　affiliated

가정　assumption

가청의　audible

각개격파　defeat in detail

간결한, 명료한　concise

간접 접근　Indirect approach

간접화력　indirect fire

감도 점검　radio check

감독 및 평가　supervise and assess

감독하다　oversee

감시, 정찰　surveillance

감시태세　WATCHCON(Watch Condition)

감찰　Inspector general

강습　air assault

강압　suppress

강압 진입 작전　forced entry operation

강화된 진지 위치보고 시스템
　　EPLRS(Enhanced Position Location
　　Reporting System)

강화하다　consolidate

개머리(재고, 축적)　stock

개머리판　butt

개인호　foxhole

개활지　open space

거리측정 작업　range-finding works

거부하다　deny

거의 어려움이 없다　there is little difficulty

건의, 장점, 추천　recommendation

건전한 판단　sound judgment

격발장치를 수용하다
　　house the firing mechanism

격발장치를 작동시키다
　　release the firing mechanism

격자방안　grid square

격퇴하다　repel

견지, 입장, 관점　standpoint

결과　consequence

결심지원형판　decision support template(DST)

결함부품　defective parts

결합하다, 연합하다　combine

경계 정찰　security patrol

경계 작전　security operation

경리 장교　finance officer

경쟁, 논쟁, 다투다　contest

경쟁하다, 다투다　emulate

계량화할 수 있는　quantifiable

계획운영과
　　P&O branch(Plans and Operations branch)

고가치 표적　high-value targets(HVTs)

고결, 우아, 위엄　nobility, elegance, and dignity

고결, 청렴, 진실성 integrity

고농축 우라늄 highly enriched uranium(HEU)

고성능 폭발 high yield explosive(CBRNE)

고용, 일자리 employment

고유의, 본래의, 본질, 필연성 inherent

고주파 HF(High Frequency)

고착시키다 hold down

공간배치 space allocation

공감, 감정이입 empathy

공격 attack

공격 개시 시간 time of attack

공격 개시선 line of departure(LD)

공격 대형 attack formation

공격대기지점, 공격진지 attack position

공격방향 direction of attack

공격적인 aggressive

공격준비폭격 preassault bombardment

공군연락장교 air liaison officer(ALO)

공동경비구역 JSA(Joint Security Area)

공무장교, 공공장교 public affairs officer

공백 vacuum

공병협조 장교
      engineer coordinator(ENCOORD)

공세적 정보작전
      offensive information operation

공역 airspace

공역지휘 및 통제
      airspace command and control(AC2)

공이치기 hammer

공정(부대) airborne

과수원 orchard

관계 있는, 적절한 pertinent

관심지역 area of interest(AI)

관측소 observation post(OP)

괜찮습니다(My pleasure) It was my pleasure

괜찮아, 걱정 마 no sweat

교란 harass

교리 doctrine

교리 체계 doctrinal hierarchy

교리, 견해 tenet

교신 끝 out

교전, 개입 engagement

교전규칙 rules of engagement

교정조치 corrective action

구두전투명령 verbal combat order

구류자 detainee

구성원, 구성요소 component

구성하다, ~에 해당하다 constitute

구성하다, 포함되다 comprise

구술하다, 지령(명령)하다, 결정하다 dictate

구조, 구난 salvage

구조, 구성 architecture

구현하다, 구체화하다 embody

국지도발 local provocation of disorder

군대예절, 군인다운 용모 soldierly manner

군사법정위반 court martial offense

군사분계선 military demarcation line

군사적 결심수립절차
      military decision-making process(MDMP)

군사적 정상 military crest

군사정보 MI(Military Intelligence)

군소리, 탁탁거리는 소리 crackle

군수 패키지 LOGPAC(Logistics Package)

군수공장 armaments factory

군수품, 탄약 munition

군악대 운용 band operation

군악대 지원 band support

군인들이 병원에 가는 것 sick call

군인생명보험
      SGLI(servicemen's group life insurance)

굴뚝 연기 chimney smoke

궤도 track

규모상 ~에 상응하다
    be commensurate in size with

규정 휴대량 prescribed load

그림의, 도표의, 시각 graphic

극초단파 UHF(Ultra High Frequencies)

근무 service

근접전투 close combat

근접항공지원 close air support

급조 방어 진지 hasty defensive position

기계획 임무 preplanned mission

기관총좌 machine gun nest

기능고장 stoppage

기능불량(장애) malfunction

기다리다, 기대하다 look forward to(anticipate)

기동, 책략 maneuver

기동계획 scheme of maneuver

기동방어 mobile defense

기동부대 maneuver unit

기동포체제 mobile gun system(MGS)

기동형태 forms of maneuver

기만계획 deception plan

기만작전 장교 deception officer

기만하다 deceive

기민한 agile

기병대 cavalry

기병대대, 비행대대 squadron

기복지형 relief feature

기본교범 capstone manual

기본방위방향 cardinal direction

기본병과 basic branch

기세 momentum

기술적 능력 technical competence

기습으로 by surprise

기습의 정도 degree of surprise

기여하다, 차곡차곡 포개 넣다 nest

기풍, 기질, 도덕적 특질 ethos

기회균등 상담관
    equal opportunity advisor(EOA)

기회의 창 window of opportunity

긴급소요부족품목록
    CRDL(Critical Requirements Deficiency
    List)

긴급의 immediate

ㄴ

나를 기다리다 expect me

나타내다(represent) stands for

낙오자 처리 disposition of straggler

낙진반경 radius of fall out

남방한계선 southern boundary

내부배치 internal arrangement

넓이, 범위 extent

노리쇠 bolt

논리 logic

뇌관 primer

능가, 강적 overmatch

능력과 제한사항 capability and limitation

능선 ridge

늦어도 NLT(not later than)

늪 swamp

ㄷ

다국적 파트너 multinational partner

다양한 적 diverse enemy

단결 cohesion

단일 채널 지상 및 공중무선 체계 SINCGARS

단편명령 fragmentary order

담당자, 연락처 POC(Point of Contact)

대기(지역) staging

대기동 countermobility

대량살상무기
    WMD(Weapons of Mass Destruction)

대신하다 substitute

대신하다, 대체하다 replace

대안 alternative

대정보 counterintelligence

대중 populace

대항하다 counter

도덕적 및 윤리적 품성들
    moral and ethical qualities

도로관리 RM(Road Management)

도심지역 urban terrain

독수리 타법 hunt and peck

돌격단계 assault phase

돌격진지 assault position

돌파 penetration

돌파하다 breach

동력, 추동력 drive

동시화하다 synchronize

동정, 연민 sympathy

되풀이하다, 반복하다 reiterate

들르다 stop by, drop by, visit, come over to

등고선 contour line

똑똑히 발음하다 articulate

ㅁ

마모 wear

말 그대로의, 축어적인 verbatim

말로 이루 다 표현할 수 없는 beyond words

맞춤식으로 tailored

매복 ambush

멜빵 sling

면제된, 면제하다 exempt

명령수령 receive the mission

명령양식 order format

명시하다, 열거하다 specify

명확한 표현 clear articulation

모르고 들어가다 stumble into

모르고 지나치는 overlooking

모형, 모형 상황판 imagery

목사 chaplain

몸소 모범을 보여 인도하다
    lead by personal example

못 미쳐서 short of

무력화하다 neutralize

무선 radio

무선침묵 silence

무선침묵대기 해제 silence lifted

무선통신소 radio station

무인 항공기 UAV(Unmanned Aerial Vehicle)

무장해제 disarmament

미 본토 CONUS(Continental United States)

민간인 인사장교
    civilian personnel officer(CPO)

민간인 인사처 CPO(Civilian Personnel Office)

민간인 피수용자, 민간인 피억류자
    civilian internee

민감성 susceptibility

ㅂ

바로 right away

바비큐 BBQ(barbecue)

반격 counteroffensive

반란, 폭도 insurgent

받아쓸 준비 되었나? ready to copy?

방공포 ADA(Air Defense Artillery)

방공협조관
    air defense coordinator(ADCOORD)

방관자 bystander

방백으로(혼자 중얼거리는 소리로) aside

방법 mode

방사능에 오염되다 pick up the radiation

방사선의, 방사선 물질에 의한 radiological

방아쇠 뭉치 trigger housing group

방아쇠울 trigger guard

방아쇠, 쏘다 trigger

방안 좌표법 grid system

방책 COA(Course of Action)

방책 courses of action

방책개발 COA development

방호 protection

배속 attachment

배정되다 be assigned to

배제하다 preclude

배치 fielding

배치, 위치 emplacement

백병전 hand-to-hand fighting

범위 scope

범위, 제약, 제한사항 constraint

법무참모 SJA(Staff Judge Advocate)

변동 없음 no change

변화 variation

별개로, 홀로 in isolation

병기 ordnance

병기단 ordnance corps

병력 수송 장갑차
    APC(Armored Personnel Carrier)

병력의 절약 economy of force

병참 quartermaster

병참단 quartermaster corps

보급 supply

보병수송차량 infantry carrier vehicle(ICV)

보안장비 radiant mercury

보유, 비축, 재고 inventory

보존하다 preserve

보좌관, 행정장교, 선임장교
    XO(Executive Officer)

보초, 경계 guard

보충관리 replacement management

보충하다, 추가 supplement

복잡성 complexity

복창하라 read back

복창한다 I read back

본래의, 고유의 inherently

본부 headquarter

본부관리 headquarters management

부관 adjutant general(AG)

부관단, 부관병과 adjutant general's Corps

부대 건강 방호 force health protection

부대 단위 troop unit

부대신설 unit activation

부대원, 하급의, 부하, 하급부대 subordinate

부대의 구성 composition

부대의 배치 disposition

부대이동(도로 행군)
    troop movement(road march)

부대창설 및 해체
    activation and deactivation of units

부동산 통제 real property control

부록 appendix

부수적인 손해, 피해 collateral damage

부호, 구분하다 label

북한 인민군 KPA(Korean People's Army)

분배 및 배당표
  TDA(Table of Distribution and Allowances)

분별하다, 식별하다 discern

분쇄하다 pulp

분할된 divided

분할된 일부분 quartering party

분해결합 disassembly and assembly

불꽃신호, 섬광신호탄, 신호탄 및 신호
  pyrotechnic and signal

불만, 불평, 혐오 disaffection

비극적 영향(충격) catastrophic impact

비대칭 전력 asymmetric forces

비무장지대 DMZ(Demilitarized Zone)

비우호적인 조건, 황폐한 조건
  inhospitable condition

비율, 크기 proportion

비전투손실 non battle losses

비전투원 noncombatant

비정규적 unconventional

비축 stockpile

비포장 도로 unpaved road

비품, 장비의 설치 furnishing

빗나가게 하다, 비끼다 deflect

ㅅ

사격과 기동 fire and maneuver

사기, 훈련, 규율 discipline

사람이 거주하는 마을 inhabited village

사상자 casualty

사상자 후송 CASEVAC(Casualty Evacuation)

사심 없는 근무 selfless service

사업관리관 PM(Program Manager)

사주방어 all-round defense

사판, 모래를 이용한 모형판 sand table

사후강평 after action reviews

산개대형 skirmish line

삼각형 triangle

상당한 수준 considerable level

상륙작전 amphibious operation

상륙전 amphibious warfare

상벌 rewards and punishments

상비군, 상비육군 active army

상상하다, 계획하다 envision

상호 작용하다 interact

상호작용 interaction

상황, 환경 circumstance

색인 index

생각하다, 의견을 갖다 deem

생물학 작용제 biological agent

생산 generation

석유제품 petroleum product

선도 guide

선도 소총부대 leading rifle element

선전문구 propaganda slogan

선호도 preference

성격, 인격, 특성 character

성분, 구성요소 ingredient

성숙, 원숙 maturity

성장하다, 무성하다, 성공하다 thrive

성향, 기호, 경향 propensity

소각 burning

소산 dispersion

소산 공간 room for dispersion

소요보급률 required supply rate(RSR)

소중한, 귀중한 precious

소탕하다 wipe out

소해함 mine sweeper

소형화하다 miniaturize

속담, 격언 adage

속도 velocity

송신소 transmitting Station

송신하다 transmit

수도방위사령부
    CDC(Capital Defense Command)

수류탄 grenade, hand grenade

수반하다 entail

수상계획 awards program

수색 및 공격 search and attack

수색작전 reconnaissance operation

수색정찰대 reconnaissance patrol

수송 transportation

수송단 transportation corps

수신소 receiving station

수신양호 roger

수신여부 acknowledge

수신여부(필수) ACKNOWLEDGE(Mandatory)

수의장교 Veterinary officer

수정 분배 및 할당표
    modification table of distribution and
    allowances(MTDA)

수정 편제 장비표
    MTOE(Modified Table of Organization and
    Equipment)

수정하다, 변경하다 modify

수직의, 수직선 상의 perpendicular

수하 및 암호 challenge and password

수행하다 carry out

숙영 lodgment

숙영지 할당 quartering

숨이 차다 be short of breath

숫자 조합 number combination

숫자로 부르겠다 figure

쉬어! at ease!

스트라이커 여단 전투팀
    stryker brigade combat team(SBCT)

습격, 급습 assault

습격, 침입 raid

승무원 훈련 crew drills

시간을 절약하다 buy time

시간이 제한된 time-constrained

시계 방향 clock reference

시민 대중 civil populace

시설 facility

시설물, 설비 installation

시설피해 FACDAM(Facilities Damage)

시신처리 mortuary affair

식량, 배급량 ration

신속 rapid

신속 돌파작전 fast-breaking operation

신장된 내구력 prolong endurance

신중한, 숙고하다 deliberate

신중한, 빈틈없는 prudent

신청, 적용 application

신호에 의한 통신간섭 signal interference

신호정보 signals intelligence(SIGINT)

실시 execution

실태적 인구통계 demographics

실행 불가능한 infeasible

심리전 psychological operations(PSYOP)

심리전 장교 PSYOP officer

(십자형의) 가로로 crosswise

쌍안경 binocular

ㅇ

아주 중요한 overarching

악성코드, 악성소프트웨어 malware

악화되다 deteriorate

안도, 안심시키는 것 reassurance

안부(鞍部), 고갯마루 saddle

안전장교 safety officer

안전한 피난처 safe haven

안정화 작전 stability operation

암구어 code word

압도하다, ~보다 수적으로 우세하다 outnumber

야시장비 night vision device

야외 숙영지(bivouac로도 표기) bivouacking

야전 근무 Field service

야전 위생 field sanitation

야전 이동 취사반 mobile field mess

야전군 전술작전본부
field army tactical operations center(FATOC)

양공 feint

양동, 시위 demonstration

어려운 가능성 steep odds

어뢰정 torpedo boat

어쨌든(anyway) be that as it may

엄격한, 엄밀한 rigorously

엄폐와 은폐 cover and concealment

여러 가지이다, 다양하다 vary

여유 있는 시간 comfortable time

역경, 불행 adversity

역사담당관 historian

역설적으로 paradoxically

역습 counterattack

연결 conjunction

연결하다 link-up

연구하다, 정리하다, 계산하다 work up

연달은 고지들 chain of hills

연락장교 liaison officer(LNO)

연막 및 화염 smoke and flame

연속적인 질문 a burst of question

연습장 출입자 명단 exercise site access roster

연신하다 lift

연합군 돌파 작전
combined arms breach operation

연합부대 예행연습 combined arms rehearsal

연합부대요소 combined arms element

연합특전사
CUWTF(Combined Unconventional Warfare Task Forces)

염두로, 머릿속으로 mentally

영광, 명예 honor

영상정보 imagery intelligence

영토, 영역, 범위 domain

예규, 내규
SOP(Standing Operating Procedure)

예비군, 예비육군 army reserve

예비로, 예비대로 in reserve

예비역 reserve

예행연습 rehearsal

오래된 녹슨 기관차 old rusted locomotive

오솔길 trail

완성화, 완벽화 completeness

완전, 철저함 thoroughness

완전히 cold

외과 군의관 surgeon

용이하게 하다 facilitate

우군간 피해 회피 fratricide avoidance

우군첩보기본요소
essential elements of friendly information(EEFI)

우발상황 contingency

우선권 priority/precedence

우선정보요구
Priority Intelligence Requirement(PIR)

우세, 우월, 지배 dominance

우위, 유리, 이점 advantage

우회공격 turning Movement

울타리 fence

위기조치예규
 CASOP(Crisis Action Standard Operating
 Procedure)

위력수색 reconnaissance in force

위장하다 camouflage

위태롭게 하다 jeopardize

위험감소 통제수단
 risk reduction control measures

위험물자 hazardous material

유능한, 능력이 있는 competent

유도하다 canalize

유류(석유, 오일, 윤활유)
 POL(Petroleum, Oils and Lubricants)

유류능력보고 POLCAP(POL Capabilities)
 Report

유선 wire

유효사거리 effective range

유효성이 증명된 time-tested

육군항공협조관
 aviation coordinator(AVCOORD)

육체적으로 적합한 physically fit

음성문자 phonetic alphabet

음성문자로 송신한다 I spell

음성회로 voice circuit

응집력의, 결합시키는 cohesive

의무, 책무 obligation

의무, 책임, 투입 commitment

의무후송 MEDEVAC(Medical Evacuation)

의전 및 연락 Protocol and Liaison Branch

이동 및 기동 movement and maneuver

이동 중에 on the move

이병 private

이상 over

이야기, 서술 narrative

이용하다 capitalize

인간정보 human intelligence(HUMINT)

인공물 cultural feature

인력 personnel strength

인사근무지원 personnel service support

인사준비태세관리
 personnel readiness management

인수하다, 넘겨받다 took over

인적자원 human resource

인적자원 지원(보충)
 Human resources support

인접 부대장 adjacent commander

인접배치하다 collocate

인접 부대 adjacent unit

인증하다, 입증하다 authenticate

일관된, 고정된 consistent

일렬종대로 in single file

일반 공병과 관련된 것
 related general engineering

일부, 분할 portion

일상(상비) 암구어 running password

일상적인 결심사항들 routine decisions

일시적인 전투 중지, 소강상태 lull

임무, 적, 부대, 지형, 시간, 민간인
 METT-TC(Mission, Enemy, Troop, Terrain,
 Time, Civilian)

임무계선 line-of-duty

임무과제목록
 mission-essential task list(METL)

임무수행계획보고 debrief

임무형 지휘 mission command

임무확인 보고 confirmation brief

잉여자산 excess property

ㅈ

자격이 있다 qualify

자극하다, 유발하다 incite

자문관 자격으로 in an advisory capacity

자산 property

자유마을 freedom village

자주 self-propelled

자진해서 willingly

작업량, 업무량 workload

작전개념 concept of operation

작전명령 OPORD(Operation Order)

작전보안 OPSEC(Operations Security)

작전 성격 nature of the operation

작전수행과정 troop-leading procedure

작전지속지원 sustainment

작전지역 AO(Area of Operation)

작전통제 CHOP(change of operational control)

작전환경 OE(Operational Environment)

잔여부대 residual forces

잠수함 submarine

잠정계획 tentative plan

장갑판 armor plate

장비복구 equipment recovery

장비표 TOE(Table of Equipment)

장비하다 equip

장전된 탄약 cartridge supply

장전손잡이 charging handle

재래식 보병부대 conventional Infantry unit

재래식 전력 conventional forces

재보급 resupply

재송하라 say again

재송한다 I say again

재입대, 재모집 reenlistment

쟁취하다, 빼앗다(비틀다) wrest

저격팀 sniper team

저항하는 적 resisting enemy

저항하다 resist

적 지향 공격 enemy-oriented attack

적 포로 EPWs(Enemy Prisoner of War)

적, 적의 adversary

적당한 appropriate

적용하다 emplace

적응시키기 orienting

적절한 adequate

적절한 전진로 suitable route forward

전(全) 전역(戰域)에 걸친 theaterwide

전개 능력 deployability

전과확대 exploitation

전구공수연락장교
    theater airlift liaison officer(TALO)

전구육군, 전구군 theater army

전략군 strategic force

전력개발 force development

전령의, 의전의 heraldic

전례가 없는 unprecedented

전망하다 project

전문기술, 전문지식 expertise

전방전선 front line

전방지역 frontal area

전방진지 forward position

전방항공통제관 forward air controller(FAC)

전복시키다 subvert

전사상자 수집소 casualty collection point

전속 permanent Change of Station(PCS)

전술단위부대 tactical unit

전술작전본부 tactical operations centers(TOC)

전술적 운용 가능 작전들
    tactical enabling operations

전술적 이동 tactical movement

전술항공지원반
    tactical air support element(TASE)

전술항공통제반 tactical air control party(TACP)

전술항공통제본부
    tactical air control center(TACC)

전입 PCS in

전자전 장교 electronic warfare officer(EWO)

전장정보분석
    IPB(Intelligence Preparation of the
    Battlefield)

전쟁지속능력 war sustainment capability

전진축 axis of advance

전출 PCS out

전투 휴대량 combat load

전투근무지원 combat service support

전투기의 출격 sortie

전투력 투사 force projection

전투력의 창출 및 적용
    generating and applying combat power

전투부대 combat arm

전투수행기능 warfighting function

전투원 combatant

전투정찰 combat patrols

전투지경선 boundary

전투지역 zone of action

전투지원 combat support

전투진지 battle position

전투편성
    organization for combat, task organization

전투훈련 battle drills

전파방해 jamming

전파하다 disseminate

전환하다 shift

점 또는 지역표적 point or area target

점화시키다 ignite

접적 전진 approach march

접적이동 movement to contact

접촉선 line of contact(LC)

접촉점 contact point

정교화하다 refine

정면공격 frontal attack

정밀 도하 deliberate crossing

정밀타격 precision strike

정비, 지속, 유지 maintenance

정수 water purification

정원, 물량 quotas

정정 correction

정찰 reconnaissance

정찰, 순찰 patrols

정찰, 정찰대 recon

정찰하다 reconnoiter

정해진 한계, 범위 prescribed limit

정확한 사격(타격)을 부정확하게 만든다
    render precision fires inaccurate

정확히 상황을 평가하다
    accurately assess the situation

정확히 수신했으며 지시대로 시행하겠다
    wilco(will comply)

제2전선 second front

제거하다 knock off

제공하다, 표현하다, ~이 되게 하다 render

제대, 단계 echelon

제재 sanction

제출하다 turn in

제한된 지형 restricted terrain

조건, 평가기준, 기준 criteria

조공, 부차적 노력 secondary effort

조직 의류 organizational clothing

조합된, 연합된, 편조된 associated

존재, 영향력 presence

종결작전 terminal operation

종심지역 deep area

종심지역 작전 계획 deep area operation plan

좌표 coordinate

주공 main effort

주다, 가하다, 입히다 inflict

주도권, 선제의 initiative

주둔국 host nation

주말 외출(증) weekend pass

주 보급로 main supply route(MSR)

주요 관리 행위
　　　consequence management action

주요 참모 principal staff

주요기동부대 primary maneuver force

주요사태목록
　　　MSEL(Master Scenario Event List)

주요지휘관 세미나
　　　SLS(Senior Leader's Seminar)

주유(윤활유) lubrication

준비명령 warning order

중대 행정반, 중대 사무실 orderly room

중보병 heavy infantry

중여단 전투팀
　　　HBCT(heavy brigade combat team)

중요지형지물 key terrain feature

즉시, 곧장 immediately

증강요원 augmentee

증강하다 reinforce

지대 zone

지도 소요 map requirement

지배, 지배권, 통치, 관리 governance

지배적 predominant

지배적인, 우세한 dominant

지상전 land warfare

지상전술계획 ground tactical plan

지속능력 유지 자산 sustainment assets

지속된 sustained

지속작전, 단절 없는 작전
　　　uninterrupted operation

지역 area

지역경계(통로, 수송로 포함)
　　　area security(including route and convey

지역방어 area defense

지연, 지연전 delay

지점, 관점, 양상 aspect

지침 guidance

지탱하는 행동, 지속작전을 위한 행동
　　　sustaining actions

지형물 Geographic feature

지형부호 topographic symbol

지형적 정상 topographic crest

지휘, 통수, 명령, 구령, 사령부 command

지휘관 주요첩보 요구
　　　CCIR(Commander's Critical Information
　　　Requirement)

지휘관 우선 정보요구
　　　commander's priority intelligence
　　　requirement

지휘관 의도 intent

지휘권 승계 succession of command

지휘자 부재 leader's absence

지휘통제 시스템
　　　C2(command and control) system

지휘통제전
　　　command and control warfare(C2W)

직사각형 rectangle

직속상관 등을 칭하는 속어 old man

직접, 직접의 firsthand

직접항공지원본부
   direct air support center(DASC)

직접화력   direct fire

진지강화   consolidation

진지강화 및 재편성
   consolidation and reorganization

진지교대   relief in place

진행계획   timeline

집결지   assembly area

집착, 견지, 충실   adherence

집행, 시행   enforcement

ㅊ

차상급부대   next higher command

차장   screen

착륙지점, 상륙지점   landing zone

참모장   CofS(Chief of Staff)

참호진지를 구축하여 방어편성을 하다
   is entrenched

채우다, 가득 차게 하다   suffuse

책무   stewardship

책임, 의무   accountability

책임지역   area of responsibility

처리, 처분   disposal

척도   scale

천연두   smallpox

천천히 송신하라   speak slower

철수   withdrawal

철저한   thorough

철퇴, 전역, 하기식   retirement

첨부, 붙임   annex

첩보요구   IR(information Requirement)

초과 가시선   BLOS(beyond line-of-sight)

초단파   VHF(Very High Frequency)

초목   vegetation

초원, 목초지   meadow

초월전진   passage of lines

총검, 대검   bayonet

총구, 포구   muzzle

총몸   receiver

총열   barrel

최고점에 달하다, 완결하다   culminate

최종 협조선   final coordination line

최종상태   end state

최초 이동   Initiate movement

추격   pursuit

추리, 논리   reasoning

추종자   follower

추진시키는, 추진장약   propellant

축성   fortification

축약하는   abbreviating

충격   shock

취약점   vulnerability

취약한   vulnerable

측면의, 옆의   lateral

측방기동   lateral maneuver

치과 진료   dental surgeon

친절, 환대   hospitality

침투   infiltration

ㅌ

타격, 공격   blow

탄도미사일   ballistic missile

탄두, 탄환, 발사체   projectile

탄알집, 잡지   magazine

탄약   cartridge

탄약기본휴대량   ammunition basic load

탄약보급소   ASP(Ammunition Supply Point)

탄약할당/통제보급률
　　AA/CSR(Ammunition Allocation/Controled
　　Supply Rate)
탄저균　anthrax
탄피　cartridge case
탄환　bullet
탈영, 도망　desertion
탈영, 무단이탈　absence without leave(AWOL)
탈취　seizure
탈취 및 확보하다　seize and hold
탑승 기동　mounted mobile
토착민　indigenous personnel
통로　route
통신단　signal corps
통신보안, 신호보안　signals security(SIGSEC)
통신운용지시
　　SOI(Signal Operation Instructions)
통제보급률　controlled supply rate(CSR)
통제선　phase line
통지　notification
통합되고 동시적인 효과
　　integrating and synchronizing the effects
통합하다　incorporate
통화 약어　procedure words(prowords)
투명도　overlay
투명도 또는 요도　overlay or sketch
특수목적 공격　special purpose attacks
특수작전 협조관
　　special operations coordinator(SOCOORD)
특수작전부대　SOF(Special Operation Forces)
특유의　distinctive

Ⅲ

파견　detachment
파견부대　detaching unit

파괴, 폭파　demolition
파기하다, 무력화하다　nullify
파쇄공격　spoiling attack
판단하다　size up
퍼지다, 스며들다, 보급되다　permeate
퍼트리다　diffuse
편제의　organic
편집하다, ~을 축적하다　compile
평가하다　assess
평화, 고요, 소박함
　　peace, calmness and simplicity
폐쇄등고선　closed contour line
폐연료봉 재처리 과정
　　reprocessing spent fuel rods
포로　prisoner of war
포병　artillery
포병 포대　battery
포악, 잔학행위, 잔인성　atrocity
포위　envelopment
폭발물 처리 장교
　　explosive ordnance disposal(EOD) officer
폭발성 무기류 처치
　　explosive ordnance disposal
표적공격시간　time on target(TOT)
표적분석체계보고
　　TSAR(Theater System Analysis Report)
표창장　letter of commendation
표현, 설명　representation
필수의, 반드시 실행해야 하는　imperative

ㅎ

한도와 지침　ceilings and guidance
할당, 배당　allocation
할당표　table of allowance
할당하다　allocate

할당하다, 임명하다 assign

항공 및 반항공 사령부 air and anti-air command

항공, 비행 aviation

항공/함포연락중대 지휘관
    air/naval gunfire liaison company
    (ANGLICO) commander

항공기의 공격방향 attack heading

항공지원작전본부
    ASOCS(Air Support Operation Center)

항공차단 air interdiction

해독, 제독제 decontamination

해상박명종
    End of Evening Nautical Twilight (EENT)

해상박명초
    Beginning of Morning Nautical Twilight
    (BMNT)

해상병참선 sea lines of communication

해상저격여단 maritime sniper brigade

해안경비정 coastal patrol boat

핵심, 중심 nucleus

핵심이익 vital interest

허위정보 disinformation

헌병사령관(장교), 법무장교 provost marshal

헌신, 구금, 투입 commitment

현역 active duty

현재의 조건 present term

현저하게 radically

현지 언어 native language

현지 인력 및 장비조사
    on-site manpower and equipment surveys

협조지시 coordinating instruction

형성하다, ~을 틀로 만들다 mold

형판, 상황판 template

호출부호 call sign

혼합되다. 섞이다 intermingle

화력 지원반 fire support team(FIST)

화력지원 협조장교
    fire support coordinator(FSCOORD)

화력지원협조관
    FSCOORD(Fire Support Coordinator)

화력지원협조본부
    fire support coordination center(FSCC)

화생방 및 핵폭발
    CBRNE(chemical, biological, radiological,
    nuclear explosive)

화학장교 chemical officer(CHEMO)

확대하다 amplify

확산 proliferation

확산, 전파 diffusion

확산방지 counterproliferation

확신하는, 자신 있는 confident

확인 identification

확인보고 confirmation briefing

확인점 check point

확인한다 I verify

확장된 작전 범위 extend operational reach

환경 조성 environmental manipulation

환경문제협조관
    ENCOORD(Environmental Coordinator)

회수지점 pickup zone

획득 procure

획득 및 계약 procurement and contracting

획득, 징발, 청구 requisition

획일적이고 자유가 없는 monolithic

후방지역작전 rear area operation

후송 및 의무계획
    evacuation or hospitalization plans

후퇴작전 retrograde operation

훈련지침 training guidance

휘장, 표장, 훈장 insignia

휴가   leave

홈 없는, 완벽한   flawlessly

기타

2개의 항공저격여단
   two air force sniper brigades

3차원 경계, 보안   three-dimensional security

3 침투 땅굴   3rd invasion tunnel

~에 기인하다   result from

~에 기초하다, 바탕을 두다   base on

~을 경유해서, ~에 의하여   via

~로 향하는 북쪽 능선   ridgeline north to

~에 구애 없이, 상관없이   regardless of

~ 라고 불리다   be referred to as

~ 에 신물이 나다, ~에 질리다   sick of

~ 에 익숙하다   be familiar with

~ 에 직면한   faced with

~ 와 결합하여, 짝지어   in combination with

~ 와 관련된, 연관된   associated with

~와 나란히, 밀접한 관계를 가지고
   side by side with

~와 비교하여, ~에 관하여   in relation to

~으로 전속되다   transferred to

~을 꽉 막다   stuff up

~의 수단으로, ~으로   by means of

~하기 위하여   in order to

~ 하기로 되어 있다   be supposed to

~에 대하여   as to

~에 배속되다   be attached to

~에서 나오다, 발산하다   emanate from

~에서 벗어나다   be clear of

~에서 벗어나다, ~을 없애다   get rid of

~와 관계된   concerned with

~와 상의하다   consults with

~으로 구성되다   consist of

~을 고착시키다   pin down

~을 이용하다, ~에 편승하다   capitalize on

~을 최대한 이용하다   take advantage of

Reference

1. 국내 서적

국방부, 『국방백서 2020』(국방부, 2020. 12. 31.).

────, 『국방백서 2020』(영문판, 국방부, 2020. 12. 31.).

서경석, 『전투감각』(서울: 샘터사, 2003).

육군사관학교 영어과, 『Military English I』(서울: 도서출판 봉명, 2008).

연합사, 『Practical Military English II』(비매품)

2. 미 교범

ADRP 6-22(FM 6-22), *Army Leadership*(Headquarters, Department of the Army, Washington, DC, 2012).

Army Training Publication(ATP) 3-21.8, *The Infantry and Squad*(Fort Benning, 2016), http://www.benning.army.mil/infantry/DoctrineSupplement/ATP3-21.8/, 검색일 2016. 8. 27.

ATTP 5-0.1, *Commander and Staff Officer Guide*(Headquarters, Department of the Army, September, 2011).

FM 3-21.5, *Drill and Ceremonies*(Department of the Army, Washington, DC, January 2012).

FM 3-21.8, *The Infantry and Squad*(Headquarters, Department of the Army, Washington, DC, 28 March 2007).

FM 3-21.10(FM 7-10), *The Infantry Rifle Company*(Headquarters, Department of the Army, Washington, DC, July 2006).

FM 3-25.26, *Map Reading and Land Navigation*(Headquarters, Department of the Army, 30 August 2006).

FM 6-02.53, *Tactical Radio Operations*(Headquarters, Department of the Army Washington, DC, 5 August 2009).

FM 6-0, *Commander and Staff Organization and Operations*(Headquarters, Department of the

Army, May 2014).

FM 101-5, *Staff Organization and Operation*(Headquarters, Department of the Army, July 4th 2009).

Joint Publication 1-02, *Department of Defense Dictionary of Military and Associated Terms*(15 January 2012).

TRADOC Pamphlet 525-3-1, *The US Army Operating Concept*(October 2014).

3. 인터넷 자료

국가지표체계, http://www.index.go.kr/potal/main/EachDtlPageDetail.do?idx_cd=1715, 검색일: 2020.1.19.

국군간호사관학교 홈페이지, http://www.kafna.ac.kr/user/indexSub.action?codyMenuSeq=81995559 1&siteId=afna&menuUIType=top, 검색일: 2023. 1. 30.

육군3사관학교 홈페이지, https://www.kma.ac.kr:461/kma/2195/subview.do, 검색일: 2023. 1. 30.

육군사관학교 홈페이지, https://www.kma.ac.kr:461/kma/2195/subview.do, 검색일: 2023. 1. 30.

합동군사대학교 국방어학원 과정 홈페이지, http://new.mnd.go.kr/user/indexSub.action?codyMenuSeq =70206&siteId=jfmu&menuUIType=sub, 검색일: 2020.1.19.

America's Army Homepage, http://www.tioh.hqda.pentagon.mil/Catalog/HeraldryList.aspx?Cate goryId=9362&grp=2&menu=Uniformed%20Services, 검색일: 2015. 7. 30.

US Army Careers: Ways to Serve in the Army 홈페이지, http://www.goarmy.com/about/what-is-the-army/history.html, 검색일: 2017. 2. 3.

US Army Homepage, http://www.goarmy.com/about/personnel.html, 검색일: 2015. 7. 29.

US Army Value 홈페이지, https://www.army.mil/values/oath.html, 검색일: 2017. 2. 3.

Index

책 속의 책

우리말 번역본

제1부 Unit 6 ~ Unit 15
원어민 음성파일 제공

Military English

제2판

군사영어

조용만 · 최병욱 지음

• 군사영어의 기초부터 연합작전까지 단계적으로 구성
• 미군의 최신 교범 내용을 엄선하여 Reading Text로 활용
• Military English 1, 2의 한글 번역본이 있어 초급자도 쉽게 학습
• 국가의 간성(干城)들이 필수로 소지해야 할 군사영어 핵심 결정판!

북코리아

군사영어
우리말 번역본

조용만 · 최병욱 지음

북코리아

Contents

Military English I

Contents

Military English
I

Unit 3 | 작전실무용어 해설 I (인사/군수분야)

⊙Useful Expressions (유용한 표현)

1. 현대의 군사 복무제도는 세 개의 광범위한 인사 분류(체계)로 이루어진다.
2. 이것(인사분류제도)들은 사병, 부사관, 장교들로 구별되는 제네바 협약에 성문화되어 있다.
3. 사병들은 임관된 계급 아래에 있는 인력들이다.
4. 부사관 계급(지휘)의 기본이 되는 상병(CPL)들은 가장 작은 육군 단위부대의 조장으로 근무한다.
5. 부사관은 하급 군인들의 관리(돌봄)와 직접 통제의 책임을 지고 있다.
6. 위관급 장교들은 일부 부대에서 참모역할을 또한 수행한다.
7. 대표적인 육군 및 해병의 영관급 장교 계급은 대령, 중령, 소령이다.
8. 장군 계급은 일반적으로 대장, 중장, 소장, 준장을 포함한다.

⊙Useful Expressions(유용한 표현)

1. 어떤 단위부대는 더 큰 집단의 하위부대로 조직된 집단이 된다.

2. 분대는 가장 작은 군대의 전술 단위부대다.

3. 분대는 보통 분대장의 지휘하에 있다.

4. 소대는 분대보다 크고 중대보다 작다.

5. 소대장은 중·소위다.

6. 대대는 중대보다 크고 여단이나 연대보다 작다.

7. 대대는 중령의 지휘를 받는다.

8. 1개 연대에는 2개 이상의 대대가 있다.

9. 여단은 다양한 대대와 지원부대들로 구성되어 있다.

10. 여단의 지휘관은 대령이다.

11. 사단은 여단보다 크고 군단보다 작다.

12. 군단은 3성 장군이나 중장의 지휘를 받는다.

13. 육군은 군대의 가장 큰 부대다.

14. JPO(합동유류사무소)는 어디에 있는가?

15. 탄약을 보관할 때 가장 중요한 것은 탄창들 사이의 안전한 거리를 유지하고, 혼합저장을 방지하며, 로트번호별로 보관하는 것이다.

Unit 4 | 작전실무용어 해설 Ⅱ(작전분야)

⊙Useful Expressions(유용한 표현)

1. 할당표란 조직 장비의 기본 할당을 규정하는 장비 할당 문서를 말하며,

장비의 인가된 재고 목록을 향상, 수정 또는 변경할 수 있는 통제를 제공한다.

2. 보유는 창고에서 실제로 사용할 수 있고 발행 활동의 책임 있는 재산 장부 기록에 포함된 품목의 양을 의미한다.

3. 인가된 인원과 보직된 인원의 차이점은 무엇인가?

4. 주한미군의 최근 병력 현황을 알려 주시겠습니까?

p. 40

⊙Useful Expressions(유용한 표현)

1. 저는 당신에게 현 상태와 작전 준비 상태에 대해 보고해 드리고 싶습니다.

2. 소규모 병력에 의한 MDL(군사분계선)의 정찰과 횡단은 최근 전방 전선 지역에서 눈에 띄는 적의 활동이었습니다.

3. 전투 시설의 검사와 지속적인 수리도 관찰되었습니다.

4. 종심 지역에서는 6월과 8월 사이에 하계 지휘통제통신 훈련이 실시되었습니다.

5. 11월에 국가 차원의 평가 점검이 완료되었으며, 그 결과 북한은 최고 수준의 전투준비태세를 달성했다고 봅니다.

6. 최근 서해안에서 주목된 활동은 침투용 함정과 소형의 잠수정을 이용한 침투 훈련이었습니다.

7. 적의 침투와 국지도발은 항상 위협으로 존재합니다.

8. 아군의 작전개념, 전투편성 또는 임무에 어떤 변경이 필요합니까?

9. 현재 상황은 상급부대의 작전계획에 묘사되어 있는 적과 아군사항이 현저하게 상이합니까?

10. 전투 지역은 증강부대 위치, 예비진지, 보급 노드 및 전술 항공 기지를 결정하기 위한 기본적인 고려 사항입니다.

11. 우리의 목표는 D+3까지 각 적군 여단의 80%를 파괴하는 것입니다.

12. 야간에 이 기동로에서 작전하는 모든 항공기는 완전히 등화관제 되어

야 합니다.

Unit 5 | 작전실무용어 해설 Ⅲ (작전/정보분야)

p. 45

⊙Useful Expressions(유용한 표현)

1. 오늘 17시에 브리핑하게 자료를 보내주셔야겠습니다.
2. 이번 임무에 관한 좀 더 자세한 정보를 주시겠습니까?
3. 위기조치예규 작성 담당자는 누구입니까?
4. 미 제7공군 본부는 어디에 있습니까?
5. 이 전술은 현재 적용되지는 않았지만 우발 시에 사용될 수 있습니다.

p. 48

⊙Useful Expressions(유용한 표현)

1. 파쇄, 소각 또는 분쇄는 비밀정보를 파괴하는 데 사용된다.
2. 모든 인원은 연습장 출입자 명단에 등록되어 있어야 한다.
3. 유엔사/연합사의 인원과 시설에 대한 테러 및 정보전 위협 요소는 무엇인가?
4. 초기 연합특전사 인간정보자산 수집 팀은 어떻게 전개되어 있고 생존율은 얼마인가?
5. 지난밤 1800시경에 특수작전부대 활동이 비무장지대(DMZ)에서 목격되었다.
6. 북한의 잔존 전투력의 배치와 전투력은?

Unit 6 | 군대의 단위부대

p. 50

Useful Expressions

1. 어떤 단위부대는 더 큰 집단의 하위부대로 조직된 집단이 된다.
2. 분대는 가장 작은 군대의 전술 단위부대다.
3. 소대는 분대보다 크고 중대보다 작다.
4. 대대는 중령의 지휘를 받는다.
5. 1개 연대에는 2개 이상의 대대가 있다.
6. 여단은 다양한 대대와 지원부대들로 구성되어 있다.
7. 사단은 여단보다 크고 군단보다 작다.
8. 군단은 3성 장군이나 중장의 지휘를 받는다.
9. 육군은 군대의 가장 큰 부대다.

p. 51-54

Reading Text

◎ 분대로부터 전구군까지의 군대조직

분대. 분대는 가장 작고 기본적인 군대의 단위부대이다. 한 분대에 할당된 인원수는 다양하지만, 8명에서 11명이고 2개 이상의 사격조로 나누어져 있다.

소대. 소대는 중소위급 장교인 소대장과 그리고 3개 이상의 분대로 구성된다.

중대. 중대는 대위가 지휘하기에 적절한 부대이다. 중대본부와 3개 이상의 소대를 포함하고 있으며, 독립된 부대로 짧은 기간 동안 역할을 수행할 수 있다. 포병부대들은 중대 대신에 포대라는 용어가 사용된다. 기병 부대에서는 troop(부대)라는 용어가 중대 대신 사용된다.

대대. 전통적으로 대대는 지휘관과 지휘관의 참모, 대대본부 요원, 그리고 2개, 3개 또는 4개의 중대/포대/부대(troop)들을 포함한다. 기병부대에서는 대대 대신 편대라는 용어를 쓴다.

여단. 여단은 지휘관, 참모, 본부 요원, 그리고 보통 3개 대대로 구성된다.

연대. 연대라는 용어는 두 가지 의미가 있다. 전술적 의미로는 장갑화된 기갑부대(기병부대)가 여러 가지가 있는데, 기병부대는 3개 기병편대(대대급)로 구성되어 있다. 그러나 이 용어는 역사적으로 전령이라고 하는 의미와 더 밀접하게 연관되어 있다.

육군의 연대체제는 전투자격이 있는 요원들이 경험을 통해 그들 연대들과 편조되어 안정성과 연속성의 (전투) 환경을 조성하기 위한 것이다. 전투부대의 연대 이외도 다양한 전투지원 및 전투근무지원 병과들이 연대 체제를 도입하고 있다. 이러한 연대에 소속된 병사들은 특색 있는 부대 휘장을 착용한다.

사단. 현재 전투 사단은 기갑, 기계화, 중/경 보병, 공정, 공중 강습 등 6가지 종류의 사단이 있다. 사단은 소장급이 지휘하기에 적절하다. 각 사단은 지휘통제, 전투, 전투지원 및 전투근무지원 요소들을 가지고 있다. 지휘통제요소는 사단본부와 4~5개 여단본부들로 포함되어 있다. 전투 요소는 사단을 구성하기 위해 다양한 종류의 전투 대대의 비율로 포함되어 있다. 부대들의 조합은 특정 과업을 수행할 수 있도록 더욱 맞춤화할 수 있다.

군단. 군단은 군단본부, 2개 이상의 사단, 그리고 임무에 필요한 다른 조직들로 구성된다. 추가 부대들은 포병, 항공, 공병부대, 의무부대 및 기타 부대들로 구성될 수 있다.

`야전군.` 야전군이 필요한 경우, TDA(분대 및 할당표)의 본부들과 2개 이상의 군단, 그리고 지속적인 야전 작전에 필요한 모든 종류의 조직으로 구성된 조직이 될 수 있다.

`전구군.` 전구 작전에서 미군의 통합된 지휘부의 육군 구성 요소를 의미한다. 군단 조직의 상위 제대인 전구군은 전구 내에서 미군의 전투 및 전투지원 부대에 전투지원과 전투근무지원을 제공한다. 전구군은 각 전구에 맞춤화되어야 한다.

◎ 미군은 무엇으로 이루어졌는가?

미육군은 병사가 강하기 때문에 강하다. 미군은 어떤 임무를 수행하든, 혹은 어떤 계급이든 간에, 각각의 개인은 미국의 안보를 유지하는 역할을 한다. 675,000명 이상의 병사가 현재의 육군을 구성하고 있는데, 여기에는 현역 488,000명, 예비역 189,000명이 포함된다.

`구조.` 육군은 이처럼 많은 수의 군인으로 구성되어 있기 때문에, 각각 자신의 지휘자와 보고 체계를 갖춘 부대로 편성되어야 한다. 각 부대 — 부대 또는 사단 — 는 그 규모나 복잡성에 상관없이 어떤 임무에도 대응할 수 있도록 창설되어 있다.

`구성.` 육군은 크게 두 가지 요소로 이루어져 있는데, 현역과 예비역이다. 또한 사병, 부사관, 준위 그리고 임관된 장교들로 구성되어 있다.

Unit 7 | 소총부품 및 탄약

Useful Expressions

1. 소총은 탄알을 발사하거나 사격을 할 수 있도록 고안되었다.
2. 반자동화기는 방아쇠를 당길 때마다 한 발씩 발사된다.
3. 자동 소총은 네가 방아쇠에 압력을 유지하는 한 사격이 계속된다.
4. 가늠자는 목표를 직접 조준하는 데 사용된다.
5. 총몸은 격발장치(사격장치)를 수용하기 위해 설계되어 있다.
6. 방아쇠울은 방아쇠가 잘못으로 손상되거나 압력을 받지 않도록 보호한다.
7. 약실은 탄약을 유지하는 총열의 한 부분이다.
8. 기능고장은 어떤 화기가 만족스러운 작동의 실패를 말한다.

Reading Text

소총은 보병의 기본 무기다. 소총은 탄알을 발사하거나 사격을 할 수 있도록 고안되었다. M1소총은 반자동의 견착식 화기다. 이는 어깨에서 소총을 발사하는데 방아쇠를 당길 때마다 한 발씩 사격되는 것을 의미한다. 반면에 M16은 자동소총이다. 자동소총은 네가 방아쇠에 압력을 유지하거나 총몸에서 탄약이 공급될 때까지 계속 발사된다.

먼저, 소총의 몇 가지 부분을 설명하기로 하자. 총열은 탄약이 발사되는 금속관이다. 총구는 총알이 나오는(발사되는) 총구의 앞쪽 끝부분이다. 가늠자는 총열 위에 돌출되거나 튀어나와 있다. 이것들은 2개의 가늠자인데 가늠자(뒷부분)와 가늠쇠(앞부분)이다. 가늠자는 (총열의) 뒷부분 끝에 가늠쇠는 총열의 앞

부분 끝에 있다. 이 두 가늠자는 직접 목표를 조준하는 데 사용된다. 개머리는 소총을 유지하고 조준하고 발사하는 데 사용된다. 개머리판은 개머리의 뒷면이다. 착탈식 멜빵은 소총을 안정되게 운반하고 고정시키는 데 도움이 된다.

총몸은 격발장치(사격장치)를 수용하기 위해 설계되어 있다. 사격장치(격발장치)는 방아쇠, 공이치기, 공이치기 핀으로 구성된다. 압력에 의해 작동하는 방아쇠는 사격장치(격발장치)를 해제하는 것이다. 공이치기는 공이치기 핀을 작동하도록 설계되어 있고 공이치기 핀은 뇌관을 치도록 설계되어 있다. 소총수가 방아쇠를 (짜듯) 당기면 탄알이 발사된다. 방아쇠울은 방아쇠 뭉치를 분리할 수 있는 금속 고리이다. 그것은 방아쇠가 잘못으로 손상되거나 압력을 받지 않도록 보호하기 위해 사용된다.

다음으로, 탄약에 대해 이야기해보자. 카트리지는 탄환이다. 탄약의 완전한 둥근 형태는 뇌관, 탄피, 추진 장약, 발사체(탄두) 또는 탄환으로 구성된다. 탄두(발사체)는 표적을 타격하는 한 부분이다. 장약(추진제)이나 장약(추진제) 분말은 탄환을 앞으로 밀어내고, 스스로 타거나 폭발하고, 팽창하는 가스를 형성함으로써 에너지를 제공한다. 탄피 통은 뇌관과 장약(추진제)을 유지하고 추진체(장약)를 고정할 수 있는 용기다. 뇌관은 장약을 점화하는 데 사용된다.

마지막으로, 정비에 대해 간단히 살펴보자. 정비는 화기의 정지(사용 못함)나 오작동을 방지한다. 정지란 의도하지 않은 화기의 작동 순환의 중단이나 방해를 의미한다. 만약에 소총의 공이치기 핀이 구부러지거나 부러지면 화기의 무작동을 경험하게 된다. 오작동은 화기가 만족스럽게 작동하지 않는 실패를 의미한다. 예를 들어 방아쇠에 압력을 가할 때 안전장치가 풀릴 경우 오작동이 발생할 수 있다. 따라서 소총병은 소총의 사격 상태를 양호하게 하기 위해 항상 일상적인 총기손질, 세부적인 부품 검사, 수리, 기름칠 등의 모든 조치를 취해야 한다.

대부분의 기능고장(정지)은 더러워지거나 마모되거나 파손된 부품과 윤활유 부족으로 발생한다. 더러운 부품은 깨끗하게 해야 한다. 마른 부분은 깨끗이 닦고 기름칠을 해야 한다. 더럽고 건조한 부품은 둔하게 또는 느리게 작동하는 반면에 깨끗하고 기름칠이 제대로 된 부품은 부드럽고 쉽게 작동한다. 따라서 소총수는 항상 둔하거나 느리게 작동하는 문제점을 예방하기 위하여 자신의 무기의 작동 부분을 적절히 기름칠하고 깨끗이 유지해야 한다. 사용 또는 마모에 의해 손상된 마모 부품은 교체해야 한다. 부러진 부품은 교체해야 한다. 결함이 있는 부품의 기능고장(정지)이 있기에 소총수는 항상 이러한 결함을 주시하고 이를 제거하거나 제거하기 위한 교정 조치를 취해야 한다.

Unit 8 | 부대 병과 및 부호

p. 69

Useful Expressions

1. 직사각형은 단위부대를 나타내는 군대부호이다.
2. 깃발은 지휘소 또는 본부를, 그리고 삼각형은 관측소, 점(dot)과 수직선 및 X도 부대의 크기를 나타내는 데 사용된다.
3. 육군의 각 병과는 전투, 전투지원, 전투근무지원으로 분류된다.
4. 전투부대들은 직접적으로 실질적인 전투의 행위에 관여하는 장교와 사병들을 보유한 병과들이다.
5. 전투지원 부대들은 전투부대에 작전적 지원을 제공한다.
6. 전투근무지원 또는 근무지원은 기본적으로 장교와 사병들이 군에 행정 및/또는 군수지원을 제공하는 데 관심이 있는 병과들이다.
7. 보병부대는 훈련되고 장비되고 도보로 전투할 수 있도록 조직되어 있다.
8. 기갑부대들은 탑승하여 기동 지상전을 수행하기 위해 훈련되고 장비되고 조직되어 있다.

Reading Text

각 부대마다 고유의 군대부호가 있다. 직사각형은 단위부대를 나타내는 군대부호이고, 깃발은 지휘소 또는 본부를, 그리고 삼각형은 관측소, 점(dot)과 수직선 및 X도 부대의 크기를 나타내는 데 사용된다. 예를 들어 직사각형 위에 있는 점 하나는 분대를 나타내는 군대부호이고 점 2개는 반, 점 3개는 소대이다. 직사각형 위에 있는 하나의 수직선은 중대를 나타내고, 두 개의 수직선은 대대를, 세 개의 수직선은 연대를 나타낸다. 위에 두 개의 X가 있는 직사각형은 사단을 나타낸다. 군단의 상징은 직사각형 위에 세 개의 X로 이루어져 있다. 그리고 육군은 직사각형 위에 네 개의 X로 상징된다.

육군에는 많은 기본 병과가 있다. 육군의 각 병과는 전투, 전투지원 또는 전투근무지원으로 분류된다. 전투부대들은 직접적으로 실질적인 전투의 행위에 관여하는 장교와 사병들을 보유한 병과들이다. 전투병과는 방공포병, 기갑, 야전포병, 보병 등이다. 전투지원 부대들은 전투부대에 작전적 지원을 제공한다. 그들(전투지원부대)은 화학단, 공병단, 군사경찰단, 그리고 통신단 등이다. 전투근무지원 또는 근무지원은 기본적으로 장교와 사병들이 군에 행정 및/또는 군수지원을 제공하는 데 관심이 있는 병과들이다. 그들(전투근무지원부대)은 부관단(한국군은 인사행정병과로 통합됨), 경리단, 병기단, 병참단, 그리고 수송단 등이다. 육군의 모든 병과는 육군의 임무를 전체적으로 완수하기 위한 각자의 기능과 임무를 가지고 있다.

보병은 기본병과이고 육군의 부대이다. 보병은 다른 부대와 전투근무지원부대들이 주변에 그룹화되어 육군 전투력의 핵심을 형성한다. 보병부대는 훈련되고 장비되고 도보로 전투할 수 있도록 조직되어 있다. 소총은 보병의 기본화기이지만 기관총, 박격포, 수류탄 등도 운용된다. 공세작전에서 보병부대들은 적을 격파하거나 포로로 잡기 위하여 화력과 기동으로 적에게 근접한다. 방어 작전에서는 적의 공격을 화력, 근접전투, 역습 등으로 격퇴한다. 보병의 군대부호는 십자형 소총이다. 기갑부대 역시 육군의 전투력이며 기본병과에 속한다. 기갑부대들은 탑승하여 기동 지상전을 수행하기 위해 훈련되고 장비되고 조직되어 있다. 그들은 전차와 기타 장갑차량으로 장비되어 있다. 전차들은 승무원이나 병사들을 보호하기 위해 장갑판으로 둘러싸여 있다. 그들은 중궤도(차량)와 자주 전투차량에 탑승하기도 한다. 기갑의 주요 임무는 결정적인 작전을 획득하기 위해 장갑으로 보호된 화력, 기동력, 충격 효과 등을 이용하여 적과 기갑 전투작전을 수행하는 것이다. 기갑의 군대부호는 전차궤도이다.

야전포병과 방공포병은 육군의 전투력이며 기본병과들이다. 야전포병은 보병전력에게 화력지원을 제공하기 위해 조직되고 훈련되어 있다. 야전포병은 대포와 미사일로 장비되어 적 표적에 재래식 화력이나 핵을 투하(placing)한다. 그들은 적의 위험표적을 파괴하거나 무력화함으로써 전투부대에게 연속적이고 적시적인 시간에 화력지원을 제공한다. 야전포병의 군대부호는 탄환 또는 발사체로 표시한다. 방공포병은 대포와 미사일로 장비되어 있어 핵이나 비핵 화력을 적의 표적에 투하한다. 방공포병의 주요 임무는 적대적인 공정부대 수송기와 미사일과 교전하여 파괴하거나 그 효과를 무력화 또는 감소시키는 것이다.

공병단(公兵團)은 육군의 전투지원부대 중 하나이다. 공병부대들은 건설, 철거(폭파), 도로 및 교량 공사, 위장 등을 관리한다. 폭파란 화력, 수력을 사용하거나 폭발물, 기계 또는 다른 수단을 사용하여 어떤 것(things)들을 파괴하는 것이다. 공병대는 교량을 자신의 군대부호로 사용한다.

통신단은 병과의 장교들이 통신, 기상, 사진 및 사거리 탐지 작업 등에 관련된 업무를 하는 전투병과이며 전투근무지원 병과이다. 통신부대들은 통신 및 전자 장비를 갖추고 있다. 통신부대의 주요기능은 야전에서 육군의 임무에 긴요한 전투지원 통신, 모든 기타 육군, 기갑, 목표 작전에서 요구되는 통신과 전자지원을 제공한다. 통신단의 군대부호는 번개섬광이다.

화학단은 육군의 기본병과 중 하나이다. 화학부대는 화학, 방사능, 연막과 화염 작전 및 생물학전 방어를 책임지고 있다. 화학단 장교는 군사 전술에 있어 기본적인 자격을 갖추어야 하고 화생방 활동과 환경에서 병력과 화기의 전술적, 전략적 운용과 방어에 특히 자격을 갖춰야 한다.

군사경찰단은 전투, 전투지원, 전투근무지원 임무를 수행한다. 군사경찰은 군법, 명령, 규정의 집행과 더불어 범죄의 예방과 조사를 담당한다.

병기단은 기술 근무지원 병과이다. 병기단은 주로 전쟁에 사용되는 모든 무기와 탄약을 책임진다. 병기단은 또한 장비나 화기의 정비에 사용되는 보급을 책임지고 있다. 병기부대의 군대부호는 폭탄을 사용한다.

수송단은 기술 또는 부대의 전투근무를 지원한다. 수송단은 육군의 부여된 임무 완수를 위해 요구되는 인력과 물자의 이동을 담당하고 있다. 물자(군수품)는 모두 군사 활동의 장비, 유지, 작전(운용), 공급에 필요한 품목들이다. 수송부대의 군대부호는 바퀴이다.

병참단은 근무지원 병과다. 병참단의 주요기능은 육군 물자를 획득, 공급 및 관리하고, 모든 제대에서 육군에 대한 군수 근무지원을 제공한다. 병참단은 열쇠를 자신의 군대부호로 사용한다.

Unit 9 | 소대와 분대

p. 82

Useful Expressions

1. 보병 소대와 분대의 기본 임무는 적군에 근접하는 것이다.

2. 보병 소총소대와 분대들은 공세작전, 방어작전 그리고 안정화 작전이나 민간 권한 업무를 방어적으로 지원하는데 최적화되어 있다.

3. 보병 소총소대와 분대원들은 METT-TC에 근거하여 단독으로 또는 연합전투부대로서 임무를 수행할 수 있도록 편성을 할 수 있다.

4. 보병부대를 운용하기 위한 근본적인 고려사항은 부대의 임무, 유형, 장비, 능력, 한계 및 조직에서 비롯된다.

5. 이 집중화된 권위는 그(지휘자)가 부대의 사기와 단결을 유지하고 결정적으로 행동할 수 있게 해준다.

Reading Text

◎ 소병소총소대와 분대의 임무

보병 소대와 분대의 주요임무는 화력과 기동의 수단으로 적을 격파, 포획 또는 화력으로 적의 습격을 격퇴, 근접전투, 역습을 하기 위하여 적에게 근접하는 것이다. (작전에) 성공하기 위하여, 보병소대와 분대들은 공격적이고 육체적으로 적합하고 사기충천하고 그리고 잘 훈련되어 있다. 보병부대의 고유한 전략적 기동성은 상이한 작전 환경에서 상황에 대응하여 신속한 운용에 준비될 필요성을 요구한다. 이 장에서는 작전환경에 대한 간략한 논의와 통일된 지상 작전의 작전개요, 지상전 준칙에 대해 설명한다. 이장은 보병 소대와 분대 내의 임무와 책임뿐만 아니라 역할과 편성에 초점을 맞추고 있다.

보병 소총소대와 분대들은 공세작전, 방어작전 그리고 안정화 작전이나 민간 권한 업무를 방어적으로 지원하는 데 최적화되어 있다. 보병 소총소대와 분대는 전 세계에 배치(운용)될 수 있고 통일된 지상 작전을 수행할 수 있다.

◎ 편성

보병 소총소대와 분대원들은 METT-TC에 근거하여 단독으로 또는 연합 전투부대로서 임무를 수행할 수 있도록 편성을 할 수 있다. 전차, 브래들리 전투차량(BFV)과 스트라이커 보병 수송차량(ICV) 공병, 기타 지원요소 등을 포함한 연합군의 상승효과를 통해 그 효율성이 증대된다. 보병 소총 소대와 분대는 연합군으로서 그 제한점을 최소화하면서 팀 요소의 강점을 활용할 수 있다.

보병부대들은 모든 지형 및 기상 조건에서 운용될 수 있다. 그들은 신속한 전략적 운용(배치) 때문에 지배적인 전투력이 되는지도 모른다. 그럴 경우, 조기에 주도권을 획득하고 취할 수 있으며, 육지를 탈취하고 확보할 수 있으며, 적을 저지하기 위해 대규모 화력을 퍼부을 수 있다. 보병부대는 특히 도시 지형에 효과적이며, 적진 후방으로 침투해 신속하게 이동할 수 있다. 지휘자는 헬기와 공중수송을 이용하여 이동성을 향상시킬 수 있다. 보병부대를 운용하기 위한 근본적인 고려사항은 부대의 임무, 유형, 장비, 능력, 한계 및 조직에서 비롯된다. 기타 능력들은 부대훈련 프로그램, 리더십, 사기, 인력의 강점, 그리고 많은 기타 요소들로부터 기인한다. 이들의 다른 능력들은 계속해서 현재 상황에 기초하여 변화된다.

◎ 임무와 책임

1) 소대장

소대장은 개인적인 시범을 보임으로써 소대를 지휘하며 부하들의 전반적인 것에 대한 완벽한 권한을 갖고 모든 소대가 하는 일이나 실패에 대한 책임이 있다. 이 집중화된 권위는 그가 부대의 규율(사기)과 단결을 유지하고 결정적인 행동을 할 수 있게 해준다. 그(소대장)는 모든 상황에서 중대장의 의도 내에서 특별한 지침 없이도 주도권을 행사할 준비가 되어 있어야 한다. 소대장은 그의 병사들과 소대의 운용(배치) 방법, 소대의 화기, 그리고 그 시스템을 잘 알고 있어야 한다. 소대 선임하사의 전문성을 신뢰하고 소대장은 모든 소대 문제에 대해 정기적으로 그와 상의해야 한다. 작전기간 동안 소대장은 ―

- 소대원들이 상급 본부 임무들을 지원하도록 이끌어야 한다. 소대장

은 자신의 행동을 그에게 부여된 임무, 상급 지휘관들의 의도와 작
전개념에 근거를 두게 된다.

- 부대지휘절차(작전수행과정)에 따라 수행한다.
- 기동 분대들과 전투 요소 (통제)
- 분대들의 노력을 동시화한다.
- 소대의 다음 "이동"을 예견한다.
- 지원 자산 요청 및 통제
- 분대와 소대에 임무형 지휘 시스템이 가용하도록 운용
- 전면, 3차원 경계 유지가 강화되도록 분대장들 점검
- 주요 화기 시스템의 배치를 통제하는 화기분대장의 점검
- 정확하고 시기적절한 보고서들의 발행
- 임무를 완수하기 위해 가장 필요한 위치에 자기 자신을 위치시킴
- 명확한 업무와 목적을 분대들에게 부여
- 2단계 상급(중대 및 대대) 지휘관의 임무 및 의도 이해
- 계획을 수립하는 동안 소대 선임하사와 분대장들로부터 현보유 상
  태 보고서를 받음
- 장애물 계획 발전에 대한 협조 및 지원
- 재산 관리에 대한 책임 및 감독

　　소대장은 상황 이해를 발전시키고 유지하기 위해 작업한다. 다음은 어떤
산물을 (생산하기) 위한 4가지 요소이다. 첫째, 소대장은 현 상황 조건의 아군,
적군, 중립군 그리고 지형 상황에서 무슨 일이 일어나고 있는지 파악을 시도
해야 한다. 둘째, 그는 임무를 완수해야 하는 최종상태를 알고 있어야 한다.
셋째, 그의 부대가 현재로부터 최종상태로 이동하는 동안 발생할 주요 행동
(조치사항)들과 사건들을 결정해야 한다. 마지막으로 그는 전체적인 위험을 평
가해야 한다.

2) 소대 선임하사관(한국군은 부소대장)

소대 선임하사관은 소대에서 가장 경험이 많은 부사관이자 2인자로 소대 장병들의 리더십, 규율, 훈련, 복지에 대한 책임을 맡고 있다. 그는 매사에 모범이 된다. 그는 기준과 소대 규율을 유지함으로써 소대장을 보좌한다. 그는 매사에 모범이 된다. 그는 기준과 소대 규율을 유지함으로써 소대장을 보좌한다. 그의 전문성은 전술적 기동, 화기 및 시스템의 운용, 작전지속지원, 행정, 경계, 책임, 전투 기능 방호, 병사 관리 등을 포함한다. 2인자로서 소대 선임하사관은 소대장이 규정한 것 외에는 공식적 업무를 담당하지 않는다. 그러나 전통적으로 소대 선임하사관은 ―

- 전투 전 점검 및 검사를 감독하는 것을 포함하여 소대가 임무를 완수할 준비가 되어 있는지 확인한다.
- 적절한 보고서와 상급사령부에서 필요한 차후 보고서들에 대한 소대장 보고사항을 최신화한다.
- 소대장의 역할과 책임을 떠맡을 준비를 한다.
- 전술 작전 간 소대 내에서 임무분할, 급습 또는 공격 간 요원들에 대한 지원 그리고 경계정찰과 같은 제한되지도 않지만 포함될 수 있는 과업위주 편성요소들에 대한 책임을 맡는다.
- 소대의 사기, 규율 및 건강에 대한 관찰
- 교전에 도움이 되는 가장 필요한 곳에 위치(화력의 기저가 되거나 공격 요소에 필요한)한다.
- 분대장들의 행정, 군수, 정비보고서를 받고 식량, 물, 연료 및 탄약을 요청한다.
- 상급 사령부에 군수지원을 요청하며, 통상 중대 선임하사관이나 보좌장교와 협조한다.
- 병사들이 모든 장비를 유지 관리하도록 보장한다.
- 소대가 목표에서 진지강화 후 그리고 소대가 재편성된 후에 탄약과

물자가 적절히 균등하게 분배되도록 보장한다.

- 작전하기 이전에 부대 전투휴대량을 관리하고 작전간 군수 상태를 관찰한다.
- 부대의 전사상자 수집소를 설치 및 운영한다. 여기에는 소대 의료진과 구호/들것조를 지휘하여 전사상자를 이동시키는 것, 소대 병력 수준의 정보 유지, 소대 전사상자 보고서의 통합 및 전달, 보충병의 수령 및 배치 등이 포함된다.
- 분대 및 소대에 사용 가능한 디지털 임무지휘 시스템을 운용한다.
- 소대장의 지침과 지시에 따라 병사들에게 보급품이 분배되도록 보장한다.
- 병사들에 대한 장비와 보급에 책임을 진다.
- 병사들에 대한 지도, 상담 및 멘터 역할
- 표준과 소대의 규율 유지
- 2단계 상급부대(중대 및 대대)의 임무와 지휘관의 의도 이해

Unit 10 | 중대편성

Useful Expressions

1. 보병, 중보병, 스트라이커, 그리고 유격 등 네 종류의 보병 소총 중대로 구성되어 있다.
2. 보병 소총 중대의 대부분 전투력은 고도로 훈련된 분대와 소대에 달려 있다.
3. 보병 부대들은 대부분의 지형과 기상조건에서 효과적으로 작전할 수 있다.

4. 신속돌파 작전에서 그들은 신속한 전략적 전개능력 때문에 우세한 전투력이 될 수 있다.

5. 유격부대들은 어떤 환경에서도 모든 군종별 특수 작전 부대들과(또는 지원을 받아서) 합동 타격 작전을 실시할 수 있도록 신속한 전개가 가능하고 훈련되었고 공정작전 능력이 있다.

6. 중보병 부대들은 브래들리 전투 장갑 차량에 탑승한다.

7. 스트라이커 여단 전투팀(SBCT)의 대대들은 주요 기동부대 역할을 한다.

Reading Text

보병소총중대들의 유형과 특성

보병, 중보병, 스트라이커, 그리고 유격 등 네 종류의 보병 소총 중대로 구성되어 있다. 이들 중 일부는 공정작전과 공중강습과 같은 전문화된 능력을 가지고 있다. 그들 사이에는 차이가 존재하지만 편성, 전술, 운용 등에서 어느 정도 유사성을 지니고 있다. 주요한 차이점들은 수송의 수단과 전장에서, 그리고 유기적인 지원 자산의 가용성에 있다.

보병 소총 중대의 대부분 전투력은 고도로 훈련된 분대와 소대에 달려 있다. 중대는 모든 유형의 지형과 기상 그리고 가시조건 하에서 기동성이 있고 모든 형태의 이동을 이용할 수 있다. 중대들은 또한 야시장비와 감시 장비들을 사용한다.

◎ 보병

보병 부대들은 대부분의 지형과 기상조건에서 효과적으로 작전할 수 있다.

신속돌파 작전에서 그들은 신속한 전략적 전개능력 때문에 우세한 전투력이 될 수 있다. 그럴 경우, 조기에 주도권을 획득하고 취할 수 있으며, 육지를 탈취하고 확보할 수 있으며, 적을 저지하기 위해 대규모 화력을 퍼부을 수 있다. 보병부대는 특히 도시지형에 효과적이며, 적진 후방으로 침투해 신속하게 이동할 수 있다. 지휘관은 헬기와 공중수송을 이용하여 이동성을 향상시킬 수 있다.

◎ 유격

유격부대들은 어떤 환경에서도 모든 군종별 특수 작전 부대들과(또는 지원을 받아서) 합동 타격 작전을 실시할 수 있도록 신속한 전개가 가능하고 훈련되었고 공정작전 능력이 있다. 그들은 국가 정책과 목표를 지원하기 위해 특별한 군사 작전을 계획하고 수행한다. 그들은 또한 지리적 전투 지휘관들을 지원하기 위한 직접 행동 임무를 수행하고 다른 연합 부대 요소들과 통합될 때는 재래식 보병부대들로서 작전하기도 한다. (FM 7-85는 유격작전용 기준교범이다.)

◎ 중보병

중보병 부대들은 브래들리 전투 장갑 차량에 탑승한다. 이들 부대들은 중여단 전투팀(HBCT)의 연합군 대대에 있는 M1 에이브람스 전차와 함께 임무 위주로 조직된다. 이 중부대들은 엄청난 연합부대 화력을 보유하고 기동성이 높다. 그들은 기갑화된 적에 대항하여 다소 제한적인 지형과 전투에 가장 적합하다.

◎ 스트라이커

　스트라이커여단전투팀(SBCT)의 대대들은 주요 기동부대 역할을 한다. 이 대대는 3X3, 즉 각각 3개 소총소대로 편성된 3개 소총중대로 구성되어 있다. 중대들은 60mm 편제반과 분리형 81mm 박격포, 이동식 대포시스템(MGS) 소대, 저격팀으로 구성된 연합 부대로 전투한다. 스트라이커여단전투팀 부대들은 스트라이커 보병 수송 차량(ICV)으로 장비되어 있다. SBCT(스트라이커여단전투팀) 대대는 다른 보병들의 대부분 능력에 추가하여 스트라이커 차량의 이동성을 보유하고 있다. 스트라이커 중대들은 현대 전투 작전의 전 영역에 걸쳐 작전이 가능하다. 그들은 제한된 지역이나 심하게 제한된 지역 내에서도 전술적 융통성을 유지하도록 편성되어 있다.

◎ 추가적인 능력 및 제한사항

　다음은 보병 소총 중대의 능력과 제한사항을 보여준다.

1) 능력

- 주로 야간에 모든 종류의 환경에서 공세적이고 방어적인 작전들을 수행한다.
- 지형의 탈취, 확보, 점령 및 유지
- 적군의 격파, 무력화, 진압, 저지, 교란, 차단, 유도, 고착
- 적 장애물 돌파
- 적을 기만하기 위한 양동 및 시위
- 아군에 대한 차장 및 보호
- 정찰, 거부, 우회, 소탕, 포위 및 격리 (이러한 업무들은 지형과 적 모두를 지향할 수 있다.)

- 소부대 작전 수행

- 공중강습작전에 참여

- 공정작전에 참여(공정 및 유격 중대들)

- 탑승 또는 특수작전부대와 연계하여 작전

- 상륙작전에 참여

2) 제한사항

- 제한된 전투지원(CS) 및 작전지속지원 자산

- 제한된 차량 이동성

- 개활지에서 작전할 경우 적의 기갑, 포병, 항공 자산에 취약

- 제한된 제독 능력 때문에 적 화학, 생물, 방사능, 핵 및 고성능 폭발물(CBRNE) 공격에 취약

◎ 편성

유격부대들을 제외하고 모든 보병소총중대 편성은 동일한 장비표(TOE)를 가진다. 공중 강습과 공정작전 훈련을 받은 중대들은 독특한 능력과 관련된 몇 가지 특수 장비를 필요로 한다. 그러나, 이러한 몇 가지 차이에도 불구하고, 임무와 운용 시 고려사항과 전술들은 거의 동일하다.

Unit 11 | 독도법

Useful Expressions

1. 지도는 지구 표면의 일부를 축척으로 그린 그래픽(도식적) 표현이다.
2. 지도는 지구 표면을 선으로 그린 것이다.
3. 인공물들(문화적 특징)은 인간이 만든 것들이다.
4. 지형물(지리적 특징들)은 자연적으로 조성된 것들이다.
5. 방안좌표법은 지도 위에서 지점들의 위치를 찾는 데 사용된다.
6. 좌표는 격자 방안 내의 지점을 식별하는 데 사용된다.
7. 안부는 두 언덕 꼭대기 사이의 능선이다.
8. 지형적(지리적) 정상은 언덕 꼭대기에서 가장 높은 고도를 말한다.
9. 군사지도는 방안좌표법을 통해 당신의 정확한 위치를 파악할 수 있다.
10. 당신은 이곳으로부터 떨어져(또는 벗어나게 되어) 있어서 행운이다.

Reading Text

  지도는 지구 표면의 일부를 축척으로 그린 그래픽(도식적) 표현이다. 지도는 지상에서 발견되는 형상을 나타내기 위해 색상, 부호, 표식(라벨)들을 사용한다. 지도는 인구 밀집 장소와 이동 경로 및 통신 경로와 같은 지상의 특징적인 것들 사이의 존재, 위치 및 거리에 대한 정보를 제공한다. 또한 지형의 변화, 자연적 특징물의 고도 및 초목 두께의 범위를 나타낸다.

  지도는 지구 표면의 전부 또는 일부를 도식한 일종의 선 그림이다. 지도상에서는 문화적 그리고 지리적 표면 특징들을 보여준다. 문화적인 특징(인공물)들은 인간이 만든 것이다. 건물, 학교, 전신선들은 인공물에 속한다. 지형물(지리적 특징들)은 자연적으로 조성된 것들이다. 산, 늪, 호수는 지형물들이다. 이러한 자연적, 인위적 특징들이 지도상에 부호에 의해 표시된다. 따라서 지도 판독의 핵심은 기호(부호)에 의해 지상의 형상들을 식별하는 방법을 아는 것이다.

색깔들은 때때로 지도를 읽는 데 중요한 역할을 한다. 만약 당신이 당신의 지도상에 있는 색상이 어떤 종류의 특징을 나타내는 것인지 안다면, 당신은 그것을 쉽게 판독할 수 있다. 문화적 혹은 인공적 특징은 통상 검은색으로 나타나지만, 빨간색은 인간이 만든 특징물들을 유형이나 용도에 대해 분류하는 데도 사용된다. 예를 들어 주요 도로, 건설된 지역, 특수한 기능물 등이 그것이다. 지리적 특징은 파란색, 녹색, 갈색과 같은 다른 색으로 나타난다. 지리적 특징(지형물들)은 파란색, 녹색, 갈색과 같은 다른 색으로 나타난다. 푸른색은 호수, 강, 늪과 같은 물의 특징을 나타내는 데 사용된다. 녹색은 숲, 과수원, 포도밭 등과 같은 식물을 식별하는 데 사용된다. 갈색, 또는 때때로 회색은 등고선과 같은 기복지형들을 묘사하는 데 사용된다.

군사지도는 군대부호와 지형부호들을 사용한다. 군대부호는 특정 군부대의 활동이나 시설물를 식별하는 데 사용된다. 지형 부호들은 언덕, 계곡, 강, 호수, 운하, 다리, 도로, 도시 등을 포함한 지역의 표면을 식별하는 데 사용된다. 환언하면, 지형부호는 지리적 특징뿐만 아니라 문화적인 모습들을 보여주기 위해 사용된다.

지리적 특징들은 군사 지도상에 등고선으로 묘사된다. 예를 들어, 언덕 꼭대기는 지도상에서 폐쇄된 등고선으로 그려진다. 지상에서, 그것은 언덕의 정상이 된다. 만약 당신이 언덕 꼭대기에 있다면 지면들이 사방으로 경사져 내려간다. 그것(언덕 꼭대기)은 지리적 정상이나 군사적 정상을 가지게 된다. 지형적 정상은 언덕 꼭대기에서 가장 높은 고도에 있지만, 군사적 정상은 언덕 기슭(언덕 하단부분)까지 경사면을 관찰할 수 있는 언덕의 전방 경사면의 선상이 된다. 골짜기는 U자 또는 V자의 기저부분에서 더 높은 지표면을 가리키는 U자- 또는 V자 등고선으로 그려진다. 계곡은 언덕이나 산 사이에 있는 낮은 육지의 넓은 지역이다. 그것(계곡)은 보통 강이나 시냇물을 가지고 있다. 당신이 계곡에 있다면 지면이 세 방향으로 경사져 있고 한 방향은 아래(하단)로 내려간다.

당신이 보다시피, 산등성이(산맥)는 길고 좁은 지상의 높은 곳이다. 환언하면, 산맥은 산이나 고지의 정상이 길게 연장된 길고 좁은 융기된 형성물이라고 할 수 있다. 당신이 능선에 서 있다면, 지면은 한 방향으로는 오르막으로 갈 것이고 그 밖의 세 방향은 아래로 향할 것이다. 지도에서는 U자 또는 V자의 밑부분이 더 높은 지면에서 멀어지는 것을 가리키는 U자 또는 V자 모양의 등고선으로 그려진다. 안부는 두 개의 언덕꼭대기나 산 정상의 사이에 있는 산등성이다. 다시 말하면, 두 봉우리나 정상 사이에 위치한다. 당신이 안부에 있다면, 2개의 반대 방향으로 더 높은 지표면이 있고 2개의 반대 방향으로는 더 낮은 지표면이 있다. 지도상에서는 8자 모양의 등고선으로 나타난다.

전투지역이나 지도상에서 길을 잃지 않기 위해서 우리는 정확한 위치나 주소를 찾는 방법을 알아야 한다. 전투 시에는 거리 주소가 없지만, 군사지도는 방안좌표법의 방법으로 당신의 정확한 위치를 알아낼 수 있다. 군사지도에는 검은색 평행선이 상하(남북)로 나 있고 (동서로) 교차하고 있다. 이 선들은 격자라고 불리는 작은 정사각형으로부터 왔다. 그 선들은 지도 그림의 바깥 가장자리를 따라 번호가 부여되어 있다. 우리는 그 숫자들을 사용하여 각각의 사각형의 이름을 지어줄 수 있다. 일정한 격자방안의 정확한 숫자를 알려면 먼저 왼쪽으로부터 오른쪽으로 읽고 나서 위쪽으로 읽으면 된다. 예를 들면, 왼쪽에서 시작하여 당신 위치의 전반부인 11이 될 때까지 오른쪽으로 읽고 나서, 마지막 절반인 81까지 위로 읽으면 된다. (즉) 당신의 위치는 격자 방안 1181 어딘가에 있다. 격자 방안 1181은 당신의 일반적인 근처를 제공하지만, 그 격자 방안 안에는 많은 지점들이 있다. 당신의 위치를 더 정확하게 하기 위해, 우리는 첫 번째 전반부에 다른 번호를 추가하고 나머지 반에 또 다른 번호를 추가한다. 그렇게 되면 당신의 주소는 4개 대신 6개의 번호들을 가지게 된다. 이 6개의 숫자들은 당신의 좌표라고 불린다. 만약 당신이 항상 당신의 정확한 좌표들을 안다면, 당신은 절대로 길을 잃을 수 없다.

Unit 12 | 통신

Useful Expressions

p. 118

1. 메시지는 한 사람이 다른 사람에게 보내는 보고서, 명령 또는 다른 정보를 말한다.
2. 간결한 메시지는 간단하고, 불필요한 말들은 전혀 포함하고 있지 않다.
3. 송신(전송)은 들릴 수 있게 전달되어야 한다.
4. 유선과 무선은 메시지들을 전달하는 주요 수단들이다.
5. 전파방해는 송신의 수신을 막기 위한 고의적인 의도된 간섭이다.
6. 음성문자는 음성송신 간 혼동이나 오류들을 피하기 위해 사용된다.
7. 숫자들은 숫자 하나하나로 발음한다.
8. 잠깐만 기다리세요, 제가 그를 데려올게요.
9. 문의 사항이 있으면, 탱고 4129로 전화하세요.

Reading Text

p. 119-122

메시지는 한 사람이 다른 사람에게 보내는 보고서, 명령 또는 다른 정보를 말한다. 대부분의 메시지는 유선이나 무선으로 전송된다. 전선은 한 전화기를 다른 전화기와 연결하는 데 사용된다. 무선은 한 무선 세트와 다른 무선 세트를 연결하는 데 사용된다. 잘 준비된 메시지는 명확하고 완전하며 간결한 세 가지 요건을 충족해야 한다. 명확한 메시지는 쉽게 이해된다. 완전한 메시지는 무엇을, 언제, 어디에서라는 질문에 잘 응답된다. 간결한 메시지는 간단하다. 즉, 불필요한 말들을 포함하고 있지 않다.

메시지는 들을 수 없다면 가치가 없다. 즉, 송신은 잘 전달되어야 하며 들을 수 있어야 한다. 하지만, 소리 또는 신호 간섭으로 인해 송신이 들리지 않을 수 있다. 간섭은 바람직하지 않은 자연적 또는 인공적 소음이거나 또는 송신 수신을 어렵게 하는 신호들을 말한다. 전파방해는 송신의 수신을 막기 위한 고의적인 의도된 간섭이다. 다시 말하면, 전파방해는 신호들의 수신을 고의적으로 간섭한다. 적의 전파방해는 무선 통신소 감독관에게 상세히 보고해야 한다.

음성문자는 음성송신 간 혼동이나 오류들을 피하기 위해 사용된다. 이 알파벳은 오해받을 수 있는 단어들이나 어려운 단어들을 철자(스펠링)로 말하는 데 사용된다.

숫자들은 숫자 하나하나로 말해지지만, 수백, 수천은 이런 방법으로 말해진다. 즉 2,500은 "tu faif hʌndrəd(투 하프 한드레도)"이고, 15,000은 "wʌn faif θáuzənd(완 하프 싸우전드)"로 말한다. 당신이 기억하다시피, 지도 좌표들도 숫자 하나하나로 발음한다.

무전 교환원들은 긴 문장을 대신해서 통화약어(proword)를 사용한다. 그들은 음성송신을 가능한 짧고 명확하게 유지하기 위해 통화약어를 사용한다. 여기에 음성 전송에 일반적으로 사용되는 통화약어들이 있다.

수신여부	네가 이 메세지를 수신했고 이해했는가를 나에게 알려 달라.
정정	내가 이 송신에서 실수를 했다. 정확한 정보는 ...이다.
숫자로 부르겠다	숫자들 또는 숫자들이 뒤따른다.
내가 복창한다	다음은 당신의 지시에 따르는 나의 응답이다.
재송한다	나는 지적된 전송(또는 부분)을 반복한다.
음성문자(스펠링)로 송신한다	나는 다음 단어를 음성으로 철자화해서 말할 것이다.
확인한다	다음 메시지(또는 일부)는 당신의 요청에 따라 확인하는 것이며 반복한다. (확인하는 것은 정확성을 점검하는 것이다.) VERIFY(확인)에 대한 회신으로만 사용한다.
교신 끝	이것이 당신에게 보내는 내 송신의 끝이며 어떠한 대답도 요구되거나 기대되지 않는다.

이상	이것은 당신에 대한 내 전송의 끝이며 너의 응신이 필요하다. 계속 송신하라.
감도체크	내 신호의 강도와 가독성은? 즉, 내 말 어떻게 들려?
복창	당신이 받은 대로 모든 전송을 다시 나에게 정확히 반복하라.
수신양호	당신이 그것을 수신한 것처럼 나도 나에게 보낸 당신의 마지막 전송을 수신했다.
재송	당신의 송신을 모두 반복하라.
무선침묵	즉시 송신을 중지하라.
무선침묵대기 해제	정상적인 전송을 재개(시작)하라.
천천히 말해라	전송의 속도를 줄여라.
정확히 수신했으며 지시대로 시행하겠다	나는 너의 신호를 받았고, 그것을 이해했고, 따를 것이다. 수신인만 사용할 수 있음. ROGER(수신양호)의 의미는 WILCO(시행할 것임)의 의미에 포함되기 때문에, 통화약어는 더 이상 함께 사용되지 않음.

AN/PRC-150 1 무전기 ─ 그림 12-1 참조 ─ 는 부대들에게 신속한 이동성, 넓은 작전지역의 지원으로 고주파 무전 능력의 상태를 제공한다. 고주파 신호들은 초단파(SINGGARS: 단일 채널 지상 및 공중무선 체제)나 극초단파(EPLRS: 강화된 진지위치 보고 시스템)보다 지상에서 더 먼 거리를 이동한다. 왜냐하면 고주파 신호들은 지형과 식물과 같은 요인들에 의해 덜 영향을 받기 때문이다. AN/PRC-150 I 및 AN/VRC-104(V) 1 및 (V) 3 차량 무선 시스템들은 혼잡한 통신 전장에서 위성 가용성에 의존하지 않고도 부대들에게 초과가시선(BLOS) 통신들을 제공한다. 그 시스템 휴대용과 차량용 배치(무전기)들은 부대들이 이동간 믿을 만한 통신과 데이터 및 영상의 신속한 송신을 허용하고 보장해 준다.

Unit **13** | 전투훈련

Useful Expressions

1. 1개 소대가 505 고지 정상에 참호를 구축하였다.
2. 'A' 중대는 언덕 남쪽의 평지에서 대형을 갖추고 있다.
3. 적 방어의 가장 약한 지점은 서쪽 경사면에 있다.
4. 목표는 접근(로)을 차단하고 있는 적의 진지다.
5. 과업은 화력으로 적을 고착시키는 것이다.
6. 그 중대에는 박격포 반이 배속되어 있다.
7. 3소대는 예비이다.
8. 안개 속을 틈타 그들은 언덕의 기슭에 도달했다.
9. 저항 거점은 소탕되어야 한다.
10. 그것은 "적을 끝내라"는 의미이다.

Reading Text

◎ 전투준비

　보병중대들은 적에 근접하여 적을 사살하고 적 장비를 파괴하고, 저항하려는 적의 의지를 산산조각 낼 수 있도록 조직되고 장비되어 있다. 이 긴밀한 개인의 전투력은 숙련된 병사들과 지휘자를 가진 전투 준비가 된 부대들을 필요로 한다. 이들 부대들은 강인하고 철저하며 힘든 훈련을 통해 기민한 전투력으로 발전한다. 이것은 보병 부대의 복잡한 작전환경에서 보병부대들의 효율적인 운용을 이해하는 지휘자들을 요구한다. 모든 부대들은 수색정찰 기술을 익히는 광범위한 훈련을 받는다. 이를 통해 철저한 상황 파악이 가능해져 보병 중대장들이 적의 의사결정 주기 내에서 압도적이고 정확한 전투력 투입을 보장한다. 이러한 전투력과 민첩성의 정밀한 적용은 시설과 비전투원의 피해를 감소시키는 데 도움이 된다.

◎ 병사

지상 전투의 성공적인 결과는 보병에게 달려 있다. 훈련되고 잘 지도된 팀으로 형성된 각개 병사들은 전투 준비가 된 군대를 만든다. 보병 병사들보다 더 다양한 전투기술을 숙달한 병사들은 없다. 병사들은 기본 총검에서 첨단 박격포와 다목적 미사일에 이르기까지 무기 사용에 관한 권위자다. 필요에 따라 병사들은 기술자, 의사, 대공 방어자, 선임 무선 운용자(교환병), 외교관, 컴퓨터 전문가, 정비사, 건설 전문가 등의 역할을 동시에 할 수 있다. 병사들은 생존자들이다. 왜냐하면 어떤 조건하에서도 작전을 수행할 수 있고 어려운 조건에서도 승리를 획득하기 때문이다. 또한, 모든 병사들은 하나의 센서로서 작전지역에서 지휘관 주요첩보 요구(CCIR)와 관련된 세부사항들을 적극적으로 관찰하도록 훈련받았다는 것을 의미하며, 그들의 보고는 유능하고 간결하고 정확하다. 그들의 지휘자들은 적시에 정보를 생성하기 위해 어떻게 그들의 부대에서 정보의 수집, 처리 및 배포를 최적화할 수 있는지를 이해한다. 개인 병사는 보병의 가장 귀중한 자원이다.

◎ 전투훈련

시원한 아침이다. 'A'과 'B' 중대들은 전투 훈련을 위해 야외에 있다. A 중대는 공자, B중대는 방자이다. 'B'중대의 1개 소대가 505고지 꼭대기에서 참호를 구축하고 있다. 다른 2개의 소대들은 언덕 산맥 너머 계곡에 위치한 마을을 점령하고 있다. 'A' 중대는 언덕 남쪽의 평지에서 대형을 갖추고 있다. 집결지 지역은 안개에 가려져 있다.

악천후에도 불구하고 적군의 위치를 파악하기 위해 제1소대의 수색정찰팀이 조금 일찍 출동했다. 그들은 적이 505고지를 점령하고 있으며, 그들 방어의 가장 약한 지점이 서쪽 경사면에 있다는 것을 알아냈다. 소대장은 방금 공격 명령을 수령했다. 목표는 (아군의) 접근을 저지하고 있는 마을 외곽에 있는 적의 진지다. 다음 임무는 화력으로 적을 고착시키는 것이다. 이를 위해 박격포 반이 추가로 배속되었다.

제1소대의 기관총과 박격포 반의 화력이 진지에서 적을 제압하고 있는 동안 제2소대는 돌격진지로 접근하고 있다. 제3소대는 예비이다. 그 순간에, 제2소대의 병사들이 일렬종대로 초원을 가로지르고 있다. 짙은 안개 때문에 그들은 서로를 거의 볼 수 없다. 반면 이 안개는 적군이 정확하게 조준하지 못하도록 방해하기 때문에 유리하다. 돌격 진지에서 병사들은 전개하라는 명령을 받는다. 그들은 접적대형(산개대형)으로 개활지를 가로지르고 있다. 그들은 안개 속에서 아무런 전사상자 피해 없이 언덕 기슭에 도착했다. 그곳에서, 그들은 잠시 멈춘다. 임무의 가장 힘든 부분은, 어쨌든, 아직 완수되지 않았다. 머지않아, 그들은 언덕을 올라가 적의 진지를 탈취해야 할 것이다.

이제 그들은 경사지의 반쯤 올라가고 있다. 그들은 현재 그들 아래에 있는 안개 보호 층에서 벗어나서, 가능한 모든 은폐와 엄폐를 최대한 이용해야만 전진할 수 있다. 산 정상의 적은 여전히 육중한 박격포 화력에 의해 진압되고 있지만, 공격 소대 위에는 기관총 진지가 있어 북쪽 경사면의 왼쪽에서 그들에게 사격을 개시하고 있다. 이 저항 거점을 먼저 소탕해야 했다. 소대원 세 명이 후방에서 그쪽으로 접근하여 기습으로 (기관총) 조원들을 제압하는 데 성공한다.

한편, 박격포 사격은 연신되었다. 마지막 돌격으로 그 병사들은 참호의 가장자리에 도달했다. 그들은 마침내 수류탄과 총검으로 근접전투로 적의 진지를 점령하고 격파하고 있다.

전투 임무가 완수되었다. 중대들은 언덕 근처의 숲 가장자리에서 재집결을 하고 있다. 그곳에는 이동 야전 취사가 그들을 기다리고 있었다. 병사들은 피곤하고 배고프지만, 음식 냄새를 맡으면서 조금 더 행복함을 느낀다. 그들은 따뜻한 식사를 제공받는데, 야외에서 매우 맛이 좋다. 힘든 하루였지만 초가을에 있을 기동훈련에 유용한 훈련이었다.

Unit 14 | 전술통제수단

Useful Expressions

1. 지휘관은 전술통제수단으로 기동부대와 화력지원을 통제한다.
2. 전술통제수단은 기동부대와 지원화력 사이의 그리고 그 부대들 내에서 협력(teamwork)과 협조를 보장한다.
3. 집결지는 차후행동에 대비하기 위해 부대가 집결하는 지역이다.
4. 공격개시선은 지상에서 쉽게 식별할 수 있는 특징이어야 하며, 우군부대의 통제하에 있어야 한다.
5. 공격 개시 시간은 항상 기동 및 화력 지원 요소들을 통제하기 위해 전투명령에 명시된다.
6. 전투지경선들은 전진하는 측방 기동 부대 및 인접부대와 화력들을 통제하기 위한 선들이다.
7. 지휘관은 그의 전투지역 내에서 모든 적 부대의 위치 확인과 격파의 책임이 있다.
8. 확인점 30 주변의 지형은 엄폐와 은폐를 제공한다.

Reading Text

전술통제수단은 일반적으로 전투지대를 가로질러 신장된 두드러진 지형적 특징을 따라 군사작전의 통제와 협조를 위해 사용된다.

지휘관은 전술통제수단으로 기동부대와 지원사격들을 통제한다. 전술통제수단은 기동부대와 지원화력 사이의 그리고 그 부대들 내에서 협력(teamwork)과 협조를 보장한다. 그들은 통제된 전투력의 사용을 보장함으로써 각개격파(당하는 것)의 가능성을 최소화할 뿐만 아니라, 규정된 한도 내에서 지휘관의 최대 행동의 자유를 허용한다. 통상 전술통제수단은 공격개시시간, 지결지, 공

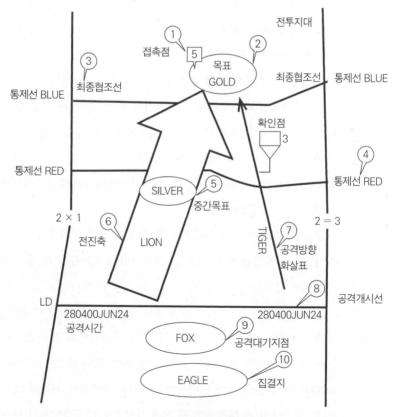

그림 14-1. 전술통제수단

격대기지점, 공격개시선, 전투지경선, 전투지역, 전진축, 공격방향, 확인점, 접촉점, 통제선, 최종협조선, 중간목표, 목표 등을 포함한다.

집결지는 차후행동에 대비하기 위해 부대가 집결하는 지역이다. 집결지는 추가 조치에 대비하기 위해 명령이 조립되는 구역이다. 집결지는 일반적으로 차상급 부대에 의해 지정된다. 예를 들어, 중대장은 소산된 소대 집결지를 지정한다. 집결지에서는 공격명령이 내려지고, 정비와 보급이 이루어지며, 전투편성이 완성된다. 집결지는 상황 및 시간이 허락되는 범위까지 사주방어가 되도록 배치하고 준비되어야 한다. 집결지들은 또한 은폐, 소산 공간, 적절한 전방 이동로, 지상과 공중에서의 경계가 제공되어야 한다. 가능하면 집결지들은 대부분의 적 간접화력 화기의 유효사거리로부터 벗어나야 한다.

공격 대기지점은 공격개시선 못 미처 마지막 지점이며 소총 요소들이 최초공격 대형을 전개하고 최종협조를 완성하는 곳이다. 공격대기지점은 적의 관측과 직접 사격으로부터 엄폐와 은폐를 제공하고, 지상에서 쉽게 식별이 가능해야 하며, 초기 공격대형의 공격요소들을 충분히 수용할 수 있을 정도로 커야 한다. 공격대기지점은 사용하지 않더라도 지정되어야 한다.

공격대기지점에서의 정지는 집결지나 이동 중에 최종 준비를 완료할 수 없는 경우에만 이루어진다. 공격대기지점에서의 불필요한 지연은 불필요하게 부대를 적의 화력에 노출시키고, 그렇지 않으면 달성할 수 있는 기습의 정도를 감소시킨다. 중대장은 보통 그의 공격소대들에게 공격대기지점의 정확한 위치를 지정해 준다.

공격개시시간은 공격 부대의 선두 소총 요소가 공격개시선을 넘는 시간이다. 공격개시시간은 항상 기동 및 화력지원 요소들을 모두 통제하기 위해 전투 명령에 명시된다.

공격개시선은 공격개시를 협조하기 위해 지정된다. 공격개시선은 지상에서 쉽게 식별할 수 있는 특징이어야 하며, 일반적으로 공격 방향에 수직으로, 우군부대의 통제하에 있어야 하고, 가능하면 적에 가깝게 있어야 하고, 적의 직접화력이나 관측 하에 있어서는 안 된다. 중대장이 지정한 LD(공격개시선)가 중대의 요소들에게 부적합할 경우, 중대장은 대대공격개시선 못 미처 중대공격개시선을 선정하여 사용할 수 있으나, 대대 명령에 명시된 시간에 중대의 요소들이 대대공격개시선을 통과하는 것은 피할 수 없는 것이다. 공격개시선이 지형에 고정될 수 없을 경우에는 접촉선이 공격개시선으로 지정될 수 있다. 접촉선은 우리의 부대들이 적과 접촉하고 있는 전방을 연한 선이다. 만약 접촉선이 공격개시선으로 사용될 경우, 이는 호(arced)를 이루는 선의 각 끝에 'LD/LC'로 표시한다.

전투지경선은 부대들에 대한 책임 지역을 기술하고 전진하는 측방 기동부대 및 인접부대와 화력들을 통제하기 위한 선들이다. 공격작전에서 전투지경선은 전투지역으로 언급된다. 방어 및 후퇴작전에서 전투지경선들은 책임지역으로 언급된다. 전투지경선들은 통상적으로 강, 계곡, 도로, 수목이 없는 곳과 같이 지상에서 식별이 용이한 지형의 특징들을 따라 위치하게 된다. 가능하면 주요 지형의 특징적인 것들과 접근로들은 통제 책임을 분할하지 않도록 하기 위하여 한 개 부대의 전투지역에 완전히 포함시켜야 한다. 전투지경선은 최소한 목표를 넘어 목표의 탈취 및 진지강화에서 화력의 협조에 필요한 종심까지 확장되어야 한다. 전투지경선은 소대들 간의 시각적 협조를 달성할 수 없거나 다른 이유로 인해 소대들의 혼재가 발생할 것 같은 경우를 제외하고 보통 소대 수준에서는 사용되지 않는다. 부대들은 일시적으로 전투지경선들을 넘어 이동하거나 사격할 수 있지만, 인접 지휘관과의 협조 후에나 그리고 차 상급 지휘관에게 통지한 후에만 가능하다.

전투지역은 더 큰 공격 지역의 전술적 일부(세분화)가 된다. 일반적으로 두 전투지경선 사이의 지형이며, 전투지경선들의 전방과 후방 한계는 전투지역의 전방과 후방 한계에 해당한다. 한 부대를 위한 전투지역은 해당 부대의 예하 (작전)요소들에게 적절한 기동 공간을 제공하며 부대능력의 크기에 비례한다. 인접 부대 간의 긴밀한 협조가 필요한 경우 또는 부대의 임무가 공격이 진행됨에 따라 해당 지역의 적을 제거해야만 하는 경우와 같이, 책임지역을 명확히 기술해야 할 때, 전투지역이 할당된다. 전투지역을 할당될 때 그 지휘관은 상급본부가 구체적으로 떠맡는 것을 제외한 전투지역 내에서 수행되는 모든 군사작전에 대한 책임이 있다. 지휘관은 그의 임무를 완수하기 위해서 그 전투지역내에서 그의 (작전)요소들을 기동시키는 것은 자유이다. 지휘관은 자신의 전투지대에 있는 모든 적 부대의 위치를 찾아서 격파할 책임이 있으며, 이는 지휘관의 임무 달성과 그 부대의 경계와도 일치한다.

Unit 15 | 근접항공지원 요구

Useful Expressions

1. 근접 항공 지원(CAS) 임무들에 대한 요청들은 기계획 또는 긴급으로 분류된다.
2. 전형적인 기계획 임무들은 공격준비폭격과 주요 교량 및 병참선의 항공 차단이다.
3. 전술항공통제본부(TACC)는 육군이 수립한 우선순위/우선권에 따라 쏘티(전투기 출격)를 할당한다.
4. 긴급한 요구사항들을 수행하기 위해 피지원 지상군 지휘관들의 요청에 따라 긴급 임무들이 이행된다.
5. 모든 상황에서 피지원 지상군 지휘관이나 그의 대리인은 모든 긴급항공 지원요청들을 승인하거나 거부한다.
6. 표적에 대한 교정은 완벽해야 하지만 간결하고 신속해야 한다.
7. 기본적인 방위방향들은 시계방향 교정이 선호된다.
8. 사단은 우리에게 근접 항공 지원의 우선권을 주었다.
9. 당신의 소대는 가장 전방 진지에 있다.

Reading Text

근접항공지원은 아군에 근접해 있는 화력 및 전투부대의 이동에 각 항공임무의 세밀한 통합이 요구되는 적대적인 표적들에 대하여 고정익 및 회전익 항공기에 의한 공중조치이다. 또한 CAS라고도 한다. 항공 차단, 긴급임무요청, 기계획 임무 요청을 참조할 것(합동교범 3-0)

근접 항공 지원(CAS) 임무들에 대한 요청들은 기계획 또는 긴급으로 분류된다. 기계획된 임무는 요구사항이 예견될 수 있는 임무다. 그(기계획)들은 지상 전술 계획과의 세부계획, 통합 및 협조를 가능하게 한다. 대표적인 기계획 임무는 주요 교량 또는 병참선의 사전 폭격과 항공 차단이다. 기계획 임무는 효율적인 활용의 관점에서 보면 가장 바람직하다. 왜냐하면 탄약들이 표적에 정확하게 맞춤식으로 사용될 수 있고 완전한 임무계획이 달성될 수 있기 때문이다.

기계획 근접 항공 지원 요청은 작전 채널을 통해 화력지원 협조본부(FSCC) 또는 전술작전본부(TOC)로 전달된다. 각 제대의 지휘관은 보고서를 평가한다. 즉 공역, 화력 및 정보와 같은 요구사항들을 협조하고 통합한다. 그리고 승인되면, 요청에 대한 우선순위/우선권을 부여한다. 그런 다음 그(지휘관)는 기존의 음성 회로나 무선 네트워크에 의해 승인된 요청을 차 상급 제대로 전달한다. 이러한 과정이 진행되는 동안, 공군 전술항공통제반(TACP)은 해당 지역에 위치한 육군 부대에 조언과 지원을 제공한다.

야전군 전술작전본부(FATOC)의 전술항공지원반(TASE)이 기계획 근접항공 지원 요청을 최종 통합하고, 승인한다. 그런 다음 요청서는 공군 전술항공통제본부(TACC)에 제출된다. 여기서 육군 연락반은 전구 전체의 요청을 통합하여 TACC에 육군 요청서들을 전달한다. TACC는 육군이 수립한 우선순위/우선권에 따라 소티(전투기 출격)를 할당한다.

긴급 임무들은 예상할 수 없었던 다급한 요구사항들을 이행하기 위해 피지원 지상군 지휘관의 요청에 따라 수행된다. 지상작전 중 예견치 못한 우발

상황에 대처하기 위해, 공군 지휘관은 보통 그의 공중지원의 일부를 예비로 유지한다. 항공기가 비행하는 동안 긴급임무의 세부사항들이 일반적으로 협조된다.

긴급 요구사항들은 어떤 수준에서든 개시될 수 있으며 다음 요소들을 포함해야 한다 :

    a. 관찰자 식별

    b. 준비명령(근접항공지원 요청)

    c. 표적 위치

    d. 표적의 종류(유형) 및 수량

    e. 표적의 활동 또는 이동상태

    F. 점표적 또는 지역표적

    g. 요구되는 결과(무력화, 파괴 또는 교란)

    h. 원하는 표적 타격 시간(TOT: 일제사격)

대대급 이하에서 시작되는 긴급요청은 가능한 가장 빠른 방법으로 대대 지휘소로 전달된다. 여기서 승인되면 그 요청은 TACP(전술항공통제반)로 전달된다. TACP는 해당 요청을 군단의 전술 항공지원반과 함께 있는 직접항공지원본부(DASC)로 직접 전송한다. TACP(전술항공통제반)에는 ALO(공군연락장교)와 FAC(전방항공통제관)가 포함될 수 있다. 그러나 이러한 항공 요소의 구성원은 단지 자문관 자격으로 활동한다. 모든 상황에서 피지원 지상군 지휘관이나 그의 대리인은 모든 긴급 항공지원 요청을 승인하거나 거부하게 된다. ALO, 화력지원협조관 및 부대장은 일반적으로 합동(또는 인접)으로 배치되어 작전 중에 함께 이동이 가능하다.

긴급 CAS 임무를 요청할 때, 피지원 지상군 부대는 표적위치와 우군의 위치를 FAC(전방항공통제관)에 전달하고, FAC는 이를 타격 항공기에 전달한다. FAC 통제의 항공타격들은 지상이나 공중의 위치로부터 이뤄진다. FAC이 부재 시는 지상 인원 즉, 화력지원반(FIST)의 장이 표적에 타격 항공기들을 지시한다. 적의 전파방해 가능성 때문에 표적에 대한 교정은 완벽해야 하지만 간결하고 신속해야 한다. 기본적인 방위방향들은 시계방향 교정이나 항공기의 공격방향 교정들이 선호된다. 포병이나 박격포 사격을 교정하는 관찰자 표적방법은 빠르게 움직이는 항공타격에서는 위험할 정도로 혼란스러울 수 있다.

Military English

II

Unit 1 | 참모편성 및 운용

Useful Expressions

1. 참모들은 지휘관이 결정을 내리고 실행하는 데 도움을 주기 위해 존재한다.

2. 모든 참모장교는 자신 직책의 모든 면에서 유능해야 하며, 구체적인 임무와 책임을 누구보다 잘 알아야 한다.

3. 참모장교는 요구사항들을 예상하기 위한 주도권을 가져야 한다.

4. 지휘관은 항상 문제에 대한 새롭고 혁신적인 해결책을 찾는다.

5. 참모장교는 변화하는 요구사항과 우선순위로 인해 압도당하거나 좌절하지 않도록 성숙하고 정신력(또는 침착성)이 있어야 한다.

6. 충성심이 있다면 참모장교는 지휘관이 듣고 싶어 하는 것보다 올바른 정보를 지휘관에게 보고하게 될 것이다.

7. 참모장교는 그의 건의가 병사들에게 어떤 영향을 미치는지 잊지 않아야 한다.

8. 첫 번째는 상황 인식 정보로, 이는 결심을 하는 기초로서 상황에 대한 이해를 형성하는 것이다.

p.
164-
170

Reading Text

참모들은 지휘관이 결정을 내리고 이행하는 데 도움이 되기 위하여 존재한다. 저항하는 적에 대하여 국가의 의지를 강요하는 군인들의 생명에 대한 위험보다 더 중요한 지휘결심은 없으며 더 어려운 것이 없다. 참모 조직과 절차는 지휘관의 중요 첩보 요구 사항을 충족하도록 구성되어 있다. 따라서 참모와 조직, 책임 및 절차를 이해하려면 먼저 지휘관이 어떻게 지휘하는가를 이해하는 것이 첫 번째이다. 군대는 국가 전쟁에서 성공적으로 싸우고 승리하기 위해 존재하기 때문에, 명령을 이해하는 것은 군대가 어떻게 싸우는지를 이해하는 것으로 시작된다. 전쟁 시에 지휘와 관련된 기량, 절차 및 기술은 평화 시에 군대 조직 관리에도 적용될 수 있다. 그러나 우리의 교리는 전투에 초점을 두어야한다.

협조참모는 아래와 같은 직책으로 구성된다.

- 참모장 보좌 인사참모(인사과장)
- 정보
- 작전
- 군수
- 기획
- 통신
- 관리, 재무, 경리
- 민사

- 화력
- 방호
- 작전지속지원

화력반장, 방호반장, 작전지속지원반장 등은 사단급과 군단급에서 권한을 부여받는다(편성된다). 그들은 주 지휘소 내의 기능 반들을 통해 지휘관을 위한 각자의 전투 기능들을 협조한다.

◎ 참모장교의 특성

1) 능력

모든 참모 장교는 그의 직책의 모든 면에서 유능해야 하며, 그의 구체적인 과업과 책임을 누구보다 잘 알아야 한다. 그는 또한 지휘관을 위한 최선의 건의에 부합하기 위해 수직적, 측면적 협조를 수행하는 다른 참모들의 과업에도 익숙해야 한다. 지휘관은 참모장교들이 각각의 문제를 적절히 분석하고, 정확한 답을 알고, 추측을 하지 않고, 건의할 것으로 기대한다. 참모장교는 어떤 질문에도 정확한 답을 알지 못할 때 인정할 수 있는 도덕적 용기를 가져야 한다.

2) 주도권 및 판단

참모장교는 요구사항들을 예측하는 주도권을 유지하고 있어야 한다. 그는 또한 상황을 신속하게 평가하기 위해, 그리고 무엇이 중요한지 결정하기 위해, 그리고 해야만 할 필요한 일을 하고 있는지를 평가하는 훌륭한 판단력을 사용해야 한다. 그는 지휘관이 언제 어디서 조치해야 할 행동에 관한 특별한 지침을 주기를 기다릴 수 없다. 그는 지휘관이 임무를 완수하기 위해 무엇을 필요로 하는지와 지휘관이 정보에 입각한 결심을 하기 위해 질문할 문제점을 예상해야 한다.

3) 창의성

지휘관은 항상 문제에 대한 새롭고 혁신적인 해결책을 찾고 있다. 참모장교는 어렵고 독특한 상황에 대한 해결책을 찾는 데 창의적이어야 한다. 창의적 사고와 비판적 추론은 각각 방책들을 개발하고 분석하는 데 있어 참모장교에게 도움이 되는 기술이다. 만약 그가 한 방향이나 지역에서 하나의 방책만을 건의할 수밖에 없다면, 그는 하나의 대안을 찾아야 한다.

4) 융통성

참모장교는 요구사항과 우선순위를 변경하여 압도당하거나 좌절하지 않도록 하기 위해 성숙함과 침착성을 갖춰야 한다. 지휘관은 그의 (상급)지휘관으로부터 추가 정보나 새로운 요구 사항을 받게 되면 자주 마음이나 방향을 바꾸게 될 것이다. 지휘관은 왜 갑자기 마음이 바뀌었는지 참모장교와 자주 (의견을) 나누지 않을 것이다. (그래서) 참모장교는 유통성을 유지하고 지휘관의 필요와 욕구들에 적응해야 한다.

5) 확실성

비록 지휘관이 결과적인 건의를 거절하더라도, 참모 장교는 모든 참모 업무가 지휘관을 위해 근무하는 것이라는 것을 이해하는 정신수양과 확실성(믿음)을 가져야 한다. 참모장교는 지휘관이 그 건의에 대해 동의하지 않을 것이라고 생각하기 때문에 "반 노력"으로 제안해서는 안된다. 참모장교의 과업은 지휘관이 최선의 가능한 결심을 하는 데 지원해 왔다.

6) 충성심

참모장교는 지휘관에게 충성해야 한다. 충성심을 고수하는 것은 참모장교가 지휘관이 듣고 싶어 한다고 생각하는 것보다 올바른 정보를 지휘관에게 제공하는 데 도움이 될 것이다. 참모장교는 지휘관에게 '좋은' 그리고 '나쁜' 소식을 말할 수 있는 도덕적 용기가 있어야 한다. "나쁜 소식은 나이를 먹어도(시간이 지나도) 나아지지 않는다"는 옛 속담이 모든 참모장교들에게는 적절한 것이다.

참모장교는 또한 군인(병사)들에게 충성해야 한다. 작전계획(OPLAN)이든 훈련 이벤트든 모든 참모업무는 결국 군인(병사)들에게 영향을 미칠 것이다. 군인(병사)들은 참모장교의 건의를 지휘관이 그 건의를 승인하면 실행해야 할 것이다. 참모장교는 그의 건의가 군인(병사)들에게 어떤 영향을 미칠지 절대 잊지 말아야 한다.

7) 팀 플레이어(협력 작업자)

참모장교는 팀 플레이어(협력 작업자)가 되어야 한다. 그는 참모 조치사항들과 참모과업을 공백상태에서는 완수할 수 없다. 그는 다른 요원들과 조언하고 상담하고 협력해야 한다. 그는 그들이 마치 그 자신의 것인 양 다른 결정들을 대변할 준비가 되어야 한다. 그가 그렇게 하지 않으면 얻지 못할 결과를 얻는 데 도움이 될 것이기 때문에 현명한 참모장교는 또한 기분 좋은 성향(기질)을 유지해야 한다.

8) 효과적인 의사전달자

참모장교는 효과적인 의사 전달자가 되어야 한다. 효과적인 의사소통은 참모장교에게 중요하다. 참모장교는 지휘관의 의도와 결정을 구두로, 서면으로, 시각적으로(차트와 그래프로) 분명하게 표현해야 한다.

◎ 참모의 역할

　지휘관과 그의 참모들은 적보다 신속하게 결심하고 행동하기 위하여 전장의 활동들을 예측하고 인지하는 데 중점을 두어야 한다. 모든 참모 조직과 절차들은 지휘관이 방대한 양의 정보를 관리할 수 있도록 조직, 분석 그리고 제시하기 위하여 존재한다. 지휘관은 적보다 더 신속하게 전장 정보로부터 전장의 이해나 상황 인식을 하기 위해 그의 참모진에 의존한다. 일단 결심이 되면 지휘관은 적절한 장소와 시간에 적에 대한 지휘관의 비전이나 의지를 달성하기 위해 지휘권 내에서 필요한 능력을 신속하게 집중시키는 방식으로 부하들에게 의사결정을 전달하는 데 있어서 그의 참모들에게 의존하게 된다.

　참모들이 지휘관, 그리고 부하 지휘관들을 위해 생산해 내는 주요 생산물은 이해력, 또는 상황 인식에 관한 것이다. 사실에 입각한 이해는 지휘관들에게 제공되는 정보가 결심을 내릴 수 있는 기초가 된다. 공식적인 참모활동 절차는 (상황)이해 및 의사결정과 관련된 두 가지 유형의 정보를 제공한다. 다른 모든 참모활동들은 부차적인 것이다. 첫 번째는 상황 인식 정보인데 이는 결심을 내리는 기본으로서 상황에 대한 이해를 창출한다. 간단히 말해 자신, 적, 그리고 지형과 환경에 대해 이해하는 것을 말한다.

　두 번째 정보의 유형, 즉 실행 정보는 결심이 이루어진 후에 작전의 비전과 요망되는 결과를 분명히 이해하는 의사소통이다. 실행정보의 예는 결론, 건의사항, 지침, 의도, 작전개념 명시 및 명령 등이 된다.

　모든 지휘관은 부대와 자원의 배분과 투입 그리고 교전에 관한 결심을 해야만 한다. 이어서, 작전을 하는 동안 지휘관 의도의 범위(제한) 내에서, 지휘관은 그의 참모들에게 일상적인 결심들을 할 수 있는 권한을 주어야 한다. 지휘 및 통제(C2) 시스템은 지휘관이 그의 결심들을 예하 지휘관들에게 신속히 배분하는 하나의 도구이다.

　지휘관은 그의 참모들을 엄격하게 훈련시켜, 그가 중요하다고 여기는 정보를 이해하기 위해 함께 작업할 수 있는 응집력 있는 집단으로 만들어야 한다. 참모장교들은 후속 임무에 대한 개념을 개발하기 위해 현재 작전의 결과를 예측할 수 있어야 한다. 그들은 또한 그들의 임무를 실행함에 있어서 일반적으로 이해되는 교리를 이해하고 적용할 수 있어야 한다.

Unit 2 | 인사참모(업무)

Useful Expressions

1. 인사참모는 인적 자원(군사 및 민간인)에 관련된 모든 문제에 관한 주요 참모장교이다.
2. 인사준비태세 관리는 현 전투능력을 결정하기 위한 인력 데이터(자료) 분석을 포함한다.
3. 건강 및 인사근무 지원에는 오락 및 체력단련 활동을 포함한 사기 지원 활동과 같은 참모 계획과 감독이 포함된다.
4. 본부관리에는 이동, 내부배치, 공간 배치, 행정지원과 같은 협조와 감독이 포함된다.
5. G1 또는 S1의 임무 중 하나는 휴가, 외출, 상담 그리고 인사문제를 포함한 군인 및 민간인을 위한 행정지원에 대한 참모계획과 감독이다.

Reading Text

G1(S1)은 인사준비태세, 인사근무, 본부관리 등을 포함한 인적자원(군사 및 민간인)에 관한 모든 문제를 담당하는 주요 참모다. 인사 장교는 대대로부터 군단까지 모든 제대에 위치해 있다. 일반적인 참모 임무와 책임은 이전의 장

에 실려 있다. 다음은 G1(S1)의 구체적인 책임분야와 활동들이다.

인사관리에 포함되는 것들 ―
- 인사 준비태세 관리에 포함되는 것은
    - 현재 전투 능력을 판단하기 위한 인력 자료 분석.
    - 향후 요구사항 전망
- 병력준비태세(사기, 조직의 분위기, 헌신, 응집력 등과 같은)에 영향을 미치는 데이터를 관찰, 수집 및 분석하는 것을 포함한 부대 전투력 유지.
- 부대 전투력 상태 관찰
- 전투력을 유지하기 위한 계획 수립
- 인사보충 관리에 포함되는 것들은
    - 수용, 계산, 처리, 병력인도.
    - 개별적 보충 및 보충 시스템 운용과 관련된 사항들에 대해 지휘관 및 참모에게 조언.
    - 예상 사상자, 비전투 손실, 그리고 예측 가능한 행정적 손실을 기준으로 한 인력 보충 요구들에 대한 판단서 준비
    - 보충인력 배정을 위한 계획 및 정책 준비
    - G3 우선순위에 따른 개별 보충 요청 및 할당
    - G4의 장비보충계획, G3의 훈련계획과 G1의 인사보충계획 통합
    - 준비태세 과정, 이동 지원, 보충 처리 부대들의 위치에 대한 조정 및 관찰
    - 전투근무 부적합 판정을 받은 인력에 대한 정책 수립 및 협조(예: 의료사유)
- 전사상자 보고, 통지, 그리고 지원 ; 업무 계선 결정, 유해 상태 보고; 전사상자 우편 협조 등이 포함된 전사상자 운영 관리.
- 근속(재모집)
- 적군 포로(EPW) 부상, 병, 부상률 평가 및 기록
- 민간인 배치

- 민간인 담당 인사장교(CPO)와 협조하여 민간인력 활용
- 군 인력 배치 관찰

건강 및 인사근무지원에 포함되는 것들 —
- 참모 계획 및 감독은 다음 항목 포함 —
    - 오락, 체력단련 활동을 포함한 사기 지원 활동
    - 공동체, 가족 지원 활동 및 프로그램
    - 삶의 질 프로그램.
    - 적 포로 우편 서비스를 포함한 우편 운영(운영 및 기술적 통제)
    - 군악대 운영.
    - 시상 프로그램.
    - 군기행정.
- 재정, 기록보존, 군인단체생명보험(SGLI) 등 인사지원, 종교활동지원, 법률서비스, 지휘정보 등을 포함한 인사근무지원.
- 사기상태 평가 및 저하된 사기강화 프로그램 건의
- 상호 업무와 협조 -
    - 육군과 공군의 교환 근무, 예를 들면 영화 상영
    - 미국 적십자사와 같은 지시를 수행하는 비전투 기관

본부관리에 포함되는 것들 —
- 본부의 조직 및 행정 관리.
- 인력 할당 건의.
- 협조 및 감독.
    - 이동.
    - 내부 배치.
    - 공간 배치.
    - 행정적 지원.

참모계획 및 감독은

- 휴가, 외출, 상담, 개인사정 등이 포함되는 군인과 민간인에 대한 행정지원.
- 증원인원들에 대한 행정지원(비미군, 외국 국적, 민간인 피수용자).
- 무단 이탈, 탈영, 군사법정 위반, 전출요구, 보상과 처벌, 그리고 낙오자 처리 등을 포함한 군기행정, 법과 질서(G3(군사경찰참모) 협조하에).
- 정보참모에게 정보요구에 대한 건의(추천)

아래와 같은 특별참모에 대한 참모책임의 협조사항

- Adjutant general(AG).(부관)
- Civilian personnel officer(CPO).(민간인 인사장교)
- Dental surgeon.(치과 진료)
- Equal opportunity advisor(EOA).(기회균등 상담관)
- Finance officer.(경리 장교)
- Surgeon.(외과 군의관)
- Veterinary officer.(수의장교)

> **노트** 이러한 특별참모장교들의 임무와 책임은 FM 101-5, 4-17쪽에 있는 특별참모장교 부분에서 확인할 수 있음.

다음과 같은 특별 및 개인참모 장교들의 참모책임의 협조(협조 필요시)

- Chaplain.(목사)
- Inspector general.(감찰)
- Public affairs officer.(공무장교)
- Staff judge advocate.(법무참모)

Unit 3 | 정보참모(업무)

Useful Expressions

1. G2(S2)는 군사정보(MI)와 대(對)정보, 보안작전, 군사정보훈련 등 모든 문제를 총괄하는 주요참모장교이다.

2. 군사정보(MI)는 적절한 방법으로 지휘관들과 다른 사용자들에게 정보를 전파하는 것을 포함한다.

3. 군사정보(MI)는 평가된 적의 수집능력과 기만에 대한 민감성에 근거하여 표적과 목표를 추천함으로써 G3(기만 장교)가 기만계획을 수립하는 데 도움을 주는 것을 포함한다.

4. 대정보(CI)는 인간정보(HUMINT), 신호정보(SIGINT), 영상정보(IMINT) 및 부대에 대한 타격 노력과 같은 적 정보수집 능력을 식별(파악)하는 것을 포함한다.

5. 보안작전에는 부대 및 인원보안 프로그램에 대한 감독이 포함된다.

6. 정보훈련에는 부대 정보 훈련계획을 준비하고 정보통합, 대정보, 작전보안, 적(조직, 장비 및 작전) 및 전장 고려사항의 정보준비를 다른 훈련 계획들에 통합하는 과정이 포함된다.

Reading Text

G2(S2)는 군사정보(MI)와 대(對)정보, 보안작전, 군사정보훈련 등 모든 문제를 총괄하는 주요 참모장교이다. 정보장교는 대대부터 군단까지 모든 제대에 위치해 있다. 공통적인 참모 임무와 책임은 앞 장에 실려 있다. 다음은 G2(S2)의 구체적인 책임 분야와 활동들이다.

군사정보에 포함되는 것들 —

- 지휘관 등 다른 사용자들에게 적시에 정보 전파
- 정보 수집, 처리, 생산, 전파
- 전장정보준비(IPB) 시행 및 협조
- 부대 관심지역 건의 및 부대 전장공간의 규정에 대한 참모 지원
- 전장환경이 아군 및 적 능력에 미치는 영향에 대한 기술
- 위협 평가(적의 교리, 전투요소 서열, 고가치 목표(HVT), 능력 및 약점)
- 가장 가능성이 높고 가장 위험한 방책 및 주요 사태 결정
- 지휘관의 주요 정보 요구에 대해 모든 참모들과 협조하고 PIR(우선정보요구) 건의
- 참모 계획, 의사 결정 및 표적 설정에 대한 IPB(전장정보분석) 생산에 참모 입력 정보 통합
- EPW(적 포로) 및 민간인 피억류자로부터 취득한 (정보 목적) 자료 처리를 위한 G3(PM: 사업관리관)와 협조
- 다른 수집 자산과의 지상 및 공중 정찰 및 감시 작전 협조
- 표적회의 참여
- 적의 통제로부터 귀대하는 인원(첩보요원)에 대한 복명
- G3(공병협조관)와 협조하여 아군을 방해하거나 장기작전 목표를 위태롭게 하는 수단으로써 환경을 조성할 수 있는 적의 능력 분석
- 기술정보 활동 협조 및 정보전파
- 표적 정보 수집을 위한 표적 획득 활동 계획 시 G3 지원

- 핵 · 생물 · 화학(NBC) 무기의 사용에 대한 적의 능력과 예측 가능성을 분석하기 위해 화학장교와 협조
- 후송 또는 입원 계획에 영향을 미칠 수 있는 적 상황에 대하여 G1과 협조
- 군수작전에 영향을 줄 수 있는 적의 상황에 대하여 G4와 협조
- 민사작전에 영향을 줄 수 있는 적 상황에 대한 G5와 협조
- 평가된 적의 수집능력과 기만에 대한 민감성에 근거하여 표적과 목표를 추천함으로써 G3(기만 장교)의 기만계획 수립 지원
- 지휘통제전(C2W) 포함하여 정보작전에 대한 G3 지원
- G3 및 화력지원계획수립자들과 협조하여 정보 수집 작전 계획수립 및 관리
- 지휘관 우선정보 요구와 정보요구에 부합되는 전 출처 정보를 생산하기 위해 수집된 정보를 기록, 평가 및 분석
- 적 및 환경요소 그리고 IPB 및 정보평가의 최신화 관련 현 상황 유지
- 지도 및 지형 형판 제작을 담당하는 G3(공병협조관)와 협력하여 지도 및 지형 형판의 소요결정, 획득 및 분배 관리

대정보에 포함되는 것들 —
- 인간정보(HUMINT), 신호정보(SIGINT), 영상정보(IMINT) 및 부대에 대한 타격 노력과 같은 적 정보수집 능력을 식별(파악)
- 작전보안(OPSEC)지역, 대정보, 신호 보안(SIGSEC), 보안작전, 기만 계획, 심리전(PSYOP), 후방지역 작전, 부대방호 등에 영향을 미치는 적의 정보 능력 평가
- 보안 및 부대방호를 위한 대정보 연락 활동
- 부대방호 자원 작전에 대한 대정보 활동

보안작전에 포함되는 것들 —
- 부대 및 인원 보안 프로그램 감독

- G3를 지원하기 위한 물리적 보안 취약성 평가
- 토착민 보안점검 협조

특수보안 사무실에 대한 참모 계획 및 감독

정보 훈련에 포함되는 것들 ─

- 부대 정보 훈련계획 준비 및 정보통합, 대정보, 작전보안, 적(조직, 장비 및 작전) 및 전장 고려사항의 정보준비를 다른 훈련 계획들에 통합
- 부대 정보훈련 프로그램에 대한 군사정보(MI) 지원의 참모 감독 시행

특별참모 장교에 대한 참모책임의 협조, 기상장교(SWO). (기상장교의 임무 및 책임은 특별 참모 장교 부분(section)에서 찾을 수 있음)

Unit 4 | 작전참모(업무)

Useful Expressions

1. G3(S3)는 훈련, 작전, 계획과 관련된 모든 문제뿐만 아니라 전력개발 및 현대화에 대한 주요 참모장교이다.
2. G3의 훈련 임무는 지휘관을 보좌하여 부대 임무 과제 목록(METL)을 개 발하고 훈련시키는 것을 포함한다.
3. G3의 업무 가운데 작전과 계획에 관련된 과업들은 다른 참모부서에도 도움이 되는 부대 SOP, 작전계획(OPLAN), 작전명령(OPORD), 단편명령 (FRAGO), 그리고 준비명령(WARNO)에 대한 준비, 협조, 증빙, 출판 그리

고 분배하는 것들이 포함된다.

4. 작전과 계획은 G2와 G4와 협조하여 탄약소요보급율(RSR)을 발전시키는 것을 포함한다.

5. 전력개발과 현대화에는 부대신설, 활성화, 조직, 해체, 그리고 재편성(전투력 결산)에 대한 진행절차가 포함된다.

Reading Text

p. 196-202

G3(S3)는 훈련, 작전 및 계획, 전력개발과 현대화에 관한 모든 문제를 담당하는 주요 참모장교이다. 작전 장교는 대대부터 군단까지 모든 제대에 배치되어 있다. 공통적인 참모의 임무와 책임은 앞 절에 기술되었다. G3(S3)의 구체적인 책임 분야와 활동은 다음과 같다.

훈련에 포함되는 것들 ―

- 부대(지휘) 훈련 프로그램 감독
- 지휘부 내 훈련 실시에 대한 준비 및 감독
- 지휘관 승인 및 서명을 위한 훈련지침 준비
- 부대 임무과제목록(METL) 개발 및 훈련 시 지휘관 지원
- 부대의 임무과제목록(METL) 및 훈련상태에 근거하여 훈련소요 파악
- 전투조건 및 표준화(기준)에 부합되는 훈련소요 적응 강화
- 훈련자원의 소요 결정 및 할당
- 부대 내 교육기관 편성 및 실시, 외부 교육기관의 쿼터(몫, 할당량) 획득 및 배분
- 훈련점검, 시험, 평가 계획 및 실시
- 부대 내 각 부대의 부대전투준비태세 유지
- 적절한 훈련 기록 및 보고서 작성

작전 및 계획에 포함되는 것들 —

- 다른 참모부서에도 기여하는 부대 SOP, 작전계획(OPLAN), 작전명령 (OPORD), 단편명령(FRAGO), 그리고 준비명령(WARNO)에 대한 준비, 협조, 증빙, 출판 및 분배
- 연습에 대한 계획, 협조, 감독
- 표적회의에 참여
- 예하부대의 계획 및 명령 검토
- 전 참모 부서들과 전술 작전 동시화
- 전 작전계획 및 작전명령의 동시화 및 완성도에 대한 검토
- 전투(상황, 지역 등) 관찰
- 시기와 장소에 요구되는 필요한 전투지원(CS) 소요의 제공 보장
- G5와 민간 정부 수립을 위한 전술부대의 사용에 관한 협조
- G2와 협조하여, 가용 자산을 보유한 임무수행부대를 포함하여, 지휘 관 우선정보요구를 수집하기 위한 수색정찰 및 감시 부록 작성
- G2에 첩보요구사항(IR) 추천
- 모든 작전에 화력 지원 통합
- 부대이동로 선정, 이동 우선순위, 이동시간, 경계 제공, 야영지, 할당, 대기지역, 이동명령 준비 등 부대 이동 계획 수립
- 제한되지 않는 것에 대한 다음과 같은 주요 부대 자원 할당의 우선 순위 건의
  - 시간(사용 가능한 계획 시간)
  - 탄약 기본휴대량 및 탄약통제보급률(CSR)
  - 인력과 장비 보충
  - 전자 주파수 및 주요보안목록
- G2 및 G4와 협조하여 탄약 소요 보급률(RSR) 개발
- 작전 채널을 통한 부대교체 요청
- 재편성(전투력 복원) 작전을 위한 기준(조건) 수립
- 기만 목적에 필요한 자원을 포함하여 기동 및 지원을 완수하기 위한

자원 사용 건의

- 지형관리 협조 및 지도(모든 지상 관리자)
- G1 및 G4와 협조하여 전투근무지원(CSS) 자원 소요 결정
- G2 및 화력지원협조관(FCOORD)과 함께 방책 및 결심지원형판(DST) 개발에 참여
- 공병협조관(ENCOORD), G2, G5 및 군의관과 환경 취약성 보호 수준을 수립하기 위한 협조
- 전투부대에 인원 할당 및 주요무기체계 보충을 위한 우선순위 부여
- 지휘소 일반 위치 건의
- 다음 항목에 포함되는 부대편조 및 예하 요소에 임무 할당
    - 부대목록 개발, 유지, 수정
    - 조직되어야 할 부대들의 수와 유형 그리고 인원과 장비의 단계적 투입 및 교체 우선순위 판단을 포함한 부대들의 조직 및 장비화
    - 파견부대, 파견대, 또는 팀의 배치, 배속 등
    - 필요에 따라 부대의 오리엔테이션, 훈련, 재조직을 포함한 부대, 파견대, 팀의 접수
- 전술작전에 민간인 포함 여부를 G1(CPO: 민간인 인사처)과 협조

전력개발과 현대화에 포함되는 것들 —

- 계획되거나 프로그램화된 부대 구조에 대한 검토, 분석 및 건의
- 부대창설, 해체, 구축, 중단 및 재조직(전투력 결산)에 대한 절차 진행
- 신무기 및 장비 시스템의 야전배치(전투력 현대화)
- 병력과 민간인의 적절한 운용과 소요(인력 활용 및 요구사항)를 보장하기 위한 조직구조, 기능, 작업량 등의 평가
- 설정된 한도와 지침 내에서 예하부대에 인력 자원 할당(인력 할당)
- 수정편제장비표(MTOE)와 수정및분배할당표(MTDA)의 변경 사항을 문서화하기 위한 부대 전투력 데이터 개발 및 개정
- 공식적인 현지 인력 및 장비조사 계획 및 시행

- 정보, 기획 및 프로그래밍, 할당 및 정당성(인력 보고서)을 위한 데이터 기록 및 보고
- 할당된 임무를 수행하는 데 필요한 최소 필수 및 가장 경제적인 장비가 반영되도록 수정및분배할당표(MTDA)와 수정편제장비표(MTOE) 문서 보장

G3는 새로운 장비와 시스템을 위한 질적 및 양적 인력 소요들을 결정한다.

참모계획 및 감독에 포함되는 것들 —

- OPSEC(작전보안), 부대의 작전보안 태세 분석, 우군첩보기본요소(EEFI) 결정 및 작전보안의 취약점, 대정찰작전 계획 및 대책, 통신참모(C6)와 통신보안 대책 협조, 작전보안 조사 실시, 그리고 부대방호 대책의 효과성 평가 등이 포함됨
- 부대방호
- 공역 지휘 및 통제(AC2)
- 정보 작전, C2W(지휘통제전)에 포함
- 파괴된 지역 통제
- 후방지역 작전(G3: 후방지역작전 부록 준비)
- 군기, 법질서(군기, 법질서를 다루는 행정절차에 대해 G1과 협조)
- 부대 창설 및 해체
- 동원 및 동원 해제
- 군사경찰 부대장과 협조하에 EPW(적포로) 및 민간인 피역류자에 대한 작전

아래와 같은 특별참모에 대한 참모책임의 협조사항

- Air defense coordinator(ADCOORD).(방공협조관)
- Air liaison officer(ALO).(공군연락장교)
- Air/naval gunfire liaison company(ANGLICO) commander.(항공/함포 연락중대 지휘관)

- Aviation coordinator(AVCOORD).(육군항공협조관)

- Chemical officer(CHEMO).(화학장교)

- Deception officer.(기만작전 장교)

- Electronic warfare officer(EWO).(전자전 장교)

- Engineer coordinator(ENCOORD).(공병협조 장교)

- Explosive ordnance disposal(EOD) officer.(폭발물 처리 장교)

- Fire support coordinator(FSCOORD).(화력지원 협조장교)

- Historian.(역사담당관)

- Liaison officer(LNO).(연락장교)

- Provost marshal(PM).(군사경찰대장)

- Psychological operations(PSYOP) officer.(심리전 장교)

- Safety officer.(안전장교)

- Special operations coordinator(SOCOORD).(특수작전 협조관)

- Theater airlift liaison officer(TALO).(전구공수연락장교)

노트	특별참모장교의 임무와 책임은 특별참모 장교 부분(section)에서 찾아볼 수 있음

Unit 5 | 군수참모(업무)

Useful Expressions

1. G4(S4)는 부대에 보급, 정비, 수송, 전투근무지원의 통합을 협조하는 주요 참모장교이다.

2. G4에 대한 군수작전과 계획에 관련된 업무들에는 IPB(전장정보준비)에 포함시키기 위해 적 군수작전에 관한 정보를 G2(S2)에 제공하는 것이 포함된다.

3. G4에 대한 보급업무는 지휘관의 우선순위에 따라 VIII종(의무)을 제외한 모든 종별 보급에 대한 협조를 포함한다. VIII종은 의무 보급 채널을 통해 협조된다.

4. G4의 정비 분야 중 하나는 장비준비태세를 관찰하고 분석하는 것이다.

5. 군수참모(ACOS, G4)의 수송 과제 중 하나에는 종결작전뿐만 아니라 이동통제와 방법을 지원하기 위한 작전 및 전술 계획을 시행하는 것을 포함한다.

6. 군수참모는 지역 민간인, 전쟁포로(EPW), 민간인 피억류자 및 억류자 사용에 대한 요구사항 및 제한사항의 식별에 대한 참모 계획 및 감독을 수행해야 한다.

p. 209- 213

Reading Text

G4(S4)는 부대에 보급, 정비, 수송, 전투근무지원의 통합을 협조하는 주요 참모장교이다. G4(S4)는 지원부대와 그의 지휘관, 그리고 나머지 참모들과 연계되어 있다. G4(S4)는 지원부대장이 지휘관 및 나머지 참모들과 군수의 가시성을 유지하는 데 도움을 준다. 또한 G4(S4)는 G3(S3)와 밀접하고 지속적인 협조를 유지해야 한다. 군수 장교는 대대부터 군단까지 모든 지휘제대에 위치하고 있다. 여단과 대대급에서 S4는 활동들을 협조하는 것뿐만 아니라 지휘관과 부대에 대한 요구사항들을 실행한다. 공통적인 참모 의무와 책임은 앞 절에 기재되었다. G4(S4)의 구체적인 책임 분야와 활동들은 다음과 같다.

군수작전과 계획(일반적)에 포함되는 것들 —

• IPB(전장정보준비)에 포함시키기 위해 G2(S2)에 적 군수작전에 관한 정

보 제공

- 작전을 지원하기 위해 G3와 함께 군수계획 발전
- 인원과 부대의 장비화 보충에 관한 G3 및 G1과 협조
- 해당 부대의 현재 및 미래 지원 능력에 관해 지원부대 지휘관과 협조
- 공병협조관(ENCOORD과 협력하여 주보급로(MSR) 및 군수 지원 분야들의 선정 및 건의를 G3로 협조
- 지원부대와 협조하여 전장의 군수준비(사항) 시행
- G2에 IR(첩보요구) 추천
- 잉여자산과 구조(물품)의 수거와 처리를 위한 부대 방침 건의
- 표적 회의에 참여

보급에 포함되는 것들 ―

- 보급 요구사항 결정(의무 요구사항 제외). 이 기능은 지원부대 지휘관 및 G3와 공유
- OPLAN(작전계획) 및 OPORD(작전명령)의 발간을 위한 보급 및 보급 우선순위, 통제보급률 건의
- 지휘관의 우선순위에 따라 VIII종(의무)을 제외한 모든 종별 보급 협조. VIII종은 의무 보급 계통을 통해 협조됨
- 보급 및 장비의 요청(징발), 획득 및 저장, 군수품의 정비 기록에 관한 협조
- 군사경찰 지휘관과 협력하여 보급과 장비의 책임과 경계가 적절하도록 보장
- G3에게 기본 및 규정 휴대량에 대한 계정 및 건의, 소요보급률 결정 시 G3 지원
- 초과, 잉여, 구난 물자 및 장비의 수거 및 배분을 조정하고 감시
- G2와의 조정 후 포획된 적물 및 장비 폐기 지시
- 예하부대들에 대한 유류 제품의 할당 협조
- 외국 및 주둔국 지원 요구사항을 지원하기 위한 G5(S5)와 협조

정비에 포함되는 것들 ㅡ

- 장비 준비태세 상태 관찰 및 분석
- 지원 부대와 정비 작업소요 결정(의무는 별도)
- 지원 부대와 장비 복구 및 후송작전 협조
- 정비 일정 계획 결정

수송에 포함되는 것들 ㅡ

- 이동 통제 및 방법, 종결작전을 지원하기 위한 작전 및 전술 계획 수립
- 다른 전투근무지원에 대한 수송 자산 협조
- 주둔국 지원을 위한 G5(S5)와 협조
- G1 및 G3(PM: 군사경찰)와 보충 인원 및 EPW(적포로) 수송 협조
- 지휘소 이동을 위한 특수 수송 요구사항 협조
- G3와 전술부대 이동에 대한 군수계획 협조

근무지원에 포함되는 것들 ㅡ

- 축성 및 통신체계를 제외한 설비 및 시설의 건설 협조
- 야전위생 협조
- 교환을 위한 그리고 개인야전장비(TA-50: 할당표) 교체를 위해 편성상 피복 및 개인 장비 작전 수립을 위한 행동 관련 협조
- 식사 준비, 정수, 시신처리, 항공수송, 세탁, 샤워, 피복 및 경직물 수선 관련 협조 또는 제공
- 위험물자 또는 위험폐기물의 수송, 보관, 취급 및 처리에 관한 협조
- 부대 유출 예방 계획 협조

참모계획 및 감독에 포함되는 것들 ㅡ

- 군수지원작전에 있어서 지역 민간인, 전쟁포로(EPW), 민간인 피억류자 및 억류자 사용에 대한 요구사항 및 제한사항의 식별

- 전장 획득 및 계약
- 계약의 법적 측면에 대한 SJA(법무참모)와 협조
- 계약의 재정적 측면에 대한 RM장교 및 재정 장교와 협조
- 부동산 통제
- 식사 지원
- 화력 방호
- 목욕과 세탁 지원, 피복 교환
- 시신처리

특별참모에 대한 참모책임의 협조사항

수송 장교 (수송 장교의 의무와 책임은 특별한 참모 장교 편, FM101-5 4-29쪽에서 찾을 수 있다.)

Unit 6 | 군사적 결심수립 절차

Useful Expressions

1. 결심이란 지휘관이 자신의 최종상태에 대한 비전을 행동으로 옮기는 수단이다.
2. 군사적 결심수립과정(MDMP)은 하나의 확립되고 입증된 분석 과정이다.
3. MDMP는 지휘관과 참모진이 전장 상황을 점검하고 논리적인 결정에 이르도록 돕는다.
4. 과정을 축약하는 대신 완벽한 MDMP(군사적 결심수립 절차)를 사용하는 이점은 최선의 가능한 아군의 방책 식별을 시도하기 위해 다중의 아군 방

책과 적군의 방책을 분석하고 비교한다는 것이다.

5. 지휘관은 군사적 결심수립 절차를 책임지고 각 상황에서 어떤 절차를 사용할지 결정한다.

6. 지휘관은 MDMP 기간 중 전 참모들을 동원하여 개연성이 있고 가능성이 있는 적과 아군 방책(COA)의 전 범위를 탐색하고, 자신의 조직 능력을 분석하여 적과 비교한다.

7. 참모장 또는 보좌관(COFS(XO))은 참모를 관리, 조정, 훈련하고 양질의 통제를 제공한다.

8. 중요한 새로운 정보를 수신하거나 상황이 크게 변화할 때 평가요소들이 수정된다.

p.
221-
226

Reading Text

의사결정(결심수립)을 하는 것은 결정 여부를 알고, 그다음에 언제 무엇을 결정해야 하는지를 아는 것이다. 그것은 결정의 결과를 이해하는 것을 포함한다. 결정은 지휘관이 최종상태에 대한 비전을 행동으로 옮기는 수단이다. 의사결정은 과학과 예술이다. 군사 작전의 많은 측면들 즉 이동 속도, 연료 소모, 무기 효과 등을 수량화할 수 있기 때문에 전쟁 과학의 일부분이다. 리더십의 영향, 작전의 복잡성, 적의 의도에 관한 불확실성 등 다른 측면은 전쟁술에 속한다.

군사적 결심수립절차(MDMP)는 하나의 확립되고 검증된 분석 과정이다(그림 6-1 참조). MDMP는 문제 해결에 대한 육군의 분석적 접근방식으로 적용(채택)한 것이다. MDMP는 지휘관과 참모들이 판단과 계획을 개발하는 데 도움을 주는 도구다. 본 장에서 설명한 공식적인 문제 해결 절차는 임무 수령에서 시작하여 명령의 발간을 목표로 할 수 있지만, MDMP의 분석 양상은 작전 실시 중 모든 수준에서 계속된다.

MDMP는 지휘관과 그의 참모들이 전투 상황을 점검하고 논리적인 결정을 내리도록 돕는다. 그 과정은 그들이 결정을 도출하기 위해 철저함, 명확성, 건전한 판단력, 논리력, 전문적인 지식을 적용하는 데 도움을 준다. 전체 MDMP는 적절한 계획 시간과 충분한 참모 지원이 가능하여 수많은 아군 및 적의 방책(COA)을 철저히 검토할 수 있을 때 상세하고 신중하며 순차적이고 시간이 많이 소요되는 절차이다. 이는 일반적으로 지휘관의 판단 및 작전계획(OPLAN)을 개발할 때, 완전히 새로운 임무를 계획할 때, 연장된 작전 중, 그리고 MDMP를 교육하도록 특별히 설계된 참모 훈련 중에 발생한다.

MDMP는 시간적 제약 환경에서 계획을 기반으로 하는 토대이다. 전체 MDMP 동안 창출된 산출물은 철저한 재점검을 위해 시간이 가용하지 않을 때 기존의 METT-T 요인은 크게 변하지 않은 후속 계획 수립시간(sessions) 시 사용될 수 있으며 사용되어야 한다. (시간제한 환경에서의 의사결정에 대한 논의는 FM 101-5, 5-27쪽 참조)

MDMP는 특히 FM 101-5-1에서 발견되는 용어와 기호들(그래픽) 및 교리에 의존한다. 승인된 용어와 기호를 사용하면 절차에 사용된 용어와 기호의 의미에 대한 혼동을 최소화함으로써 상황의 신속하고 일관된 평가와 계획 및 명령의 작성 그리고 실행을 용이하게 한다.

절차를 축약하는 대신에 완전한 MDMP를 사용하는 이점은 다음과 같은 것들이다.

- 그것(MDMP)은 가능한 최선의 아군 방책 파악을 시도하기 위해 다수의 아군 및 적군의 방책을 분석 및 비교하게 한다.
- 그것은 작전을 위한 최대한의 통합, 협조, 동시화를 산출하고, 작전의 중요한 측면을 간과할 위험을 최소화한다.
- 그것은 상세한 작전명령 또는 작전계획을 가져온다.

완전한 MDMP를 사용할 경우 시간이 많이 소요되는 단점이 있다.

◎ 지휘관과 참모의 역할

    지휘관은 군사적 결심수립절차를 책임지고 각 상황에서 어떤 절차를 사용할지 결정한다. 계획 과정은 그(지휘관)의 전장 시각화에 대한 명확한 표현에 달려 있다. 그는 개인적으로 계획을 세우고, 준비하며, 작전을 실행할 책임이

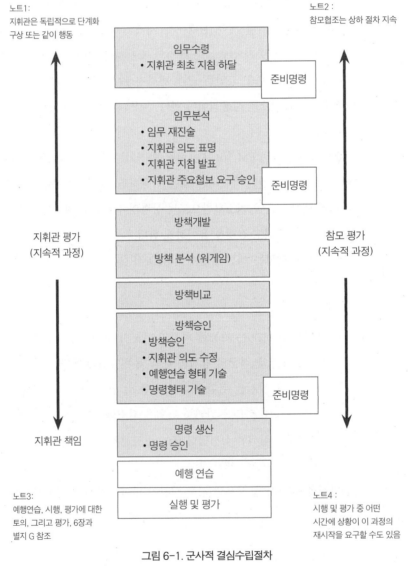

그림 6-1. 군사적 결심수립절차

있다. 처음부터 끝까지 지휘관의 개인적 역할이 중심이 된다. 즉, 그 과정에 참여하는 것은 그의 참모들에게 중점과 지침을 제공한다는 것이다. 그러나, 거기에는 지휘관 혼자만의 책임과 결심이 있다는 것이다(그림 6-1 참조). 그(지휘관)가 직접 참여하는 양은 시간의 가용성, 개인적 선호도, 그리고 참모의 경험과 접근성에 의해 작동된다. 가용시간이 적을수록 참모들의 숙련도도 떨어지고, 참모들의 접근성도 떨어지며, 일반적으로 지휘관이 더 많이 관여하게 된다. 증가된 지휘관 개입의 토론 사례들은 시간이 제한된 환경의 결심수립에서 발견된다.

지휘관은 MDMP 기간 중 개연성이 있고 가능성이 있는 적과 아군 COA(방책)의 전반적 범위를 탐색하기 위하여 전 참모를 활용하며, 자신의 조직 능력을 분석하여 적과 비교한다. 이러한 참모의 노력은 하나의 목적을 가지고 있는데, 그것은 지휘관의 결심을 돕기 위해 정보를 건전한 교리와 기술적 경쟁력과 집합적으로 통합하여 궁극적으로 효과적인 계획을 이끌어내는 것이다.

참모장 또는 보좌관(COFS(XO))은 참모를 관리, 조정, 훈련하고 양질의 통제를 제공한다. 그(참모장)는 전 과정을 감독하기 때문에 지휘관의 지침을 이해해야 한다. 그는 참모들이 필요한 정보, 지침 및 시설을 갖추도록 보장한다. 그는 참모에게 시간계획을 제공하고, 간단한 백브리핑 시간과 장소를 정하며, 어떤 특별한 지시를 하기도 한다.

지휘관과 CofS(XO)는 지침을 내리고 공식 및 비공식 브리핑에 참여함으로

- 1 단계. 임무 수령
- 2 단계. 임무 분석
- 3 단계. 방책 개발
- 4 단계. 방책 분석
- 5 단계. 방책 비교
- 6 단계. 방책 승인
- 7 단계. 명령 생산

그림 6-2. 결심수립절차 7단계

써 결심수립절차 통해 참모들을 지도한다. 이러한 상호 작용은 참모들이 문제를 해결하는 데 도움이 되며 전체 참모가 전 과정에 참여하게 된다. 선택된 방책과 작전명령의 실행은 지휘관과 참모 모두가 MDMP의 각 단계를 얼마나 잘 완수하는지에 직접적으로 관련되어 있다.

군사적 결심수립절차는 7단계가 있다(그림 6-2). 그 절차에 있는 각 단계는 이전 단계의 수립된 어떤 입력으로 시작된다. 각 단계는 차례로, 그 단계의 산출물이 있고, 후속 단계를 이끈다. 절차에서 조기에 투입된 오류들은 후속 단계에 영향을 미치게 된다.

평가는 MDMP에 중요한 입력물들을 지속적으로 제공하기 위해 계속된다. 지휘관과 각 참모부서는 평가를 한다. 평가는 중요한 새로운 정보를 받거나 상황이 특별히 바뀌게 되면 수정하게 된다. 그것들은 계획과정을 지원하기 위해서뿐만 아니라 임무수행 동안에도 시행된다.

Unit 7 | 부대지휘절차(작전수행과정)

p.
231

Useful Expressions

1. 부대지휘절차(작전수행과정, TLP)는 지휘자들에게 작전의 계획 및 준비단계에서 의사결정을 위한 틀(framework)을 제공한다.

2. 그러나 작전의 템포는 특히 하위 제대 수준에서 이러한 이상적인 순서를 불가능하게 하는 경우가 많다.

3. 임무를 받자마자 지휘자들은 상황에 대한 초기 평가를 수행한다.

4. 그 과정에서 그들은 가용한 계획과 준비시간의 약 3분의 1을 자신에게 할당한다.

5. 지휘자들은 예하부하들에게 최대한의 계획과 준비 시간을 주기 위해 가능한 한 빨리 초기 준비명령(WARNO)을 발행한다.

6. 지휘자들은 임무 준비를 계속하거나 실행하기 위해 부대 배치를 위해 필요한 이동을 시작한다.

7. 시간과 상황이 허락할 때마다 지휘자들은 개인적으로 중요한 임무 측면의 정찰을 수행한다.

8. 보병 소대와 부대장들은 보통 그래픽과 다른 통제수단을 이용하여 보충 구두 전투명령을 내린다.

9. 일반적으로 부대 SOP는 개별 책임과 준비 활동의 순서를 명시한다.

p. 232-239

Reading Text

부대지휘절차(작전수행과정, TLP)는 지휘자들에게 작전의 계획 및 준비단계에서 의사결정을 위한 틀(framework)을 제공한다. 이 8단계 절차는 작전 진행의 계획과 준비 기능을 위한 가시적인 논리, 구상 및 방향을 적용하게 한다. 부대지휘절차(작전수행과정)의 단계는 다음 내용들을 포함한다.

- 임무수령
- 준비명령(WARNO) 발행
- 잠정적인 계획 수립
- 이동 개시
- 정찰 실시
- 계획 완성
- 명령 발행
- 감독 및 평가
- 잠정계획 작성에 대한 전반적 논의는 FM 3-21.8의 6장을 참조한다.

◎ 명령 수령

지휘자들은 일련의 준비 명령(WARNO), 작전 명령(OPORD) 및 브리핑을 통해 지휘자/지휘관으로부터 여러 가지 방법으로 임무를 수령한다. 그러나 작전의 템포는 특히 하위 제대 수준에서 이러한 이상적인 순서를 불가능하게 하는 경우가 많다. 이는 지휘자들이 준비명령(WARNO)이나 단편명령(FRAGO)만 받는 경우가 많다는 의미지만 그 과정은 동일하다.

명령을 수령한 후에, 지휘자들은 보통 그들의 더 높은 지휘관에게 확인 브리핑이 요구될 수도 있다. 이것은 지휘관의 임무, 의도와 작전 개념에 대한 그들의 이해뿐만 아니라 작전 내에서 그들의 역할을 명확히 하기 위하여 행해진다. 지휘자는 필요시 상급 사령부 계획의 어떤 부분에 대하여 설명을 득하기도 한다.

임무를 수령한 지휘자들은 임무에 중점을 두고, 더 큰 작전에서의 부대 역할, 그리고 계획 및 준비 시간을 할당하는 등 상황(임무, 적, 지형, 부대-시간, 민사 [METT-TC] 분석)에 대한 초기 평가를 수행한다. 이 초기 평가에서 가장 중요한 두 가지 산물은 최소한 부분적으로 재진술된 임무와 시간사용계획이 되어야 한다. 지휘자들은 이 첫 번째 평가와 시간 할당에 대해 초기 준비명령(WARNO)을 발표한다.

그들의 지식에 기초하여, 지휘자들은 임무를 위한 계획과 준비를 위해 가용한 시간과 판단한다. 그들은 가능한 한 상세한 잠정적인 시간사용계획을 발행한다. 그 과정에서 그들은 가용한 계획과 준비시간의 약 1/3을 자신에게 할당하고 나머지 2/3는 예하부대에 할당한다. 급변하는 작전 동안에, 계획과 준비 시간이 극도로 제한될 수 있다. 미리 이러한 것을 알게 되면 지도자들은 이러한 상황에서 그들에게 도움이 되는 작전예규(SOP)를 만들게 한다.

◎ 준비명령 발행

지휘자들은 부하들에게 최대한의 계획과 준비 시간을 주기 위해 가능한 한 빨리 초기 준비명령(WARNO)을 발행한다. 그들은 추가 정보를 기다리지 않는다. 준비명령은 아래와 같이 야전명령 형식 5개 항에 따라 가능한 한 많은 세부사항을 포함한다. 최소한 예하부대들은 이동의 가장 빠른 시간과 같은 중요한 시간들, 그리고 언제 작전을 수행할 준비가 되어 있어야 하는지를 알 필요가 있다. 지휘자들은 최초 준비명령의 발행을 지체하지 말아야 한다. 더 많은 정보가 입수될수록 지휘자들은 추가적인 준비명령을 발행할 수 있고 또한 발행해야만 한다. 최소한 준비명령은 일반적으로 다음을 포함한다.

- 작전의 임무 또는 성격
- 작전명령 발행을 위한 시간과 장소
- 작전에 참여하는 부대 또는 요소들
- 부대 SOP에서 다루지 않는 특정 과업
- 작전을 위한 시간사용계획
- 예행연습 지침

◎ 잠정계획 수립

일단 그가 초기 준비명령을 발행하고 나면, 지휘자는 계속해서 잠정적인 계획을 발전시킨다. 잠정적인 계획을 세우는 것은 기초적 의사결정 방법의 가시화, 구상, 지침, 그리고 육군 표준 계획절차 등을 따른다. 이 단계는 임무 분석, 방책개발, 방책분석, 방책비교, 방책선택 등 부대결심수립절차의 2~6단계를 결합한 것이다. 보병 소대 수준에서 이러한 단계는 염두(머리)로 수행되는 경우가 많다. 소대장과 분대장은 특히 방책개발, 분석 및 비교 과정에서 그들의 주요 예하부대로 포함될 수 있다.

잠정 계획을 수립하기 위해 육군 지휘자들은 임무 분석을 수행한다. 이 임무 분석은 초기 부대지휘절차(작전수행과정) 1단계에서 시행되는 최초 평가를 지속하면서 METT-TC 양식을 따른다. 이 단계는 FM3-21.8의 6장에 상세하게 나와 있다.

◎ 최초 이동

부대이동은 부대지휘절차(작전수행과정, TLP)와 동시에 발생할 수 있다. 지휘자들은 임무준비를 계속하거나 실행부대를 배치하기 위해 필요한 어떤 이동을 시작한다. 그들은 그렇게 할 수 있는 충분한 정보를 얻거나 차후 임무를 위해 그 부대가 그 위치로 이동해야 할 때 바로 이것을 한다. 이동은 집결지, 전투위치 신 작전지역 또는 공격 위치로 이동할 수 있다. 여기에는 정찰 요소, 지침들 또는 임무할당 부분의 이동이 포함될 수 있다. 보병 지휘자들은 그들의 잠정적인 계획에 근거하여 이동을 개시할 수 있고 새로운 장소에 있는 부하들에게 명령을 내릴 수 있다.

◎ 정찰실시

시간과 상황이 허락할 때마다 지휘자들은 개인적으로 중요한 임무 측면의 정찰을 수행한다. 아무리 계획을 세워도 그 상황에 대한 직접적인 평가를 대신할 수는 없다. 불행히도, 많은 요소들이 지휘자들이 개인 정찰을 하는 것을 막을 수 있다. 그러나 지휘자가 자신의 가시성을 개발하고 확인할 수 있는 몇 가지 방법이 있다. 그것들은 내부 정찰 및 감시 요소, 무인 센서, 상급 부대의 정보, 감시, 정찰(ISR) 요소, 인접 부대, 지도 정찰, 영상, 정보 산물 등을 포함한다. 정찰을 실시할 때 가장 어려운 측면 중 하나는 지휘자가 알아야 할 사항(첩보요구[IR])을 파악하는 과정이다.

◎ 계획완성

이 단계에서 지휘자들은 계획과 순서를 완성하기 위하여 정찰 결과를 자신들이 선택한 방책(COA)에 통합한다. 여기에는 투명도 준비, 간접화력 표적 목록의 정비, 작전지속지원 및 C2 요건 협조, 정찰 결과를 잠정 계획에 최신화 등이 포함된다. 소대 및 분대 수준에서 이 단계는 일반적으로 잠정 계획에 포함된 정보를 확인하거나 최신화하는 것들만이 포함된다. 시간이 허락되면, 지휘자들은 명령을 내리기 전에 인접 부대 및 상급 본부와 최종 협조를 한다.

◎ 명령 발행

보병 소대와 분대장들은 보통 그래픽과 다른 통제 수단으로 보완된 구두 전투 명령을 내린다. 순서는 표준 5개 항 야전명령 양식을 따른다. 보병 지휘자들은 명령을 전달하기 위해 많은 다양한 기술을 사용한다(6장 참조). 전형적으로, 소대장과 분대장들은 지휘관 의도를 발표하지 않는다. 그들은 자신들의 중대장과 대대장의 의도를 반복한다.

명령 발생을 위한 이상적인 위치는 목표와 지형의 다른 양상을 잘 관찰할 수 있는 작전지역의 한 지점이다. 지휘자는 정찰을 수행하고 명령을 완성한 다음에 부하들을 특별한 장소에서 그것을 수령하도록 소집한다. 때때로, 경계 또는 다른 제약 조건이 지형 위에서 명령을 내릴 수 없도록 하기도 한다. 그런 경우에, 지휘자들은 작전지역과 상황을 묘사하기 위해 사판, 자세한 스케치, 지도, 항공 사진과 영상, 그리고 다른 제품들을 사용하기도 한다.

◎ 감독 및 평가

부대지휘절차(작전수행과정)의 마지막 단계는 매우 중요하다. 보통 부대의

SOP에는 개인의 책임과 준비 활동의 순서가 기술되어 있다. 작전 명령 발행 후에, 소대장과 그의 부하 지휘자들은 임무 수행 전에 적시적인 방법으로 요구되는 활동과 과업이 완성되도록 강화해야 한다. 장교와 부사관들이 성공적인 임무완수를 위해 중요한 모든 것을 확인하는 것은 꼭 필요하다. 그 과정에 포함되는 것은:

- 각 요소의 지휘에서 두 번째로 강화해야 할 것은 그들의 지휘자가 부재 시의 실행을 준비하는 것
- 예하부대 작전 명령 청취
- 병사들의 임무 수행에 필요한 사항과 작전명령에 명시된 특수한 사항만을 휴대토록 보장하기 위해 휴대계획을 확인하는 것
- 화기의 상태와 사용 가능성 확인
- 예하부대의 정비활동 확인
- 지역 경계 유지 보장
- 예행연습 시행

소대와 분대는 5가지 유형의 예행연습을 사용한다.

(1) 임무확인 보고
(2) 백 브리핑
(3) 연합부대 예행연습
(4) 지원부대 예행연습
(5) 전투훈련 또는 SOP 예행연습

Unit 8 | 전장기능

p. 244

Useful Expressions

1. 전장기능은 지휘관들이 임무와 훈련목표를 달성하기 위해 사용하는 공통의 목적에 의해 결합된 과업과 시스템(인원, 조직, 정보, 과정)의 그룹이다.
2. 지휘관은 전장기능의 관점에서 작전 및 훈련을 시각화, 구상 및 지도하고 이끈다.
3. 정보 전장 기능은 적, 지형, 날씨, 민간인 고려사항에 대한 이해를 촉진시키는 관련 업무와 시스템을 포함한다.
4. 이동과 기동은 지휘관들이 전투력을 집중시켜 기습, 충격, 기세 및 우세를 얻는 수단이다.
5. 방호 전투 기능은 지휘관이 최대 전투력을 적용할 수 있도록 병력을 유지하는 관련 업무와 시스템을 포함한다.
6. 작전지속지원은 정비, 수송, 공급 등과 관련된 업무를 포함한다.
7. 지휘와 통제는 지휘관과 지휘통제체계라는 두 부분으로 나뉜다.
8. 전투를 위한 부대 전투력의 핵심에는 화력, 기동력, 방호와 경계 등 세 가지의 유효성이 증명된 근접전투의 요소가 있다.

p. 245- 251

Reading Text

전장기능은 지휘관들이 임무와 훈련목표를 달성하기 위해 사용하는 공통의 목적에 의해 결합된 과업과 시스템(인원, 조직, 정보, 과정)의 그룹이다. 전장기능에는 정보, 이동 및 기동, 화력, 방호, 작전지속지원 그리고 지휘 및 통제가 있다. 이러한 전장 기능은 전장작전체제와 같은 것이다.

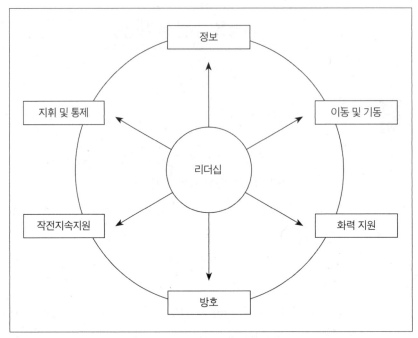

그림 8-1. 전투력의 전장기능 요소

　　지휘관은 전장기능의 관점에서 작전 및 훈련을 시각화, 구상 및 지도하고 이끈다. 결정적이고, 형태를 만들고 그리고 지속시키는 작전은 모든 전장기능을 결합한다. 어떤 기능도 독점적으로 결정적이거나 형태를 만들거나 유지되지 않는다. 그림 8-1은 전투력의 전장(기능) 요소들을 보여준다.

◎ 정보

　　정보 전장기능은 적, 지형, 날씨, 그리고 민간인 고려사항에 대한 이해를 촉진하는 관련 업무와 시스템을 포함한다. 그것은 정보, 감시, 정찰과 관련된 업무를 포함한다. 정보 전장기능은 절차, 인력, 조직 및 장비의 유연하고 조정 가능한 구성을 결합하여 지휘관들에게 지역의 위협, 시민 대중 및 환경과 관련된 정보와 산출물을 제공한다.

◎ 이동 및 기동

이동 및 기동의 전장 기능은 적과 관련된 유리한 위치를 달성하기 위하여 전투력을 이동하는 과업과 시스템에 관련된 것들을 포함한다. 그것은 직접 화력 혹은 화력의 잠재적(기동), 전투력 투사(이동), 그리고 기동 및 대기동과 결합된 전투력 배치와 관련된 과업들을 포함한다. 이동과 기동은 지휘관들이 전투력을 집중시켜 기습, 충격, 기세 및 우세를 얻는 수단이다.

◎ 화력지원

화력지원 전장기능은 육군의 간접화력, 합동화력 및 공세적 정보작전의 집중적이고 협조된 이용을 제공하는 것과 같은 관련 업무와 시스템을 포함한다. 여기에는 작전 및 전술적 목적을 달성하기 위하여 다른 전장 기능과 함께 유형별 화력 효과를 통합하고 동시화 시키는 것과 관련된 업무들을 포함한다.

◎ 방호(보호)

방호 전장기능은 지휘관이 최대 전투력을 적용할 수 있도록 전투력을 보존하는 관련 업무와 시스템을 포함한다. 전투력 보존에는 인력(전투원 및 비전투원), 물질적 자산, 미국과 다국적 파트너의 정보를 보호하는 것이 포함된다. 방호 전장기능에 포함되는 과업은 다음과 같다.

- 안전
- 우군 간 피해 회피
- 생존 가능성
- 공중 및 미사일 방어

- 대테러
- 화학, 생물, 방사능, 핵 및 고성능 폭발 화기들과 관련된 반확산과 주요관리 행위
- 방어적 정보작전
- 부대 건강 방호

◎ 작전지속지원

작전지속지원 전장기능은 행동의 자유를 보장하고, 작전 범위를 확장하며, 신장된 내구력을 보장하기 위한 지원과 근무지원을 제공하는 관련 업무와 시스템을 포함한다. 작전지속지원은 다음과 관련된 업무를 포함한다.

- 보수
- 수송
- 보급
- 야전 전투근무지원
- 폭팔성 무기류 처치
- 인적자원 지원(보충)
- 재정관리
- 건강 근무 지원
- 종교 관련 지원
- 군악대 지원
- 일반 공병과 관련된 것

작전지속지원은 보급 시스템, 보수 및 기타 근무지원과 같은 적절하고 지속적인 군수지원을 통해 중단 없는 작전을 가능하게 한다.

◎ 지휘 및 통제

지휘 통제 전장 기능은 연습 권한과 방향에 관해 지휘관을 지원하는 업무와 시스템을 포함한다. 거기에는 아군정보 획득, 관련 정보 관리, 그리고 예하 부대를 지휘(지시)하고 선도하는 업무들이 포함된다.

지휘와 통제는 두 부분으로 나뉘는데, 지휘관과 통제시스템이 있다. 정보 시스템은 통신 시스템, 정보 지원 시스템 및 컴퓨터 네트워크를 포함하며 지휘 및 통제 시스템을 지원한다. 그들은 지휘관을 그들의 작전 지역의 어느 곳에서든 예하부하를 이끌게 한다. 지휘와 통제를 통해 지휘관은 모든 전장기능을 주도하고 통합한다.

◎ 전투력

전투력은 한 부대의 싸울 수 있는 능력이다. 전술적 차원에서 리더십의 일차적 과제는 임무를 완수하기 위한 결정적인 지점에 전투력을 창출하고 적용하는 기술을 숙달하는 것이다. 지휘자들은 전투력을 창출하기 위해 작전과정(계획, 준비, 실행 및 평가)을 이용한다. 그들은 전투력을 적용하기 위해 찾고(Find), 고착(Fix)시키고, 끝내는(Finish) 마무리(Follow-through) 모델을 시행한다.

한 부대 전투 능력의 핵심에는 세 가지의 유효성이 증명된 근접 전투 구성요소가 있는데:

(1) 화력
(2) 기동
(3) 방호(보호)/경계(보안)이다.

이러한 구성요소들은 여러 가지 이름으로 군대 역사 전반에 걸쳐 적과 싸워 승리하기 위해 필요한 중심요소들로 나타났다. 화력은 적에게 사상자를

내는 데 사용되는 무기들로 구성된다. 이동 없는 화력만으로는 결정적일 수 없다. 기동은 전장에서의 이동능력으로서 전투력의 속도, 템포, 전술적 배치에 영향을 준다. 화력과 기동성에 모두 내재(본질)된 것은 적의 화력과 기동력으로부터 방호의 필요성이다. 지휘자들은 그들 부대의 싸울 수 있는 전투능력을 보존하기 위해 방호와 경계 수단을 적용한다. 그들은 부대 화력과 기동성의 창조적인 조합으로 적의 방호를 거부한다.

◎ 상황

모든 전투 상황은 독특하다. 지휘자들은 상황을 정확하게 평가하고 그들의 부대를 운용하는 것에 대한 훌륭한 결정을 내리기 위해 최선을 다한다. 전투 환경, 군사 원칙의 적용, 바람직한 육군 작전의 종료 상태는 보병 소대와 분대의 근접전투로 절정에 이른다. 지휘자는 더 큰 군사적 목적과 그의 행동과 결정이 대규모 작전의 결과에 어떻게 영향을 미칠지 이해해야 한다.

Unit 9 | 공세작전

Useful Expressions

1. 그림 9-1은 교리적 체계 구조와 하위 작전 형태와 유형의 관계를 보여준다.
2. 실제로 많은 이런 종류의 작전들은 대대나 여단, 사단급 수준에서만 실시된다.

3. 공세 작전은 적을 격파하거나 격퇴하는 것을 목표로 한다.

4. 효과적인 공세작전은 적군, 기상, 지형에 대한 정확한 정보를 필요로 한다.

5. 격파란 적 부대(군인들과 그들의 장비)가 더 이상 싸울 수 없는 결과를 말한다.

6. 소대 및 분대 수준에서 이러한 공세작전들은 기본적으로 계획하고 준비하고 실행하는 동일한 것들이다.

7. 공격 작전의 4가지 형태는 접적 이동, 공격, 전과확대 및 추격을 포함한다.

Reading Text

◎ 작전의 교리적 체계

그림 9-1은 교리적 계층 구조와 하위 작전 형태와 유형의 관계를 보여준다. 그림 9-1은 교리적 계층 구조와 하위 작전 형태와 유형의 관계를 보여준다. 작전의 지배적인 특성은 공격, 방어, 안정화 또는 민간인 지원 작전으로 구분하지만, 해당 작전에 포함된 다른 부대들은 서로 다른 유형과 하위 형태의 작전을 수행할 수 있다.

이러한 단위들은 종종 한 유형 또는 하위 형태에서 다른 유형으로 빠르게 전환된다. 지휘관은 최대의 효과를 위해 그의 전투력을 배치하는 동안 지속적으로 적의 균형을 깨기 위하여 한 가지 유형이나 작전 형태에서 다른 형태로 빠르게 전이한다. 전환의 융통성은 성공적인 작전에 기여한다.

보병 소대들과 분대들은 교리적 체계에 나열된 모든 유형의 작전을 실시한다. 하지만, 보병 소대 및 분대들은 거의 항상 더 큰 부대의 한 부분으로 그들의 하위 형태와 유형의 이러한 작전들을 실시할 것이다. 사실, 이러한 작전 유형의 다수는 대대, 여단 또는 사단급 수준에서 수행된다. 보병 소대 및 분

공세(공격) 작전들	
• 접적 이동 　– 수색 및 공격 　– 접적 전진 • 공격 • 특수 목적 공격들 　– 매복 　– 시위(양동) 　– 양공 　– 파쇄공격 • 기동형태 　– 포위 　– 정면공격 　– 침투 　– 우회공격	• 수색 작전 　– 지역 　– 통로 　– 지대 　– 위력 수색 • 경계 작전 　– 차장 　– 보초 　– 지역 경계(통로 및 수송로 포함) • 연합부대 돌파작전 • 초월 전진 • 진지 교대 • 부대 이동(도로 행군)
방어 작전들	
• 지역 방어 • 후퇴작전 　– 지연전 　– 철수 　– 철퇴	• 정찰 　– 전투 정찰 　– 수색 정찰 　– 경계 정찰 • 전술적 이동 • 전투 훈련 • 승무원 훈련

그림 9-1. 작전의 교리적 체계

대에 적용 가능한 작전의 유형들은 이 교범에서 더 다루어진다.

◎ 공세(공격) 작전

공격(공세) 작전은 적을 격파하거나 격퇴하는 것을 목표로 한다. 그들의 목적은 적에게 미국의 의지를 부여하고 결정적인 승리를 달성하는 것이다(FM 3-0, 작전). 공격의 우세는 미군 작전 교리의 기본 원칙이다. 방어가 군사행동의 더 강한 형태인 반면 공격은 결정적인 형태다. 전술적 고려사항은 육군 병력이 일정 기간 동안 방어 작전을 수행하도록 요구할 수 있다. 하지만 지휘자들은 끊임없이 공세 쪽으로 방향을 바꿀 방법을 찾고 있다. 공세 작전은 공백 속에 존재하지 않는다. 그것들은 방어와 전술적 가능 작전들과 나란히 존재한다. 지휘자들은 그들의 부대 임무가 전체적인 개념에 어떻게 자리 잡는지 (기여하는지) 결정하기 위해 임무를 두 단계 상향(2단계 상급부대)으로 분석한다. 예를 들어, 보병 소대장은 중대와 대대 임무들을 분석하게 된다.

효과적인 공격 작전은 적군, 기상, 지형에 대한 정확한 정보를 필요로 한다. 그런 다음 지휘자들은 (적과) 접촉하기 전에 유리한 위치에 그들의 병력을 배치한다. 결정적인 행동 이전에 적군과 접촉하고, 결정적인 행동을 위한 최적의 상황을 형성하도록 신중하게 계획한다. 결정적인 행동은 갑작스럽고 맹렬한 것으로서, 예하부대의 주도권을 이용하는 것이다. 따라서 보병 소대장과 분대장들은 기습, 집중, 속도, 대담성으로 공세작전을 수행한다.

공격과 공격을 실시하는 것 사이에는 미묘한 차이가 있다. 공격은 매일 사용하는 일반적으로 적이나 진지에 대한 화력과 이동의 근접 전투행위를 의미한다. 공격은 모든 종류의 작전 중 전장에서 빈번히 일어난다. 공격을 실시한다는 것은 구체적인 교리적 의미와 요건을 갖춘 공세 작전 4가지 형태의 하나를 의미한다.

◎ 공세(공격) 작전의 목적

부대가 어떻게 공격 작전을 수행할 것인가 하는 방법은 임무의 목적과 전반적인 의도에 따라 결정된다. 공격에는 네 가지 일반적인 목적이 있다: 적을 균형을 잃게 하고, 적의 능력을 압도하며, 적의 방어를 교란하고, 적들의 패배나 격파를 보장하는 것이다. 실제로, 이러한 각각의 목적은 적군과 지형에 대한 방향(지향성, 의미)을 가지고 있다. 구분은 단지 작전의 지배적인 특성을 묘사할 뿐이다.

◎ 적에 대한 지향

지휘자들은 적의 대형과 능력을 격파하기 위해 적 지향적 공격을 운용한다. 격파란 적 부대(군인들과 그들의 장비)가 더 이상 싸울 수 없는 결과를 말한다. 공격이 성공할 수 있도록 병력 지향적 공격을 위해 모든 것을 파괴해야 된다는 것은 아니다. 그것은 일반적으로 적의 능력 또는 부대의 응집력에 초점을 맞추면 충분하다. 이 공격들은 적의 취약점에 대해 가장 잘 운용된다. 일단 파괴가 일어나면 기회의 창은 열린다. 이것은 지역적 그리고 일반적인 전과 확대와 추격을 통해 적의 불균형을 이용하는 것은 지휘자의 몫이다.

◎ 지형에 지향

지휘자들은 지형이나 시설을 확보하기 위해 지형을 중심으로 공격을 감행한다. 지형을 중심으로 공격을 수행하는 부대는 기회의 창을 활용할 수 있는 행동의 자유가 적다. 부대의 최우선 과제는 지형이나 시설이다. 적의 취약점에 대한 공격(공적)은 지형이나 시설의 경계가 더 이상 의문의 여지가 없는 경우에만 발생할 수 있다.

◎ 전술적 가능성과 보병 소대 행동

비록 아군들이 항상 적에 초점을 두고 남아있다 하더라도 성격상 공세적이거나 다른 작전들을 구상하고, 구체화하고, 유지할 수 있는 아군이 수행할 많은 행동들이 있다. 지휘자들은 작전의 전반적인 목적을 지원하기 위해 전술적으로 가능한 작전들을 운용한다.

◎ 공세(공격) 작전의 형태(유형)

공격작전의 유형(형태)은 작전을 둘러싼 맥락(지형 또는 병력 지향)에 의해 기술
된다. 소대와 분대 수준에서 이러한 공격 작전들은 기본적으로 비슷하게 계
획되고 준비되고 실행된다. 4가지 유형의 공격 작전들에 포함되는 것은:

(1) 접적 이동 – 적과 접촉을 획득하거나 재획득하기 위해 시행(병력 지향)
(2) 공격 – 결정적인 결과를 달성하기 위해 시행(지형 지향 또는 병력 지향)
(3) 전과확대 – 성공적인 공격의 이점을 활용하기 위해 시행(병력 지향)
(4) 추격 – 도망가는 적을 격파하기 위해 시행(병력 지향)

공세작전의 이 순서는 정상적인 발생 순서에 따라 나열되기 때문에 신중
한 것이다. 일반적으로 지휘자들은 적을 찾기 위해 접적이동을 한다. 지휘자
가 적에 대해 성공하리만큼 정보를 충분히 획득하면 공격을 감행한다. 성공
적 공격이란, 지휘자가 적의 무질서함을 이용하여 공격의 성공을 전과 확대
하는 것이다. 전과학대가 성공한 후에, 지휘자는 도망가는 적을 포획하거나
차단하여 격파를 완성하는 추격을 실행한다. 비록 보병 소대들과 분대들이
전과확대와 추격 작전에 참여하지만 계획을 세우지는 않는다.

Unit 10 | 방어 작전

Useful Expressions

1. 방어 작전은 적의 공격을 격퇴하거나, 시간을 절약하거나, 병력을 절약

하거나, 공세 작전에 유리한 조건을 개발한다.

2. 부대가 방어를 수립하는 방법은 임무의 목적과 의도에 따라 결정된다.

3. 지휘관들은 위험의 감수 없이 작전을 수행하고자 하는 모든 전투력을 거의 보유하지 않는다.

4. 그 결과 지휘관들은 다른 지역의 기동방어 및 공격작전을 위한 유리한 여건을 조성하기 위하여 공간과 시간에 병력을 준비한다.

5. 아군의 전투력을 보존하기 위한 방어는 아군을 보호(방호)하고 주요 아군 자산이 파괴되는 것을 예방하기 위한 것이다.

6. 적의 취약점에 대한 공격(공적)은 지형이나 시설의 경계가 더 이상 의문의 여지가 없는 경우에만 발생할 수 있다.

7. 후퇴는 상급 수준의 지휘관들이 적과의 접촉을 유지하거나 단절하기 위해 사용하는 기술이다.

8. 후퇴란 공격적 전과확대나 추격에 대한 방어의 대응이다. 후퇴에 사용되는 세 가지 기법이 있다.

p.
268-
273

Reading Text

◎ 방어 작전들

방어 작전은 적의 공격을 격퇴하거나, 시간을 절약하거나, 병력을 절약하거나, 공세 작전에 유리한 조건을 개발한다. 방어 작전만으로는 일반적으로 결정적인 것(승리)을 달성할 수 없다. 그들의 가장 중요한 목적은 육군 전투력이 주도권을 되찾을 수 있도록 하는 반격의 여건을 조성하는 것이다(FM 1-02). 방어 작전은 공백 속에 존재하지 않는다. 그것들은 공격, 전술적으로 가능한 작전들, 그리고 보병 소대 활동들과 나란히 존재한다. 지휘자들은 그들 부대의 임무가 전체적인 개념 내에서 어떻게 차지하는지(기여하는지) 결정하기 위해 임무를 2단계 위(상급부대)까지 분석한다.

　전술 기동 원칙은 방어에도 적용된다. 결정적이 되려면 방어 전술도 양개 요소를 보유해야 한다. 이동성을 방어의 일부로 유지하는 것은 지휘자의 가장 큰 도전요소들 중 하나이다. 방어 전투력이 공자의 타격을 기다리고 공격을 성공적으로 회피하고 격퇴한다는 것은 사실이지만, 방어가 하나의 소극적인 활동이라는 의미는 아니다. 지휘자들은 항상 그들의 방어 활동에 이동을 통합하는 방법을 모색한다.

　작전을 시행하는 동안, 형태와 무관하게, 아군 전투력은 그 부대가 정지하거나 이동을 재개할 것을 요구받는 많은 전환을 해야 한다. 이동하지 않는 보병 소대와 분대들은 방어를 하고 있는 것이다. (공격 중) 이동을 정지하는 부대들은 즉각 방어로 전환한다. 이 전환은 부대가 신속하고 모든 군인들과 그들의 부대들에게는 제2의 천성이 되어야 한다. 이것은 그 부대가 수적으로 우세하거나 생존을 위해 전투하고 있는 곳에서 전술적 상황이 신속하게 전환되어야 하는 보병 소대 및 분대 급에 특히 관련이 있다.

◎ 방어 목적들

　어떤 부대가 방어를 구축하는 것은 임무의 목적과 의도에 따라 결정된다. 방어를 시행하는 데는 4가지 일반적인 목적들이 있는데 이는, 적의 공격을 격퇴하거나, 한 지역에서 아군병력을 절약하여 다른 지역에 전투력을 집중하기 위해서나, 시간을 절약하거나, 공격작전을 재개하기 위하여 유리한 조건을 개발하기 위함이다. 실제로, 방어 수행을 위한 이러한 각각의 명시된 목적들은 모든 방어(작전)에서 고려된다. 그 범주들은 지배적인 목적을 기술할 뿐이다. 보병 소대와 분대들은 또한 주요 지형이나 시설과 같은 특정 지역을 방어하는 과업을 수행할 수도 있다.

◎ 공격하는 적의 격퇴와 공세작전을 위한 조건 개발

　방어는 아군의 전투력을 보존하면서 적의 공격을 격퇴하는 것이다. 적의 공격을 격퇴하기 위해서는 그 자신을 방어 행동으로 전환하는 것을 요구받는다. 이런 일이 발생하는 동안, 아군 전투력을 위한 기회의 창도 생길 수 있다. 국지적 그리고 일반적인 역습(반격)을 통해 적 불균형의 이점을 이용하는 것은 지휘자의 몫이다.

◎ 병력을 절약하여 다른 지역에 집중

　지휘관들은 거의 위험의 감수 없이 작전을 수행하고자 희망하는 모든 전투 병력을 보유하지 않는다. 병력절약은 조공에게 최소 필수 전투력을 할당하는 것으로 정의된다(가능하다)(FM 1-02). 그것은 결정적인 작전에서 — 압도적인 효과 — 우월성을 달성하기 위해 선택된 지역에서는 신중한 위험을 감수할 것을 요구한다. 결과적으로 지휘관들은 다른 지역에서의 기동방어 및 공격작전에 유리한 여건을 조성하기 위해 공간과 시간에 병력을 조정한다.

◎ 시간절약

　아군 전투력을 보존하기 위한 방어는 아군 전투력을 보호하고 주요 아군 자산 파괴를 예방하기 위한 것이다. 부대가 스스로를 보호하기 위해 방어를 구축할 때는 시간적 여유가 있다. 비록 아군은 항상 적에 초점을 맞추고 있지만, 부대를 유지하기 위해 아군이 수행하는 많은 행동들이 있다. 작전지속력을 위한 행위들은 일반적으로 그 부대가 활동을 수행하는 동안 방어 태세 구축을 요구한다. 예를 들면 진지강화와 재편성, 재보급/군수패키지, 탑승지점/착륙지점, 그리고 사상자 후송/의무후송 등이 포함된다. 방어의 이러한 형태는 집결지에서의 행동, 전투력을 건설하기 위한 숙영지 구축이나 수적으로 우세한 적군을 직면했을 때와 연관시킬 수 있다.

◎ 공세작전 재개를 위한 유리한 조건 개발

적은 전투력이나 진지 등의 분야에서 아군보다 유리한 점을 가질 수 있다. 이는 전투력을 증강하기 위해 아군이 방어하는 (장소에서) 강압진입작전을 하는 동안 자주 발생한다.

◎ 주요 지형 및 시설

특정 지역에 대한 적의 접근을 거부하는 방어는 특정 위치, 핵심지형, 또는 시설을 보호하기 위해 계획된다. 보병 소대들은 언덕 정상에서부터 주요 기반시설에 이르는 지역과 종교지역까지 방어하는 임무를 부여받을 수 있다. 왜냐하면 방어는 지형을 지향하기 때문에, 지휘자들은 기회의 창을 이용하는 데 있어서 행동의 자유를 덜 가질 수 있다. 그 부대의 최우선 과제는 지형이나 시설이다. 적의 취약점에 대한 공격은 지형이나 시설의 경계가 더 이상 문제가 되지 않을 경우에만 발생할 수 있다.

◎ 방어 작전의 유형

방어 작전은 다음 3가지 범주 중 하나로 분류된다.

(1) 지역 방어 - 특정 기간 동안 지형을 유지하는 데 초점을 둠 (지형 지향)
(2) 기동방어 - 고착부대로 적의 공격을 저지하고 타격부대로 적을 격

멸(사단급 이상의 작전) (병력지향)

(3) 후퇴 – 적으로부터 이탈하는 조직적인 이동을 포함하는 방어 작전의 일종. 후퇴작전의 3가지 유형은 지연, 철수 그리고 철퇴

◎ 지역 방어

지역 방어는 전술적 수준(여단 이하)에서 수행하는 가장 일반적인 방어 작전이다. 이는 9장(FM3-21.3)에서 논한다.

◎ 기동 방어

기동 방어는 보통 군단 차원의 작전이다. 기동 방어에는 고착부대, 타격부대, 예비부대 등 3가지 부류의 병력이 있다. 기동 방어의 결정적인 작전은 타격부대다. 고착부대로 지정된 부대는 본질적으로 지역 방어를 수행한다. 타격부대로 지정된 부대는 본질적으로 공격을 실시한다. (기동방위에 대한 자세한 내용은 FM 3-90, 전술 참조)

◎ 철수

철수는 상급 지휘관들이 적과의 접촉을 유지하거나 단절하기 위해 사용하는 기술이다. 이것은 주도권을 되찾고 적을 격퇴할 수 있는 여건을 조성하기 위한 더 큰 작전 계획의 일환으로 행해진다. 후퇴는 현재의 상황을 개선시키거나 상황이 악화되는 것을 막는다. 이러한 작전들은 목적을 위한 수단이지, 그 자체가 목적이 아니다. 상급 지휘관의 후퇴 작전에서 보병 소대의 전투는 두 가지 기술 중 하나를 사용한다: 적과 싸우거나 새로운 위치로 이동하는 것

이다. 지휘자들은 철수가 아군 부대의 사기에 잠재적으로 비극적 영향을 미친다는 것을 알고 있어야 한다. 철수는 공격적 전과확대나 추격에 대한 방어와 같은 개념이다. 철수에 사용되는 세 가지 기법은 :

- 지연전 – 시간을 위한 공간의 거래(적군의 속도 저하를 시도)
- 철수 – 공간을 위한 시간 거래(적과 최대한 멀리 접촉 단절)
- 철퇴 – 적과 비접촉하에서의 이동

Unit 11 | 작전 명령 양식

Useful Expressions

1. 전투편성은 작전을 위해 부대가 어떻게 조직되는가를 설명한다. 이전 전투편성에 변경이 없는 경우에는 "변동 없음"을 표시한다.
2. 상황은 예하부대 지휘자의 상황 이해에 필수적인 정보를 제공한다.
3. 임무는 완수해야 할 과제와 그 목적을 명확하고 간결하게 기술한다.
4. 실시사항은 지휘관의 의도, 작전개념, 이동 및 기동계획, 화력계획, 전사 상자 후송, 예하부대 과업, 전투지원부대 과업으로 구성된다.
5. 작전지속지원에는 군수, 인사근무지원, 육군의무체계지원이 포함된다.
6. 지휘 및 통제는 지휘, 통제 및 통신으로 구성된다.

Reading Text

명령은 상급부대에서 예하부대로 전달하는 지시(지침)사항으로서 구두, 서면 또는 신호로 하는 의사소통이다. 지휘관들은 구두 또는 서면으로 명령을 내린다. 5항 형식(상황, 임무, 실시, 작전지속지원, 지휘 및 통신)은 명령 발행의 표준으로 유지된다. 명령(구두 또는 서면)을 내릴 때 사용하는 기법은 지휘관의 재량에 달려 있으며, 각각의 기법은 시간과 상황에 따라 다르다. 육군 부대들은 3가지 형태의 명령을 사용하는데, 이는 작전명령(OPORD), 단편명령(FRAGO), 준비명령(WARNO)이다.

작전명령 양식

(비문 표시)

(구두 명령과 변동사항, 필요시) (선택사항)

사본 번호

발행 본부

발행 장소

서명 일자 및 시간

참조 문서 번호

부대편성: 작전을 위해 부대가 어떻게 편성되는지 설명. 이전 과업편성과 변동이 없을 시는 "변동 없음"으로 표시

1. 상황

예하부대 지휘자들의 상황에 대한 이해에 중요한 정보 제공

- 관심지역

- 작전지역

(1) 지형

(2) 기상

a. 적군. 투명도나 요도 참조시킴. 상급부대 본부와 기타 사실에 의해 제공된 관련 있는 정보 및 적에 대한 가정 포함. 이 분석은 결론 및 아래 내

용으로 명시됨.

(1) 배치, 구성 및 전투력

(2) 최근 활동

(3) 위치 및 능력

(4) 가장 가능성 있는 방책

b. 아군. 예하부대가 그들의 과업을 완수하는 데 필요한 정보 제공.

(1) 상급부대 임무 및 의도. 제2항의 상급부대 임무 및 제3a항의 작전개 념에 기술된 축약된 내용

(2) 좌측 부대 임무

(3) 우측 부대 임무

(4) 전방 부대 임무

(5) 예비 또는 후속 부대 임무

(6) 상급 부대의 지원 또는 증강되는 부대들

c. 배속 및 파견. 부대편성에 보이지 않으면 여기에 목록화 또는 부록에 명 시하고, 소대로부터의 배속 및 파견 부대들은 유효시간 함께 명시.

2. 임무

완수해야 할 과제와 그 목적(누가, 무엇, 언제, 어디서, 왜)에 대한 명확하고 간 결한 서술을 제공한다. 지휘자는 그의 임무 분석에서 임무를 도출한다.

3. 실시

의도. 작전의 목적과 병력, 적, 지형 중에서 관련 있는 것과 명시된 비전 을 제시한다.

a. 지휘관 의도

b. 작전개념

(1) 기동

(2) 화력

(3) 수색 및 정찰

(4) 정보

(5) 공병

(6) 방공

(7) 정보 작전

c. 이동 및 기동계획

e. 화력 계획

f. 예하부대의 과업

g. 전투지원부대 과업

(1) 정보

(2) 공병

(3) 화력지원

(4) 방공

(5) 통신

(6) 화생방 및 폭발무기

(7) 군사경찰대장

(8) 군사 정보지원작전, 이전 심리작전 또는 심리전 작전

(9) 민군

h. 협조지시

(1) 계획이나 명령의 효력발생 시간 또는 조건

(2) 지휘관 주요 첩보요구

(3) 우군첩보기본요소

(4) 위험감소 통제수단

(5) 교전규칙

(6) 환경 고려요소

(7) 전투력 방호

4. 작전지속지원

a. 군수

(1) 작전지속지원 투명도

(2) 정비

(3) 수송

(4) 보급

(5) 야전 근무

b. 인사근무지원

(1) 적포로 표시 및 취급요령

(2) 종교근무

c. 육군 위생체계 지원

(1) 의무 지휘 및 통제

(2) 의무치료

(3) 의무후송

(4) 예방의무

5. 지휘 및 통제

a. 지휘

(1) 지휘관 위치

(2) 지휘권 승계

b. 통제

(1) 지휘소

(2) 보고서

c. 통신

(1) 유효한 통신운용지시 색인표

(2) 통신방법 우선순위

(3) 신호탄과 신호

(4) 암구어

(5) 수하 및 암호

(6) 숫자 조합

(7) 일상 암구어

(8) 약정 인식 신호

수신여부(필수)

이름(지휘관 마지막 이름)

계급(지휘관 계급)

공식(선택)

부록들: 문자와 제목 순서별 부록 목록

부록 A(전투편성)

부록 B(정보)

부록 C(작전투명도)

부록 D(화력지원)

부록 E(교전규칙)

부록 F(공병)

부록 G(방공)

부록 H(통신)

부록 I(전투근무지원)

부록 J(화학, 생물학)

부록 K(군사경찰)

부록 L(수색 및 정찰)

부록 M(종심지역작전)

부록 N(후방지역작전)

부록 O(공역 지휘 및 통제)

부록 P(지휘 및 통제전)

부록 Q(작전 보안)

부록 R(심리전)

부록 S(기만작전) 지시

부록 T(전자전) 지시

부록 U(민군 작전)

부록 V(공보)

(특정 부록을 사용하지 않는 경우, 부록 문자 옆에 "사용하지 않음"이라고 명시)

준비명령 양식 및 내용: 작전명령 양식 번역 참조

단편명령 양식 및 내용: 작전명령 양식 번역 참조

Unit 12 | 미래 작전 환경

Useful Expressions

1. 다양한 적들은 미국의 안보와 핵심이익을 위협하기 위해 전통적, 비전통적, 그리고 혼합 전략을 운용할 것이다.

2. 국가 및 비국가 행위자들은 통신, 장거리 정밀 화력, 감시 분야에서 미국의 장점들을 교란시키는 기술을 적용할 것이다.

3. 인터넷과 소셜미디어를 통한 정보의 확산은 사람, 정부, 군사, 그리고 위협 간의 상호작용을 증폭시키고 가속화시킨다.

4. 강적은 상대가 효과적으로 대응할 수 없게 만드는 방식으로 능력이나 전술을 적용하는 것이다.

5. 광범위한 행위자들의 배치는 우주와 사이버 공간에서 합동군 행동의 자유에 도전한다.

6. 내부 이주 및 높은 출산율은 도시화를 증가시키는 데 기여한다.

Reading Text

◎ 미래 작전환경과 예상되는 위협

다양한 적들은 미국의 안보와 핵심이익을 위협하기 위해 전통적, 비전통적, 그리고 혼합 전략을 운용할 것이다. 위협은 국가나 초국가적인 테러리스트, 반란군, 그리고 범죄 조직과 같은 비국가 행위자들로부터 나올 수 있다. 적들은 단순하고 이중적인 사용 기술(즉석 폭발 장치와 같은)뿐만 아니라 첨단 기술을 계속 적용할 것이다. 적들은 전통적인 대응책(분산, 은폐, 민간인과의 혼합과 같은)을 통해 미국의 강점(장거리 감시 및 정밀 타격과 같은)을 회피할 것이다. 새로운 군사 기술이 더 쉽게 이전됨에 따라 잠재적 위협은 미국의 전력투사에 대응하기 위해 미국의 군사 능력을 모방하고 미국의 행동 자유를 제한할 것이다. 이러한 능력에는 정밀 유도 로켓, 포병, 박격포, 그리고 미국의 전통적 강점을 공중 및 해양영역에서 표적화하는 미사일 등이 포함된다. 적대국들은 방어체계를 압도하고, 우발사태나 위기에 개입하기 위해 미국에 높은 비용을 부과하려 할 수도 있다.

국가 및 비국가 행위자들은 통신, 장거리 정밀 화력, 감시 분야에서 미국의 장점을 교란시키기 위해 기술을 적용할 것이다. 적의 행동은 지상, 공중, 해양, 우주, 사이버 공간 영역에서 미국이 지배력을 달성하고 있는 능력을 감소시킬 것이다. 또한, 정치적 목적을 달성하기 위해 적 조직은 미국 본토로 작전을 확장할 것이다. 적과 적대세력들은 물리적 전장을 넘어 작전하게 되고 적들은 공공의 인식에 효과를 주기 위해 선전과 허위 정보를 이용하면서 미군과 파트너 군의 침투(예: 내부자 위협)를 통해 (우리의) 노력을 전복할 것이다. 역설적으로 미국 내의 네트워크 기기의 연결성은 이용할 수 있는 취약성과 함께 적대세력들을 보여주고 있다.

미래 작전환경의 다음과 같은 5가지 특성은 지상군 작전에 상당한 영향을 미칠 가능성이 있다.

1) 인간의 상호 작용과 사건의 증가된 속도와 가속도

정보가 전 세계적으로 다양한 수단을 통해 발산하는 스피드는 속도, 가속도(추진력), 그리고 사람들 간의 상호 작용 수준을 증가시킨다. 인터넷과 소셜미디어를 통한 정보의 확산은 사람, 정부, 군사, 그리고 위협 간의 상호작용을 증폭시키고 가속화시킨다. 정보에 대한 접근은 조직들이 지방, 지역, 그리고 전 세계적으로 인력과 자원을 동원할 수 있게 한다. 허위정보와 선전은 정치적 목적을 지원하는 폭력을 조장한다. 제때에 사건을 압축하려면 주도권을 잡고, 이야기를 통제하고, 그리고 질서를 강화하기에 충분한 규모로 신속하게 대응할 수 있는 전투력을 필요로 한다.

2) 강적의 잠재성

강적은 상대가 효과적으로 대응할 수 없게 만드는 방식으로 능력이나 전술을 적용하는 것이다. 기술 면에서 차별적인 이점을 획득하기 위해 잠재적 적들은 투자하고 강함을 달성하기 위한 미국의 능력을 잠식한다.

이러한 기술에는 장거리 정밀화력, 대공방어 체제, 전자화력, 그리고 무인항공기 체제(UAS) 등이 포함된다. 반접근 및 지역거부 능력은 공중과 해양 영역으로부터 지상에 전투력을 투사하는 능력뿐만 아니라 공중우세권과 해양통제를 달성하고자 하는 합동군의 능력에 도전한다.

잠재적 적들은 지장을 초래하고 파괴적인 악성코드와 같은 사이버 공간기능과 미국의 통신과 기동의 자유를 방해하는 반위성무기와 같은 우주공간능력을 개발할 것이다. 적의 강적화를 막기 위해 능력을 모방하거나 교란하려는 적의 노력을 예상하면서 육군은 새로운 능력을 개발해야 한다. 강함을유지하기 위해 합동군은 기술을 연합하고 여러 영역에 걸친 노력을 통합하여적을 복합적 진퇴양난에 놓이게 해야 한다.

3) 대량 파괴 무기의 확산

화학, 생물학, 방사능, 핵 및 고성능 폭발물 무기 형태로 다양한 국가와 비국가 행위자들에게 대량 살상 무기 확산은 미국과 국제안보에 증가된 위협을 부과하고 있다.

적대세력들은 CBRNE 지식, 기술, 그리고 설비를 공유한다. 극단주의 조직으로서 내전을 부추기고 영토, 인구, 무기에 대한 통제를 확립함에 따라 핵 자산의 증가에 대한 통제를 상실할 위험이 증가한다. 게다가, 유도된 에너지와 정교한 CBRNE 무기는 적들에게 미군과 민간인들을 대량 사상자로 위협할 수 있는 전례 없는 능력을 줄 수 있다. CBRNE 위협에 대항하려면 비우호적인 조건에서 작전할 수 있는 능력을 갖추고, 무기의 존재를 확인 또는 거부하기 위해 정찰을 실시하고, 그러한 무기들을 보유한 적군을 격파하고, CBRNE 부대가 감소 또는 그들이 무력화될 때까지 그러한 무기를 억제하기 위해 영토를 확보하는, 특수 훈련되고, 장비되고, 조직된 육군 병력이 필요하다.

4) 발달된 사이버공간의 확산과 대 우주공간 능력

사이버 공간과 우주공간 영역은, 비국가 행위자뿐만 아니라 지구적 또는 지역의 경쟁자들이 그들의 접근을 보호하고 다른 이들에 대한 접근을 방해하거나 거부하는 능력에 투자함에 따라, 중요성이 커지고 있다.

광범위한 행위자들의 배치는 우주와 사이버 공간에서 합동군 행동의 자유에 도전한다. 적과 적대세력들은 경쟁자로서 공간과 사이버 공간을 확장하고 전술작전에 영향을 주는 협력하고 있다. 예를 들면 적의 전 지구 위치에 있는 위성의 전파방해 능력은 정확한 화력을 부정확하게 만든다. 육군 지휘관들은 그들 자신의 시스템을 보호하고 작전하는 적의 능력을 방해해야 한다. 육군 부대는 통신 성능이 저하되고 사이버 및 우주 기능에 대한 접근이 감소된 상태에서 작전을 수행해야 할 것이다. 육군은 지상에 근거한 적의 우주 공간과 사이버 공간 능력을 파괴하기 위해 정찰, 공세작전 또는 습격을 통해 합동작전을 지원해야 할 것이다.

5) 인구, 도시, 그리고 복잡한 지형 간의 인구집단 및 작전

2030년까지 도시 지역에서 세계 인구의 비율은 60%로 증가할 것이다. 내부 이주 및 높은 출산율은 도시화의 증가에 기여한다.

적대세력들은 미국의 군사적 이점을 피하기 위해 이러한 도시지역과 다른 복잡한 지역의 사람들 사이에서 작전하며, 전쟁은 정치적 현상으로서 본질적으로 사람에 관한 것이기 때문에 그들은 도시에서 작전한다. 도시가 성장함에 따라, 많은 정부는 적절한 보안, 고용, 사회기반시설 및 서비스를 제공하는 데 실패한다. 무장 단체들은 대중의 불만과 취약한 통치 방식을 이용할 것이다. 도시 지역은 테러리스트, 반란군 또는 범죄 조직의 안전한 피난처와 지원 기지가 된다. 도시 지역은 대량 잔학행위의 잠재적인 현장이다. 적들은 미국뿐만 아니라 동맹국을 위협하는 장거리 미사일의 발사 플랫폼(대)으로 도시를 이용할 수도 있다. 도시 환경은 위협을 정확하게 조준하는 능력을 저하시키기 때문에, 합동작전은 그러한 위협을 격퇴하기 위해 혼잡하고 제한된 도시 지형(지하, 지표면, 초표면 포함)에서 작전할 수 있는 지상군을 필요로 할 것이다.

도시 환경의 기술적, 지리적, 정치적, 그리고 군사적 도전의 이해는 복잡하고 불확실한 환경에서 번성하는 혁신적이고 적응력 있는 지휘자와 응집력이 있는 팀들을 요구할 것이다. 도시 환경에서의 작전은 분권화된 연합군 및 합동능력이 필요하다.

Unit 13 | 군대 리더십

Useful Expressions

p. 298

1. 리더십은 임무를 완수하고 조직을 개선하기 위한 목적, 방향, 동기를 부여함으로써 사람들에게 영향을 미치는 과정이다.

2. 이것은 야간, 주말, 그리고 예하 부대원이 근무하고 있는 어떤 조건이나 장소에서든 리더십의 존재를 포함한다.

3. 개선을 위한 평가에서 예하 부대원을 포함시키는 2개의 검증된 기법은 진행 중 검토와 사후 조치 검토(AAR)이다.

4. 사람의 도덕과 윤리적 자질들로 구성된 성격은 무엇이 옳은지 결정하는 데 도움을 주며, 상황이나 결과에 관계없이 지도자에게 적절한 일을 하도록 동기를 부여한다.

5. 성격은 사람이 누구인지, 어떻게 행동하는지를 결정하고, 옳고 그름을 판단하는 데 도움을 주며, 옳은 것을 선택한다.

6. 국가와 기관에 봉사할 것을 맹세함으로써, 사람은 새로운 가치인 육군 가치에 따라 살고 행동하는 것에 동의한다.

7. 순서대로 읽을 때, 육군 가치의 첫 글자들은 "LDRSHIP"라는 약자를 형성한다.

8. 육군 지휘자들은 다른 사람의 상황, 동기, 감정과 진정으로 연관되어 있을 때 공감을 나타낸다.

9. 개인 차원의 규율(수련)은 주로 자기 수양, 즉 자신의 행동을 통제할 수 있는 능력이다.

Reading Text

◎ 리더십의 정의

리더십은 임무를 완수하고 조직을 개선하기 위한 목적, 방향, 동기를 부여함으로써 사람들에게 영향을 미치는 과정이다. 전투력의 한 요소로서, 리더십은 전투력의 다른 요소들(정보, 임무 명령, 이동과 기동, 지능, 화력, 작전지속지원과 방호)을 통합한다. 자신감 있고, 유능하며, 정보에 입각한 리더십은 전투력의 다른 요소들의 효과를 심화시킨다.

영향력 영향력은 — 군인 및 민간인, 정부 및 비정부 파트너, 또는 심지어 방관자 같은 지역 주민들 — 사람들이 요구되는 것을 하도록 한다. 영향력은 단순히 명령을 전달하는 그 이상을 수반한다. 말과 개인적인 시범을 통해서 리더들이 목적, 방향 및 동기를 소통하게 한다.

목적 목적은 부하들에게 원하는 결과를 얻을 수 있는 이유를 준다. 지휘자들은 추종자들에게 분명한 목적을 제공해야 한다. 지휘자들은 요청이나 명령을 통해 목적을 전달하는 직접적인 수단을 사용할 수 있다.

방향 명확한 방향을 제시하기 위해서는 임무의 우선순위를 정하고, 완성에 대한 책임을 부여하고, 부하(예하부대)들이 표준을 이해하도록 하는 등 임무를 완수하기 위해 해야 할 일을 의사소통하는 것이 포함된다. 부하들이 방향을 원하고 필요로 하지만, 그들은 도전적인 업무, 양질의 훈련, 그리고 적절한 자원을 기대한다. 그들은 적절한 행동의 자유를 가져야 한다. 명확한 방향을 제시하면 추종자들은 지휘관의 의도 내에서 훈련된 진취성을 통해 계획과 명령을 수정함으로써 변화하는 상황에 적응할 수 있다.

동기 동기부여는 임무를 완수하기 위해 필요한 일을 할 의지와 진취성을 제공한다. 동기부여는 내부에서 나오지만, 다른 사람의 행동과 말은 그것에 영향을 미친다. 동기부여에서 지휘자의 역할은 다른 사람들의 필요와 욕구를 이해하고, 개인의 욕망을 팀 목표로 조정하고 고양시키며, 다른 사람들이 그러한 더 큰 목표를 달성하도록 고무시키는 것이다. 어떤 사람들은 일을 성사시키기 위한 내부적인 동기부여가 높은 반면, 다른 사람들은 더 많은 확신과 긍정적인 강화 그리고 피드백을 필요로 한다.

동기부여에 대한 간접적인 접근은 직접적인 접근만큼이나 성공할 수 있다. 개인적인 예를 들면 다른 사람들에서도 추동력을 지속시킬 수 있다. 이것은 지휘자들이 어려움을 함께할 때 명백해진다. 부대가 배치를 준비할 때, 모든 핵심 지휘자들은 힘든 일을 분담해야 한다. 여기에는 야간, 주말, 부하(예하부대)들이 근무하고 있는 어떤 조건이나 장소에서나 리더십의 존재가 포함된다.

조직 개선 미래에 대한 개선은 진행 중이고 완료된 프로젝트와 임무의 중요한 교훈을 포착하고 실천하는 것을 의미한다. 개선은 효율적이고 효과적인 조직을 만들기 위해 노력하는 관리적 행동이다. 개발적인(계발적인) 상담은 부하(예하부대)들의 업무 수행을 향상시키고 미래의 책임에 대비하는 데 중요하다. 상담은 약한 분야뿐만 아니라 강한 분야도 다루어야 한다. 3부에서는 상담에 관한 정보를 제공한다. 개선을 위한 평가 시 부하가 참여하는 2개의 검증된 기법은 진행 중인 검토와 사후검토(AAR)이다.

육군 지휘자 특성의 기초 사람의 도덕적, 윤리적 자질들로 구성된 성격은 무엇이 옳은지 결정하는 데 도움을 주며, 상황이나 결과에 상관없이 적절한 일을 하도록 지휘자에게 동기를 부여한다. 육군 가치와 일치하는 정보에 입각한 윤리적 양심은 지휘자들이 어려운 문제에 직면했을 때 올바른 선택을 하도록 강화한다. 육군 지휘자들은 이러한 가치들을 구체화하여 다른 사람들도 그렇게 하도록 고무시켜야 한다.

성공적인 리더십을 위해서는 인격이 필수적이다. 그것은 사람들이 누구인지, 그들이 어떻게 행동하는지, 옳고 그름을 결정하는 데 도움을 주고, 옳은 것을 선택하게 한다. 지휘자의 핵심에 대한 내부 및 중심 요소는 다음과 같다.

- 육군의 가치관
- 공감
- 전사 기풍과 근무 기풍
- 규율

육군의 가치관 군인과 육군 민간인은 유년기에 발달하여 수년간 개인적인 경험을 쌓으면서 길러진 개인적 가치관을 가지고 군대에 들어간다. 국가와 기관에 봉사할 것을 맹세함으로써, 사람들은 새로운 가치인 육군의 가치관에 따라 살고 행동하기로 동의한다. 육군 가치는 성공적인 육군 지휘자들에게 필수적이라고 여겨지는 원칙과 기준, 그리고 자질들로 구성되어 있다. 그들은 어떤 상황에서도 군인과 육군 민간인들이 올바른 결정을 내리도록 돕는 데 필수적이다. 가치관을 가르치는 것은 육군 가치관과 예상 기준에 대한 공통의 이해를 창조하는 중요한 지휘자의 책임이다.

육군은 모든 육군 구성원이 발전시켜야 할 7가지 가치를 인정하고 있다. 순차적으로 읽을 때, 육군 가치의 첫 글자는 "LDRSHIP"라는 약어를 형성한다.

- 충성: 미국 헌법, 육군, 당신 부대, 그리고 다른 병사들에 대한 진실된 믿음과 충성을 지켜라.
- 책무: 의무를 이행하라.
- 존중: 그들이 대접받아져야 하는 대로 대접하라.
- 사심 없는 근무: 국가, 육군과 부하들의 복지를 자기보다 우선시하라.
- 명예: 육군의 가치에 부응하라.
- 정직성: 합법적, 도덕적으로 옳은 일을 한다.
- 개인적 용기: 두려움, 위험 또는 역경을 직시(물리적 · 도덕적)하라.

◎ 공감

군 지휘자들은 그들이 다른 사람의 상황, 동기, 감정과 진정으로 연계되어 있을 때 공감을 보인다. 공감은 반드시 다른 사람에 대한 동정을 의미하는 것이 아니라, 보다 깊은 이해로 이끌어지는 식별을 의미한다. 공감하는 것은 지휘자가 다른 사람들이 경험하고 있는 것을 예측하고 결정이나 행동이 그들에게 어떤 영향을 미치는지 상상하도록 한다. 공감 경향이 강한 지휘자들은 이를 육군 민간인, 군인 및 그 가족들, 지역 주민, 적 전투원 등을 이해하는 데 적용할 수 있다. 다른 사람의 관점에서 무언가를 보고, 함께 인식하고, 다른 사람의 감정과 감동 속으로 진입하는 능력은 육군 지휘자가 다른 사람들과 더 잘 상호작용하는 것을 가능하게 한다.

지휘자들은 임무 완수에 필요한 훈련, 장비, 지원을 제공함으로써 군인들과 육군 민간인들을 돌본다. 작전 중에 공감적인 육군 지휘자들은 그들의 계획과 결정이 현실적이었는지를 측정하기 위해 어려운 일을 함께 한다. 그들은 군인들과 육군 민간인들에게 훌륭한 사기와 임무 효과성을 유지하기 위해 적당한 위안과 휴식 기간을 제공할 필요성을 인식하고 있다.

◎ 전사 기풍과 근무 기풍

전사 기풍은 미국 병사를 특징짓는 전문적인 태도와 신념을 말한다. 그것은 국가, 임무, 부대, 그리고 동료 군인들에 대한 한 병사의 사심 없는 헌신을 반영한다. 육군 민간인들은, 전투병은 아니지만, 그들의 임무 수행을 동일한 태도, 신념, 헌신으로 온통 퍼지게 하는 서비스 기풍을 통해 전사 기풍의 원칙을 구현한다. 전사 기풍은 규율, 육군 가치에 대한 헌신, 그리고 육군의 유산에 대한 자부심을 통해 개발되고 유지된다. 군인들에 의해 살고 육군 민간인들의 지원을 받는 전사 기풍은 이 기관(제도)에 스며드는 승리 정신의 토대가 된다.

나는 미국 병사다.
나는 전사이자 팀의 일원이다.
나는 미국 국민들을 위해 봉사하고 있으며, 육군 가치관에 산다.
나는 항상 임무에 우선할 것이다.
나는 결코 패배를 인정하지 않을 것이다.
나는 절대 그만두지 않을 것이다.
나는 결코 쓰러진 전우를 남겨두지 않을 것이다.
(전사 기풍)
나는 단련되어 있고, 육체적으로나 정신적으로 강인하며, 훈련도 받고, 전사들의 임무와 훈련에도 능숙하다.
나는 항상 나의 무장, 나의 장비 그리고 나 자신을 유지한다.
나는 숙련자이고 전문가다.
나는 미국의 적들을 근접전에서 운용되고, 교전하고, 격파할 준비가 되어 있다.
나는 자유와 미국인의 삶의 방식에 대한 수호자다.
나는 미국 병사다.

그림 13-1. 군인 신조

◎ 규율

개인 차원의 규율은 주로 자기 수양, 즉 자신의 행동을 통제할 수 있는 능력이다. 규율은 군대의 가치관이 요구하는 것을 표현한다. 즉 옳은 일을 기꺼이 한다.

규율은 부대나 조직이 군사적 기능을 수행할 수 있는 능력에 도달하고 이를 유지하기 위해 지속적이고 체계적인 행동을 연습할 수 있는 사고 방식이다. 이것은 종종 조직의 주요 업무보다 덜 긴급하지만 효율성과 장기적 효과에 필요한 조직과 행정의 세부사항에 참여하는 것을 포함한다. 효과적인 부대 보급 훈련 프로그램, 조직 검사 프로그램 그리고 훈련 관리를 예로 들 수 있다.

표 13-1. 특성에 관련된 태도 요약

	개인의 핵심을 구성하는 지휘자의 내부적, 중심적 요소들
육군 가치관	• 가치관은 성공적인 지휘자에게 고려되는 필수적인 원칙, 기준 또는 자질이다. • 가치관은 어떤 상황에서도 사람이 옳고 그름을 판별하는 데 도움이 되는 기본이다. • 육군은 모든 육군의 개인이 발전시켜야 할 7가지 가치관이 있는데 그것은 충성, 의무, 존경, 사심 없는 봉사, 명예, 진실성(청렴), 개인적 용기이다.
공감	• 다른 사람의 관점에서 어떤 것을 경험하는 경향 • 다른 사람의 감정과 감동을 파악하고 진입할 수 있는 능력 • 병사들이나 기타를 돌보고 보살피고자 하는 갈망
전사 기풍/ 근무 기풍	• 군인과 육군 민간인 모두를 위한 동일한 육군의 직업정신을 구현하는 내부적으로 공유된 태도와 신뢰
규율	• 육군 가치에 따른 자신의 행동 통제; 행정, 조직, 훈련, 그리고 작전 임무에서 훌륭한 질서의 실천을 강요하고 따르려는 마음가짐

Unit 14 | 북한의 위협과 전투력 (브리핑 샘플)

p. 308- 312

Briefing Text

안녕하십니까? 여러분을 모시고 북한의 위협과 군사력에 대한 브리핑 기회를 갖게 된 것을 기쁘게 생각합니다.

여러분이 잘 아시다시피 북한은 김정은이 집권한 이후 유일통치를 공고히 하고 체제 안정에 힘을 집중해 왔습니다. 남북관계의 주도권을 잡고 국제사회의 제재와 고립에서 벗어나기 위해 끊임없이 도발-대화 전술을 사용해 왔습니다. 북한은 핵무기와 탄도 미사일과 같은 대량살상무기를 개발하고, 전통적 전투력 증강, 적과 접촉 지역에서의 무장도발 행동, 그리고 사이버 공격과 소형의 UAV 침투와 같은 지속적인 도발을 수행하는 등 대한민국과 국제 사회에 심각한 위협 제기를 계속하고 있습니다.

먼저, 북한의 전투력에 대해서 알아보겠습니다. 우선, 북한군의 70%가 평양-원산선 남쪽에 위치하고 있으며 또 지상군은 1,100,000명의 현역과 7,620,000명의 예비군을 보유하고 있는 것으로 추정됩니다. 다른 북한의 육군 무기 자산은 4,300대의 전차, 2,500대의 장갑차, 5,500대의 다련장 로켓, 8,600문의 포병화기, 그리고 5,500대의 방공포병화기 등이 있습니다.

이들 병력 중 약 20만 명은 특수정찰부대인데 그들의 임무는 정찰, 재래식 작전 지원, 적 후방지역에 제2전선 형성, 북한지역에서 적 특수작전 부대에 대응, 그리고 내부보안 유지 등이 되겠습니다.

다음은 북한 해군과 공군의 전투력입니다. 먼저 북한 해군조직의 위치와 전투력입니다. 해군사령부 예하에 편성된 해군은 동, 서 해상의 2개 함대 사령부, 13개 전대, 2개의 해상 저격여단으로 구성되어 있습니다. 북한 해군 중 60%는 평양-원산선 남쪽에 전진 배치돼 기습공격 능력을 유지할 수 있습니다.

함대 사령부는 토조동과 남포에, 해군기지는 나진, 완산, 비파곶에 위치하고 있습니다. 6만여 명의 인력과 810여 척의 함정이 있으며 잠수함, 상륙전, 어뢰정, 해안경비정, 소해정 등이 있습니다. 이것들은 모두 해상 병참선에 대한 위협입니다.

다음은 북한의 공군에 관한 정보입니다. 북한 공군 사령부는 항공과 반항공 사령부로 이름이 바뀌었습니다. 사령부 예하에 4개의 비행사단, 2개의 전술 수송 여단, 2개의 공군 저격 여단과 방공 부대 등이 있습니다.

북한 공군은 4개의 다른 권역에 전력을 배치했습니다. 북한 공군 항공기는 대부분 구식 모델입니다. 전투기 820대 중 40% 정도가 평양-원산선 이남에 전진 배치돼 있습니다. 북한공군 재고에는 전술 전투기 810여 대, 폭격기, 수송기, 헬기 등 1,340여 대가 투입되어 있습니다.

공군은 항공기의 추가 배치나 조정 없이 한국의 통제 및 지휘 시설, 방공 자산, 산업 시설에 대한 기습 공격을 할 수 있습니다. AN-2 항공기와 헬리콥터는 침투용 대규모 특수작전부대를 수송할 수 있습니다. 공군은 최근 정찰과 타격용으로 무인정찰기를 제작, 배치하고 있습니다.

북한은 육·해·공군 외에, 만약 전쟁이 발발한다면 많은 사상자를 남길 전구 탄도 미사일, 화학 무기, 핵 능력이 있습니다. 전구 탄도 미사일에는 세 가지 종류가 있습니다. 스커드 미사일은 사거리가 500km이고 1,300km까지 도달할 수 있는 노동 미사일, 최근에는 3,000km 이상의 목표물을 타격할 수 있는 무수단 미사일을 보유하고 있습니다. 이런 배치에 따라 북한은 한국, 일본, 괌 등 기타 주변국에 대한 직접 타격 능력을 갖췄습니다. 대포동 미사일은 사거리가 10,000km 이상이어서 북한이 미국 대륙을 위협할 수 있는 능력이 있는 것으로 추정됩니다.

북한은 1980년대부터 화학무기를 생산하기 시작했으며, 비축량은 2,500~5,000t 정도인 것으로 추정됩니다. 북한은 탄저균, 천연두, 페스트 등 각종 생물 무기를 자체 배양하고 생물학 무기로 생산할 수 있는 능력도 있는 것으로 보입니다.

북한은 여러 차례 핵실험을 했습니다. 북한은 폐연료봉을 여러 차례 재처리한 후, 핵무기 제조에 사용할 수 있는 플루토늄 약 00kg을 보유하고 있는 것으로 추정되며, 고농축 우라늄(HEU) 프로그램도 진행 중인 것으로 평가됩니다. 북한의 핵무기 소형화 능력도 상당한 수준에 이른 것으로 보입니다.

전략 로켓사령부는 지상군, 해군, 항공 및 반공군 사령부와 같은 수준으로 군종 사령부로 승격하는 등 전략군으로 명칭이 바뀌었습니다. 전략군은 중국 제2포병부대와 러시아의 전략미사일부대 등과 유사한 기능을 수행할 가능성이 높습니다. 비대칭 전력을 증강하기 위한 이들의 노력은 앞으로도 계속될 전망입니다.

다음으로 저는 여러분들에게 북한의 전쟁 지속 능력에 대해 설명드리겠습니다. 북한은 경제적 어려움에도 불구하고 전쟁 지속 능력을 유지하기 위해 군수 산업 발전에 최우선 순위를 두고 있습니다. 약 300개의 군수 공장을 보유하고 있으며, 전시에 군비 생산으로의 전환을 위해 지정된 민수 공장은 단기간에 이러한 전환을 할 수 있습니다.

북한의 전시 물자의 대부분은 지하 저장 시설에 저장하고 있으며 이러한 물자의 비축량은 약 1-3개월을 지속할 수 있는 것으로 추정됩니다. 그러나 추가적인 구매나 외부의 지원 없이 장기전을 지속할 수 있는 북한의 능력은 제한될 것 같습니다.

지금, 우리가 오늘 논의된 모든 요소들을 고려한다면, 남한 전체 인구의 1/5인 1,000만 명의 서울에는 몇 가지 취약점들을 가지고 있습니다. 서울은 역사적, 문화적 중심지로서 DMZ에서 불과 22마일 떨어져 있으며, 적 포병 사정거리 안에 있고, 해상 침투에도 취약합니다. 이런 점들이 바로 우리가 주한미군과 협력하여 항상 높은 수준의 대비태세를 유지해야 하는 이유입니다.

Unit 15 | 구두 지형 설명(도라 전망대)

Briefing Text

여러분, 안녕하십니까? 김 소위입니다. 여러분을 뵙게 되어서 반갑습니다. 지금부터 전방지역 상황을 보고드리겠습니다.

여러분들은 지금 도라 관측소에 계시며, 이 관측소는 비무장지대 남방 한계선 상에 위치하고 있습니다. 저희 10사단은 남북한의 군사적 긴장상태를 이해시킬 목적으로 민간인들에게 이 관측소를 포함하여 전방지역, 별공관 및 제3땅굴을 공개하고 있습니다. 서울은 남쪽으로 43km 떨어져 있으며, 북한의 도시 중 하나인 개성은 북쪽으로 8km 떨어져 있습니다.

먼저 군사분계선에 대해서 설명드리겠습니다. 여러분의 전방을 주목해 주시기 바랍니다. 북한 선전 문구가 새겨진 작은 언덕을 보실 수가 있을 것입니다. 우리 한반도를 남한과 북한으로 나누고 있는 군사분계선은 그 언덕 밑을 지나갑니다. 울타리가 없고, 단지 황색 표지판들이 200m 간격으로 설치되어 있습니다.

원래 군사분계선은 제2차 세계대전 후에 북위 38도선에 미군과 러시아군에 의해 나누어진 것입니다. 이는 일본군의 무장해제를 용이하게 하기 위해 설치한 것입니다. 한국전쟁이 일어난 지도 거의 ○○년이 지났고 현재 우리나라는 냉전의 결과로 분단된 유일한 국가입니다. 동서 진영 간의 냉전은 더 이상 존재하지 않고 있지만 북한은 아직도 무력에 의한 한반도 적화야욕을 버리지 않고 있습니다.

이곳으로부터 전방 약 35km 지점이 남방한계선입니다. 그곳이 우리의 최전방 전선입니다. 우측 방향을 주목해 주시기 바랍니다. 여러분은 비포장도로를 연하여 설치된 철조망을 보실 수가 있습니다. 2시 방향을 보시면 여러분들은 북한기, 즉 '인공기'를 보실 수가 있습니다. 그 깃발은 폭이 15m이며, 길이가 30m입니다. 북한의 선전마을인 기정동이 그곳에 위치하고 있습니다.

건물들은 창문이 없습니다. 모든 불빛은 동일한 색깔이며 동시에 불이 들어오고 나갑니다. 어떠한 굴뚝 연기나 세탁물들도 보이지 않습니다. 많은 건물들이 우리들에게 보여 주기 위해서 세운 것입니다. 단지 군인들과 관리인들만이 이 마을을 지키기 위해 거주합니다.

오른쪽으로 약 3km 지점을 보십시오. 우리의 자유의 마을이라고 부르는 대성동이며 비무장지대 내에 주민이 거주하는 유일한 마을입니다. 여러분들은 또 다른 높은 탑과 '태극기'를 보실 수가 있습니다. 약 ○○세대로 구성된 ○○명의 주민이 그곳에 거주하며 그들은 국방 및 납세 의무가 면제됩니다.

깃발 오른쪽으로부터 2km 지점을 주목해 주십시오. 여러분들은 숲속의 흰 건물을 보실 수가 있습니다. 그곳이 공동경비구역이라고 부르는 판문점 내의 '평화의 집'입니다.

왼쪽을 보시면, 한국전쟁 이전에 남한과 북한을 운행했던 숲속에 있는 기관차를 보실 수가 있습니다. 그러나 지금은 평화통일에 대한 한국인의 염원의 상징으로 서 있습니다. 한국전쟁이 발발한 지 거의 ○○년이 지났습니다.

이상 보고를 마치겠습니다. 이제 양측에 설치되어 있는 쌍안경을 이용하여 전방지역을 살펴보시기 바랍니다. 감사합니다.